THE McMAHON LINE

THE McMAHON LINE

A CENTURY OF DISCORD

J.J. SINGH

HarperCollins *Publishers* India

First published in hardback in India in 2019 by
HarperCollins *Publishers*
A-75, Sector 57, Noida, Uttar Pradesh 201301, India
www.harpercollins.co.in

2 4 6 8 10 9 7 5 3 1

Typeset in 11.5/15 Dante MT (T1) at
Manipal Digital Systems, Manipal

Printed and bound at
Thomson Press (India) Ltd.

For
Anupama, Vivek and Urvashi
and
the people of Arunachal Pradesh

Contents

Preface

The Sino-Indian border dispute has had a profound impact on the contemporary history and modern-day evolution of the two Asian giants, China and India. It was over this dispute that the two countries fought a brief but fierce war in October–November 1962, and it is this issue that has been the cause of skirmishes and stand-offs between the border forces on both sides both before and after this war.

The genesis of the boundary problem lies in a web of complex issues, fundamental among them being the partly undemarcated, partly delimited and, at many places, undefined, albeit traditionally accepted, boundary that has existed for many centuries between the two great civilizations.

The arena where all this has played out is visually dramatic. The two countries are separated by the grandest mountain chains in the world—the Karakoram, the Kunlun and the Himalayas. And sandwiched between the countries (and also further complicating their confrontation) is the ancient kingdom of Tibet, which has now become an autonomous region of China (as highlighted in Figure 1). The Sino-Indian boundary of over 4,057 kilometres averages the height of the Alps, at places being even higher than Mont Blanc. It traverses perhaps the most desolate and uninhabited yet picturesque high-altitude regions on the globe where nothing but frontier zones had existed for centuries.

Considering these factors, a study of the geopolitical and historical dimension of the region where India, the Tibet Autonomous Region and China meet will help us understand the complexities of the boundary problem that has severely impacted relations between the two emerging powers of Asia for more than half a century now.

Four aspects had to be considered for this study: first, the effect of geography on this region; second, the question of how far one must go back in history so that the 'boundary fixing' is relevant to the realities of the present times; third, the significance of the McMahon Line drawn up during the Tripartite Conference involving British India, Tibet and China during 1913–14; and fourth, the defining parameters for arriving at a reasonable, fair and mutually acceptable Sino-Indian boundary. After this we consider the way forward.

Given the considerable lack of accurate historical records or maps on the subject, the ever-changing notions of where the boundary should lie, dictated by the political climate in this region over the last two-and-a-half centuries, have ensured that neither China nor India, both successor states in the larger sense of the term, has yet convincingly proved to the other the historical, traditional and legal rights by which each claims its boundaries. Fortunately, since the 1980s the leadership of both nations has adopted a statesman-like and visionary approach to constructively engage on and resolve the vexed boundary issue in a peaceful and pragmatic manner, thereby preventing another conflict. This disputed border has not witnessed any conflict during the last five-and-a-half decades.

As far as the India–China boundary issue is concerned, the focus of this work has been limited to the McMahon Line and to India's north-eastern frontier. The other areas of the boundary have been given briefer treatment. A meaningful analysis of the frontier region of north-east India, east Tibet and south-west China must also take into account the strategic compulsions of the British Indian empire that extended from Afghanistan to Burma (now Myanmar) a century ago. What has emerged from this study is a clearer perspective of the Chinese grand design of a direct link connecting Yunnan province with Lhasa, cutting across northern Burma and the tribal territories of upper Assam, thus bypassing the steep, snow-covered parallel ranges and treacherous canyons formed by the Irrawaddy, Salween, Mekong and Yangtze rivers and also evading the region inhabited by the fierce Khampa tribe. As discussed later, this work covers the little-addressed geopolitical and geostrategic dimensions that need to be kept in mind for any sound resolution of the border dispute.

To understand the evolution of the McMahon Line, one must also study the corresponding political developments during the latter half of the first decade of the twentieth century in south-east Tibet, north Burma, Bhutan and Sikkim. These developments were the fallout of the Younghusband expedition to Lhasa and the Chinese 'forward policy' along the Sino-Tibetan frontier region, also called the Marches, the Assam frontier and northern Burma. The reaction of the British along the frontier regions of both north Burma and north-east India manifested in measures to ensure the security of the Indian north-eastern frontier—the tea industry in Assam in particular—and north Burma. At that point in time, neither the Chinese nor the British appeared to be concerned about the western part of the Indo-Tibetan frontier (the Ladakh region), having already fixed the frontier at the Karakoram Pass. As the Russian threat had subsided and no financial investments were at stake, there was no urgency to put in place a demarcated boundary between Ladakh and Tibet as far as the British Empire was concerned. An undefined boundary highlighted by a colour wash on the map was all that represented the north-western frontier of British India up to 1947, and surprisingly, this representation continued till 1954.

In the case of China, the geostrategic imperative to link both Sinkiang (presently Xinjiang) and Yunnan provinces with Lhasa was the driving force behind its claim and occupation of Aksai Chin along the western periphery and the raison d'être for its conception of Hsikang province to link Yunnan with Lhasa by carving out portions of Tibet proper, some parts of the tribal territories south of the Himalayas and some northern parts of Burma. The latter strategic design of the Chinese has escaped the attention of most analysts and, unfortunately for the Chinese, this fictitious dream of Chao Erh-Feng died a sudden death with the downfall of the Manchu Empire and the breakout of the October 1911 revolution. These events led to the eviction of the Chinese and an end to their authority over Tibet for the next four decades till the 'de facto independent' Tibet was 'liberated' in 1951 by the army of People's Republic of China.

The twenty-first century has been predicted to be dominated by the two Asian giants under discussion. Whether it turns out to be one of conflict, a protracted contest or a genial tango between the dragon and the elephant, as they are referred to, is not easy to forecast. Yet, unquestionably, the focus of the world would be on Asia during this century. About three centuries ago, over 40 per cent of the world's gross domestic product was generated by India and China. Today the world seems to be moving once again in that direction, slowly but surely.

During my military career and my subsequent tenure as a governor in the north-east spanning over half a century (1961–2013), I had ample opportunity to serve in the Arunachal Pradesh (the erstwhile North-East Frontier Agency, or NEFA) and Sikkim regions, and in the Uttarakhand and Ladakh regions of India's northern frontier. I acquired through these years first-hand and intimate knowledge of the history, geography, ethnic diversity, traditions and culture of the people living in these regions along the Sino-Indian boundary. My stint in the army and as governor in these regions has therefore considerably helped me in this project.

Importantly, my experience of about four years as additional director general of military operations at the Army Headquarters, whose major responsibility was—and continues to be—the handling of all operational issues related to the security of the external boundaries of the nation, my later tenure as chief of army staff, and my few visits to China, official and unofficial, have given me wide exposure and insight in Sino-Indian matters. My five-and-a-half years as governor of Arunachal Pradesh brought me excellent opportunities to visit the far-flung corners of this strategic front-line north-eastern state of India, and helped me know the people and understand the geostrategic and political features of this region.

In a tripartite convention among Britain, Tibet and China 105 years ago, Sir Henry McMahon drew a 'red line' on a small-scale map (1 inch to 60 miles) in Simla that delineated the frontiers or limits of Tibet. The British objective at this conference at Simla during 1913–14 was to secure for Tibet a fully autonomous status under a nominally suzerain China and to determine the Sino-Tibetan frontier to put an end to the state of war in eastern Tibet by drawing a 'blue line' and, incidently, delineating the Indo-Tibetan frontier in the process. Having a benign Tibet as a neighbour and a buffer state would guarantee the security of the north-eastern frontier of British India. The reluctance of the British to support full independence for Tibet and their insistence on Chinese suzerainty over Tibet even after 1913, when there was absolutely no presence of the Chinese in all of Tibet, was based on imperial geopolitics and economic reasons—the impact for Britain on the freedom struggles of its own colonies not being the least! Besides, the British were seeking an arrangement that would continue to keep the Russians at bay, something that they had achieved to a large degree by the Anglo-Russian treaty of 1907. Although these British aims could only be partially achieved as the Chinese declined to sign the Simla agreement even though they concurred with most of the articles of the draft convention, in hindsight many benefits accrued to the British—the delineation of the Indo-Tibetan boundary along the Himalayas (the McMahon Line) and the restoration of their image as the most significant global empire, besides other intangible gains.

Of greater consequence to British India was the portion of the red line that demarcated the boundary between Tibet and British India from Bhutan to Burma. Definitely more important from the Chinese perspective was the lesser known blue line drawn by McMahon on the same map. This line divided Greater Tibet into two parts: the first, a fully autonomous state, though one nominally under Chinese suzerainty and called, ironically, 'Outer Tibet', comprising Lhasa, west and central Tibet; and the second, an 'Inner Tibet', marching with the frontiers of Szechuan and Yunnan provinces of China, which would be under full control of China but would fall short of being classified as akin to a Chinese province. While China did not raise any objections to the portion of the red line depicting the Indo-Tibetan boundary, it mainly contested the alignment of the blue line separating Outer Tibet from the Chinese Inner Tibet. China also had some issues concerning the red line (not related to the frontier with north-east India) which defined the limits of Tibet. Besides, China also wanted some Tibetan territory in the Kokonor, Kansu and Amdo regions to be included in China proper. It was on account of these reasons that the Chinese refused to ratify the Simla convention of 1914.

Differences in the on-ground perception and interpretation of this red line—now famously known as the McMahon Line—and the Aksai

Chin area of Ladakh unilaterally claimed by China were the principal reasons that triggered the Sino-Indian war of 1962. The war had disastrous consequences for India and for Jawaharlal Nehru, India's first prime minister. These reasons continue to constitute the major bone of contention between India and China as the two nations traverse the journey towards resolution of the boundary issue pertaining to the Karakoram and Kunlun ranges and the Great Himalayas.

In this work the focus, as mentioned earlier, has been limited to the north-eastern frontier of India. The McMahon Line, by and large, follows the crest of the eastern Himalayas and delimits the northern frontier of Arunachal Pradesh in India. It extends eastwards from the tri-junction of Bhutan, China and India to Myanmar and beyond. Could the century-old McMahon Line provoke another conflict in the region, as predicted by some experts? An endeavour has been made in this book to address this question and suggest the possible way forward.

Within a month of conclusion of the Simla conference on 4 August 1914, Great Britain got drawn into the First World War. For the next five years, 'empire building' and 'safeguarding of the empire' were put on the back burner, and matters like Tibet and the McMahon Line almost went into oblivion. By a fortuitous turn of events, and because of the alacrity of Olaf Caroe, a British official in the external affairs department in Delhi in the mid-1930s, the McMahon Line maps and the Indo-Tibet Agreement of 3 July 1914 were literally dug out from the dust-laden almirahs of the department and brought out. Surprisingly, these historical documents had not been formally shared with the administrative authorities in Assam, including the lieutenant governor at Shillong. It is my belief that events such as the outbreak of the Great War riveted the attention of the world powers on central Europe, which then became the centre stage of global developments, reducing the Tibetan issue to a petty affair of the British Empire. Consequently, the enforcement of decisions taken at the historic convention of July 1914 at Simla was put on the back burner. The Tibetans, who at that time were de facto independent, were well aware of and content with the boundary defined by the McMahon Line. The Indo-Tibetan Agreement of 1914 had clearly delineated the boundary eastwards from Bhutan up to the tri-junction of India, Tibet and Burma and beyond, to the Isu Razi Pass on the Irrawaddy watershed.

The date 3 July 2014 signalled the completion of 100 years of the signing of the much underrated yet now historical McMahon Line and the Simla Convention.

On the surface, relations between India and China appear to be on the right trajectory. Trade between them is burgeoning, and estimated to touch 100 billion USD in the near future. They are in close cooperation in diverse fields relating to world trade and the World Trade Organization, counter-terrorism, security of sea lanes, global warming, strengthening of the UN to make it more representative, and improvement of military-to-military ties. However, there are the negatives in their relationship, such as the intractable boundary issue, the tension-filled face-offs between their armed forces, the reported diversion of river waters and construction of dams, the adverse balance of trade as far as India is concerned, the Tibet and Dalai Lama factors, and the Sino-Pakistan relationship.

India–China ties, however, have an overarching impact on peace, prosperity and stability in the region, and perhaps the world too. Undoubtedly, Sino-Indian relations are going to be under the gaze of the international community for a better part of this century. Hence the interest generated by the subject will have contemporary relevance for decades to come.

India and China may have a strategic and cooperative partnership in place. Our leaders may have adopted a statesman-like approach and agreed to resolve our boundary dispute and other problems in a peaceful, mature and pragmatic manner. Nonetheless, the unresolved boundary problem that led to the 1962 Sino-Indian war along the Himalayan borders had intensely bedevilled our relations for almost three decades, from the late 1950s to 1988 (the visit of India's prime minister Rajiv Gandhi to China after thirty-four years), and continues to be the most daunting of our problems. The scars of the border war have left their impression on an entire generation of Indians, but the same generation in China perhaps has nothing more than a faint memory of it, although they may remember the Mao era better for other reasons.

Having examined the impact of geography and history in keeping the Himalayan region and Tibet isolated and autonomous for centuries and having also determined how far one must go back in history to determine the status of Tibet and her borders with China and India, this study moves on to describe the evolution of the McMahon Line and the nuances of British India's Tibet policy from the eighteenth century up to India's independence in 1947. Thereafter, the narrative focuses on Sino-Indian relations during the first decade after Independence—a peaceful one, until the conflicting boundary claims emerged like a sinister monster and led to the fierce and fateful border war in October–November 1962 between the two nations. This war proved to be a decisive debacle for India.

This account deliberately does not delve into the details of this war as a number of books have been written on the subject. Instead, it takes forward the debate on India–China boundary negotiations to our contemporary times and concludes with recommendations for the way ahead for resolution of this territorial dispute. The study has analysed how China has resolved boundary disputes with twelve of its neighbours, particularly those with Russia and Vietnam which resulted in major skirmishes with the former, and a border war involving a huge loss of life and property with the latter. It also indulges in a bit of crystal gazing, analysing the future of the relationship between the two Asian powers who, creditably, never experienced a 'clash of civilizations' despite having been neighbours for over 3,000 years.

Acknowledgements

Writing about the boundary problem between two ancient civilisations that were not neighbours in a strict sense till the mid-twentieth century because Tibet acted as a buffer has been a daunting task. The source material has not been easy to come by. While, on the Chinese side, the closed system allows access to researchers in a highly controlled manner, the Indian archives have been carefully shrouded and many documents pertaining to the period from our Independence for three decades are not in the public domain, although they have leaked through in bits and pieces.

Soon after the launch of my book *A Soldier's General*, my publisher Krishan Chopra broached the subject of my next project. Almost instinctively I replied that something which has engaged my imagination and interest for almost half a century is what I would endeavour to write about. The McMahon Line and the India–China boundary problem is a vexatious issue that has defied resolution despite the brief border war between the two large neighbours. 'We should go ahead with it' was Krishan's measured response, the astute publisher that one finds him to be. My grateful acknowledgement of his support and constructive suggestions as this work progressed during the past five years. My gratitude goes to the team at HarperCollins, especially Siddhesh Inamdar, who was my editorial anchor for this project.

I am immensely grateful to Lieutenant General V.R. Raghavan for his valuable comments and guidance for this work. I was also facilitated greatly in my research by the excellent staff of the British Library and Archives and the director and his dedicated team of the Arunachal Pradesh Museum and Archives at Itanagar. The staff of the libraries at the Institute of Defence and Strategic Analysis and the Delhi Gymkhana Club, particularly Mukesh Jha and Joginderpal Goswami respectively, were extremely efficient and helpful in sourcing material for research of this book. The secretarial team in Arunachal Pradesh and Delhi proved to be a great asset, particularly, Rana, Amol A. Sawant, who helped immensely in cataloguing and retrieving the reference material and associated computer work and rendered valuable advice while working on the drafts, and Dattatray Redekar, who made some wonderful sketches and illustrations. I am indeed grateful to Shanta Serbjeet Singh and her son Karamjeet Singh for kind permission to use the panoramic painting by reknowned artist Serbjeet Singh of the Kameng region that has been adapted as the backdrop of the cover. I would like to specially thank Colonel Raman Yadav, 1/8 Gorkha Rifles for kind permission to use adaptations of some photographs taken during the Younghusband Expedition of 1903–04.

A project of this nature cannot be accomplished without the encouragement and support of friends and well-wishers. I have been fortunate to have a wealth of such friends, many of whom wish to remain anonymous. I am deeply indebted to all of them, most of all my close family who had to bear my pre-occupied disposition for a long time with patience and understanding, especially Seerat and Anne-Tara, who kept me humoured whenever I was out of sync with my surroundings.

It is my pleasure to place on record the contribution, in terms of valuable ideas, generosity and willingness to give their time, of my friends and close ones: Pema Khandu, Hardeep Singh Puri, Chowna Mein, Chattrapati Shahu Maharaj, P.J.S. Pannu, Anil Malhotra, Ramesh Bhatia, Sambaji Raje, Satish Kapur, Ankur Garg, Sushil Gupta, Harsh Sethi, Y.K. Joshi, Gurchi Kochhar, Satish Lakhina, Lakshminarayanan, Dr Amarjeet Singh Marwah, Vikramjeet Singh Sawhney, Naresh Gujral, Raj Loomba, Ranjit Singh, Nirupama Kaur, Vikramjit Sen, Shakti Sinha, Ashok K. Kanth, Vivek Chadha, Shivaji Mahadkar, Ashok Mehta and Maroof Raza. To them I shall be deeply indebted. I owe gratitude to my friends from Arunachal Pradesh, particularly Governor B.D. Mishra, the Dorjee Khandu family, Nabam Tuki, Y.D. Thongchi, Mamang Dai and many others who readily shared the source material and first-hand accounts relating to the historical, etymological, and cultural dimensions of the tribal societies that have inhabited the densely forested and splendrous mountains of the Himalayas.

A special word of thanks to former President of India Dr A.P.J. Abdul Kalam, who, before his passing in 2015, had a look at an early draft of this book and wished it success. He was happy to know that it was in the works and graciously noted that it would be of great value to readers, soldiers, the youth and the nation at large.

Finally, my grateful thanks to all of you for making this work a reality.

PART I

WHERE TIBET, CHINA AND INDIA MEET

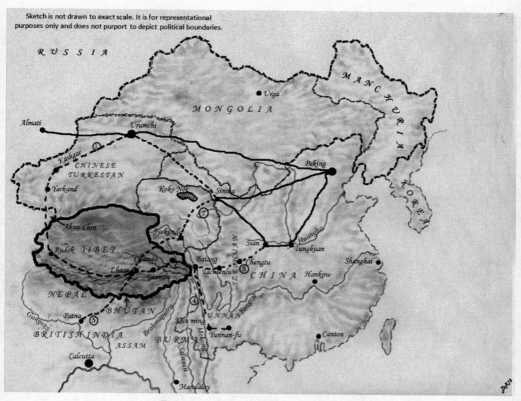

Figure 1: East Asia—early twentieth century

1

Roof of the World: Geography of Tibet

'Civilisation exists by geological consent, subject to change, without notice.'

—*Will Durant*[1]

The Indian subcontinent sheared and drifted from the supercontinent[2] of Gondwanaland about 120 million years ago. The name Gondwanaland has possibly been derived from the Sanskrit *'gondavana'*, meaning 'forest of the Gonds'. Around 45–50 million years ago, the Indian plate collided with Asia, which was a part of the northern supercontinent, Laurasia. This collision resulted in an upwards 'buckling' of the southern crust of Asia in two principal directions—north and north-east, towards the part of the globe that comprises Sinkiang province in China, Tibet and South-East Asia. The great ocean, called Tethys, that lay between the two supercontinents for over 100 million years ceased to exist as a result of this gigantic collision and the tectonic movement of the earth.

Part of the Indian plate was subsumed under the Asian continent. The results of this geographical phenomenon were: first, the creation of the mountain ranges of the Himalayas, Pamirs, Karakoram and Kunlun; second, the elevation, compression, corrugation and crumpling of the vast Tibetan land mass averaging 4,500 metres above sea level, and which had enormous deserts and innumerable saltwater lakes; and third, its impact on the topography, biological development and climate of the entire region comprising the Indian subcontinent, Tibet, western China and the

3

northern part of South-East Asia. In the Himalayan region, the presence of marine limestone embedded with fossils that date back millions of years has corroborated the theory of geologists that almost all of Tibet was once at or just below sea level.[3]

Tibet Autonomous Region (TAR) neighbours India on the north and has the longest shared boundary with India along the Himalayas. The 'Roof of the World', as the Tibetan region is called, and the Himalayan range were the outcome of one of earth's most fascinating geological events described earlier. This high-altitude region of Asia has the highest and arguably the most striking mountains on the globe and is the fountainhead of major river systems like those of the Indus, the Sutlej, the Ganga, the Brahmaputra (Tsangpo in Tibet), the Irrawaddy, the Salween, the Mekong, the Yangtze and the Huang Ho (Yellow River), as shown in Figure 2. These river basins have spawned the great civilizations of India, China, Tibet, Mongolia and many other South-East Asian countries. As eloquently described by Mike Searle in his authoritative book *Colliding Continents*, 'The Himalaya is the greatest mountain range on earth: the highest, longest, youngest, the most tectonically active, and the most spectacular of all.'[4] The Himalayas are reverently called *'deva bhoomi'* in India, meaning 'land of the gods'.

'In a hundred ages of the gods I could not tell thee of the glories of the Himalaya,' say the Puranas, the 'ancient stories', myths, and legends of India, transmitted orally and first recorded in texts dating back before the Mahabharata. It is not surprising that all the Asian religions worship and revere the mountains. The Himalaya, the 'abode of snow', was where the unknown forces lived that controlled everything on Earth.[5]

Tibet is the epicentre of East Asia. It is an elevated land mass in the shape of a pear, with its narrow end radiating outwards from the Pamir knot like a petal (see Figure 1). The Karakoram and the Himalayan mountain chains form an impressive necklace to the south of the Tibetan massif. One-third the size of America,[6] Tibet lies between two ancient civilizations and has acted as a kind of natural divide and buffer zone between them.

Historically, traditionally and culturally, independent Tibet comprised four distinct regions: Ngari, U-Tsang, Amdo and Kham, besides the northern permafrost desert called Changthang, which no longer exists in the same form. This ancient land has been truncated and reconfigured by China into Tibet Autonomous Region (TAR), consisting of an area of 1,228,000 square kilometres (approximately 12.8 per cent of China's land mass).[7] TAR is less than half of the original Tibet and has only one-third of the Tibetan population. Most of Amdo, Kham and other outlying regions have been merged with Sinkiang, Quinghai, Sichuan and Yunnan provinces of China.

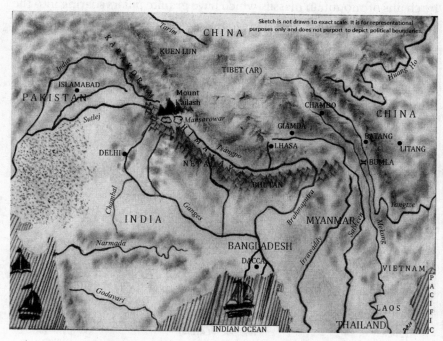

Figure 2: Important rivers originating from Tibet

Unlike the common perception of its being some kind of a raised tableland, the Tibetan plateau mostly lies at an altitude of 4,000–5,000 metres, with peaks rising up to 7,000 metres and many passes at over 5,000 metres. It has mountain ranges, lakes, rivers, deserts and marshes. Parts of Tibet have terrain that is serrated or crumpled with mountain chains such as the Kunlun, Altyn Tagh, Nyenchen Tanglha, Tangula, Ningjing and Shule Nanshan.

This mineral-rich plateau[8] (40 per cent of China's mineral resources lie therein) has a very small percentage of arable land, on account of which it has historically been able to support only a sparse population. It is the source of major Asian river systems such as those of the Indus, Sutlej, Brahmaputra (Tsangpo), Salween, Mekong, Yangtze and Huang Ho (the Yellow River). The major population centres in the lower reaches of this region are cradled in these river valleys, which have over the centuries spawned many civilizations en route their long journeys hundreds of miles downwards to the oceans. Geographically shielded from all sides by chains of mountain massifs which have granite pillars soaring into the sky, the Tibetan civilization evolved mostly on its own. To illustrate how inaccessible Tibet is, between Assam and Mongolia, over a spatial distance of about 2,600 kilometres, there are seven high mountain ranges, most of them over 6,000 metres in altitude, and at least six major rivers with deep valleys and gorges, as illustrated in Figure 3. Before the modern era, it would generally take eight months or more to traverse such distances over such difficult terrain. This resulted in the isolation of Tibet.

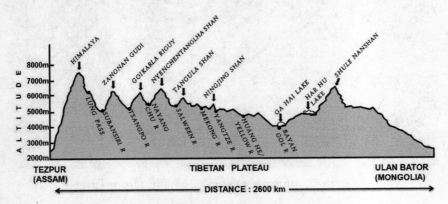

Figure 3: Tibetan topography: A cross section

Buddhism, which permeated across the Himalayas, was instinctively customized by the Tibetans to suit their local conditions. This resulted in the evolution of a 'modified' version of Buddhism, one that is deeply treasured by all Tibetans. While their spiritual needs were met from India, they looked mainly to China for their material requirements. However, as compared with their association with the Chinese, the Tibetans had a closer and special relationship with Mongolia.[9]

The northern fringe of Tibet is encompassed by the Kunlum, Altyn Tagh and Nan Shan ranges. Hemmed in by these mountain chains is the great high-altitude desert region of Changthang, about 1,000 kilometres wide and spread out laterally over 2,000 kilometres in the east–west direction. This desolate and inhospitable area was largely unexplored till the twentieth century and presented a formidable barrier to invaders from the north. With most of it lying at an average altitude of around 4,500–5,000 metres, this wind-swept region of permafrost produces nothing worthwhile to humans except grass, which too appears only when the land is free of snow. 'The greater part of Tibet is icebound during seven or eight months in the year; even the inhabited areas can be cultivated for a few months only.'[10]

The nomadic inhabitants of this region, the Changpas, are herders and eke out a pastoral living. In his vivid description of the climate he experienced in the northern escarpment of the Tibetan plateau, Sven Hedin, a famous explorer of the nineteenth century, writes: 'Those who have never been in one of those storms, can form no conception of what it is like. It is as though the entire volume of the atmosphere were concentrated into this great trough of the earth's surface and forced through it like a roaring tide. The clouds drove overhead at racing speed; drift sand and even small stones were caught up from the ground and hurled point-blank into our faces.'[11]

To the east and south-east of central Tibet lie the regions of Amdo and Kham. Looking south from the Koko Nor area, one can see the high-altitude mountainous landscape with its deep canyons and ravines formed by the great rivers of the region, which, except for the Huang Ho, run north–south, as do the Irrawaddy, Salween, Mekong and the Yangtze. In this region, these very long rivers flow parallel to each other, the distance between one river and the next ranging from 50 to 100 kilometres. In this region also lie 'three mountain ranges, the length of the Alps and much higher that were still almost totally unknown',[12] said Mike Searle (Figure 2). On the map these rivers appear quite like the fingers of a hand that don't join. They disgorge millions of litres of water along with soil and sediments on to vast flood plains and eventually flow into the different seas of South-East Asia. They are unbelievable hurdles to movement in the east–west direction as the defiles created by the intervening ridges rise up to formidable heights of 4,000–5,000 metres (about 13,000–16,000 feet). The eastern frontier of Tibet is not easy to describe as there are no distinctive and continuous geographical features except for these rivers. The difficult terrain makes for a kind of buffer between China and Tibet. This region was inhabited by hostile tribes who at times displayed token allegiance to China or Tibet, and in certain areas to neither. Both China and Tibet kept attempting to impose their writ over these tribes, but without great success. Historically, the routes from east to west passing through these areas had been vulnerable to raids by the tribes living here. Thus it was that the Sino-Tibetan frontier in this region kept shifting from one river basin to the other, between the Yangtze, Mekong and Salween.

In southern Tibet, the comparatively fertile Indus and Tsangpo Valleys situated along the suture created by the continental collision developed as the cradle of the Tibetan civilization. Known as 'U-Tsang', it is the core of Tibet proper. This was the habitat of the prosperous Tibetan community where their culture, traditions and commerce evolved and thrived. The semi-nomadic tribes living in the northern slopes of the Himalayas in Tibet are known as *Drukpas*. This region—its heights ranging from around 4,500 to 5,500 metres—rises gradually from the Tsangpo basin to the watershed of the Himalayas. The steep southern face of the Himalayas with its stupendous rampart-like structure and the very high snow-covered peaks and massive glaciers of this region tower over the Ganga and the Brahmaputra basins and the plains of north and east India. The Himalayas have remained the natural divide between China and India over centuries.

From the north-east of India, the Great Himalayas extend westwards in a crescent shape for almost 3,000 kilometres and link up with the Indus basin at the south-western edge of Ladakh. The traditional southern frontier of Tibet generally lies along the northern slopes of the main Himalayan range going from east to west from the Isu Razi Pass on the Irrawaddy–Brahmaputra divide to Demchok in the Indus basin where the river exits the Tibetan plateau. From the tri-junction of India, Burma and Tibet, it follows the Himalayan watershed for 1,070 kilometres along the Assam frontier region (now Arunachal Pradesh), then runs westwards through the northern part of the kingdom of Bhutan for over 500 kilometres before finally coming down to Chumbi Valley. It follows the watershed of the Teesta for about 200 kilometres across Sikkim, then runs for about 1,350 kilometres along the Himalayan ramparts in northern Nepal, and another 700 kilometres or so along the Kumaon, Garhwal and Himachal regions (also referred to as the middle sector) to Demchok in eastern Ladakh, which borders the western region of Tibet called Ngari. Before the tenth century, this region formed part of the kingdom of Ladakh, and its traditional boundary with Tibet was at the watershed formed by the Mayum La.[13] This area includes the famous Hindu pilgrimage sites of Mount Kailash and Manasarovar.

From Demchok, the western frontier of Tibet cuts across the Indus and continues northwards across the huge saltwater lake of Pangong Tso and the high-altitude wastelands of western Changthang, flanking Aksai Chin (desert of white stones), which it runs past to finally join the Kunlun and Karakoram ranges. The approximate distance of this stretch of the frontier is 900 kilometres up to the historical Karakoram Pass. North of the Indus basin, the eastern Ladakh region is very sparsely populated, and beyond Rudok one encounters the uninhabitable, bleak and windy western periphery of the Changthang high-altitude desert where 'not a blade of grass grows'. An ancient caravan route leading northwards through Aksai Chin crosses the Kunlun range to Shahidulla, Yarkand and Kashgar in Chinese Turkestan.

Practically inaccessible from all directions a century ago, Tibet, the 'hidden land of the Lamas', would demand months of arduous trekking just to reach its periphery, the only exception being from the south, where despite the Himalayan wall there existed routes over passes leading to the heart of Tibet in a much shorter time. But only the most daring, adventurous and hardy travellers made it to Tibet, and even fewer were privileged to set their eyes on Lhasa, the sacred but 'forbidden city'. Many never returned alive. Hence, up to the early twentieth century, Tibet remained somewhat both an enigma and a 'Shangri-La' (a mystical, beautiful, faraway place) in the popular imagination.

Although the two belligerents, Tibet and China, concluded peace treaties (which have been inscribed on pillars) in the eighth and ninth centuries, laying down their common borders, Tibet's boundaries were still 'ill-defined and frequently non-existent'.[14] This was particularly so to the north and east.

A brilliant and fairly accurate geostrategic analysis of the frontiers of Tibet is contained in the military report of the Imperial General Headquarters of British India, published in 1910. While describing the frontiers and mountain systems of Tibet, this report mentions only the mountain chains to the north of the Himalayas, which include the Kunlun, Altyn Tagh, Nan Shan, Kokoshili, Tangla, Nyenchen Tanglha, Karakoram and the Great Himalayas.[15] Tibet lies between the first and the last mentioned ranges. These surveys and research were done over a century ago. Significantly, the absence of any mention or depiction of the Himalayas by ancient Chinese historians, Chinese map makers or in Chinese folklore does not help strengthen China's claim to Himalayan or cis-Himalayan regions. On the other hand, the Kunlun range does figure prominently as the southern limit of China. Zhou Enlai, the first premier of the People's Republic of China, himself told Jawaharlal Nehru, the first prime minister of independent India, in November 1956 that the Chinese looked upon the Karakoram with the same sentiment that India looked upon the Himalayas.[16] Perhaps this was to justify the Chinese claim to Aksai Chin. Historically and traditionally, Tibet's southern jurisdiction extended at best up to the northern slopes of the Himalayas and very rarely, at any period in history, extended beyond that to the southern glacis. The Tibetan highlanders could never take to the thickly forested, hot and humid southern Himalayan slopes and definitely could not adapt to the climate of the foothills or the plains.

Tibet had been isolated and secluded for thousands of years because of its geography. Access to Lhasa, the heart of Tibet, was principally by five routes; they were from the north-west, north-east, east, south-east and south. Till the middle of the twentieth century, there were hardly any worthwhile means of surface transportation within Tibet or even roads leading to it from the neighbouring regions, except for two or three caravan routes and bridle paths in a few areas. There were mainly foot tracks and yak, camel or pony trails across the sparsely populated areas, with little logistics support along the way. Journeys across Tibet were fraught with danger and adventure, and it would take months for men and material to reach Lhasa, unless they took the access route from the south. There are exciting descriptions of these hazardous voyages made in the eighteenth and nineteenth centuries by adventurers, pilgrims, surveyors, traders and spies from Britain, France, Russia and other European nations, and from India, Japan and China. As elaborated in the report of the general staff of the army headquarters of British India, 1910, 'It is only in the case of the *Janglam*—the great high road connecting Peking with the Tibetan capital, and continuing westward into Ladakh—that any effort has been made to maintain a roadway suitable for commercial traffic.'[17]

There were no metalled roads connecting Lhasa till the middle of the twentieth century. There were five historical caravan or trade routes, as shown in Figure 1. Two of these routes were from the north and skirted the Changthang Plateau. One was from Urumqi in Xinjiang (Sinkiang) province to Lhasa via Kashgar, Aksai Chin, Mayum Pass and Shigatse. Kashgar and Yarkand figured prominently as nodes along the silk trade route from China and Tibet to Central Asia and beyond. Marching along the western extremity of the Takla Makan desert and the Kunlun range, this route climbs up to the Tibetan plateau along the northern slopes of the Kunlun and traverses through the Aksai Chin area. It rises from an elevation of about 1,000 metres at Urumqi to 5,000 metres on the Tibetan plateau, covering a distance of over 4,000 kilometres to do so, threading its way across a number of mountain ranges. The rainfall in this region is scanty, and varies from 100 to 500 millimetres per year. Till about the mid-twentieth century, it took eight to nine months to complete this journey on foot.

The second northern route connects Lanzhou in Gansu province with Lhasa along the historical alignment via Xining in the famous Koko Nor lake region and Golmud. This route negotiates six major mountain ranges and passes at altitudes of about 5,000 metres (16,400 feet), the Tanggu La, at 5,220 metres (17,000 feet), being the most daunting of them. This route traverses a more rugged and desolate terrain than the first and is even more sparsely inhabited than many other Tibetan regions. Although the distance from Lanzhou to Lhasa is only 2,200 kilometres, much shorter than the north-western route, even at a conservative estimate it would take four to five months of arduous trekking to do this journey. The rise in elevation of about 3,000 metres from the Sichuan basin across ravines and gorges adds to the challenge of movement of man, material and related logistics along this route.

The third major axis connecting Peking with Lhasa is through Chengdu, Derge, Chamdo and Nagchuka, a distance of about 2,210 kilometres. A southern alignment of this route takes off from Chamdo, joins the road coming from Yunnan at Gartok and then proceeds westwards to Lhasa. Though they pass through areas with relatively larger populations, these axes from Sichuan province to Tibet run through some of the most challenging terrains in the world. Between the mountain ranges here tapering off from the Tibetan massif in the south-eastern direction flow the major rivers of South-East Asia and southern China (the Irrawaddy, Salween, Mekong and Yangtze and their numerous tributaries). As mentioned earlier, these rivers flow through extremely narrow valleys and deep canyons, posing a formidable challenge for lateral movement against the 'grain' of the country in the east–west direction.

In order to appreciate the degree of difficulty involved in travelling this route, one must know that over a spatial distance of about 500 kilometres between the Yangtze and the Tsangpo river valleys, there are at least seventeen ridges or mountain ranges that have to be negotiated, with elevations yo-yoing between 2,500 metres and 5,000 metres. Till the mid-twentieth century, it would take many months, perhaps even up to half a year, to cover this distance on foot or on horseback. Going up and down every ridge and the steep ascents and descents took a heavy toll of men and material. The fierce, semi-nomadic tribes living in this forested mountainous region were a law unto themselves and made travel here that much more difficult. Provision for security for travel in this region had always been a major concern, and remained so till even a few decades ago. To add to all this, the heavy precipitation (1,000–1,500 millimetres annually) and even snow in the higher reaches of these mountain ranges often resulted in snow avalanches and mudslides that would wash away bridges and even segments of roads.

The route from the south-east linking Yunnan to Tibet too is a very challenging and difficult one. Of approximately 2,170 kilometres, it connects Kunming to Lhasa via Dali and Gartok, where it joins the southern Sichuan–Tibet road. From Dali it proceeds northwards along the valleys of the Yangtze and Mekong rivers and passes through difficult, heavily forested mountainous terrain. This region too had its proud tribes, and security along this route too had always been a big challenge. Heavy precipitation of up to 1,000 millimetres annually along this route results in enormous erosion of riverbanks and floods. Frequently, massive landslides occur, carrying the roads along with them.

The last route left to describe is the one from the southern direction, from India to Tibet—to Lhasa in particular. Since the ancient times, Tibet's proximity to India had resulted in exchanges of culture, ideas, trade and commerce between the peoples of the two regions. Buddhism spread across the Himalayan passes from India to Tibet. The core of Tibet and the Lhasa region are just 500 kilometres to 1,000 kilometres away from many places in north India, requiring only a month or two to reach by foot or on horseback from there. In fact, from Kalimpong and Darjeeling, Lhasa is only about 400 kilometres away as the crow flies, while Kolkata (earlier Calcutta) is 600 kilometres distant. The only barriers between the two regions are the mighty Himalayas and the Tsangpo river.

2

History and Geopolitics

'When Tibet was free, we took our freedom for granted. We had little
sense that it was something we had to prove or even defend, because we
were unaware that it was under threat … Our physical isolation lulled
us into a sense of complacency … In former times Tibetans were a war-
like nation whose influence spread far and wide. With the advent of
Buddhism our military prowess declined.'

—*Dalai Lama*[1]

Geography isolated Tibet from the world, and its history was a construct thereof. Till 1951, when the Chinese assimilated Tibet into its fold, and with brutal force when the situation called for it, Tibet witnessed either periods of independence or some form and degree of vassalage to the Chinese kingdom, depending upon the waxing and waning of imperial China.

Tibetans have been acclaimed as a race of ferocious warriors and were militarily aggressive. In fact, Tibet was an important military power in Asia till the seventh century. During brief periods in its history it even held sway over parts of China, Turkestan, Mongolia and Hindustan.[2] It was on account of the advent and spread of Buddhism from the fifth to the eighth century that the Tibetans commenced their transformation into a pacific society. Once they embraced Buddhism, their military prowess gradually diminished to such an extent that they were hard put to even defend their own nation. The Tibetans were naive in the extreme and believed that spiritual strength and non-aggressive intent would guarantee them a peaceful existence. They eventually realized that religion and a 'strong national faith' were no substitute for military power. Interestingly, a unique *choe–yon*, or priest–patron relationship, as some kind of a security shield, came into being, first between the Tibetans and the Mongols in the mid-thirteenth century, when it was established between the Sakya guru, Phagspa, and Kublai Khan, the Mongol prince, in 1254, and later between the Tibetans and the Chinese.[3]

Ancient Tibetan history is shrouded in obscurity. Tibetans believe in their mythological origin from the union of a divine male monkey reincarnation of Chen-re-zi, an avatar of Avalokitesvara, the Bodhisattva of compassion, and a 'mother cliff-ogress'. Their six offspring were believed to be the first inhabitants of Tibet.

There is some evidence to show that human settlements existed in this elevated plateau from palaeolithic times. Nomadic tribes who were fierce hunter-gatherers and herders came into Tibet from northern China, Koko Nor and Zhang Zhung (Amdo) and settled in this region. It is also probable that some frontier tribes from western Sichuan and from the northern parts of Yunnan and Burma moved northwards along the major river valleys and established habitats here and in the uplands of eastern and south-eastern Tibet. It is clear that as they were scattered across this vast, inhospitable and desolate land mass, their civilization took a long time to evolve and emerge.

Tibet having no written language, the oral records of its history and civilization assumed a mystical and mythological dimension. Some accounts derived from the annals of Chinese historians and from later reports of the intrepid travellers and explorers to Tibet from around the fifteenth century have helped trace the origin and history of this 'hidden land' and its people. The Tibetans were a prosperous people who lived in the agricultural river valleys and in towns in the central, southern and south-eastern regions of their land; these people consisted of the elite, the lamas, the landed gentry and the laity. There were also the nomads who inhabited the vast Changthang Plateau and the northern, western and eastern highlands. And, lastly, there were the people who lived on the northern glacis of the Himalayas and led a pastoral existence. By and large, the average Tibetan led a simple and fun-loving life. A Tibetan saying aptly portrays this facet of their lifestyle: 'If you have beer [a local brew] you will get a headache, and if you don't have it you will get heartache.'

Civilization, as the world understands it, began in Tibet with the founding of a large Tibetan empire during the reign of the illustrious Songtsan Gampo in the seventh century. A powerful king, he 'overran upper Burma and western China and forced the Chinese emperor to a humiliating peace'. As part of the terms of this peace with China in AD 640, 'he received a Chinese princess [named Wencheng] in marriage'.[4] Reportedly, his first wife was Bhrikuti, a Nepalese princess. Both wives happened to be zealous Buddhists and were able to prevail upon their husband to adopt Buddhism and spread this faith throughout Tibet. 'He sent his minister Thomi Sambhota to India with sixteen students to study Buddhism and Sanskrit. On their return, they created a new script derived from a Gupta script, which is still used today, to render the Buddhist scriptures into Tibetan.'[5] He is also credited with moving the capital from Yarlung to Lhasa and constructing a palace on Potala hill.

Buddhism got established as a state religion under the subsequent kings. The new religion prevailed despite great resistance from the older Bon faith associated with the ancient Zhang Zung culture. The new faith could not gain acceptance among the laity without some kind of its synthesis with the traditional Bon religion. 'The deities that ruled their environmentally harsh and hostile surroundings needed pacification, and many of the local spirits and deities and their complicated, extremely localised reverence rituals were absorbed into the Buddhist pantheon. Many of these local spirits were made into local protectors of the Buddhist religion.'[6]

During this period, Tibet's relations with China deteriorated time and again, resulting in conflicts. Peace treaties of significance were concluded in AD 783 and 821; they were inscribed bilingually on pillars and tablets. The AD 821 treaty has even broadly demarcated the border between China and Tibet.[7] This treaty's terms were engraved on three stone pillars—the first erected at the boundary, the second at the Jokhang temple at Lhasa, both of which exist today, and the third at the Chinese capital of that time, Chang'an, currently known as Xian or Sian.

Here are some relevant snatches from the inscription:

Tibet and China shall abide by the frontiers of which they are now in occupation. All to the east is the country of Great China; and all to the west is, without question, the country of Great Tibet ... Between the two countries, no smoke nor dust shall be seen ... This solemn agreement has established a great epoch when Tibetans shall be happy in the land of Tibet, and the Chinese in the land of China.[8]

As a matter of fact, H.E. Richardson, the last British resident in Lhasa, has said in his authoritative book *A Short History of Tibet*, 'Tibet and China, it is clear, were then two powers on an equal footing. In fact, the Tibetans were regularly the aggressors and, in general, had the upper hand.'[9]

Richardson says that in time, the power and authority of the lamas (priests) became supreme, beginning with the Indian scholar Atisha, who was invited by the king of western Tibet in the early part of the eleventh century. Chiefly due to the wisdom, knowledge and ability of Atisha, the first of the 'chief priests', ecclesiastical rule firmed in its roots in Tibet. Subsequently, during the Mongol (Yuan) rule in China, Kublai Khan, son of the famous Genghis Khan, summoned to his court the head priest of the Sakya monastery 'who stayed for twelve years with the Great Khan'. He prevailed upon the emperor to accept the Buddhist faith, and, for his services as 'the consecrator and coronator of the emperors of China', was conferred sovereign powers over the entire territory of Tibet comprising the U-Tsang, Amdo and Kham provinces. This was the beginning of spiritual and temporal rule by the Sakya lamas, the 'red hat' sect, in Tibet during the eleventh century.

With the downfall of the Yuan dynasty, the Mongols retreated into outer Mongolia and established their own Buddhist religious order with their grand lama located at Urga, near the great lake of Lob Nor. As a result of withdrawal of patronage of the imperial court, the authority of the Sakya lamas diminished considerably. In the meanwhile, a reformist movement in Tibetan Buddhism, the 'yellow hat' sect, was founded by Tsong Khapa, a famous Buddhist teacher. This period, the fourteenth century, witnessed the founding of the three famous monasteries of

Lhasa—Sera (The Wild Rose Fence), Ganden (The Joyous, located about twenty-six miles from Lhasa) and Drepung (The Rice Heap, the largest in the world, near Lhasa). Due to the unsettled political situation, the Gelug school was declared as a new sect and gained strength and recognition as the predominant strain of Buddhism in Tibet.

Eventually, Sonam Gyatso, believed to be the reincarnation of the first two chief priests of the Gelug sect, was the first to be formally anointed with the title of Dalai or 'Tale' (Vast as the Ocean) in 1578 by the Mongolian king Altan Khan. Thus began the tradition of the Dalai Lama. The fourth Dalai Lama was from Mongolia. During his scholarship in Tibet he became a disciple of the reputed Lama Lobsang Chosgyan of Tashilhunpo (The Mount of Blessing) monastery near Shigatse. This 'guru' later became known as the Panchen Lama, 'Great Gem of Learning', and was given the spiritual status of a Grand Lama by the Dalai Lama. Also referred to as Tashi Lama, this line of chief priests had no temporal power, but was revered for its piety and ecclesiastical acumen. The Tashi Lama played an important role in the selection and approval of the new Dalai Lama and in ordaining him, as was done by the Grand Lama of Lhasa for the Tashi Lamas. As borne out by history, the two Grand Lamas from the same yellow hat sect have been frequently set against each other as part of a 'balancing game' by the bigger players or external powers.[10]

The Mongol prince, Gushri Khan, who was a firm follower of the Gelug sect, invaded Tibet in 1640, and in the next two years established his writ over Amdo, Kham and the 'U' regions. Assisted by Sonam Rapten, the Dalai Lama's regent, he disempowered the ruling clan of Tsangpa and ended the era of dynasties, firmly putting in place instead theocratic rule by the Dalai Lama in Tibet.[11]

The fifth Dalai Lama, Lobsang Ngawang Gyatso, ruled for thirty-five years. He united Tibet once again. With the help of his patron, Gushri Khan, he became the supreme spiritual and temporal leader of all Tibet—a combination of priest, God and king in the seventeenth century.

He was also received by the Chinese emperor Shunzi in January 1653 with elaborate protocol and stayed in the specially built Yellow Palace.

During his reign, the Great Fifth, as he was called, brought in many reforms and established the Ganden Phodang, a new form of government, with the Dalai Lama as its head and a Kashag or council of ministers.[12] (This temporal administrative structure remained in vogue till the Chinese takeover in 1951.) It was the Great Fifth who commenced construction of the Potala palace and spurred enhancement of the powers of the monasteries of Tashilhunpo, Ganden, Sera and Drepung.

Tibet went into turmoil after this relatively peaceful period and was invaded by the Dzungar tribe of Mongols in 1717. Lhasa witnessed rape and pillage, and the Tibetans appealed to the Chinese emperor K'ang Hsi for help. His army evicted the Dzungars and installed the next Dalai Lama. This aid came at a price, in that K'ang Hsi assumed formal suzerainty over Tibet in 1720, and positioned a Chinese Amban who represented the Manchu emperor and had vast powers at Lhasa with an armed escort, taking away the temporal powers of the Grand Lama. This was the first armed intervention carried out by the Chinese in Tibet. As time passed, the powers of the Ambans and of their appointees, the regents of the successive Dalai Lamas, increased phenomenally.

The Sino-Tibetan boundary in the early eighteenth century was edified by the erection of pillars bearing inscriptions that demarcated the frontier, as mentioned in the famous British explorer Eric Teichmann's account.[13]

> In 1727 the Chinese erected a boundary stone on the Bum La (Pass) to the west of Batang which indicated that they regarded this border as more or less following the Mekong-Yangtze watershed ...[14]
>
> As narrated by Alastair Lamb in *The McMahon Line*, Volume 1

East of this line the Chinese exercised nominal control over the Tibetan districts except for the main communication arteries. With the decline of the Chinese Empire in the latter part of the nineteenth century, even main roads were at times controlled by the local tribals.

During certain phases of the eighteenth and nineteenth centuries, the machinations of the Ambans and the regents to retain their hold on power ensured that the young Dalai Lamas never attained adulthood and died as minors.[15] 'It is perhaps more than a coincidence that between the seventh and the thirteenth holders of that office, only one reached his majority,' said Thubten Jigme Norbu, the older brother of the present Dalai Lama.

British India's earliest contact with Tibet took place in 1774 when Warren Hastings, the first de facto Governor General of India, sent his emissary George Bogle to Tibet at the request of the Panchen Lama. Bogle met with the great lama of Tashi Lhunpa in response to Tashi Lama's missive interceding on behalf of the Bhutanese. The second contact of the British with Tibetans was when Captain Samuel Turner, a cousin of Warren Hastings, visited Shigatse in 1783, endeavouring to build on the rapport established with the Tashi Lama by Bogle. Cordial relations were thus established between the two sides, which led to an increase in commerce and trade between them. However, this development was short-lived as the first Gurkha–Tibet war started in 1790; the Gurkhas, in a surprise offensive, crossed the Himalayas and captured Shigatse. They plundered and damaged the Tashilhunpo monastery too. The Tibetans appealed to the Chinese once again, and a large army was sent to Tibet by the Manchu emperor. Eventually, the Gurkhas were not only defeated but pushed back into the precincts of Kathmandu by the combined forces of the Chinese and the Tibetans and made to sign an 'ignominious treaty' as recorded by Teichmann. This was the second occasion when the Chinese army advanced into Tibet. As a result of this campaign, 'by Imperial Decrees of 1793 two Ambans were appointed, given equal rank with the Dalai and Panchen Lamas, and made responsible for the superintendence of the administration of the country'.[16]

The unfortunate outcome of this war was the Tibetan adoption of the 'policy of exclusion' under Chinese pressure as they felt there was a British hand behind the Gurkha campaign. This kept Tibet isolated from external influences, particularly the British, for almost a century. However, it goes to the credit of Thomas Manning—the first British adventurer who cleverly and ingeniously managed to reach Lhasa in 1811 without any encouragement or official support from British India—that he was able to gain the audience of the seven-year-old Dalai Lama and secure a high degree of standing amongst the Chinese and Tibetan officials. But after Manning's return in 1812, following its age-old custom of keeping foreigners out, Tibet once again became the 'Forbidden Land'.

Tibet was invaded in 1841 by a Dogra force from Ladakh led by General Zorawar Singh of the Sikh army of Maharaja Ranjit Singh. Zorawar Singh advanced along the Indus Valley and captured areas up to Taklakot in the proximity of Lake Manasarovar and Mount Kailash. In retaliation, a combined force of Chinese and Tibetan armies was dispatched from Lhasa and the battle was joined by 10 December 1841. After an intense fight, during which Zorawar Singh was mortally wounded, the Dogra forces suffered a decisive defeat. The Dogra army of 6,000 under the Lahore flag was practically destroyed by both the enemy and Tibet's murderously cold conditions. Reinforcements arrived from Kashmir by the spring of 1842 and the battle was joined once again near Chushul. The Chinese and Tibetan forces were prevented from capturing Leh and subsequently defeated. The Tibetan general was killed, and his forces retreated to Tibet. 'Thus ended the war, and since its occurrence peace has remained undisturbed. In 1842, the frontier was demarcated by a party of Dogra and Chinese officials, together with Captain Cunningham and Lieutenant Strachey.' At that time, the treaty of Chushul signed by the Chinese and the Sikhs clearly contained the words: '... to respect the old boundaries of Ladakh.'[17] These boundaries, apparently, were well known to both sides, at least along the traditional routes and areas of settled populations. The gist of this treaty is given below (details in Appendix 1):

On this auspicious occasion, the second day of the month Asuj in the year 1899 we—the officers of Lhasa, viz. firstly, Kalon Sukanwala, and secondly Bakshi Sapju, commander of the forces of the Empire of China, on the one hand, and Dewan Hari Chand and Wazir Ratnu, on behalf of Raja Gulab Singh, on the other—agree together and swear before God that the friendship between Raja Gulab Singh and the Emperor of China and Lama Guru Sahib Lassawala [of Lhasa] will be kept and observed till eternity; for the traffic in shawl, pasham, and tea. We will observe our pledge to God, Gayatri, and Pasi. Wazir Mian Khusal Chu is witness.

In 1888, the British took advantage of a Tibetan incursion into Sikkim in the area of Jelep La and launched a military expedition to evict the

Tibetans. Led by Colonel Graham, the British forces stormed the Tibetan stockade and entrenchments and drove the Tibetan forces over the Jelep La and into the Chumbi Valley, following them into it. But later, the British army were recalled to the Sikkimese side of the frontier in order to avoid complications with the Chinese. However, skirmishes and minor clashes continued for some time afterwards.

Apparently, the *casus belli* for the Tibetan incursion was the British penetration of Sikkim and their road developments there, the British possession of Darjeeling, issues relating to British India's trade with Tibet and perceived loss of the sphere of influence of the lama king. From a British perspective, their military actions were undertaken to consolidate their acquisitions in the Darjeeling area and secure the flanks of Sikkim, which was their protectorate. After almost two years of negotiations, a treaty was signed between China and Britain in Calcutta on 17 March 1890. The Tibetan claim to suzerainty over Sikkim was given up, and the Sikkim–Tibet boundary was delimited. It was decided that trade issues would be settled later. However, as the Tibetans were neither a party to this convention nor concurred with it, they refused to comply with the terms of the agreement. Notwithstanding the Tibetan response, after hard bargaining by the two sides, the British and Chinese signed a 'set of trade regulations' on 5 December 1893. However, these were not allowed to be implemented by the Tibetans, who were in connivance with or had the tacit approval of the Chinese themselves![18]

The intransigence of the Tibetans and the cold-shouldering by the Dalai Lama and his officials of British overtures to develop cordial relations and trade with Tibet led to strained relations between the two sides. Even letters from the office of the viceroy of India in 1900–01 were returned unopened from Tibet, an insult not easy for the British Empire to swallow. On the other hand, during the same period, the Grand Lama was corresponding with the Russian Tsar through his special envoys. This communication channel was facilitated by Lama Dorjieff, a suspected Russian plant in the Dalai Lama's inner council and the mastermind of Russian intrigue and influence in Tibet. Though a Russian subject from the region of Lake Baikal, he was a Mongolian Buriat, and was to play an important role in Tibetan politics. He had been a monk at the famous

Drepung monastery since 1880, and by 1888 had worked his way up to become the tutor and confidant of the young Dalai Lama. In 1901, he even led a group of Tibetans as the 'Envoy Extraordinary of the Dalai Lama' and was granted an audience by the Tsar.

The British were growing apprehensive of Russia gaining a hold over Tibet while the Chinese feared that Tibet might become a protectorate of the British. The 'Great Game East' was in full play; it was a period of high intrigue and machinations by Russia, China and Britain to bring Tibet into their respective spheres of influence. The Chinese Manchu Empire had been weakened by successive wars, beginning with the Opium Wars of 1839–42 and 1856–60, the Sino-French war of 1883–85, and the Sino-Japanese War of 1894–95. All these wars culminated in humiliating treaties being thrust on the Chinese. The impact of these treaties and subsequent events on the psyche of the Chinese led to the coinage of the phrase 'a century of humiliation', in reference to the period from the late 1840s to 1949, when the communists took power in China.

By virtue of the British Indian empire, with its headquarters at Calcutta, being the closest 'power' to Tibet proper, it took upon itself the responsibility of keeping all the other powers away, Tsarist Russia in particular. Though Lord Curzon had strong views on China's questionable control over Tibet, which he described as a 'constitutional fiction', Whitehall did not see eye to eye with its Indian administration with regard to recommendations coming from India, which called for greater British involvement and presence in Tibet.

The British policy on Tibet swung from one extreme to another. Sometimes it was one of non-interference in or indifference to the internal affairs of Tibet, and sometimes it was to build cordial relations with Tibet in order to enhance the empire's trade and commerce with it. From another standpoint Britain sometimes dealt with Tibet as if it were an independent entity and sometimes as if it were a country under Chinese suzerainty. There were many factors simultaneously at play, not easily comprehended by the policy initiators in British India, but which restrained the home government in England. On one occasion, in a rebuke, John Morley, the Secretary of State for India, had this to say to Lord Minto, the Viceroy and Governor General, in July 1906,

'Britain *"cannot have two foreign policies* (emphasis added)". The decision
to discuss Central Asian questions with Russia had been made, and the
Indian Government would have to abide by that decision. *"Be we right or
wrong,"* he declared, *"that is our policy* (emphasis added)".[19] The Foreign
and India Offices of the home government believed they were able to see
the big picture, and therefore were the unquestioned keepers of British
imperial interests. The international power play, particularly Britain's
agreements on power, trade and influence-sharing with Russia, China,
France and Japan, as also the impact of events in Tibet on developments
in Afghanistan, Persia, Mongolia and South-East Asia had to be weighed
and analysed before any actions could be taken on the ground. The image
of Great Britain and the British Empire had to be upheld.

The Tibetans, the thirteenth Dalai Lama in particular, were extremely
wary of British expansionism as they had witnessed the forced acquisition
by the British of Darjeeling and Kalimpong areas from Sikkim and Bhutan,
respectively, the British eviction of the intruding Tibetan army from
Natong (presently called Nathang) in east Sikkim in 1888 by the use of
overwhelming force, and British forays into Bhutan. At the same time,
under the advice of Dorjieff, the Dalai Lama was emboldened to adopt
a policy of indifference towards both the British and the Chinese, on the
premise that he could depend on a benign Tsarist Russia for protection.
The stage for Younghusband's expedition to Lhasa was thus set.[20]

PART II

THE YOUNGHUSBAND EXPEDITION

Colonel F.E. Younghusband

3

Clouds over Lhasa

At the turn of the nineteenth century the British Raj in India was at its zenith. India was the jewel in the crown of the British Empire. In China, on the other hand, the Qing dynasty was on its last legs. And Tibet, under the thirteenth Dalai Lama, Thubten Gyatso, was witnessing a period of absolute autonomy veering towards independence. The Tsarist Russian Empire was expanding southwards in an endeavour to exercise control over trade along the silk routes and to seek an outlet in the warm waters of the Indian Ocean. The Great Game was being played out in the Central Asian highlands by the British and the Russians. Both powers were eyeing Tibet and intriguing and jockeying for influence in Lhasa. At this juncture, China's influence in Tibet was almost non-existent. Nonetheless, all three players were keeping an eagle eye on the activities of the Dalai Lama.

Tibetan society, as at the dawn of the twentieth century, was lucidly described by Charles Bell thus:

> It is the priests who exercise the check on the feudal lords. For the Tibetans believe devoutly in their form of Buddhism, and the powerful influence embraces all. Even Buddha himself can do but little without the priests ... Thus it comes that this people, simple but intelligent, independent yet orderly, hospitable yet suspicious, fear foreign intrusion as they fear little else.[1]

The Viceroy of India at that time, Lord Curzon, needed no stimulus to demonstrate Britain's determination to show the obstinate Dalai Lama his place and establish a hold on Tibet, and at the same time secure trading rights that were as beneficial to Britain as possible. The Russophobe that he was, keeping the Russian bear at bay was the pivot of his Tibet policy, even if that involved helping China regain its stature and prestige in Tibet. A categorical statement in an important communication to the home government on 8 January 1903 by Curzon explains his stance:

We regard the so-called suzerainty of China over Tibet as a constitutional fiction—a political affectation which has only been maintained because of its convenience to both parties.[2]

The weakening of the Chinese empire's hold on Tibet at the turn of the century, coupled with British apprehensions about the expanding Russian influence over Tibet and the indifferent attitude evinced by the Grand Lama towards them, resulted in the famous British venture—the expedition led by Colonel F.E. Younghusband to Lhasa in 1903–04. This civil–military mission crossed the frozen heights of Jelep La in Sikkim in the winter of 1903 and entered Tibet through the Chumbi Valley. Their advance met with unexpected success and did not face any worthwhile resistance, except at Gyantse. Eventually, they pushed on to Lhasa, even though the expedition was not initially authorized to penetrate so deep into Tibet. This was the beginning of British involvement in the affairs of the hidden kingdom of Tibet. Though the Dalai Lama fled from Lhasa before the expedition arrived at the gates of the 'Forbidden City', Younghusband was able to extract a treaty from the Tibetans that gave the British far-reaching influence in Tibetan affairs, greater presence in Tibet and greater trade between British India and Tibet.

Younghusband's expedition provided an excellent opportunity to the British to launch a number of exploratory missions to uncharted tribal territories, both to the south as well as to the north of the Himalayan crest line. The aim of the British was to determine their natural and political boundary with Tibet, as also the northern limit of the sub-Himalayan tribal territory. (Among other things, the mystery of the Tsangpo river and its great bend, which was reported to cut across the Himalayas through one of the greatest gorges in the world, in the Pomed region, had to be conclusively resolved!) The Chinese reaction to this turn of events brought about an increased presence of their army and administration in south-eastern and central Tibet and also led to the fierce subjugation of eastern Tibet. A reign of terror was unleashed by the Chinese army under General Chao Erh-feng. His campaigns in the Marches in the Kham and other areas along the northern slopes of the eastern Himalayas are remembered to this day for their savage repression of the people. In fact, the resurgence of Chinese power in Tibet led to the thirteenth Dalai Lama fleeing to India in 1910. These events set in motion a chain reaction, and, for the first time, Chinese activity was witnessed in one or two places in close vicinity of the traditional border during 1910–12 in the hitherto unexplored tribal territories in the southern slopes of the Himalayas. The British surveyors and explorers were the first outsiders to enter this remote and extremely rugged, mountainous, high-altitude terrain inhabited by fiercely independent tribes. It is important to highlight that there was no credible presence of the Chinese ever in the territories south of the formidable Himalayan massif.

The 'incremental invasion' (more commonly referred to as 'expedition') of Tibet by British India, led by F.E. Younghusband in 1903–04, was an epochal mission. The strength and scope of the expedition also increased as it ventured deeper into Tibet. It ended Tibet's seclusion and commenced a complex relationship between British India and Tibet. The reasons for the launch of this mission have been described earlier, but this event is historically significant as far as the geopolitics of the Tibetan and Indo-Tibetan frontier region is concerned, and it has had an enormous fallout over a full century and a decade, its reverberations being felt even today.

Cautious as the British were in their relations with China while safeguarding their 'imperial interests', primarily not wanting to upset their commerce and trade in the Shanghai region, the home government at first authorized a peaceful 'expedition' to Khamba Dzong in mid-1903. Khamba Dzong is an important border settlement, two days' march into Tibet from north Sikkim across the 5,030-metre Kongra La. A British commission led by then major F.E. Younghusband was tasked with proceeding to Khamba Dzong to discuss and resolve trade and other contentious matters arising from non-adherence to the Sino-British Convention of 1890 and the Trade Agreement of 1893 by the Tibetans. The meeting had been agreed on by the three parties—British India, Tibet and China. Khamba Dzong was accessible only by an extremely difficult foot track going upstream along the Teesta river. Connecting the small villages of Lachen and Giaogong, going past the 'crumbling mountain', where temperature variations and the mildest of tremors of the earth send huge boulders and rocks rolling off the mountains even today, the track ascends to altitudes of over 4,500 metres, almost going up to the source of the Teesta in the glaciers of north Sikkim.

Khamba Dzong was probably chosen by the Tibetans to keep the negotiations away from the public eye and prevent the 'firangis' (the British) from entering the Chumbi Valley along the more frequented trade route from Darjeeling to Lhasa. It had been decided that the Tibetans would depute officials of appropriate status or rank to meet the British at the designated meeting point. In fact, the Chinese government had assured the expedition that their Amban would participate in these deliberations along with high-ranking Tibetan officials. Despite a wait of almost five months, it became apparent that neither the Chinese nor the Tibetans intended to honour their commitment to meet the British commission. As no high-ranking and influential Chinese official had been deputed, and those commissioners who arrived at the rendezvous were 'uninfluential and of inferior rank', the British referred the matter to Peking. They received a vague reply that indicated no firm date for the arrival of the Amban. Underscoring their indifference, the Tibetans too only sent low-ranking and 'unapproachable' officials to Khamba Dzong many weeks later. Meanwhile, a Tibetan force of about 3,000 was amassed, demanding withdrawal of the British mission that comprised, in addition to Younghusband, J.C. White, the resident of Sikkim, two officer-interpreters and an armed escort of 200 soldiers of the Sikh Pioneer Regiment. There was a backup reserve force of 300 British soldiers on the Sikkim side at Tangu. However, the stand-off remained peaceful.

As the Khamba Dzong mission had become abortive, in November 1903 the Government of India ordered occupation of Chumbi Valley and resumption of negotiations at Gyantse.

Lord Curzon was thus able to drive home the necessity of launching an armed mission into Tibet in order to restore the prestige of the British Empire, bring to heel the Tibetan Grand Lama and his ministers and set the almost defunct commercial and trade relations between British India and Tibet on an even keel. This mission would also endeavour to prevent the Russians from consolidating their influence over Tibet and, the British hoped, put a stop to the intrigues being indulged in by Dorjieff and others at the Dalai Lama's palace in Lhasa. 'In fact, Agvan Dorjiev had met with Czar Nicholas in 1898, 1900 and 1901, each time having been sent by the Dalai Lama to establish closer relations with Russia. Dorjiev had convinced the Dalai Lama that the Russian Czar was sympathetic to Buddhism,'[3] as narrated by Warren W. Smith.

According approval on 6 November 1903 to Lord Curzon's recommendations based on his perceived aims, the home government of Britain assigned three tasks to the mission. The first was for it to advance without delay as far as Gyantse, using force if necessary, and insist that the Tibetans fulfil their treaty obligations. The second was to occupy the Chumbi Valley to display the earnestness of the mission, and the last was to withdraw as early as possible once 'reparation' had been 'exacted from the Lamas'.[4] This expedition was to be led by F.E. Younghusband, a commissioner with an acting rank of colonel, and its military component by Colonel James Ronald Leslie Macdonald, an officer from the Royal Corps of Engineers who was given the temporary rank of brigadier-general and placed under the command of Younghusband. At the same time, Macdonald began reporting directly to the commander-in-chief, India, from 29 September 1903.[5]

In the beginning, this force comprised about 1,150 of all ranks, with four guns (artillery) and two Maxim machine guns, besides a gargantuan logistics set-up consisting of a 'field hospital, engineer field parks, telegraph, postal and sundry detachments'. Transportation of loads for this force, a herculean task indeed, was planned on a multimode basis, with about 10,000 porters, over 7,000 mules, ponies, yaks, etc. The weapons and equipment carried by this force were far superior to anything the Tibetans possessed. The Maxim machine guns, recently introduced in European armies, were a great force multiplier. With a cyclic rate of firing of 600 rounds a minute, they were an advanced weapon system of that time. The force also had two antiquated light guns (seven-pounders) named 'Bubble' and 'Squeak', which had been in service for over forty years.[6] The 'Tibet Mission Force' was commanded by a sapper officer, as perhaps, militarily, the challenge posed by the terrain was far greater than the threat of the Tibetan army. In resource-deficient Tibet, construction of roads, cart tracks, bridges, culverts, river-crossing expedients and habitat demanded a wide range of engineering skills and advance planning for many types of equipment and resources. For example, the expeditionary force carried foldable 'Berthon boats' manufactured at Bengal Engineering Group Centre in Roorkee, India, to cross the Tsangpo in case the local boats were sunk.

On 12 December 1903, the historic Younghusband expedition took off from Kupup, located at an altitude of about 4,000 metres, and climbed to the Jelep La at an elevation of 4,267 metres, and from there took a sharp drop of about 1,500 metres to the Chumbi Valley over a distance of a few kilometres. There was no track in certain stretches. The movement of bodies of men across these steep slopes has been graphically described by Lieutenant Colonel Austine Waddel, Army Medical Corps, who was a member of the mission:

> Diving down this slope, we got out of the wind almost immediately, and then sliding and slipping down the loose shoot of frost-splintered rocks which here formed our track, along with the heavily-laden coolies who stumbled foot-sore and weary and bruised by the rocks, we passed a small frozen lake of green ice; thence descended some 2000 feet more, and across frozen side-torrents, now solid ice, till we reached the black pine-forest.[7]

Brigadier Macdonald's force entered Chumbi Valley proper on 13 December and, surprisingly, met with no resistance during the initial phase of the expedition. There was no sign of the Tibetan regular army.

This was probably because the large Tibetan contingent, assembled as a show of force opposite the British mission at Khamba Dzong, continued to remain there, tricked into believing that a larger British force was likely to ingress along the same route and proceed to Shigatse, and thence to Lhasa. It was a master stroke of British strategy that the Younghusband expedition chose to advance along the shortest and most direct approach to Lhasa through the Chumbi Valley while the mission at Khamba Dzong kept the Tibetans engaged there. The mission was to remain peaceful; it had specific instructions against use of force until the Tibetans commenced hostilities.

The force established their first camp in Tibet at the base of a hill in a pine forest at a place called Langram. Learning of their presence, an assortment of Chinese and Tibetan officials, along with the Tibetan governor of Chumbi Valley, came up and met Younghusband. They protested the intrusion. Not succeeding in persuading Younghusband to agree to fall back to India with his force, and unable to match the military capability of the invading force, they quietly went their way.[8] Next day, the mission advanced further, establishing a firm base beyond Yatung, naming it 'New Chumbi'. After a few days, Macdonald's force advanced even further and secured Phari Dzong—an important fortress village—on 18 December 1903. Their occupation of the fort, with its dominating location, caused a great deal of consternation among the Tibetan Dzongpons, Chinese officials, the monks and the people. This act was contrary to Younghusband's earlier assurance to the Tibetans and adversely impacted the credibility of the firangis among the people here.[9]

The next phase of the invasion involved the advance to Gyantse across the Tang La (5,060 metres) on the ridge that divides Chumbi Valley from the Tibetan plateau. As a matter of fact, Chumbi Valley and the Amo (also known as Mo) Chu which flows through it are on the southern slopes of the Himalayas. This river flows southwards along the Sikkim–Bhutan border to eventually join the Teesta in the plains of north Bengal. Geographically, this tract of land blends naturally with the cis-Himalayan states of Sikkim and Bhutan rather than with the Tibetan plateau, offering a strategic advantage to the side that controls it. With this in mind, Younghusband and Curzon had intended to keep it under occupation on a long-term basis even after Younghusband's mission was accomplished. It is my view that imperial Britain neither gave due consideration to this intent at that juncture nor pursued it further because of its ramifications on their relations with China, Russia and other nations. Basically, India's security interests were often overlooked and were subordinate to those of the British Empire. Imagine Chumbi Valley being in India's posession till 1979!

Towering over the area to the east of the Tang La is the majestic peak of Chomolhari, 'Mountain of the Goddess Lady', its height at 7,314 metres. The ridge that connects this mountain with another 7,000-metre peak to the west of the Tang La makes it the natural divide.

Macdonald received reports of a concentration of Tibetan armed soldiers numbering approximately 3,000 at a place known as Guru, which lay midway between Yatung and Gyantse. The Tibetans had laid out a stockade comprising a stone fortification blocking the road to Shigatse in the proximity of Guru. On the spur of the hill to the west of the stockade were stone sangars and other elementary fortifications that were coordinated with the road block. To the east of this position was a low-lying area with a lake, which made it difficult for the British mission to outflank the defensive position astride the road.

On 31 March 1904, the advancing British forces were confronted by a group of Tibetan officers a few kilometres out of Guru and told to stop and return. Later, these forces were joined by a Tibetan general and some others, including a Depon and a lama. Some of the Tibetan soldiers were carrying Russian-made rifles. After a futile discussion with them, the British told the Tibetans that their mission would continue its advance to Gyantse, and that though it was intended to maintain peace, force would be used if deemed required. On reaching the wall and the fortifications blocking the road, Brigadier Macdonald gave orders to his force to physically evict the Tibetans from their positions and disarm them.

As the burly Sikh soldiers proceeded to take away their weapons, the Tibetans resisted violently, leading to scuffles between them. During this melee, a shot was fired by a Tibetan general, severely wounding a Sikh soldier; and this act started the battle. Both sides began discharging their weapons. This was an unequal fight in which the Tibetans suffered very heavy casualties. The British troops were equipped with better rifles, and their Maxim machine guns and artillery guns decided the outcome within minutes. In fact, the British soldiers appear to have used excessive force and, inexplicably, continued to engage even when the Tibetans, having thrown down their arms, were fleeing. A comparison of the casualties on the two sides speaks for itself. There were about 600 killed (including the Drepon), 300 wounded and 200-odd prisoners from among the Tibetans, against only thirteen wounded on the British side. The battle could be described as a mindless and unjustified mass slaughter by the British, and this subsequently continued to haunt the leadership of the Younghusband expedition. However, it is to the credit of the British force that many wounded Tibetan soldiers were evacuated and provided medical care and treatment by the British doctors and nursing assistants. Nonetheless, the British had overstepped their bounds. An indicting account of this engagement is given below:

> The Tibetans were mown down by the Maxim guns as they fled. 'I got so sick of the slaughter that I ceased fire, though the general's order was to make as big a bag as possible,' wrote Lieutenant Arthur Hadow, commander of the Maxim guns detachment. 'I hope I shall never again have to shoot down men walking away.'[10]

Thereafter, the victorious force marched into Guru and secured it. Guru was being held by a small force of Tibetans, who capitulated without much resistance. The mission's advance to Gyantse from here involved a few skirmishes and clearing actions in which the Tibetans hardly gave a fight, except at the great gorge of 'Red Idol' at Dzam-tang on 10 April, where too the Tibetans were outfought and had to withdraw with heavy losses. Again, the one-sided nature of the engagement is borne out by the casualty count on the two sides—three wounded on the British side, against 150 killed and wounded and over 100 prisoners, many of them monks, on the Tibetan side. The next day, the British force neared Gyantse. Its fort, or Dzong, loomed large on the horizon. It was no doubt strategically located on a dominating height astride the east–west highway connecting Lhasa with Shigatse. These are the two largest and monastically most important towns of Tibet, both in the prosperous U-Tsang region. Gyantse had to be secured for gaining control over all movement in the Tsangpo Valley before the British could move towards the capital town of Lhasa.

Figure 4: The imposing Dzong of Gyantse

Brigadier Macdonald ordered his force to camp about a little over 3 kilometres short of the fort. He then dispatched an emissary with a note asking the Tibetans to surrender and hand over the fort. After a suspenseful night, the next morning, on 12 April, goes Waddell's account, Macdonald's force was getting into position to storm the fort when 'a small party of officials rode out from the fort, led by General Ma under his crimson umbrella with the Jongpon and their minions. The Chinese general reported that all the Tibetan troops had been withdrawn.'[11]

Soon the British force advanced into the Dzong and secured it. The British flag was flying over the highest rampart of the fort. Gyantse was in British hands as the Tibetan garrison had indeed abandoned the Dzong. However, the mission decided not to occupy the Dzong for tactical and logistical reasons, and instead chose a large country house and farmland of the noble Changlo family nearby as its headquarters. Since the country house was close to a river, water would be easily available here. Thus ended the second phase of the mission.

As planned at the outset, Colonel Younghusband decided to hold discussions with the Tibetan and Chinese representatives at Gyantse to address the issues the mission had set out to resolve. Meanwhile, satisfied with the overall security situation prevailing in Gyantse, Brigadier Macdonald decided to leave a force of about 600 of all ranks as escort for the mission headquarters at Changlo Manor and fall back with the rest of the force to 'New Chumbi'. Thereby, he conjectured, he would be better able to protect the 240-kilometre line of communication up to Gyantse by establishing more posts and also considerably reduce his logistic burden by having a smaller force deployed at Gyantse. This proved to be a miscalculation, as later events demonstrated.

Brigadier Macdonald departed from Gyantse on 19 April with the major part of the force. The Changlo post was strengthened by a wall and other fortifications and the field of fire cleared on all sides. The town and the countryside appeared peaceful, and things seemed back to normal. As time passed, the negotiations between Younghusband and the Tibetans and Chinese continued but did not make much headway. A degree of complacency had crept into the mission headquarters at Changlo Manor. In one of his despatches in April, Younghusband conveyed to his superiors at Calcutta that 'on the 12th April all resistance in this part of Tibet is ended', and added, 'neither General, nor soldiers nor people have wished to fight'.[12] Taking advantage of the situation, the Tibetan army gradually re-established their control over the fort. They were also emboldened by the return of the larger part of the British force with Brigadier Macdonald to Chumbi Valley. An impression had also gained ground that the aggressors did not have any intention of proceeding beyond to Lhasa. In view of all this, the lamas not only planned to attack the isolated and apparently vulnerable Changlo position but also to disrupt the tenuous line of communication from Chumbi to Gyantse. They also urged the Tibetans to rise against the invaders.

Younghusband now received intelligence reports that the Tibetan army was concentrating a force at Karo La, a high-altitude pass about 48 kilometres to the east of Gyantse along the road to Lhasa. A mounted infantry surveillance detachment that came under fire near the pass on 1 May reported the presence of about 3,000 Tibetan soldiers. After consultations with Younghusband, Lieutenant Colonel Brander moved out on 3 May with about two-thirds of the force with two guns and the Maxim machine guns to clear the Karo La. When Brigadier Macdonald learnt of this plan, he tried his best to stop it. Unfortunately, by the time his wire reached Younghusband, Colonel Brander had already set off on his mission. Unknown to them, every step being taken by the British mission at Changlo was being carefully monitored by the Tibetans.

That something was amiss became evident from the eerie calm that pervaded in the town on 4 May. Premonition that something dangerous was imminent now hung thick in the air, and desertion by the local servants and even the patients from the hospital that was established near the mission forewarned the British garrison of the storm that was about to hit them. Taking cognizance of these developments, Younghusband wisely summoned the governor of the town, the Dzongpon, and detained him like a hostage in the camp. Early next morning the Tibetans attacked the Changlo position. Despite the warning signs, surprise was still achieved to some extent by the attackers. However, the Tibetans did not press home their attack into the walled enclosure of Changlo Manor even though they had great numerical advantage. Once again, the British Indian Army's superior leadership, training, weapons and valour turned the tables in their favour. After a bitter and hard-fought battle, the Tibetan attack was repulsed with heavy losses to them (120 killed and forty wounded). There were only four casualties on the British side, none of them fatal. In the meanwhile, Lieutenant Colonel Brander and his force, having routed the Tibetans from Karo La, once again with heavy losses to the opposing side, rejoined the force at Changlo Manor.

During the next month and a half, there circulated reports of a concentration of the Tibetan army from various regions in the vicinity of Gyantse advancing towards Changlo to beleaguer the comparatively small and isolated British force there. Meanwhile, the fortifications in the Dzong were being strengthened. There were skirmishes and raids by both sides every other day. Firing by the Tibetans from the Dzong by artillery and other weapons and from localities in the neighbourhood of Changlo Manor continued unabated. The British force retaliated for effect and remained on high alert, particularly during the hours of darkness. The lamas were sparing no effort to mobilize the masses against the foreign occupants, going from village to village and telling them it was a religious war.

At the same time, Younghusband continued his efforts to enter into a meaningful dialogue and negotiations with Tibetan and Chinese officials, but to no avail. Exhausting all means of resolving the issues he had come to settle, he sent an ultimatum to the Tibetans that unless negotiators of appropriate stature and authority arrived at Gyantse for talks by 25 June, the British mission would start their advance to Lhasa. They now received word through an intermediary, Tongsa Penlop, the regent and wielder of supreme temporal power over the whole of Bhutan,[13] that the Dalai Lama was deputing two peace delegates for talks. One of them was already at Gyantse, while the other, Shape Ta Lama (the Lama Member of Council), was on his way, along with the Grand Lama's chief secretary, Lopu Tsang.

Accordingly, an armistice was agreed on for a few days. On 26 June, before the talks, Brigadier Macdonald returned to Gyantse at the head of additional troops and reinforcements, including guns, and the British forces captured and cleared the Tibetan strongholds of Naini and Tse Chen monastery, establishing a cordon around the town. The talks were held on 3 July but proved to be abortive once again as the Tibetan delegates did not have sufficient authority to take major decisions. The Tibetans were now asked to vacate the Dzong within two days and if they didn't, they were told, there would be consequences. When this period ended, the British force launched an attack on the Dzong on 5 July, and by 6 p.m. the next day the fort was finally captured after overcoming stout resistance from the defenders. Lieutenant J.D. Grant of the 8th Gurkhas received the only Victoria Cross awarded for this campaign for displaying conspicuous gallantry during this action. Havildar Pun of the 8th Gurkhas was awarded the highest decoration an Indian soldier could get—the Indian Order of Merit Class I.

Earlier, on 27 May, Younghusband had sent a detailed report to the secretary to the Government of India, including in it a review of the current situation in the Gyantse area, an assessment of the intention of the Tibetans, and his recommendations for the future course of action and British policy on Tibet. The recommendations made by him, some of them watered down by the home government in Britain, did find a place in the memorandum of 1904 signed on 7 September at Lhasa.

4

Tibet on Its Knees

'Om mani padme hum'[1]
(An adaptation of Thangka painting)

Having seen through the game the Tibetans had been playing so far, the British government gave the go-ahead to Colonel Younghusband to take his expedition to Lhasa and compel the Tibetans to sit at the negotiating table and resolve issues relating to the political status of Tibet, the boundary between Tibet and Sikkim and Indo-Tibetan trade. Brigadier Macdonald had anticipated the requirement of additional

41

troops and artillery for this next phase of the mission. Therefore, as soon as the reinforcements of one and a half battalion of infantry and eight guns with supporting elements arrived at Chumbi, they were moved forward to Gyantse. The advance of the force to Lhasa was planned by Brigadier Macdonald, leaving behind sufficient troops for defence of the garrison at Gyantse. He had catered for the crossing of the Tsangpo, even providing for the possibility that the Tibetans might dismantle the boats or ferries plying there. The track beyond Gyantse had not been set foot on by any Britisher, except for Manning, who had travelled this route over a hundred years prior.[2]

The advance of the British force over 256 kilometes of Tibetan territory for the final phase of 'Mission Lhasa' commenced on 14 July 1904. Macdonald took with him two companies of mounted infantry, three infantry battalions, a battery and a half of mountain artillery, half a company of sappers, logistic echelons numbering about 2,000 combatants and an equal number of camp followers, and a large number of pack animals.[3] He anticipated some opposition at the Karo La which had been cleared by Lieutenant Colonel Brander's force just over two months ago. He also gave utmost importance to seizing intact the ferry site and boats at Chaksam. The force carried four Berthon boats for crossing the Tsangpo river. Both tasks were accomplished without much difficulty as abundant precautions had been taken to ensure minimum casualties if opposed. Had the British force's crossing of the Tsangpo been opposed and the ferry site along with the boats not handed over to them on a platter, there would have been a considerable number of casualties and delay in the mission reaching Lhasa. However, it soon became clear that there existed no plans by the Tibetan army to hold the river and thwart the mission's crossing of this formidable obstacle. The Tibetan military leadership had apparently given up, but being afraid of the repercussions of disobeying the lama elite, token resistance was put up at a few places, Karo La being an example.

Eventually, on 3 August, the Younghusband mission reached the capital of mystical Tibet, Lhasa, the 'Forbidden City', and the phenomenon of The Nechung Oracle—a sacred 'spirit' that appears through a medium, a person called Kuoten—was being unveiled to the world by an alien force without the need for secrecy and disguise adopted by previous adventurers to the city. Brigadier Macdonald set up camp about 2.5 kilometres away from the Potala Palace of the Dalai Lama. It is true that on many occasions and at many places along the mission's adventurous journey, the Grand Lama's envoys met with Younghusband and enjoined upon him to desist from advancing to the sacred city of Lhasa and to return. They indicated their readiness to hold negotiations at the camp site itself. However, after having given them adequate time, including a few weeks at Gyantse, Younghusband saw the futility of such an exercise because of the lack of earnestness on the part of the Tibetans to resolve the matters he had come to fix. He also realized that they were not adequately empowered to conclude meaningful treaties. He had therefore made up his mind to hold talks only on reaching Lhasa.

Figure 5: The Potala Palace, Lhasa, the Forbidden City

Younghusband was not taken by surprise when it was confirmed on his arrival at Lhasa that the Dalai Lama had already fled. He was given an indication of this by the Ta Lama and his delegation at Chaksam ferry around the end of July when the British forces were crossing the Tsangpo. The delegation that met him at the crossing site comprised the Grand Lama's chamberlain, the abbott of Drepung, the largest monastery of Lhasa, and many others who prayed that the mission should not proceed further and should carry out negotiations at that spot itself. The same delegation reappeared once again when the force camped on the outskirts of Lhasa on 2 August, and made the same appeal!

On 30 July, when it had become clear that the British force was determined to continue its advance up to Lhasa, the Dalai Lama, along with Dorjieff and a small retinue, sped northwards towards Mongolia. Before leaving, the Dalai Lama handed over his seal to the Ti Rimpoche, the head lama of Ganden monastery, telling him that he was proceeding on a 'religious retreat'.[4]

On 4 August 1904, the British mission, led by an impressive and disciplined force, paraded down the streets of Lhasa up to the Chinese residency to return the call made by the Amban the previous day. The procession was led by the Amban's bodyguard and pikemen in traditional costume and weapons. It made its way to the Yamen, where they were given a ceremonial reception at the Amban's residence.[5] The procession's subtle show of force and its imperial regalia, combined with Chinese acceptance of British intervention in the very shadow of the Potala Palace, left the Tibetans awestruck.

During the next few weeks, Younghusband held negotiations with the Tibetans and the Chinese Amban, Yu T'ai, and was able to hammer out this Anglo-Tibetan Treaty of 1904, a treaty which not only fulfilled, to a large extent, the mandate given to him, but went far beyond it in some respects. Both Curzon and Younghusband were looking to maintain some sort of permanent British presence in Tibet, contrary to the policy enunciated by Whitehall. Expectedly, the home government took no time to water down certain provisions of this treaty, much to the disappointment of Younghusband.

There were two principal goals which Great Britain had set out to achieve through the Younghusband mission. The first was to establish their predominant position in the region because of the British Indian empire's geographical proximity to the heart of Tibet, and therefore to impress upon the Tibetans the need to respect the Sino-British treaty of 1890 and the Trade Agreement of 1893. This would end the vacillation of the Tibetans as far as accepting the Sikkim–Tibet boundary was concerned, and facilitate establishment of a trade mart and related facilities for the British at Yatung. The second was part of the agenda of the Great Game—to put an end to Russian influence and intrigue in Tibet, facilitated particularly by the cosy relationship between the Dalai Lama and the Russian Buriat monk Dorjieff, and to stop the reported arms deliveries from Russia to Lhasa.

The Anglo-Tibetan Treaty of 1904

Thubten Gyatso, the thirteenth Dalai Lama, quietly slipped out of the Potala Palace as news of the impending crossing of the Tsangpo river by Younghusband's invading force reached Lhasa. He fled to Urga in Mongolia in the company of the enigmatic Dorjieff as he neither wanted to be taken prisoner nor be a party to any British-imposed agreement or treaty. Before leaving Tibet, he sent for the hugely revered Ti Rimpoche, but, to the Rimpoche's consternation, departed before he could reach the palace. However, the Dalai Lama left his seals for the Rimpoche and a letter appointing him as the acting regent, advising him to 'face the Mission in his [Grand Lama] stead, and settle up the dispute as best he could'.[6]

In the absence of the Grand Lama, Younghusband's task of clinching an abiding and authoritative treaty was rendered extremely difficult. Undeterred, however, he single-handedly coined the treaty and the various articles it contained. He had no doubt deftly and firmly handled the consultations and negotiations with the Tibetans and the Chinese Amban. It was Younghusband's stroke of genius to have carried the Amban, Yu T'ai, with him all along, and to have garnered his support to get the Tibetans around too. In fact, he zealously induced the Tibetans to accept the treaty, even though some of its provisions far exceeded his brief. In a letter to his wife, he is reported to have said that he pushed the treaty 'down the Tibetans' throat'. His strategy went further, to acquire an endorsement of the Chinese Amban on the treaty, and he may well have succeeded but for the last-minute instructions received by Yu T'ai from Peking not to endorse the treaty. In the event, this paved the way for direct negotiations between Britain and Tibet, thereby setting a precedent.

In a formal ceremony conducted in the durbar hall of the Potala Palace on 7 September 1904, the Anglo-Tibetan treaty was read out in Tibetan and signed by stamping the respective nations' seals on the huge scroll of paper bearing the text of the treaty in three parallel columns in English, Chinese and Tibetan. The procedure and sequence of the signing ceremony were very elaborate and impressive, and the hall was filled with the officers and troops of the British mission on one side and the Tibetans on the other. To one side of the high table were seated the high-ranking officers and elite of the township of Lhasa. These included the Nepalese resident and the Bhutanese representative. The Tibetans were told to affix their seals first—the council (Kashag), followed by the abbots of the three great monasteries, Drepung, Ganden (also known as Gahldan) and Sera, and the national assembly (Tsongdu), comprising high-ranking secular and monastic officials. Then there were representatives of prominent monasteries who also affixed their seals to the document. After this the acting regent, Lo-Sang Gyal-Tsen (Ti Rimpoche), affixed the Dalai Lama's seal to the treaty, and, finally, Younghusband signed and placed his seal as commissioner on behalf of Great Britain. He handed over the document to Ti Rimpoche, saying a peace had now been made which he hoped would never be broken again.

Salient features of the treaty

The treaty comprised ten articles preceded by a brief elucidation of the state of affairs and difficulties in the observance of the Anglo-Chinese Treaty of 1890 and the Trade Regulations of 1893 which the Tibetans had refused to validate. The stated aim of the convention was to 'restore peace and amicable relations, and to resolve and determine the doubts and difficulties'.[7] It was agreed to respect the frontier between Sikkim and Tibet and open forthwith the trade marts at Gyantse, Yatung and Gartok with resident British agents and free access to British and Tibetan subjects. The 1893 Regulations would apply to these marts too, and the

Tibetan government would impose no additional levies or restrictions. The agreement provided for revision of trade regulations.

The Tibetans also agreed, after sustained coaxing and veiled threats, to the demand of the British government for reparation for the Tibetan attacks on the British mission, for violation of treaty obligations and for the costs incurred on the military expedition. An amount equivalent to Rs 75 lakh was agreed to be paid by the Tibetans to the British government over a period of seventy-five years in annual instalments of Rs 1 lakh. It was also agreed that the British would continue to hold Chumbi Valley until the indemnity was paid and the trade marts established.

The ninth article of the treaty had connotations of near 'protectorate' status for Tibet vis-à-vis Britain as it specified primacy of British dominance in Tibetan affairs to the exclusion of all other foreign powers. Without the 'previous consent' of the British, the Tibetans could have no dealings with any other foreign power as far as territorial rights, internal affairs, presence of agents, financial commitments and concessions for railways, mining, roads, telegraphs or other rights were concerned.[8] On the face of it, though not categorically stated, it implied that even China was excluded, and was therefore subject to the provisions of this article. The political implications of this article raised many an eyebrow and drew adverse comments from some of the major global powers of the time.

Not surprisingly, even the British government did not take kindly to Younghusband's overenthusiastic and determined actions and policy-making initiatives, and diluted some of the provisions of the treaty while reprimanding him at the same time. Ending Curzon's imperialistic ambitions, even though they rose from his slightly misplaced Russophobia, Younghusband's was the last 'out of empire' military invasion undertaken by the British. This historic expedition not only woke up the slumbering dragon but, importantly, resulted in a paradigm shift in the relations between Tibet, China and British India.

On completion of the signing ceremony of the treaty that took over an hour and a half, Colonel Younghusband gave a speech that was interpreted simultaneously in Tibetan and Chinese. Emphasizing the important features of the treaty and their impact on the future relations between British India, Tibet and China, the commissioner assured the gathering that 'the Treaty leaves the land, the liberties and the religion of the Tibetans untouched; that it recognises the suzerainty of China, and does not interfere with the country's internal affairs, but confers increased facilities for trade with India; and that if they [Tibetans] honestly kept the Treaty they would find the British as good friends as they had been bad enemies' (see Appendix 2 for text).[9]

Taking leave of the regent, the Amban and the other dignitaries, Younghusband's mission and its escort returned to the camp in as much ceremonial grandeur as the circumstances permitted. The parade passed by 'groups of Lamas and laity, who stood respectfully by, as the completion of the Treaty within the sacred walls of Potala had created a deep impression on the people'. This was followed by gestures of goodwill and bonhomie by release of prisoners by both sides, condoning of fines that the British had imposed and presentation of money and gifts to the monasteries and poor Tibetans.[10] It may be of interest to note that in its mention of Chumbi Valley the Tibetan version of the treaty says Tang La (the actual watershed between Tibet and Sikkim) is the start point of the valley and Phari Dzong a part of it, contrary to what the Tibetans had believed.[11]

The Chinese attitude during the entire period, from the time the British initiated the move for talks at Khamba Dzong in July 1903 till their advance through the heartland of Tibet right up to Lhasa, had been contradictory and treacherous, and definitely not in keeping with their suzerain status. Exploiting the diplomatic naivety of the Tibetans, the Chinese, without conceding anything, regained their lost grip on Tibet. The debilitating effect of successive defeats inflicted by the British on the Tibetan army helped the Chinese. But the Chinese did lose face and credibility vis-à-vis the Tibetans. This was aptly demonstrated when the Chinese Amban put up a proclamation announcing the deposing of the Dalai Lama by the imperial court of China in prominent places in Tibet, only to find these posters splattered with mud or torn to pieces by the people.

However, the graduated and punctuated nature of the British ingress, the extremely short duration of the enterprise, and the lack of wholeheartedness on the part of the British gave rise to Chinese hopes that the British would eventually leave and present them later with an opportunity to deal with a weakened Tibet as they liked. The Chinese believed that as long as Tibetan autonomy was preserved and the Russians kept at bay, the British would acquiesce to Chinese control and suzerainty over Tibet. What has perhaps escaped the attention of some historians is that while formulating their strategy, the Chinese carefully monitored the proceedings of the British Parliament as well as the Western media's views on developments in Tibet, Afghanistan, Persia and Mongolia. They had perhaps evolved a system by which they could home on to the differences relating to Tibet between the viceroy, the Government of India, the British legation in Peking, and the India and the Foreign Offices of the home government in the UK, and exploit the transparency of a democratic polity to their advantage.

For example, the massacre of hundreds of unarmed and fleeing Tibetans during the mission's action at Guru was condemned and adversely commented on in the House of Commons and by the media. This took away some of the sheen from the achievements and recognition of the Younghusband expedition. Also, the debate on whether the British should get involved in Tibetan matters or not, and if so, what their scale of involvement should be—these were cues the Chinese were desperately looking for, and they got them on a platter, courtesy of the British parliamentary debates. As a matter of fact, this pattern continues to this date, the democratic Republic of India having replaced Great Britain!

To the utter surprise of the Tibetans the Younghusband expedition began its withdrawal from Tibet a fortnight after the treaty was signed and sealed. This unexpected development was received by the people with huge awe and relief. As planned, Brigadier Macdonald, in consultation with Younghusband, decided to move back from Lhasa on 23 September. The return journey was quite uneventful and the force reached Gyantse during 5–6 October 1904 (Figure 6). Thereafter, the mission moved in smaller groups, reeling in the protective elements deployed on the road as the rear guard withdrew. The condition of the road was much better than before. It had been worked on by the sappers, who were aided by soldiers. Their work impressed the Tibetan civilian labour. By the third week of October the mission had returned to India. In this expedition to

Lhasa, every member of the mission had trekked over 1,000 kilometres in forbidding altitudes (Figure 6). In fact, some had moved even longer distances, shuttling between Gyantse and Chumbi, and later between Lhasa and Gyantse.

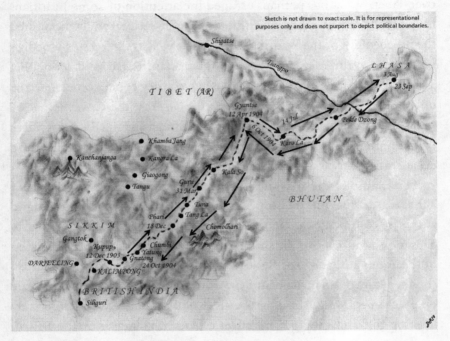

Figure 6: The Younghusband expedition: route and datelines

It is of interest to know that Whitehall sent a telegram on 19 September directing Younghusband to convey to the Tibetan authorities certain modifications to the terms of the treaty, which would result in dilution of some of the harsher conditions contained in it. These primarily involved a sizeable reduction of the indemnity and creation of a fourth trading station at Rima on the Zayul river on the Tibetan side of the north-eastern-most point along the Assam Himalayas. In a manner suggestive of disobedience, Younghusband, who received the instructions from London only on 24 September when he had left Lhasa, decided at that stage not to turn back to announce these alterations. He surmised, and rightly so, that fresh negotiations would definitely undermine the sanctity and impact of the treaty and involve a prolonged stay in Tibet for the mission.

In the final analysis, the Younghusband expedition was a turning point in Tibetan history, leading to a series of developments in the relations between Tibet, China and British India. This description of the expedition has been attempted for a clearer understanding of the events with the benefit of hindsight, keeping in mind at the same time the pulls and pressures of those times and the environment prevailing at the turn of the nineteenth century.

The mission resulted in or revealed the following:

- The British Indian Empire demonstrated its reach and determination to keep outside influences away from Tibet and maintain the status quo there, i.e., Tibetan autonomy under Chinese suzerainty.
- The status and authority of the Dalai Lama were undermined, as were his aspirations for greater Tibetan autonomy or independence from China, on the lines of Mongolia.
- The hollowness of Chinese claims of sovereignty over Tibet was exposed. Far from protecting the Tibetans, the Chinese stood by as passive and mute spectators during Britain's invasion of Tibet. At the same time, because the treaty gave the Amban some importance, China's hold on Tibet was restored to some extent, allowing the Amban to play a larger role in Lhasa affairs.
- China's subsequent hold on Tibet was facilitated by the weakening and demoralization of the Tibetan army on account of the string of defeats suffered by them during the Younghusband mission.
- The Anglo-Tibetan Treaty of 7 September 1904 that Younghusband was able to forcibly extract from the Tibetans suffered from two drawbacks. First, the Dalai Lama played a clever trick, and his absence from Lhasa prevented him from being a party to the treaty even though, legally speaking, the seals of the Dalai Lama were affixed by the regent on his behalf, and even though the head lamas of the principal monasteries, the national assembly and council gave the treaty the desired sanctity as far as the Tibetans were concerned. Second, the Chinese Amban did not endorse the document either, thus giving the Chinese a pretext to recuse themselves from the

articles in it until an adhesion agreement between the British and the Chinese was negotiated and signed.

- The influence of Tsarist Russia, though not as perfidious and pervasive as projected by Curzon, was to a large extent put an end to. The shenanigans of the Buryat monk, Dorjieff, disappeared along with him. This eventually led to the end of the Great Game, with the signing of the Anglo-Russian Convention of 1907 (see Appendix 3 for text).

- As a direct fallout of this invasion, neither the Chinese nor the Tibetans ever contemplated transgression of the customary, traditional or defined boundary between Tibet and the cis-Himalayan states from 1905 for at least half a century until the mid-1950s.

- The fear that Tibet might be made into a protectorate of Great Britain shook up the mandarins at Peking running the affairs of the Manchu Empire. The imperial court at Peking now realized the necessity of establishing Chinese presence and control in the outlying regions adjoining the provinces of Yunnan and Sichuan, particularly the Marches in the Kham and Amdo areas.

- To bring the semi-independent and irrepressible tribes living in these regions under some semblance of control of imperial China, an army was dispatched under a ruthless but dynamic commissioner, Chao Erh-feng, the Taotai (a high official who has control over the military and civil administration). He was appointed the commissioner of the Marches, the dark and shadowy frontier territories between China and Tibet. One of his principal tasks, other than to re-establish Chinese administration over these recalcitrant regions, was to open the roads linking Sichuan and Yunnan with Lhasa over which these tribes held undisputed sway. It is to his credit that during the six-year period from 1905 to 1911, he was able 'to transform completely the political landscape in eastern Tibet'.[12]

- For the first time in history, Chinese presence was reported in the Pome and Pemako areas of south-eastern Tibet during 1910–11, particularly in the isolated and undiscovered lower Tsangpo Valley and areas bordering the wild tribal territory on the southern slopes of the Assam Himalayas. It was during this period that Chao Erh-feng sent his probes to explore the cis-Himalayan tribal territories. This activity rang alarm bells in the British-administered and governed Brahmaputra Valley and raised the spectre of Chinese presence close to the prosperous tea-producing country in upper Assam.

- The myth of the 'Forbidden Land' was shattered and the veil over mystical Lhasa lifted as the soldiers of the British army literally kicked up the dust in the placid streets of Lhasa as they pounded down them with their boots. For the first time in Tibetan history, a Western army was seen by the curious lamas and the laity, who were left awestruck; the people of the city lined the streets and hung out on the balconies of Tibet's capital to watch it march past. The last Shangri-La was laid bare and presented to the world by the telegraphic reports sent by the expedition. Colonel Sir Thomas H. Holditch, a famous British geographer, writing in *Tibet, the Mysterious*, some years after the return of the Younghusband mission, said: 'It may be doubted whether even now the fascination of Tibetan travel is dead. But the glamour of it has undoubtedly faded somewhat since the streets of Lhasa have been trodden by the spurred and booted Englishman and his ruthless hand has exposed the mystic shams of that quaint and squalid city.'

- Once the mission achieved its objectives in Lhasa, the opportunity to explore for the first time the upper and lower Tsangpo regions was fully exploited, and a good amount of survey work was done along the Tsangpo Valley.

- The British were able to showcase their military capabilities and impress not only the Tibetans, but also the Nepalese, Bhutanese, and other cis-Himalayan kingdoms or principalities. The stock of the British Empire rose to a peak in these parts.

- Reparation of the costs incurred by the British mission in the form of an indemnity of Rs 75 lakh was to be paid by the Tibetans at the rate of Rs 1 lakh a year for seventy-five years. The British had the right to occupy Chumbi Valley as security till this debt was repaid.[13] One can imagine the advantage that would have accrued to India if it had control and presence there till 1979!

- The fact that the land they held sacred was trespassed with force by the British was never forgotten in Tibet. There is a very apt Tibetan saying, uncomplimentary to the British victory, that gained currency during those times: *'Lion! Do not fight with dog! Lion, though victor, is lion defeated.'*[14]

- By the terms of the 1904 Lhasa treaty, the British secured the trading privileges that had been one of their ostensible reasons for invading Tibet. They granted themselves extremely favourable terms for trade with Tibet, being allowed to open trade marts at Yatung, Gyantse and Gartok, and to position a British trade official at Gyantse, giving Great Britain hold over Tibet *sans responsibility*.[15]

- The Russians were to be excluded from Tibet under the treaty; no territory was allowed to be ceded or sold by Tibet to any foreign power; no concessions for railways, roads, telegraphs or mines could be granted; no representatives of any foreign power were to be admitted into Tibet; and no foreign power was permitted to intervene in Tibetan affairs.

The London view of the Younghusband expedition, keenly watched by the Chinese, also requires to be analysed at this stage in order to comprehend the national and international ramifications of the mission and the decision-making dilemmas that confronted the home government. It was difficult for the leadership at the field level and at the general headquarters of the British Indian Army at Calcutta, or for that matter, even for the viceroy's office, to understand the rationale for certain directions sent by Whitehall, whether from the Foreign or the India Offices. Very often the views and recommendations of the 'frontier boys', as the viceroy's team was called, were rejected with disdain by the know-all mandarins and parliamentarians at London. The sour aftertaste left by the second Boer War at the turn of the twentieth century rendered it extremely difficult for London to gain public acceptability for military expeditions such as Younghusband's. To begin with, the mission was viewed in a 'dubious light' by many a British MP. This justifies A.M.A. Hull's comments in his book, *Colonel Younghusband's Mission to Lhasa, 1904*: 'If the Younghusband Mission had been born constitutionally illegitimate, with a Russophobe birthright, the British public viewed it with a mixture of ill-ease and quiescence.' Sections 54 and 55 of the Government of India

Act 1858 were explicit on the matter of funding military operations in foreign lands:

> Except for preventing or repelling actual invasion of Her Majesty's Indian possessions, or under other sudden or urgent necessity, the revenues of India shall not, without the sanction of both Houses of Parliament, be applicable to defray the expenses of any military operation carried on beyond the frontiers of such possessions by Her Majesty's forces charged upon such revenues.[16]

During a British parliamentary debate on this enterprise in Tibet, an agitated MP termed it as the viceroy's 'bear-hunt in the Himalayas'![17] Younghusband himself retrospectively 'quite realised the difficulty which any Government at home has in securing support from the House of Commons in a matter of this kind'.[18] And of his seemingly endless wait for negotiations to start in Khamba Dzong in mid-1903, he goes on to say, 'As long as what an officer may do is contingent on the "will of men in the street" of grimy manufacturing towns in the heart of England, so long must our action be slow, clumsy and hesitating, when it ought to be sharp and decisive.'[19] The King's men at the frontier often found the orders emanating from thousands of miles away from their scene of action extremely frustrating and disappointing to follow, leading many of them to perhaps question the raison d'être of the whole exercise and ask, 'What the hell are we here for?'

5

First Exile of the Dalai Lama (1904–1909)

The progress of the Younghusband expedition was being closely monitored by the Dalai Lama ever since the British force commenced its advance on 14 July 1904 towards Lhasa from Gyantse. During this leg of the mission's journey, the Dalai Lama sent his emissaries on four occasions to persuade the British force to turn back. His first delegation met the mission at Gyantse and asked Younghusband to fall back to Yatung in the Chumbi Valley and hold talks there. As the invading force moved closer to Lhasa, the Tibetans approached Younghusband three times—once on 20 July at Nagartse Dzong, the next time at the Tsangpo ferry site around the end of July, and finally on the afternoon of 3 August on the outskirts of Lhasa—exhorting him to return to Gyantse for negotiations.

However, Younghusband was quick to realize that the delegates neither had sufficient authority to make a treaty nor the clout to implement the decisions that would be arrived at. The delegates did not include any Chinese official of rank and invariably comprised Tibetans led by 'Ta Lama, the 'Great Lama Minister of the Lhasa Council', or included some other minister, or the grand chamberlain or the important lamas of the three cardinal monasteries of Lhasa: Ganden, Sera and Drepung. The tone and tenor of the Tibetans' appeal became softer and more appeasing as the mission neared Lhasa. At the same time their desperation rose at the inevitability of British military boots trampling the sacred roads of Lhasa. The mission would bring the first European soldiers of the 'yellow-haired' race and their Indian and Gurkha counterparts to set foot on those sacred streets. But, as the British expedition progressed beyond Gyantse, Younghusband became more and more determined to lead his military expedition into the heart and soul of Tibet, carry the Curzonian doctrine to its logical conclusion and watch the Union Jack fluttering over Lhasa, make the Tibetans fall in line and ultimately secure a binding agreement on British terms from the vanquished. This historical event was to have a lasting imprint on Tibetan and Chinese minds.

Figure 7: Thubten Gyatso: the thirteenth Dalai Lama

Thubten Gyatso, the thirteenth Dalai Lama, quietly slipped out of the Potala Palace on 30 July 1904 when it had become clear that the British force were determined to continue its advance up to Lhasa. With his small retinue he fled northwards towards Urga in Mongolia in the company of the enigmatic Dorjieff as he did not want to be a party to any British-imposed agreement. Urga was the seat of the Jetsum Dampa Lama, also well known as Bagdo Gegen, the third great Hutukhtu.[1] Before leaving, as we know, he entrusted his seal and left instructions for the hugely revered Ti Rimpoche, Lobsang Gyeltsen, the head lama of Ganden monastery, appointing him his regent.

Initially, in order to keep a safe distance from the advancing British force, the Grand Lama made his way northwards across to Reting monastery, about 100 kilometres away, across two high-altitude passes.[2] From this mountain fastness he could remain in touch with Lhasa as well as be out of harm's way. Once the invading force entered Lhasa, the Dalai Lama and his entourage, including Dorjieff, took off for Nagchuka en route to Mongolia. The distance to Urga (the current Ulan Bator) was approximately 2,500 kilometres, and it took about four months for the Dalai Lama to reach his destination. It was without doubt an incredible feat—covering such a vast distance at extremely high altitudes, averaging 25 to 30 kilometres a day.

Accounts have it that in the initial stages of this arduous journey the Dalai Lama wore the dress of a Mongolian merchant in an effort to conceal his identity, also doing some hard riding in the bargain. As the journey progressed, his entourage grew larger and larger. The journey has been eloquently described by C.A. Bell in his authoritative account of the Dalai Lama's sojourn in exile: 'Having seven hundred persons in his suite, his baggage was carried by a small army of camels.' On the reception given at Urga to the Dalai Lama from Lhasa, Bell says: 'Over ten thousand citizens went several miles out of town [Urga] to meet him and prostrate themselves before him. Pilgrims flocked in from all parts of Mongolia, from Siberia, and from the steppes of Astrakhan, to do him homage.'[3]

In the meanwhile, in August 1904 itself, once it was ascertained that the Dalai Lama had fled and had no intention to return, the Amban had an imperial proclamation announced, and pasted it everywhere in Lhasa declaring the Dalai Lama deposed and nominating the Panchen Lama to act on his behalf. This edict was not accepted by the Tibetans. In many places they tore down the posters or defaced them with dung.

The freezing winters of 1904 and 1905 were spent by the Dalai Lama in Urga. He kept moving residence between three monasteries in the vicinity of the city. His preoccupations weren't 'altogether spiritual, for he is said to have been in touch with affairs in Lhasa and in Peking'.[4] His prolonged stay at Urga was a burden on its administration and the people because of the high cost of maintaining him and his enormous entourage. Moreover, after the initial euphoria of having the Dalai Lama in Mongolia, the relationship between the two Grand Lamas soured somewhat because the 'Chen-re-zi'—the Dalai Lama—appeared to command greater reverence from the people. There was also loss of revenue to the Hutukhtu of Mongolia as offerings made by the people had to now be shared between the two personages.

Some time in mid-1906, the Dalai Lama commenced his travels or his 'wanderings', as the Chinese called them, southwards to Amdo region, where he visited many monasteries, presiding over spiritual meetings and conducting discourses to spread the message of the Buddha. Giving sermons and dispensing divine blessings as the 'Inmost One' wherever he went, he reached Kanchow in Kansu province in September 1906, and three months later Sining near the Sino-Tibetan border. For the followers of his faith the Grand Lama in person was considered something of a divine vision, and everywhere they sought his blessings. For the laity in these regions it was somewhat akin to a devout Catholic being in the presence of the Pope. During 1906–07, the Dalai Lama mostly stayed at the Kumbum monastery. It was coincidental that the British and Chinese were not content to let the Dalai Lama stay for very long in Urga, apprehending unfavourable Russian and Mongolian influence, although neither wanted him back in Lhasa either. The Chinese succeeded in doing so by ensuring the return of the Grand Lama to Kumbum monastery, which was in close proximity to Sining.[5] Kumbum, meaning 'one hundred thousand images', is the birthplace of Tsongkhapa, and is considered among the most important monasteries in north-east Tibet.[6] Facilitated by the Dalai Lama's absence, the British had begun to court the Panchen Lama as the Chinese strengthened their foothold in Tibet.

The Dalai Lama, being a clever and astute temporal and spiritual leader, kept himself *au courant* on political developments in Tibet and the region while in exile. His sojourn away from his cocooned existence in Lhasa helped him expand his contacts with the outside world and increase his awareness of the role and politics being played in Asia by the world powers. With the help of Dorjieff he maintained contact with the Tsar. In fact, during his stay in Mongolia the Russians made much of him, and their consul at Urga 'carefully shepherded' the Dalai Lama[7]. The Tsar also directed M. Pokotiloff, his minister at the legation in Peking, to visit the Grand Lama, which he did in June 1906.

Dorjieff was once again dispatched to St Petersburg for an audience with the Russian emperor. However, the Russians did not offer meaningful support to Tibet against either the British or the Chinese because of their own compulsions, most importantly their war with Japan. The Dalai Lama was probably aware of the ongoing parleys between the British and the Chinese that resulted in the Sino-British Convention (Adhesion Agreement) of 1906 signed by the two nations on 27 April 1906 at Peking. On the one hand, he felt the status and future of Tibet had been forsaken in an agreement in which the Tibetans had no voice, yet on the other he felt greatly relieved as far as his personal safety was concerned, and confidently commenced preparations for his homeward journey towards Tibet during the summer of that year. He had to play his cards well and bide his time, and he did not appear to be a man in a hurry. Also, at that point the Chinese and the British were not very keen to see him back at Lhasa.

The Chinese were laboriously and ruthlessly re-establishing their control over the Marches along the frontier regions of Amdo, Kham and south-eastern Tibet, whereas the British were busy building a close rapport with the Panchen Lama so as to gain a sphere of influence in southern Tibet. The Chinese and the British were pleased to see the Dalai Lama confined to the environs of Kumbum, away from the influence of the Russians and unable to provide effective temporal leadership to the Tibetans. Seldom are there situations when every stakeholder is happy, but circumstantially, during 1905–08, the principal actors in the Tibetan drama—the Dalai Lama, the Tibetan elite, Britain, Russia and China—had something to be satisfied with … everyone but the ordinary Tibetans, as they felt forlorn and confused without their God! Maybe the Grand Lama was left with very few options and he chose the best of a bad bargain.

While in Sining in 1907, the Dalai Lama received requests from Lhasa to return and also summons from the Manchu court to present himself before the emperor and the empress dowager. He eventually decided to go to Peking and have an audience with the Chinese royalty before returning to Lhasa. He was aware of the Anglo-Russian convention of 1907 and the Adhesion Agreement of 1906 between China and Britain. The signing of the Anglo-Russian convention on 31 August 1907 at St Petersburg clearly spelt out the status of Tibet and duly emphasized 'both the "suzerain rights" of China in Tibet as well as Britain's "special interest", owing to its geographical position, in the maintenance of the status quo in the external relations of that country'.[8]

While at Wu-tai Shan—the sacred 'five-peaked mountain', which is a few days' trek from Peking—the Dalai Lama sent his emissaries to Peking with invitations to the ambassadors and heads of missions to call on him so that he could advocate to them the cause of Tibet. The Chinese were keeping a close watch on his activities and his interactions with foreigners. Having put the Great Game to an end, the Anglo-Russian convention proved to be the greatest boon for the Chinese. A free hand had been given to it to assert its authority over Tibet. Its suzerainty over Tibet had been reinforced at the cost of Tibet itself, which was being forsaken by Britain and Russia for their other, more important, imperial concerns.

Faced with this stark reality, it didn't take the Dalai Lama very long to realize that Tibet was now almost abandoned, friendless, and left to the mercy of China. Yet the wily lama wasn't entirely powerless. He knew the latent impact of his intrinsic strengths. Endowed with extraordinary mental and physical strength, he was a survivor to the core. He was not the sort to easily give up. He was becoming more worldly wise and began to understand the intricacies of the power games and the craft of international diplomacy.

At this juncture, two issues need to be discussed. Was the Dalai Lama requested or summoned by the imperial court to visit Peking, and for what purpose? Second, what was the Dalai Lama hoping to gain from the royal audience? It was while the Grand Lama was in Sining that he received the request from the monarch, and later it was while en route to Peking during his sojourn at Wu-tai Shan that he received urgent summons from the court. The Chinese aim with respect to the Dalai Lama's visit was three-fold: they wanted to demonstrate to the Tibetans and the rest of the world that Tibet was not a vassal state but a part of China; they hoped the Dalai Lama's obeisance to the throne and his being conferred a new title, albeit with a lower status than had been given to the Great Fifth, meant putting an end to the historical *choe-yon* relationship between their emperor and the Dalai Lama. The Chinese were now seeking the Dalai Lama's help to subdue the rebellious Kham region in eastern Tibet where the Chinese army was having a tough time. As far as the Dalai Lama was concerned, he was looking to establish a rapport with the dowager empress and the emperor and somehow to retain his position as the temporal and spiritual head of the Tibetan nation. Unfortunately, as we shall see later, his efforts proved to be fruitless.

At the end of 1907, the Dalai Lama left Kumbum for Wu-tai Shan, arriving there by the spring of 1908. It is believed that the Wu-tai hills, considered sacred from the times of Daoism (Taoism), were among the first regions where Buddhism gained pre-eminence in China. It has also become famous as the legendary abode of Manjushri (Buddha-to-be). Regardless of his weakened position, the sagacious and clever Dalai Lama put up a brave face and made concerted efforts to reach out to other world powers and garner their support. He had several interactions with representatives of important countries, the most significant among them being with William Rockhill, the US Ambassador to China. Rockhill described the Dalai Lama as a 'man of undoubted intelligence and ability, of quick understanding and of force of character. He is broad-minded— and of great natural dignity.' About the Dalai Lama's temperament he said, 'He is quick tempered and impulsive, but cheerful and kindly.' Another notable visitor who called on the Dalai Lama was Baron Gustaf Mannerheim, a colonel in the Russian army who subsequently rose to become president of Finland. In his impressions of the Dalai Lama, he describes him as 'as a lively man in full possession of his mental and physical faculties'. He goes on to say: 'He does not look like a man resigned to play the part the Chinese government wishes him to, but rather like one who is only waiting for an opportunity of confusing his adversary.' He presented the Grand Lama with a revolver and some ammunition and also demonstrated its use to him. In his memoirs, Mannerheim wrote, 'A revolver might at times be of greater use, even to a holy man like himself, than a prayer mill.'[9] Mannerheim also commented on the much-disliked close guard placed by the Chinese around the monastery at Wu-tai Shan to monitor the Grand Lama's activities.

The Dalai Lama also met Reginald Johnston, a British Colonial Service officer on a private journey, and a Japanese monk believed to have been 'Otani Sonyu, a monk associated with Ekai Kawaguchi, the Japanese who had spent several years in Tibet incognito'.[10] And just before his departure for Peking the Dalai Lama gave an audience to the French explorer Count Henri d'Ollone, during which he 'expressed his regrets at the barbarity of the nomads, who refused to obey him, and also his sorrow at learning of the murder of the [French] missionaries'.[11] The Dalai Lama was conscious of the fact that Tibet would need the support of the world powers to preserve its nationhood. In view of this, he even tried to smoothen the ruffled feathers (because of past events) of the British, taking pains to explain to visitors like Johnston that his (Dalai Lama's) subordinates had 'kept him in the dark as to the true circumstances of State affairs' and that he would rectify matters on his return to Tibet.

Eventually, the Dalai Lama left for Peking in September 1908. The Grand Lama, along with his vast retinue and followers, boarded the train from T'a-yan-fu, and on arrival at Peking was received in state with a ceremonial welcome, which has been eloquently described by Alastair Lamb. The Dalai Lama, 'seated on a sedan chair carried by sixteen men', moving in a procession led by 'numerous Chinese officials, a Chinese military guard of honour, hordes of mounted Tibetan monks, trumpeters and other musicians, standard bearers and footmen carrying placards bearing his titles in Chinese and Tibetan, made his ceremonial entry through the Ch'ien Men [Tien Aan Men?] gate into the Chinese capital'.[12]

The procession ended at the famous Yellow (Huang Tsu) Temple, which had been constructed to house the Great Fifth Dalai Lama in 1653 by the Manchu emperor Shunzi, who was succeeded by his son, K'ang Hsi. The 'Thirteenth' too resided there during his stay in Peking.

A problem that arose shortly after the Dalai Lama's arrival in Peking related to the protocol and procedure to be followed for his audiences with the young emperor, Xuantong, and the dowager empress, Cixi. The Dalai Lama refused to 'kowtow' to their majesties. He insisted on following the precedence established during the visit of the Great Fifth, the only audience an earlier Dalai Lama had had with a Chinese emperor. Seemingly small, but given immense importance by the Dalai Lama, these high-visibility protocol actions denoted the relative status and significance of the personalities involved. A traditional kowtow involved kneeling three times and touching the forehead to the ground nine times (described as 'head knockings').[13] However, taking advantage of the changed political situation, the Chinese snubbed the hapless Dalai Lama by insisting that he adopt a modified procedure of salutation which entailed kneeling before their royalty instead of doing the full kowtow. The meetings with the dowager empress and the emperor took place separately on 14 October 1908.

The Chinese crown diminished the Dalai Lama's status by giving him a new title of 'The Sincerely Obedient, Reincarnation-helping, Most Excellent, Self-Existing Buddha of the West' instead of 'Most Excellent, Self-Existing Buddha, Universal Ruler of the Buddhist Faith, Holder of the Sceptre, Dalai Lama' that the Great Fifth was anointed with.

The Dalai Lama had an audience with the dowager empress, Cixi, on 3 November, her seventy-fifth birthday, and once again raised the issue of his maintaining direct communications with the throne in Peking. It was conveyed to him that the procedure in vogue would continue and that the Grand Lama would be required to go through the Amban at Lhasa. Besides conferring the new title on the Dalai Lama, the empress decreed that the Szechuan treasury would be charged to pay him taels 10,000 every quarter. Unfortunately, a twin tragedy struck the royal court shortly afterwards: the young emperor met with a sudden and mysterious end within a few days of this meeting and the dowager empress too died a day after. Some accounts say the emperor's untimely death may have been caused by poisoning at the behest of the empress, who did not take kindly to his political views and did not want the throne to be occupied by him. The young king, being the de facto ruler, had been confined to the palace by her. Ironically, the Dalai Lama was called upon by the Chinese to perform the last rites for both the deceased. He wrote an impressive eulogy of the late dowager empress and also attended the enthronement of the two-year-old prince, Puyi, the last Ch'ing emperor. The Dalai Lama had meetings, without substantial results, at the Chinese Foreign Office, known as Wai-wu-pu, later renamed Wai Chiao-pu after its reorganization on the lines of Foreign Offices of contemporary Western countries during the Republican regime.[14]

However, once the period of state mourning was over and the political games and jockeying for power commenced, the Dalai Lama realized it was pointless for him to stay in Peking any longer, and commenced his return to Lhasa. He left Peking by train on 21 December 1908 for T'a-yan-fu on the way to Kumbum. Visiting various monasteries en route, he arrived there on 26 February 1909. During his stay there the Amban at Sining invested him with the new title of 'Loyally Submissive Vice-regent' of an imperial China that had 'sovereignty' over Tibet,[15] and the Dalai Lama was formally given the royal edict. Thereafter, he left for Lhasa, visiting monasteries in other parts of the region along the way, arriving in the city in late December 1909.

On his return, the people presented the Grand Lama with a new seal on which was inscribed, 'By the Prophecy of the Lord Buddha, Gyatso (Dalai) Lama is the holder of the Buddhist faith on the face of the Earth,' which was 'a symbol of Tibetan independence' and 'a mark of defiance against Chinese interference'.[16] It is amazing that this was done in the face of a mounting threat of invasion of Lhasa by the Chinese army under General Chung Ying on the orders of Chao Erh-feng, 'the butcher'. Thus ended the first exile of the Dalai Lama, which lasted from August 1904 to December 1909, during which he travelled at least 6,000 kilometres, two-thirds of it over permafrost-covered high-altitude terrain, an incredible journey by all accounts. However, neither the Dalai Lama nor the people of Tibet readily accepted Tibet's subordinate status as determined by the Chinese. Further, by then a more mature and worldly wise Dalai Lama, had no intention to be 'truly loyal and submissive'![17] Unfortunately, destiny had something else in store for him.

PART III

CHINA'S FORWARD POLICY

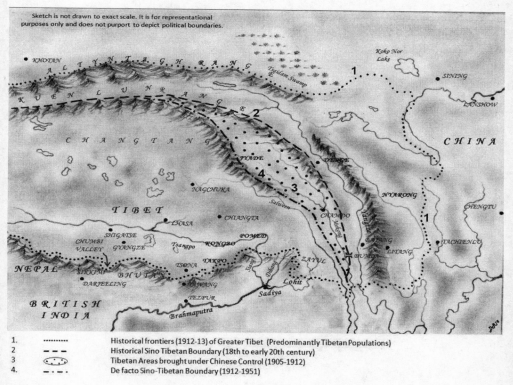

1. ⋯⋯⋯⋯ Historical frontiers (1912-13) of Greater Tibet (Predominantly Tibetan Populations)
2. ‒ ‒ ‒ Historical Sino Tibetan Boundary (18th to early 20th century)
3. ⊂∙∙∙⊃ Tibetan Areas brought under Chinese Control (1905-1912)
4. ‒∙‒∙‒ De facto Sino-Tibetan Boundary (1912-1951)

Figure 8: Sino-Tibet historical frontiers

6

Chinese Subjugation of Tibet (1905–1911)

The reactions of world powers like Russia, France, Germany, Japan, the USA and the tottering Chinese empire to the British invasion of Tibet were very interesting. Article IX of the Anglo-Tibetan Treaty of 1904 (see Appendix 2) was worded in such a manner—without, of course, actually saying it—that it appeared as if Tibet had become a protectorate of Great Britain. It even read as if China was a 'foreign power' as far as Tibet was concerned. Was Britain a special entity with special powers or a foreign power when it came to Tibet? Following this precedent, could the other powers demand similar rights or privileges elsewhere in Tibet or in mainland China? The Russians in particular demanded to know whether the British had not, in fact, violated Article IX by constructing and maintaining a telegraph line to Gyantse and by demanding an indemnity.[1] In this context, Younghusband, in a letter to his wife, had said that the Lhasa convention had been rammed down the throat of the Tibetans. And, importantly, he was convinced that he was able to achieve a settlement that bestowed 'the minimum of responsibility with the maximum of reparation'[2] for the British.

An era of heightened diplomatic power play and games followed for the next decade or two in the Central Asian and Tibetan regions. The exhausting and unpleasant experience of the Boer Wars (1880–81 and 1899–1902) had left the British with no appetite for more wars, allowing for coercion and diplomacy to take over. The Russians were licking their wounds after the Russo-Japanese War (1904–05), and the Chinese Manchu Empire, debilitated by the successive defeats and humiliation of the Opium Wars, the Sino-Japanese War (of 1894–95) and the Boxer Rebellion (1899), was on its last legs. The United States discovered a huge potential for trade with China and began to look westwards, introducing an 'open door policy' to facilitate US trade with China and to prevent other world powers from obtaining special privileges, thus ensuring a level playing field. The French were engaged in consolidating their hold on South-East Asia. Having emerged victorious in its wars with Russia and China, the Japanese were engaged in consolidating their gains. After the departure of Otto von Bismark, imperial Germany's international image and presence had shrunk considerably under Wilhelm II. Germany during this period was inward-looking and preoccupied with cementing the components of the Second Reich and strengthening its armed forces to make itself one of the most powerful nations on the globe.

These international developments spawned an era of moves and countermoves by the imperial powers—of carving out new colonies, expanding and safeguarding existing ones, and identifying 'spheres of interest' and 'buffer zones' with diplomatic finesse, intrigues, espionage, sanctions and veiled threats, particularly in Asia and Africa. These actions eventually led to agreements and conventions between the powers of the day, each trying to obtain the most favourable terms for its own empire or nation.

Four strategic imperatives drove imperial Britain's Tibet policy. The first concern was the security of India's northern border; the second was to keep the Russian bear away, preventing Russian influence and intrigues from permeating through Tibet and destabilizing Britain's relations with Nepal, Sikkim, Bhutan and other possessions; the third was the necessity for a benign neighbour like Tibet rather than an overbearing China; and the fourth was Tibet's geographical location, its proximity and ease of access from India, which made it necessary for Britain to keep that nation in its sphere of control. 'It would be madness for us to cross the Himalayas and occupy it [Tibet]. *But it is important that no one else should seize it; and it should be turned into a sort of buffer between Indian and Russian Empires* (emphasis added),' said Lord Curzon in 1901.[3]

Whitehall was prepared to allow Chinese suzerainty over an autonomous Tibet even against the wishes of the Tibetans and even though it knew what little control China actually had over that nation at the turn of the century. The British policy in a very big way helped the Chinese re-establish their hold over Tibet during 1905–11, Britain not realizing that this would be the cause of unending problems for British India in the future. The policymakers in London displayed great naivety in presuming that China would remain a benign or weak power with notional authority over Tibet. The Chinese capability to exploit the vulnerability and the impotence of Britain's Tibet policy was grossly underestimated by Whitehall. The harsh reality of the menacing presence of the Chinese along the Himalayan frontiers between 1910 and 1912, and also their intrigues with the sub-Himalayan kingdoms of Nepal and Bhutan, shook the British hard, forcing them to revise their ill-conceived 'hands off' policy on Tibet. The lack of congruence between their viceroy in India and the British government on Britain's Tibet policy quite often resulted in complications and embarrassments to both.

Despite the non-interventionist policy of the British, their frontier and trade officials maintained close contacts with both the Tibetans and the Chinese. They also had close relations with the Panchen Lama at Shigatse and worked hard to keep him under their influence. At one stage there was some talk of a separate political entity south of the Tsangpo under the Panchen or the Tashi Lama, independent of Lhasa.

Interestingly, in 1906 the Panchen Lama was presented with a Peugeot car by Captain O'Connor, the trade agent at Gyantse, on behalf of the British government. This gift was quite a novelty in a country that had no roads to speak of. It was a great feat to have it transported from the Indian border at Jelep La to Shigatse. It was the ingenuity and enterprise of O'Connor that arranged for the car to be disassembled into animal- and man-portable loads and to be taken down about 1,220 metres to the base of Chumbi Valley. It was reassembled there and taken on automotive power to Shigatse over the next few days. The journey had to be done at 'yak speed' as the fuel and lubricants were carried by these beasts!

Younghusband's Anglo-Tibetan Treaty of 1904, an underrated but landmark event, lacked two cardinal elements: the stamp of authority of the Dalai Lama and acceptance or ratification by the Chinese imperial government. Although the seal of the Grand Lama had been handed over to the Ti Rimpoche, the head lama of Ganden Monastery, and was stamped on the document, the fact that the treaty was not physically signed by the Dalai Lama or stamped in his presence made its acceptability to the Tibetans somewhat suspect.

The battered Chinese empire, meanwhile, found itself in a win-win situation following the withdrawal of the Younghusband mission from Tibet. There was a power vacuum created by the sudden departure of the British forces, which was accentuated by the absence of the Dalai Lama. The situation became further complicated by the deposing of the Dalai Lama by a Chinese imperial edict and the reluctance of the Panchen Lama to occupy his seat. The Chinese government took full advantage of this opportunity and moved rapidly to restore their lost position and prestige in Tibet. The British were perplexed to discover that the gains of the Younghusband mission were likely to be frittered away unless the Chinese were made a party to the Treaty of 1904 or by an Adhesion Agreement thereof.

Thus it was that a leaderless, weak and confused Tibet fell easy prey to its aggressive neighbour. The dying embers of the Manchu power in Tibet were fanned into life by the Sino-British Adhesion Agreement of 1906 and the Anglo-Russian 'self-denying' Convention of 1907. The latter, concluded in St Petersburg on 31 August, recognized Chinese suzerainty over Tibet and the 'special interest' of Great Britain, because of India's geographical proximity, 'in the maintenance of the status quo in the external relations of Tibet'. And importantly, in the first article itself, it was articulated that both the powers concerned would 'respect the territorial integrity of Tibet' and 'abstain from all interference in its internal administration' (Appendix 3). The subsequent articles tied British hands even tighter, giving the enfeebled Manchu Empire free rein to reassert its lost authority over Tibet.

China aggressively pushed through its plan of 'Sinification' of Tibet by ruthlessly eliminating whatever little opposition the Tibetans confronted them with. Busy safeguarding their imperial interests, the world powers kept looking the other way, despite the desperate and fervent pleas of the exiled Dalai Lama. The forsaking of Tibet did not carry a price tag anywhere close to that of having free ports and favourable trade terms with China. Subsequently, in 1915, a dismayed Lord Curzon gave vent to his strong feelings that the Russian Convention was deplorable: 'It gives up all we have been fighting for for years ... Ah me! It makes one despair of public life and the efforts of a century sacrificed and nothing or next to nothing in return.'[4]

The Chinese had subdued most of the area of the Marches along eastern Tibet; but it was only when the Chinese army's westward push crossed Chamdo, towards Lhasa, and when Chang Yin Tang's blatant violations of the trade agreements between British India and Tibet made the functioning of British agents at the trade marts in Gyantse, Yatung and Gartok almost impossible, that the British government sat up and took notice. By then the Chinese ambitions of complete overlordship of Tibet had been laid bare, and the sagacity of the advice and warnings conveyed to Whitehall by the 'frontier boys' of British India proven beyond doubt. This led to Britain reviewing its Tibet policy.

China Swoops on Tibet

The Chinese Ch'ing Empire got a rude shock from the apparent ease with which the Younghusband expedition advanced into the guts of Tibet from the exposed and vulnerable southern direction. All the Chinese officials and the Amban could do was to watch helplessly as Tibet's sovereignty was being violated. It resulted in a severe loss of face for the Chinese and deepened the scorn with which the Tibetans traditionally viewed them. The Amban, while refusing to sign the treaty that Younghusband was able to extract from the Tibetans in 1904, otherwise facilitated the proceedings and negotiations that took place during its formulation. His presence at the signing ceremony did not help the Chinese cause and showed them in a poor light as a suzerain power. The Chinese failed to protect the Tibetans or to come to their aid in any manner, thus ending the choe-yon relationship between them.[5] The facade of Chinese claims of sovereignty over Tibet was in tatters. As the events of 1911–12 and later years unfolded, the extremely dubious role played by the Chinese in fomenting problems between the Dalai Lama's regime and the British through the intrigues of the Amban in Lhasa was exposed. The Chinese actions in Tibet were two-faced and opportunistic, to say the least.

Incensed by the turn of events in Lhasa during 1904, the shaken Manchu regime in Peking, notwithstanding their weak condition, undertook urgent corrective measures to assert their authority over the semi-independent fiefdoms and tribal territories in the Marches along Tibet's eastern and south-eastern frontiers. The Manchu Empire unleashed a wave of terror to subjugate the Kham and Amdo regions in the first phase of their campaign. The Chinese strategy of destroying monasteries or curtailing their financial freedom and revenue-generation activities, and of executing the lamas and tribal leaders who did not fall in line, struck at the very roots of the Tibetan way of life and the religious beliefs of the people. As a policy, this Chinese approach may have succeeded in the short term, but as we shall see later, it sowed the seeds of conflict for years to come. This mission of pacification, colonization and assimilation of the Marches in eastern Tibet into the Chinese fold commenced as early as October 1904, on the heels of the withdrawing British expedition.

The task of bringing to heel the rebels in the Kham region was spearheaded by a set of specially selected officials. Energetic and overzealous, the newly appointed officials like Feng Ch'ang, who was appointed assistant Amban of Chamdo, and who was succeeded by Chao Erh-feng, went about their task in a ruthless and not infrequently ham-handed manner. The Tibetans, both the lamas and the laity, took great offence when Feng Ch'ang passed orders transgressing the religious and administrative tenets and rights of the monasteries, the lamas and the people. Stipulations were laid down by the Chinese restricting the number of monks that could live in the monasteries and banning fresh recruitment of monks for twenty years.[6]

Besides this, Feng's interference in the Tibetan administration of the gold-mining area in the vicinity of Ta Chien-lu heightened Tibetan resentment of the Chinese manifold. Eventually, these actions resulted in an outbreak of lawlessness, violence and disturbances in the areas around Batang and Litang, which resulted in the brutal murder of Feng and his entire Chinese escort in April 1905. Such a fate also befell a few French missionaries and many of their Christian converts, who were tortured and killed in and around Batang. This monk-led backlash against the Chinese administrators and soldiers took the form of an uprising that engulfed the region. Many more Chinese were killed in the smaller settlements and in the countryside as the rebels gained control of the area.

The Chinese retaliation did not take long in coming. A large Chinese force under General Ma Wei-ch'i laid waste the rebel-held towns and monasteries. 'So successful was General Ma in his operations and so vindictive were his punitive measures that the districts through which he passed were thrown into a state of panic, and numbers of rebels turned against their leaders.'[7]

At this stage of affairs in 1905, Chao Erh-feng was appointed as the replacement for the luckless Feng. 'Energetic, honest and ruthless to his enemies and intolerant of incompetence or misbehaviour on the part of his subordinates,'[8] he set about the implementation of administrative reforms, including the launch of projects for colonization, agricultural development, improvement of road networks and establishment of military outposts. He set up thirteen administrative centres and restored order up to the Yangtze river, including in towns such as Tachienlu, Litang, Batang and the important monastery of Sangpiling (Chantreng Gompa)[9] in the district of Hsiang Cheng. This monastery, built like a fortress, was captured after a siege of almost six months, from January to June 1906. In this siege, 'nearly all the monks were slaughtered by Chao's troops. The monastery was demolished'.[10] Soon Chao earned the ignominious epithet of 'the butcher'.

The 'Sinification' of this area had commenced with the introduction of a 'fifteen-point programme', the Batang Regulations, by Chao. This transformation programme for the Tibetans mandated adoption of Chinese surnames, wearing Chinese style of clothing, shaving their face and wearing pigtails, among other orders. The purported Chinese aim was to impose an alien but supposedly superior culture on the 'barbaric Tibetans'—the Khampas and other tribes. Great incentives were given to Chinese settlers to colonize the region, and they were even encouraged to marry local tribal women who, it was advertised, were 'extremely hard-working'. Yet there were not many takers, and only 200 Chinese made their homes in the Batang district. By the end of the first decade of the twentieth century, only a handful of them remained.

Before he could finish his mission of 'reforming' the Batang area to bring it on the lines of regular Chinese districts, Chao Erh-feng was appointed as acting viceroy of Szechuan province in early 1907. A year later he was assigned the post of imperial commissioner of the Marches along the frontiers of Szechuan and Yunnan. Coincidentally, his brother, Chao Erh-hsun, was appointed viceroy of Szechuan. The synergy between the two brothers and the power vacuum that resulted from the absence of the Dalai Lama from Tibet facilitated the effective spread of Chinese control over the whole region of the Marches (as shown in Figure 8). This was achieved by early 1910 when Chao's forces secured Chamdo, an important communication node. The exceptions were some volatile areas of the Kham region, which were brought under control only by late 1911.

The traditional system of governance in this region placed each family under the allegiance and overlordship of a particular native chief. There was a well-defined arrangement for collection of taxes and transport levies, also called *ula*, directly by the chieftains or through the deputies appointed by them. This administrative set-up was overturned and replaced by Chinese-type *hsiens*, or districts, under a Chinese magistrate during the period from 1904 to 1911. All the native chiefs were deposed and their territories reorganized into new districts. Some were executed for their perceived misdeeds while others were exiled along with their families and retinues. Most of the 'harmless' inhabitants, denuded of all power, were allowed to live in their estates. According to a Tibetan account, 'Chao Erh-feng and Ma Thi Thai, two Chinese officials, put to death the Batang Deba Nya-ngo, the Dechen Kangsar Deba, and the Litang Tseshag Deba appointed and installed by the Tibet Government ... The Chinese officials plundered the property of these three Debas and sent down their children and adherents to Szechuan.'[11]

Though the people of Tibet had more or less reconciled themselves to their fate, they had not given up hope: 'Wait,' they said to each other, 'Chao will go some day and then our turn will come.'[12] Fortunately, they did not have to wait too long for it to happen as he met with a tragic end in 1910!

The next objective of the Manchu Empire was subjugation of central Tibet and Lhasa, which appeared defenceless. The question that arose was—conquest at what cost? The unceasing military campaign in Tibet not only exhausted the Chinese army, but bled the Szechuan treasury dry. This was one of the major factors that precipitated the Revolution of 1911, and, consequently, the fall of the Manchu Empire and the end of Chinese suzerainty over Tibet.

While Chao Erh-feng and his lieutenants were subduing the area of the Marches between the Yangtze and Salween rivers with an iron hand, the Chinese set into motion steps for 'Sinification' and re-establishment of their long-lost authority over central and southern Tibet, including the Lhasa area. The British unwittingly became facilitators in consolidating Chinese power in Tibet by entering into 'self-denying' conventions and agreements with the Chinese and the Russians (the Adhesion Agreement of 1906 with China, the Convention on Tibet, Afghanistan and Persia with Russia in 1907 and the Trade Agreement with China and Tibet, albeit with a subordinate status, in 1908). Besides these factors, the absence of the Dalai Lama made the Tibetans leaderless and vulnerable.

Chinese administrators led by Chang Yin-tang, the newly designated Chinese commissioner in Tibet, and the Amban, Lien Yu, practically took over the affairs of the state from the Tibetans. Chang had arrived in Lhasa during the autumn of 1906 via Calcutta and Darjeeling (the quickest, most convenient and safe route for Chinese officials travelling from Peking to Lhasa). Lien Yu travelled overland and assumed his appointment as assistant Amban at Lhasa during the same year in September. He took over as Amban a few months later.

Chang was like a man possessed; his principal aim was to eradicate every vestige of British power and presence from central Tibet. He was equally determined to take to task and humiliate all those who had collaborated with or supported the Younghusband expedition, including the Amban, Yu T'ai, who was not only arrested but sent back to China in chains. Chang's wrath also fell on the Panchen Lama, who was isolated from British influence and cautioned against seeking assistance from Britain against China. The administrative apparatus in Tibet was reorganized on the lines of the regular provinces of China and run by

Chinese officials, with a token presence of Tibetans. The ragtag Tibetan army was to be replaced by a 40,000-strong new force.[13] As described by Hugh Richardson, the last British political officer in Lhasa:

> The Tibetan ministers who had taken part in the 1904 negotiations were dismissed; direct contact between the British and Tibetans was prohibited; obstructions were raised to the acquisition of property at the new Trade Marts by British subjects, to trade across the Sikkim border, and to postal communication with Gartok. Approaches were also made to Nepal and Bhutan in an attempt to detach them from the British sphere of influence.[14]

The meek acceptance by the British of these violations by the Chinese and Tibetans of the treaties and agreements they had made with them laid bare the impotence of Britain's flawed Tibet policy. The loss of face of the British was not confined to Tibet but also spread along the Himalayas to Nepal, Sikkim and Bhutan. The Chinese stock rose in the region as a consequence. Unfortunately, the home government and their officials in faraway London were impervious to these developments, and the hard-won gains of the Younghusband mission were surrendered or diluted one by one. The rationale trotted out by the mandarins of the Foreign Office in London, particularly during Lord Morley's time, was that since Tibet was incapable on its own to provide a stable buffer between the Russian and British empires, a Chinese-controlled Tibet was the only viable option. This policy of non-interference or 'laissez-faire' gave the Chinese free rein to consolidate their position in Tibet.

In 1909, alarm bells began to ring again for the Dalai Lama as he finally inched closer to Lhasa after his long exile. He hastened his pace, arriving in Lhasa in December of that year. Aware that it would be no more than a cakewalk for the Chinese to advance to his capital from Chamdo, he desperately sought foreign intervention and reached out to the British, Russians and Americans, but to no avail. The Tibetans on their part offered no resistance to the Chinese army as the Amban, Lien Yu, had tricked the Tibetan authorities into believing that only a force of about 1,000 troops was coming to Lhasa and central Tibet for the purpose of providing protection to the trade marts and for policing duties.[15] In the event, a Chinese force of 2,000 well-trained and equipped soldiers under a young and dynamic leader, Chung Ying, advanced rapidly over 1,000 kilometres in severe winter, crossing five or six snow-covered passes in record time. The leading elements of this force, comprising a mixed force of cavalry and infantry, heralded their triumphant arrival at the northern gates of Lhasa, entering the city on 12 February 1910. The soldiers marched on the streets, randomly firing on people; their intention was to turn the anxiety-filled but tranquil atmosphere into one of fear and awe. Unsure of their fate, the Dalai Lama and his ministers, accompanied by a small retinue, were compelled to flee in secret from the capital the same night; this time it was in the southern direction.

Tibet was never invaded by the Chinese prior to this event. On the earlier occasions that they had entered Tibet, it had been in response to requests from the Tibetans themselves or from their government. To quote from Richardson's authoritative work on Tibetan history:

This was the first Chinese army to reach Lhasa against the will of the Tibetans. The expeditions of 1720, 1728, 1750 and 1792 all came to restore order and were not opposed by Tibetans ... The Emperors on their side had been careful for nearly two centuries to do nothing to upset the ostensibly amicable basis of that relationship.[16]

The Chinese assertiveness in eastern Tibet was propelled by their apprehension that the British might some day make Tibet a protectorate. Therefore the Chinese felt the need to make their presence felt right up to the southern and south-eastern frontiers of Tibet. One of the most important aspects of consolidation of the newly subdued semi-independent tribal areas of eastern Tibet and western China was the proposal to create a new Chinese province of Hsikang ('Western Kham'). By 1911, Chao Erh-feng and his successor, General Fu Sung-mu, had established a firm grip over the entire region and had drawn up a blueprint for the new state. With thirty-three districts spread over a vast area west of the Yangtze, extending to both sides of the Salween all the way to Giamda and also including the areas of Pomed and Zayul bordering the cis-Himalayan tribal areas, this province would ably serve the purpose of a buffer between British India and the Chinese provinces of Szechuan and Yunnan. In the words of General Fu Sung-mu, as written in his book, *History of the Creation of Hsikang*, 'If Tibet be the outer fence, Kham is the house door. This being the case, the Government of China and the people of Szechuan and Yunnan can assuredly not afford to ignore Tibet; Kham, however, is of incomparably more importance to them.'[17]

During the latter period of Chao Erh-feng's campaign, a telegraph line was constructed linking the Marches to the mainland. It was first built from Tachienlu to Batang, and later, during the autumn of 1911, extended westwards to Chamdo. However, during the Revolution of 1911, this important and only link to Peking was completely destroyed by the Tibetans. There was no telegraph connectivity along the northern road or in any other region of the Marches for some time. It was later repaired during 1912–13 and put into action, but only up to Litang, beyond which messages were sent by couriers to Batang and beyond towards Lhasa. Along this route, instances were reported of Chinese postal couriers being abducted and 'skinned alive'—such was the hatred that existed between the two peoples during that period.

The Chinese grand design appears to have also provided for the worst-case scenario of an *independent or fully autonomous* Tibet in the future, and therefore China pushed hard to subdue and transform as much of eastern Tibet as possible and make it like any other province of the mainland. This would ensure that the Chinese frontier on the west would be pushed to the Mekong–Salween divide. And in south-eastern Tibet, where Lhasa's control was practically non-existent, the Chinese endeavour was to gain a foothold in the Pomed and Zayul areas by having a presence at Pome, Pemakoi, in the Tsangpo bend area, and in the frontier outpost of Rima at the head of the Lohit Valley. This area would form part of the new Hsikang province that was being conceptualized so that the Chinese frontier here would be coterminous with the frontier along the eastern end of the Assam Himalayas. Thus, for the first time, the Chinese now came into close proximity to the north-eastern frontier of India.[18]

The British apprehensions at these new developments were aptly described in an article in the *Morning Post*, London, in its issue of 28 February 1910:

> ... a great Empire, the future military strength of which no man can foresee, has suddenly appeared on the North-East Frontier of India ... The men who advocated the retention of Lhasa have proved not so far wrong ... China, in a word, has come to the gates of India, and the fact has to be reckoned with.[19]

It was also appreciated that in the 'long run', north-east India may create the same challenges and pressures on the 'defensive resources of the Indian Empire' as caused by the North-West Frontier. This laid bare the gross misjudgement and underestimation of Chinese capabilities by the British policymakers cocooned in Whitehall, who never visualized such a scenario and acquiesced to the Chinese military invasion of central Tibet, including Lhasa. The Chinese had no pretensions of obliging Great Britain by nurturing its policy of 'an autonomous Tibet under China's suzerainty'. On the contrary, realizing Britain's unenviable predicament and its inability to intervene militarily due to its self-denying agreements of 1906 and 1907, the Chinese empire ventured boldly and ruthlessly towards executing their plan to integrate Tibet with the mainland.

The Chinese were determined to stamp out every vestige of British presence and authority from Tibet; in certain quarters of the Chinese establishment there was a kind of paranoia about Tibet being given a protectorate status by the British. As a result, the Chinese adopted an obstructionist approach as far as trade between British India and Tibet was concerned. Blatant infringements of the existing trade treaties were carried out. Taking full advantage of the British predicament and their policy of non-interference, the Chinese began to interpret their 'suzerainty' as 'sovereignty' over all of Tibet. *Reneging* from the Adhesion Agreement of 1906, they *'usurped all functions of government* (emphasis added)'. Further, their expansionist designs became increasingly evident when they began to make impudent claims of suzerainty over Bhutan and Nepal too.

Despite the Chinese intransigence and acts of aggression, the British honoured their commitment to vacate Chumbi Valley, moving out their troops on 8 February 1908, consequent to payment of the final instalment of 'rupees eight lakhs, thirty three thousand, some annas and pies' (one-third of the reduced indemnity of Rs 25 lakh that had been finally agreed on after the Younghusband expedition of 1904). Thereafter, the only representatives of British India in Tibet were the British trade agents and their Indian infantry escorts, not amounting to more than fifty and twenty-five, respectively, at Gyantse and Yatung.[20]

The Chinese strategy of intransigence and aggression was zealously implemented by Chao Erh-feng, Amban Lien Yu, administrator Chang, General Chung Ying and other subordinate officials. They would most certainly have taken it to its logical conclusion but for the abrupt intervention of the Revolution of October 1911. Fortunately for the Tibetans, as a result of this the Chinese assimilation of Tibet, which was well on track, came to a grinding halt.

This section can be summed up with the words of the British minister at the legation in Peking, B. Alston, in his memorandum on Tibet:

> There can be no doubt however that the year 1910 marked the high-water mark of Chinese influence and prestige in Tibet, and just before the outbreak of the revolution in China, Chao Erh-feng's diplomatic and military measures had enabled the Chinese to hold Lhassa for nearly 2 years and to establish some form of control in the Tibetan Marches.[21]

7

Southern Frontiers of Tibet

Having subdued most of the area of the Marches along the western frontier of Szechuan and northern Yunnan by 1910, the dynamic Chao Erh-feng shifted his focus to Giamda and Lhasa on the west, and to Pomed (also known as Pome) and Zayul to the south-west. He, along with General Fu Sung-mu, wanted to put in place the new province of Hsikang without losing any more time. The Chinese army moved into the northern Zayul Valley, Pomed, Takpo and Kongbo and parts of northern Burma during 1910–12. In the Zayul Valley they did not venture beyond Rima, and in the Pomed area their reach was confined to the north of the great bend of the Tsangpo. In the Takpo and Kongbo regions, their presence was restricted to the two sides of the Tsangpo Valley. It is evident that the Chinese forces, even at the zenith of their power, did not endeavour to assert themselves beyond the customary and traditional southern frontier of Tibet.

In interviews he gave to a semi-official newspaper on 4 March and 11 March 1912, the Szechuan Kung-pao, director of a newly created office responsible for administration of the frontier at Chengdu, remarked:

What is ... a real cause for anxiety is the country to the extreme south of Chiamdo, Tsa-yu (Za-yul), which is adjacent to the British territory of Assam, and is only a dozen days' journey from Chiamdo. From Tsa-yu to Chiang-ka (Gartok) again, is not more than a dozen stages. (See Figure 9)

He went on to say:

> Should an Anglo-Tibetan question arise, and one (British) Army proceed from Shigatse and another from Tsa-yu, the whole length and breadth of Tibet for hundreds of miles would be cut through. The Frontier Office is much alarmed, and as a first step troops are being sent to occupy Tsa-yu.[1]

It is also clearly discerned from very many accounts that there was no Chinese presence in the Monyul area. The Tawang area and southern Monyul were under the temporal and monastic writ of the lamas of the Tawang monastery for most of their history. Some Chinese troops reached up to Tsona Dzong, about four days trek from Tawang to the north into Tibet in 1912 (Figure 8), and briefly halted there before withdrawing towards Lhasa. They did not venture southwards towards Tawang. Similarly, there is no evidence of the Chinese having stayed in the Tsari area, although, while advancing into Lhasa and central Tibet during 1910, they had parallely established firm control of the Tsangpo Valley from Tsethang to Pe, just short of the great bend. Simultaneously, having subdued the Takpo and Kongbo areas, the Chinese turned their attention towards Pomed and Zayul.

It was perhaps a major component of Chao Erh-feng's grand design to incorporate into China proper the regions of Pomed, Zayul and the contiguous Putao-Pienma (northern Irrawaddy Valley) area in northern Burma to make them part of the new province of Sikang (also Hsikang). This was Chao Erh-feng's dream, yet it remained a fictional project. He arbitrarily drew a line without basing it on any natural feature like a river or mountain range. It was as if the boundary was etched on sand with a sword, incorporating all the areas from Chiangta south-eastwards, cutting across the grain of the country through Pomed, Zayul and northern Burma. Areas of south-east Tibet and the northern Irrawaddy (Nmalkha) Valley of Burma (then claimed by China), where the influence of Lhasa and Rangoon was either non-existent or minimal, were the places the Chinese desired to assimilate.

The strategic gains envisaged by the Chinese through these measures were threefold: first, creation of a Chinese-controlled buffer zone between British India and China; second, denial of an avenue for British advance into China's soft underbelly; and third, securing of an alternative route to Lhasa from Yunnan province which would be shorter, easier and more secure, a direct route connecting Gongshan in the Salween Valley in north-west Yunnan with Zayul Valley, or an even more southern alignment connecting the north Irrawaddy region with the Lohit Valley in the area between Walong and Rima. This would bypass the troublesome and 'lawless' Kham territories and many high-altitude snow-bound passes and deep gorges of the Mekong and Salween en route.

Max Muller, the chargé d'affaires in Peking at the time (in the absence of Sir John Jordan, the minister plenipotentiary at the British legation at Peking), writing in April 1910 to the British foreign secretary spelt out his assessment of the general Chinese 'forward policy' being executed in Turkestan, Mongolia, Tibet and the Burmese border 'as an essentially opportunist one of asserting traditional Chinese rights, however tenuous they might be, when circumstances favoured their assertion'.[2] It may be fair to deduce that Whitehall took a rather long time to realize the portentously dangerous dimension of the Chinese game plan. Moreoever, a major restraining factor behind the disinclination of the British administration to establish their writ beyond the Himalayan watershed was Section 55 of the Government of India Act, 1858, as highlighted in Chapter 4. Jordan was from the British Foreign Service and was a key figure during the Simla conference.

Given these constraints, the Indian government watched passively and remained 'inward looking' in the face of the aggressive and ruthless Chinese assertion of their assumed sovereignty over Tibet, and their coercive and subversive strategy to create a 'sphere of influence' in the Marches between Tibet and the tribal territory along the northern glacis of the eastern Himalayas. The amazing lack of clarity until 1911 with regard to the geography of the frontier region of the eastern

Himalayas, the southern limits of Tibet, and the demography of the tribal belt was a direct fallout of the British policy of non-interference in Tibetan affairs and their reluctance to assume responsibility for the tribal belt up to the natural and traditional boundary along the highest crest line.

Even the Chinese Manchu Empire on its last legs did not fail to take cognizance of British susceptibilities and limitations and to exploit the window of opportunity that presented itself at the end of the first decade of the twentieth century. That the Chinese would have succeeded in their endeavours to overcome all resistance within central, eastern and south-eastern Tibet and bring all of Tibet under their firm control, but for the October Revolution, is without doubt.

It would be accurate to record that prior to 1910 and during the latter part of the eighteenth century, there was no Chinese activity in the Pomed or Zayul areas. The Pobas of this area were a practically independent people, and they zealously guarded all entrances to their domain, which was naturally protected in the north and the east by the snow-clad Nyenchen Tanglha and Kangri Karpo mountains (whose peaks are between 5,488 and 6,494 metres in height), the Namcha Barwa range and the Tsangpo gorge in the south. Access from the west was easily blocked by a number of rivers flowing into the Tsangpo forming a series of defiles. Strangers were denied entry. Even the Chinese army which came to survey the land and lay the road and telegraph line were told by the Pobas to return as 'they [Pobas] were *neither subject to China nor to Lhasa'*. There was an outbreak of hostilities between the two because the Chinese troops led by Chung Ying tried to force their entry here. In the fierce fighting that ensued, the Chinese suffered severe losses. There were four major engagements that took place during the spring of 1911 around Tongjuk bridge and other areas on the road to Lhasa.[3]

The Chinese returned with a battalion-sized force under Lo Ch'ing-chi, augmented by troops sent by Chao Erh-feng from the Marches and troops from Zayul Valley. They undertook a massive and ruthless retaliatory campaign that almost wiped off Showa, the capital of Pomed.

They destroyed the palace and the gompa, and eliminated the entire Poba leadership by beheading eight ministers, head lamas and four chiefs, laying waste the entire countryside by burning villages, destroying places of worship and killing men, women and children indiscriminately. The Chinese made sure that the king of the Pobas, who had escaped to Pemako, was done to death by the people while they unceremoniously dispatched two of his queens and a small daughter to Lhasa. The Chinese thereby subdued the Pomed and Pemako regions during the summer of 1911. They 'established garrisons at Yortong on the right bank of the Tsangpo and at Chimdro', during August 1911. From these bases they sent out smaller teams of soldiers to visit the more remote Tibetan villages in the countryside.[4] This Chinese attempt at Sinification of the Pomed region might well have succeeded but for the Revolution of October 1911, whose impact was catastrophic for the Chinese soldiers and for their Tibetan and Poba collaborators. At first, the exhausted, ill-fed and dispirited troops mutinied and, besides fighting amongst each other, killed many of their officers. Thereafter they resorted to arson, plunder and loot while withdrawing. By the end of 1911, most of them had met with a violent fate, and the survivors were compelled to fight their way back to Lhasa. By the end of 1913 there was no trace of the Chinese left in south-eastern Tibet, only bitter memories of their harsh and repressive acts.

In the Zayul Valley, the area up to Kyigang (Chikung) and Rima was under rudimentary administrative control of the Tibetans prior to 1910. A part of Chao Erh-feng's army came down the Zayul Valley in early 1910. A major part of this force of around 320 soldiers established its headquarters in Chikung and ousted the Tibetan administration there. It then sent a smaller detachment of about twenty to the frontier village of Rima (Figure 9).[5] As recorded in various accounts of that period, the Chinese, without much opposition, displaced the Tibetan administration and established their control in the upper Zayul Valley. But for the Revolution in 1911 the Chinese design of imposing their authority over the Meyors and Mishmi tribes inhabiting the Walong area of the Lohit Valley too might have succeeded.

Figure 9: Evolution of the McMahon Line (1913–14)—The Zayul Valley and Walong frontier region

The Chinese presence and activities in this area first came to the notice of Williamson, the daring and adventurous assistant political officer (APO) at Sadiya, in May 1910. Tungno, a tribal chief of the Miju Mishmis from the village of Pangum on the Lohit, about 32 kilometres south of Walong, arrived at Sadiya with the news given by two Tibetans that a large force of Chinese soldiers numbering 1,000 (an exaggerated figure) had recently come to Rima. They demanded taxes from the Tibetan administrator, and on being refused put him in a lock-up. He was ousted subsequently as the Chinese officers took charge of the village. The Tibetans had showed Tungno the orders of the Chinese addressed to all the Mishmi chiefs to 'cut a track from Tibet to Assam broad enough for two horsemen to ride abreast'.[6] Tungno refused to comply with these orders as his area came under the jurisdiction of the APO at Sadiya. The alarm this unsettling news created can be imagined. The peaceful and tranquil atmosphere of the Brahmaputra Valley was afire.

This was followed by another equally disturbing piece of news conveyed in July 1910 by a Miju Mishmi named Halam to Williamson. A group of Chinese comprising some officials and soldiers had recently descended from Rima, and after reconnoitring the area around Walong, planted Chinese flags at Menilkrai, a small habitation about 2 kilometres south of the junction of the rivers Yepauk and Lohit. The reason why the Chinese decided to place the boundary marker at Menilkrai, just a few miles downstream of Walong, was that beyond it the Lohit passes through a narrow defile which could be defended with a small force. From this defensible vantage point the track from Sadiya to Rima along the western (i.e. right) bank of the Lohit could be effectively dominated and entry to it denied.

Walong is where the valley opens up into large, flat, grassy areas, traditionally used by the Meyor herders on behalf of the Mishmi owners. Walong, situated about thirty miles south of Rima on the western bank of the Lohit, was never under Chinese or Tibetan administration. It offered the best location for a frontier military outpost and had been identified as such by British frontier officials and adventurers like Bailey. A few miles to its south, the Yepauk river is no mean barrier, with its vertical cliff-like banks, particularly during the rainy season when it becomes a monstrous obstacle. Hence the Chinese interest in this area and their efforts to extend the Tibetan frontier right up to Menilkrai. Importantly, this alignment would ensure that the tracks that came from north Burma through Diphu L'ka, and the Talok Pass joining the Irrawaddy and the Lohit Valleys, would come under their control. The Chinese obviously did not believe in taking into account the ethnic, customary and traditional aspects of a region while evolving their boundaries. During October 1910, it was learnt that 'the Chinese had prohibited all trade between the Miju Mishmis and Tibet'. Apparently, it was a coercive strategy to pressure the local tribes to accept Chinese terms.

These Chinese activities were confirmed six months later when the intrepid adventurer Captain F.M. Bailey reached Sadiya from Peking in the summer of 1911. He most unexpectedly announced his arrival in Assam after travelling through the Kham region and the Zayul Valley.

In an incredibly remarkable journey of about four months, he had covered over 3,200 kilometres, more than half of it through some of the most challenging terrains in the world inhabited by fierce tribes. The northern Zayul Valley and some other stretches he had journeyed through had never been set foot upon by any European before. Bailey completed his daring geostrategic recce-cum-espionage mission—which was acknowledged as of 'great value to our administration in that part of the Empire'—by deliberately exceeding his brief and the instructions of Sir Jordan. And, true to British tradition, he received both recognition and admonishment in equal measure.[7]

Trekking for two days after passing through Rima, the last Tibetan administrative centre in the Zayul Valley, Bailey met two Mishmi village chiefs at a small settlement called Tini or Tinai on the east (i.e. left) bank of the Lohit in the Walong area. They had been called to report to the Chinese officials at Chikung. They had refused to comply with an earlier summons, and this time they were threatened with 'military action' if they disobeyed and hence were on their way to meet the officials. Bailey advised them against going to Chikung and instead to seek instructions from the political officer at Sadiya; they heeded his advice and returned to their villages. On 20 July 1911, Bailey also met two Tibetans at his camp at Minzong on the banks of the Lohit. They had been directed by the Chinese, under threat of decapitation, to summon and bring all the Mishmi chiefs to Chikung. They were in the process of doing so but had exceeded the time given to them. This meeting, however, never took place as the Chinese forces were moved to the Pomed region in the west as reinforcements to the hard-pressed soldiers in that region, where the Pobas were offering fierce resistance.

Later, when the Mishmi mission under W.C.M. Dundas was launched in October 1911, the Pangum chief also reported the visit of Tibetan lamas sent by the Chinese to 'summon the Miju headmen to Rima for a purpose to be disclosed on their arrival'. The Mijus did not obey the summons either, fearing they might be required in connection with the expedition against Pomed, which the Chinese were known to be organizing.[8] Another valuable piece of information was provided by the Pangum chief; during the rainy season (May to September) in 1911, some Chinese activities had taken place in the Taraon Mishmi–inhabited Delei (Dilli) Valley. The Delei is a river that originates in the Himalayan watershed west of Rima and flows into the Lohit at an important village called Hayuliang, about 130 kilometres downstream from Walong.

The Mishmi mission was able to corroborate this news from various village headmen and concluded that the Chinese did cross the frontier from the north through the Glei Dakhru Pass (Figure 9) and had tried to assert their authority and subvert the tribals of the Taraon area, though without much success. According to a fairly authentic account provided on 30 November 1911 by the village chief of Chipa in the Delei Valley, a man called Mazanon of the Taraon Mishmi tribe, a Chinese force of fifty soldiers, led by one Ta Loh,[9] along with 100 Tibetan coolies, came over the Glei Dakhru Pass and halted at Chipa for seven days.

The Chinese ordered the villagers of the area to cut a road through the valley for their use. The villagers told them the Delei road was very bad and they should instead use the Lohit Valley road, which was better and also being used by the British. The Chinese then gave the headmen 'a piece of paper with some writing on it, which they said should be shown both to the Chinese and British'; this the Taraons did not take. Next the Chinese produced a flag and ordered the tribesmen to set it up at the confluence of the Delei and Lohit. This too they refused to do, replying that if the Chinese wished to plant flags they must do it themselves. The Chinese then produced nine loads of salt, which they gave to the villagers saying that they should eat Chinese salt as well as British. Mazanon said his people took the salt and ate half of it, leaving the other half in the village 'for fear of incurring our displeasure'.[10]

Captain Hardcastle was able to obtain a corroboration of the information provided by Mazanon and also recovered fifteen documents in the nature of authority letters or passes issued in the name of Chao Erh-feng given to the villagers to facilitate future Chinese movements for trade in Tibet. When the Taraons refused to take the hint from the Tibetan interpreters to give appropriate presents to Ta Loh, the commander of the force, the latter displayed great annoyance and threatened to send for 300 more soldiers; but they left the next day without carrying out their threat. As a matter of fact, they crossed the Glei Dakhru Pass and proceeded towards the troubled Pomed region instead. As events unfolded, the Chinese never returned to Zayul Valley again!

Dundas, who was leading the expedition in the Lohit Valley, reached Yepauk on 14 January 1912. He gathered that two days before his arrival three Tibetans had planted another Chinese flag about 70 metres north of the previous flags at Menilkrai. This flag had a four-clawed dragon, and beside it there stood a board with inscriptions in both Chinese and Tibetan, saying, 'The Southern frontier of Za-yul on the borders of the Szechuan Province of the Chinese Empire.' The Chinese carried out another similar mission to the region, now with a higher-ranking official. He examined this board and gave instructions for installation of another notification that was going to be sent. The Chinese mission did not fail to notice the two inscriptions engraved by the Sappers and Miners, who had visited earlier, on a rockface at the British camp at Yepauk,[11] and indeed took back impressions of the same with them.

The Chinese also sent probes into the adjacent Dau and Delei (Dilli) Valleys, as also to the upper reaches of the Dibang Valley, which lies to the immediate east of the Tsangpo river as it flows south of the great bend. Taking advantage of the loose political control exercised by the British administration over the hill tribes, the Chinese made a few exploratory incursions of this type south of the Himalayan watershed. They mostly used Tibetans as proxies to obtain information or to convey their pronouncements. I do not subscribe to the theory put forward by Alastair Lamb that by making these forays and coercing the Mishmi tribes to obey their diktat, Chao Erh-feng was only trying to secure his southern flank. Taking into consideration the Chinese expansionist territorial claims up to 1911, their strategic design of trying to grab areas in the southern slopes of the Himalayas to connect the Pomed and Zayul regions with Yunnan province through northern Burma falls into place perfectly.[12]

Ironically, the Chinese had never been heard of before or after this burst of forays by them in the region during 1910–12. As a matter of fact, Chinese presence in the whole of proper Tibet was eliminated by the end of 1912 and the Chinese forces were pushed back to the Salween-

Mekong watershed (shown in Figure 8). The expansionist dreams of the Manchu Empire never materialized and, in a typical anticlimax, came to a premature and abrupt end as a result of the nationalists' revolution of 1911.

Given all these events, one cannot help but commend the profound comprehension and analysis of Chinese policy in the south-eastern region of Tibet by Sir Henry McMahon, which is contained in the 'Final Memorandum on the Simla Conference', signed on 8 July 1914. This Conference has been discussed in detail later. Here are the salient extracts from McMahon's incisive report:

> No sooner had the Chinese forces arrived in Lhasa [in early 1910] than it became evident that China was scarcely in search of those peaceful and neighbourly relations between India and China, which had been contemplated by His Majesty's Government when concluding the agreement of 1906 ... The peace of our North-East Frontier was seriously menaced by a series of Chinese aggressions along the border line from Bhutan to Upper Burma.
>
> Through the hostile attitude of the Chinese a situation had arisen indeed which threatened to cancel all the advantages of our previous arrangements in regard to Tibet, and to involve grave political responsibilities and heavy military expenditure on the North-East Frontier of India.[13]

There could not have been a more telling analysis of the alarming situation obtaining on British India's north-eastern frontier than this.

8

The Dalai Lama Flees to India

The Dalai Lama, who had barely returned after five and a half years of exile from Lhasa in December 1909, had to flee once again, this time veritably saving his life by the skin of his teeth. Using subterfuge, the Chinese had tricked the Grand Lama into granting them permission to enter Lhasa unopposed, by telling him that a force of about 1,000 soldiers would be arriving in the city to provide protection to the trade marts being established there as part of the Trade Agreement of 1908. Two months later, as the Dalai Lama discerned that the advancing Chinese force was actually about 2,000 strong and was intending an occupation of Lhasa and central Tibet, he was taken aback. But at that late stage he found himself in no position to offer a fight. So on 12 February 1910, as Chung Ying's stormtroopers entered Lhasa, he took flight, along with some of his Kalons (ministers) and a small retinue, towards India. He did not want to be a puppet or, worse, a prisoner of the Chinese.

The astute Lama escaped Chinese efforts to capture him, cleverly dodging his pursuers by avoiding the well-known routes. He took the most unexpected track, along the Bhutanese border, which involved negotiating three or four high-altitude snow-covered passes to avoid his pursuers. He set out at a blistering pace in the peak of the Tibetan winter, often through deep snow and blinding mist. Eventually, he reached Gnatong (currently known as Nathang in the Jelep La area along the Sikkim border), following the Chumbi Valley route.

It was a remarkable feat by any standards, to ride about 64 kilometres in one night and make it to the Tsangpo river by early morning. Having crossed the river by boat, the Dalai sped on towards Chumbi Valley. A pursuing Chinese force of 200 soldiers was held at bay at the Tsangpo ferry by gallant rearguard action on the part of Chen-sa Nang-Kang, a youthful, spirited and loyal aide of the Grand Lama, assisted by a few poorly trained and equipped Tibetan soldiers. They had cleverly tethered the boats on the southern bank of this huge obstacle of a river, and the Chinese force was delayed here for a considerable time. Gyantse and other known Chinese garrisons en route were bypassed, and the well-known cart road from Gyantse to Yatung too was cleverly avoided by the Dalai Lama. Taking a route hugging the Himalayan mountains extending southwards to the Chomolhari peak, the Dalai Lama's entourage reached Phari Dzong, having crossed five passes over 4,500 metres in altitude and braving a snowstorm and chill winds that 'pierced the clothes of the fugitives like thorns', as described by Charles Bell in *The Portrait of Dalai Lama*. The Dalai Lama's group finally entered Sikkim after negotiating a 1,500-metre ascent to cross the Jelep La on 21 February. Amazingly, the Grand Lama and his retinue covered the distance of approximately 500 kilometres in just nine days, doing between 40 and 50 kilometres daily in those high altitudes in the peak of Himalayan winter.

In the wee hours of a wintry night in February 1910, much to the amusement and surprise of two British soldiers (one of them was Sergeant Bill Luff and the other was Humphreys) posted at the border telegraph and observation post at Gnatong, the Dalai Lama's arrival was reported by the leading elements of his weary group. *'Which blighter is the correct Dalai Lama? Yer all seem to think yer the Dalai Lama* (emphasis added),'[1] one of the soldiers asked the ragtag group in the darkness. On being indicated who the Dalai Lama was, they led him inside their shack and had a glimpse at him in the glow of the fireplace. The soldiers suggested the Dalai Lama might be more comfortable in the dak bungalow nearby, but were told that the Grand Lama would be happy to share their shack and stay put there itself. The God-king of the whole of Tibet, a state one-third the size of the United States of America, made for a pitiable sight. But, at least, once again, he had survived. The soldiers did not venture to let the

Tibetan refugees know that they had no ammunition in their weapons, as their equipment had been back-loaded for they were themselves waiting to be relieved. The night passed uneventfully. The next morning, after as sumptuous a breakfast as field conditions would permit, the two ex-sergeants, Luff and Humphreys, with bayonets fixed and still without ammunition, escorted the Dalai Lama's party a few kilometres down the slope into Sikkim. As they parted company, by a 'strange coincidence', each apparently remarked to the other, 'Thank heaven we've got the boss of Tibet off our bally hands safe and sound.'[2]

The Dalai Lama took a few days to reach the extremely picturesque town of Kalimpong, which was a centre of commerce, intrigue and espionage focused on Tibet and all that went on in that enchanted land of the lamas. It was also a refuge for retired government officials. It is a beautiful cantonment town in the present times too. There was a swell of coreligionists from Sikkim, Bhutan and Nepal, and also 'three little Scottish girls, daughters of Dr Graham, the well-known missionary and founder of the Kalimpong Homes', who had lined up on the cart track leading to the bazaar to greet the Dalai Lama. The fugitive God-king of Tibet and his entourage received a tumultuous welcome from Hindus, Christians, Muslims and prostrating Buddhists. This must have been an unbelievable experience for the Dalai Lama. He left for Darjeeling after a few days in Kalimpong, having created a record of sorts for travelling in the peak of winter from Lhasa to Gnatong (Nathang) on the Sikkim border, managing the narrowest escape from the clutches of the Chinese pursuers.

Charles Alfred Bell, an acknowledged Tibetologist of the time, was the political officer for Sikkim, Bhutan and Tibet from 1908 to 1918 and had been in charge of administering Chumbi Valley between 1904 and 1905 as a consequence of the Lhasa Convention. Naturally, the responsibility of taking care of the Dalai Lama and his entourage during their exile in India fell on his shoulders. As time would tell, he proved to be the best choice for the role. In a short period of time, he had established a personal equation with the exalted lama and had become his confidant. Soon the Dalai Lama confided to Bell: 'I have come to India to ask the help of the British Government against the Chinese. Unless they intervene, China will occupy Tibet and oppress it; China will destroy the Buddhist religion there and the Tibetan Government, and will govern the country through Chinese officials. Eventually her power will be extended into the States on the border between Tibet and India.'[3] History is proving the Grand Lama right, as far as China's extertion of its influence over smaller nations is concerned.

During this sojourn in India, the Dalai Lama was invited to Calcutta for an audience with the viceroy, Lord Hardinge. The journey by train from Darjeeling to Calcutta, including the metre-gauge 'toy train' leg to Siliguri, was a novel experience for the Tibetans. The Dalai Lama was welcomed with a seventeen-gun salute at Fort William. In his interaction with the viceroy he conveyed 'his gratitude for the hospitality he had received and his reliance on the British Government in his present difficulties'.

This is how the second exile of the thirteenth Dalai Lama, the reincarnation of the 'Chen-re-zi', commenced. Ironically, he was compelled by circumstances to seek shelter in the territory of the very same power he had considered as Tibet's sworn enemy even until half a decade ago. The British received the fugitive Grand Lama and his entourage comprising almost all the members of the Kashag, or council of ministers, with typical British 'neutral' cordiality. They put him up in a suitable cottage, named 'Hillside', on the outskirts of Darjeeling under the personal care of Charles Bell.

This time too the Chinese, on 25 February 1910, announced the deposition of the Dalai Lama. But, unlike on the earlier occasion, they declared that a new incarnation could be found. This idea was rejected outright by the Tibetans, as there was no question of searching for the incarnation of the Chen-re-zi while their Dalai Lama was still alive. The Chinese then endeavoured to replace him with the Panchen Lama. The Tashi Lama, another name the Panchen Lama is known by, had no choice but to obey the imperial command. He functioned in a perfunctory manner from the Norbulingka Palace of the Dalai Lama but did not occupy the seat of the Dalai Lama or endeavour to take over his temporal powers. Finding it impossible to handle Tibet without the Dalai Lama, the Chinese Amban, in September 1910, 'offered to rescind the deposition order', and requested him to come back to Lhasa. In a detailed reply addressed to Lo T'i-t'ai in the Manchu court, the Grand Lama recapitulated the manner in which the Chinese had invaded his nation and how the emperor had taken actions on the advice of the Amban in Lhasa without showing any concern for the 'rang wang' or independence of Tibet. Under the existing conditions, said the Dalai Lama, he could not return to Tibet. In view of the foregoing events, he added, the relationship between Tibet and China had distinctly changed. He emphasized that there was now a need for a third party to act as an intermediary to decide Tibet's future policy. Having lost confidence in the Chinese, the Dalai Lama, for the first time, suggested that Great Britain be that intermediary between Tibet and China.[4] The Dalai Lama continued to stay in Darjeeling until the middle of 1912.

During the upheaval in Tibet caused by the Revolution and the new regime's efforts to regain China's hold on its outlying frontier regions, President Yuan Shih-k'ai announced the restoration of the titles of the Dalai Lama on 28 October 1912. The presidential proclamation, loaded with political doublespeak, talked of 'a feeling of deep attachment to the mother country' on the part of the Dalai Lama and ended with 'a hope that he may prove a support to the Yellow Church and a help to the Republic'. However, after a decade of exposure to the larger canvas of world politics, the Grand Lama was now a much experienced and widely travelled leader of Tibet; he refused to be taken in and 'spurned' the Chinese offer. Riding a Tibetan revival of sorts—following a wave of successes on the part of his soldiers against the Chinese forces and the consequent Chinese retreat from the Kham region, some areas in the Marches and central Tibet—the Dalai Lama said he was not asking the Chinese government for any rank, as he intended to exercise both temporal and spiritual rule.[5] This action, coupled with a proclamation made by him asserting Tibet's unique history, including the choe-yon relationship with China, was seen by the Tibetans as an *announcement of Tibet's independence.*[6]

During his second exile, some time in 1910, the Dalai Lama, talking of the Chinese invasion, said to Charles Bell: 'The oppression of the Tibetans would recoil on themselves (the Chinese). An evil deed had been committed, and was bound to bring its own retribution sooner or later. *Karma*, irresistible *karma*, can never be over-ridden.' Commenting later, Charles Bell said, 'And in this case the retribution came soon.'[7] The Chinese emperor was dethroned in the wake of the 1911 Revolution, within two years of the Chinese invasion of Tibet.

As a matter of fact, the British—who all along wanted to see only Chinese suzerainty over Tibet—had inadvertently facilitated the Chinese in laying their foundation of sovereignty over the whole of Tibet. The fundamental flaw in the Tibet policy of Great Britain was that it had no lever with which to calibrate and control the Chinese hold and suzerainty over Tibet. There was no word such as 'suzerainty' in the political precepts of the Chinese, who understood it to mean only one thing: sovereignty. The Chinese would have almost certainly achieved their goal by 1912 but for the intervention caused by the collapse of the Manchu Empire and the Revolution of October 1911. These events happened unexpectedly, at a time when the Tibetans had reconciled themselves to their fate under Chinese rule and the British were in the process of amassing a small army along the Sikkim frontier in anticipation of a call for help from their isolated trading missions and modest military escorts at Gyantse and Yatung! Hearing the clarion call, Tibetans all across Tibet rose up in arms. With great hatred and pent-up feelings of revenge, they killed or captured the Chinese administrators and soldiery wherever they could, particularly in the remote and far-flung interiors, driving out the hapless Chinese civilians as well as the Amban and his escort from their soil.

The internecine warfare between the Chinese loyalist pro-monarchy forces and the revolutionary Nationalist army soldiers, and the several mutinies reported amongst the restive Chinese soldiery, made the task of the Tibetan avengers easier. The Chinese were on the run, and there was an exodus of them from central and western Tibet. This was the moment the cautious Dalai Lama was waiting for, and he decided to return to Tibet. The Grand Lama and his entourage left Kalimpong for Lhasa in June 1912, the day having been fixed by Tibetan astrologers. He was seen off by Charles Bell and his wife. The Dalai Lama entered Tibet through Chumbi Valley and proceeded slowly but surely, via Phari Dzong and Gyantse to Lhasa. Halting at various monasteries and dzongs en route, he finally repaired to the Samding monastery on the banks of the turquoise-blue Yamdruk Yatso, a vast lake south of the Tsangpo river. Known as 'Abode of the Abbess', this monastery was about 112 kilometres short of Lhasa. Even when apprised of the Revolution in China and its fallout in the frontier regions and outer periphery of the Chinese sphere of influence, such as Mongolia, Sinkiang and Tibet, he made cautious moves as far as returning to Lhasa was concerned. Taking no chances, the great survivor that the thirteenth Dalai Lama was, he decided to go no further till the last of the Chinese soldiery had been evicted from the capital of Tibet.

At Samding the Dalai Lama was joined by the ubiquitous Dorjieff. In order to avoid the embarrassment of associating with Dorjieff again and perhaps incurring the ire of the British because of Dorjieff's Russian connection, the Dalai Lama sent him on a mission to Mongolia, armed with the authority to build strong bonds with the newly independent Outer Mongolia.

By the end of 1912, the 'turn' of the Tibetans had come. With practically no outsiders left, *Tibet had truly and effectively become an independent state*. And so it remained for the next four decades. So much had changed in this eventful decade!

'In January 1913 the Dalai Lama finally returned to Lhasa. Tibet was free of the Chinese for the first time since 1720.'[8]

Towards the end of 1911, while it appeared that the Chinese hold over Tibet had climaxed, the uprising in China against the rule of the Manchu dynasty began, and the whole scenario changed dramatically. This historical development took the world by surprise; not just the Tibetans, who were reluctantly reconciling themselves to the overlordship of the Chinese Manchu Empire, but also, and even more so, the Chinese Amban and its army under General Chung Ying. The October Revolution in China eventually overthrew the Ch'ing emperor, who had to abdicate in February 1912, making way for Yuan Shih-k'ai as president of the new Republic of China. With mainland China in turmoil, the Chinese hold on Tibet palpably loosened. The Chinese military garrisons in the important towns of Tibet, such as Shigatse, Gyantse, Yatung and in the capital Lhasa, began to feel the heat. The insecure and restive soldiery began to display signs of indiscipline, insubordination and low morale. Reports of rampant looting and arson by Chinese soldiers began to circulate. The situation was worsened by the arrival of those stragglers that remained of the Chinese forces operating in the Pomed and Zayul areas. Tibetan resistance against Chinese authority also began to increase by the day. Skirmishes in the countryside and open clashes in the towns between the two sides had become a daily occurrence. The Tibetans effectively blocked Chinese efforts to withdraw eastwards to the mainland. Roads and telegraph communications were disrupted. News about the situation in Tibet trickled down to Sikkim via Chumbi valley and dispersed all across the world, including to China proper.

During the Dalai Lama's sojourn in the Darjeeling and Kalimpong areas from 1910 to 1912, the British were able to befriend him. And their previously sour relationship transformed into an entirely new equation. The British attitude of indifference and nonchalance towards the Dalai Lama underwent a change of heart. The rapid erosion of Chinese authority in Tibet presented an opportunity that lent itself to exploitation by both the British and the Tibetans. Whereas the Tibetans sought the support of the British to throw away the Chinese yoke forever, the British found the situation conducive to enhancement of their influence in Tibet; they charted a road map for a greater share of trade for themselves by establishing marts at Yatung, Shigatse and Gyantse, besides Lhasa.

To assuage the anger and alienation among the Tibetans caused by their ruthless and ham-handed suppression by Chao Erh-feng's army and the insensitive Chinese administrators during the invasion of Tibet in 1910–11 and the conquest of the Marches earlier, Yuan Shih-k'ai endeavoured to repair the damage. He made a proclamation apologizing for the misdemeanours and transgressions of the Chi'ing empire in Tibet. He declared that regions like Mongolia, Sinkiang and Tibet would be given the status of Chinese provinces, and he also offered to discuss greater autonomy for them. He went on to attempt to smoothen ruffled feathers by revoking the deposition of the Dalai Lama by the previous regime and restoring his position. He also conferred ceremonial titles on the Grand Lama and bestowed him generous gifts.

The Dalai Lama refused to get taken in by this stratagem of the Chinese president. Refusing to accept any honorific titles conferred by

Peking, he unequivocally conveyed to them that the relationship that existed traditionally between Tibet and China was best described as one of priest and patron, in which the subordinate or superior status of one or the other was never an issue. Richardson, in his masterful account, *History of Tibet,* said:

> ... *he wanted no rank from Peking and had resumed the temporal and spiritual government of his country. That message of the Dalai Lama is regarded by the Tibetans to be a formal declaration of their independence;* nevertheless, the Chinese, trying to be clever and blandly ignoring inconvenient facts, issued a decree on 28 October 1912 attributing to the Dalai Lama sentiments about 'affection for the Motherland', which he had never expressed, purporting to restore him to his former position (emphasis added).[9]

As early as October 1912, encouraged by the developments in neighbouring Mongolia, the Tsongdu (Tibetan National Assembly), supposedly with the approval of the Grand Lama, or at least in line with his thinking, is reported to have written to Lord Hardinge that '*the country [Tibet] had broken off its relations with Peking and would like all Chinese troops to be withdrawn* (emphasis added)'. Parshotam Mehra has commented in his well-researched account of those times that it is questionable whether this communication could be construed 'as a declaration of Tibet's independence' as it lacked 'the trimmings that go with a formal proclamation'.[10] Besides, in the absence of the seal of the temporal head of the state, as the Dalai Lama had yet to reach Lhasa, the letter did not carry the required level of authority. At the same time, the Assembly's note to Hardinge was a telling commentary of the situation then prevailing in Tibet and cannot be dismissed. Referring to the Dalai Lama's refusal to accept the titles conferred on him by the president of the Republic of China, Charles Bell wrote, 'Thus the God-king made clear his declaration of Tibetan independence.'[11] The Dalai Lama had declined the offer while he was still en route to Lhasa.

In consonance with Yuan Shih-k'ai's pet theme of a united China—a family of five races: the Chinese, the Manchu, the Mongol, the

Mahommedan and the Tibetan—he apologized to the Dalai Lama for the 'excesses' committed by Chinese troops in Tibet.

Finally, with the ignominious departure of General Chung Ying from Chumbi Valley to India over the Nathu La, along with his *'motley remnant of a half-starved and demoralised bodyguard'*, on 14 April 1913, the Chinese presence and authority in Tibet was erased.[12] This situation continued till the communist Chinese People's Liberation Army 'liberated' Tibet in 1951.

The Dalai Lama entered the portals of Lhasa in January 1913, amidst great fanfare. Without losing time, the astute Lama commenced the process of reconsolidation of his temporal and spiritual authority, which had been usurped gradually by the Chinese from 1905 to 1911. As a formal proclamation of Tibet's independence, the Grand Lama made this announcement from the hallowed precincts of the Potala Palace in January 1913:

I, the Dalai Lama, most omniscient possessor of the Buddhist faith, whose title was conferred by the Lord Buddha's command from the glorious land of India, speaks to you as follows: (select excerpts)

I am speaking to all classes of Tibetan people. Lord Buddha, from the glorious country of India, prophesied that the reincarnations of Avalokiteswara, through successive rulers from the early religious kings to the present day, would look after the welfare of Tibet.

During the time of Genghis Khan and Altan Khan of the Mongols, the Ming dynasty of the Chinese, and the Ch'ing dynasty of the Manchus, Tibet and China co-operated on the basis of benefactor and priest relationship. A few years ago the Chinese authorities in Szechuan and Yunnan endeavoured to colonise our territory ... Meanwhile the Manchu Empire collapsed ... Now, the Chinese intention of colonising Tibet under the patron-priest relationship has faded like a rainbow in the sky. Having once again achieved for ourselves a period of happiness and peace, I have now allotted to all of you the following duties to be carried out without negligence...'[13]

Interestingly, just before this proclamation was made, Tibet and Mongolia signed a treaty by which both countries jointly renounced

Chinese overlordship, declared themselves as sovereign states and enshrined their desire to strengthen the ties of friendship and religion already existing between them. 'The Dalai Lama, as Sovereign of Tibet, approved the formation of an independent Mongolian state, while the Jetsun Dampa Hutuktu acknowledged Tibet as an independent and sovereign state.'[14] They also undertook to come to each other's aid to overcome internal and external dangers.

Those who collaborated with the Chinese regime during the two exiles of the Dalai Lama were brutally tortured and put to the sword, and they included some high officials and lamas, particularly those from the seditious and pro-Chinese Drepung and Tengeling monasteries.

PART IV

BRITAIN WAKES UP

9

Tibet Policy of the British

Alarmed by the Chinese army probes into the tribal territories on the southern Himalayan slopes, particularly during the period 1910 to 1912, the British decided to review their 'hands off' policy on Tibet with a greater sense of urgency. They also warned the Chinese against interference in Tibet's internal affairs and their positioning of a large military force in Tibet, in contravention of the existing treaties. President Yuan Shih-k'ai was urged to withdraw his proclamation of 27 April 1912 declaring Tibet as an integral part of China, to be made into a province similar to other provinces of China proper. The Chinese government had also specified that all important administrative issues pertaining to Tibet would be dealt with by the central authority at Peking, contrary to the repeated assurances given by the president that it would not be so. In light of China's aggressive designs in the Marches, and also as far as the rest of Tibet was concerned, the British held out the threats of not recognizing the new Chinese republic and of closing the most convenient and secure land-cum-sea route (to Tibet) through India to the Chinese. The British also felt the need to unambiguously define the status of Tibet vis-à-vis China—both the frontiers of Tibet and the Sino-Tibetan boundary itself. Lastly, they wanted to iron out the contentious trade-related matters between Tibet and India. There had clearly emerged an urgent need to have a written agreement to resolve these issues.

The British were thus compelled to give effect to a new China policy relating to Tibet. Showing that they meant business, the first major step they took was to close the land route to Lhasa via Calcutta, Darjeeling/ Kalimpong and the Chumbi Valley in 1910, denying to the Chinese the quickest and most secure access to central Tibet. Thereafter they remonstrated with the Chinese for the armed repression and excesses by their army in the region of the Marches and for their violation of the agreements regarding intervention in the internal matters of Tibet. Realization had dawned on Whitehall that the frontier between Tibet and China needed to be defined and the Chinese cautioned against transgressing that line with their army, particularly any force intended to reinforce or rescue the besieged Chinese troops in and around Lhasa or elsewhere in central Tibet as a consequence of the 1911 Revolution. Taking advantage of the rapidly weakening position of the Chinese forces and officials in Tibet, the British policy on Tibet took on a bolder tint. The timing was propitious, as Russia was also engaged in propping up the Mongolians, and the British government could take a few liberties. Britain found it 'essential' that Tibet, 'while retaining her position as an autonomous State under the suzerainty of China, should in reality be placed in a position of absolute dependence on the Indian government, and that there should be set up an effective machinery for keeping out the Chinese on the one hand and the Russians on the other'.[1]

Accordingly, serious parleys involving John Jordan, the British minister in Peking, the Chinese president Yuan Shih-k'ai and the Chinese foreign minister took place in 1912. These led to the presentation of a memorandum to the Chinese government on 17 August 1912, seeking a meeting to resolve the issues under consideration, pending which British recognition of the Chinese regime would be withheld, followed by direct negotiations between Britain and Tibet. The Russian initiatives in Outer Mongolia indirectly paved the way for a similar approach by the British. This approach was strongly advocated by the Indian government, but Whitehall kept pussyfooting for one reason or the other and failed to exploit the situation to its full potential.

The Chinese found themselves in a most unenviable position as a newborn republic in 1912. Their greatest challenge was to stabilize the internal security situation, what with many a regional leader displaying his unbridled ambitions and wanting to break away. The Tibetans, their

army and the monk-led laity exacted a heavy toll of the Chinese soldiers
and officials. The army of the Manchu Empire was in utter disarray, and
its ill-paid, ill-fed, mutinous soldiery began to defy their officers and even
murdered some of them. As mentioned earlier, fratricide and factional
infighting between the pro- and anti-Revolution forces was reported from
many areas. This was particularly true in the case of the remote and far-
flung areas in the Marches, in Pomed and central Tibet, including Lhasa.
The beheading of Chao Erh-feng by the upstart, young and ambitious
Yin Chang-heng, a one-time protégé of Chao Erh-feng, had a disastrous
effect on the discipline of the imperial Chinese army. Many unscrupulous
and opportunistic leaders like Generals Yin and Chung Ying changed their
allegiance and joined the ranks of the republican army. Perhaps destiny
had in store a much worse fate for both these protagonists. Born into a
poor family near Chengtu (later known as Chengdu), Yin's spectacular
rise from the 'lowest stratum of society' to a position of great power was
mainly ascribed to Chao Erh-feng's fostering care. This fact 'makes his
subsequent treachery to and murder of his patron peculiarly revolting'.[2]

The outburst of the latent anger of the Tibetans and their intrinsic
hatred for the Chinese resulted in uncontrolled acts of vengeance by them
against the Chinese, and to violence and bloodshed across all of Tibet. By
the end of 1912, there remained no vestige of Chinese authority in the
whole of Tibet. Except for General Chung Ying and his close guard, who
were confined to the Trapchi barracks, and the yamen, the residence of
the Chinese Amban, in Lhasa, the rest of the Chinese army were either
killed or had surrendered their arms in exchange for safe passage to the
mainland. Also, the Chinese forces in Tibet were completely isolated,
and their direct communications with the mainland cut off. The only
link available to them for receiving mail, orders, pay, rations or even
reinforcements was through India and the Chumbi Valley. The Chinese
lifeline in Tibet was at the mercy of the British, who did not fail to
capitalize on it.

The major challenge for the Chinese republic was to rein in the
outlying dependencies like Tibet, Mongolia, Sinkiang and Manchuria.
Great Britain, Russia and Japan were stoking the fire for greater autonomy
for and independence of the regions within their spheres of interest. There

could not be more testing times for Chinese diplomacy, and it is to their credit that they endeavoured to hold their ground, although they had to give in many a time and make the best of a bad bargain. All the same, their efforts weren't always in vain, as procrastination and protracted discussions that did not culminate in any conclusions became their ploy.

Despite their constraints, the British could not remain idle bystanders while, until 1911, China went about aggressively assimilating Tibet, introducing administrative reforms as if it were another of its provinces. The Chinese unleashed an obstructionist regime that had effectively undermined trade between British India and Tibet, in contravention of the agreements signed in 1904, 1906 and 1908. Unabashedly, the Chinese forces had continued to expand their presence to the extremes of Tibet's frontiers. At this point, China became brazen enough to press its claims of suzerainty over Nepal and Bhutan. Although Britain had formally accepted Chinese 'suzerain rights' in Tibet, it was under no circumstances going to acquiesce to the Chinese taking over of the internal administration of Tibet, in violation of Article I of the Convention of 27 April 1906, or to the presence of a large number of Chinese troops in Tibet. Accordingly, a strong message was sent to Yuan Shih-K'ai, conveying Whitehall's rejection of the Chinese definition of Tibet's 'political status' and its displeasure at the overpowering and meddlesome conduct of Chinese officers in Tibet. In the Military Report on Tibet of 1910 (declassified) prepared by the General Staff, Army Headquarters, India, this was made abundantly clear:

> ... while they (British government) have formally recognised the 'suzerain rights' of China in Tibet, have never recognised and are not prepared to recognise the right of China to intervene actively in the internal administration of Tibet which should remain, as contemplated in the treaties, in the hands of the Tibetan authorities, subject to the right of Great Britain and China, under Article I of the Convention of 27th April 1906.[3]

Moreover, the British would take action to ensure the fulfilment of all guarantees by China, as per the Adhesion Agreement of 1906. Alarmed by the aggressive *forward policy* unleashed by the Manchu Empire in the wake of the Younghusband expedition of 1903–04, which was followed up in a more robust manner by the regime of the new republic during 1910–11, British India reacted vigorously, first by ejecting the policy of *non-interference*, and second by endeavouring to define the frontier with Tibet by reaching out to the less explored or unknown tribal territories on the southern slopes of the Himalayas. The Chinese actions had been prompted by an apprehension that Britain might grab central Tibet or assume the position of *protector* of Tibet, while the British reaction was spurred by a similar concern that China might take over Tibet, or that an emboldened Russia might stake her claim for Tibet to be included in its sphere of influence. In an era of power-play politics, the vacuum created by a powerless and vulnerable Tibet heralded its own dynamics.

These were the principal reasons behind the genesis of the tripartite conference. Initially, the British only wanted to play the role of *an honest broker* and offer *benevolent assistance* to the two warring sides, but eventually they realized that without their active participation, the negotiations between China and Tibet would be interminable and may end up with a situation not to Britain's liking.

The Chinese, being masters at strategic procrastination and prevarication, most reluctantly agreed to participate in this tripartite conference. They sought every method to change its format or to delay the convening of the event. For a change, Whitehall stood by the Government of India and refused to yield to China or allow itself to get disoriented by the diversionary tactics of the Chinese on matters such as the issue of the three plenipotentiaries being equals, or having separate bilateral conferences with Britain and Tibet and not necessarily in India, or the sequencing of the agenda. The Chinese insisted on discussing the status of Tibet before anything else, whereas the British were clear that the geographical expanse and boundaries of Tibet had to be decided first and foremost. The Tibetans held the same view as the British. It had to be conveyed to the Chinese in a firm manner that past precedence, such as the equation between the Tibetan and Chinese representatives during the 1908 Trade Agreement—where the Tibetans participated as subordinates of the Chinese—did not hold good in the present circumstances, when Tibet had literally declared its independence and there were no Chinese left in that country, not even the Amban! And there was no question of any bipartite agreement between Britain and China, as the Tibetans were certainly not going to honour it.

At times, when the Chinese failed to see reason, they were told that Britain would go ahead and deliberate directly with Tibet, and that China would have to forego its suzerain status vis-à-vis Tibet. Besides, they were also told the British would not lift the embargo on travel through India to Tibet and would also withhold recognition of the new republic. The Chinese were therefore left with no choice but to sit at the table with the Tibetans and the British on an equal footing to discuss issues relating to Tibet.

During the in-house discussions at Whitehall in the spring of 1913, Lord Crewe, the Secretary of State, appeared a bit apprehensive about Britain having a permanent representative in Lhasa before making amendments to the accord of 1907 with Russia, although he was on board in principle. On the other hand, as brought out by Alastair Lamb in his comprehensive account, *The McMahon Line*, Vol. II, p. 466, Lionel Abrahams, like other officials at the India Office, was more emphatic when he said:

> ... the whole lesson of the last ten years, it may possibly be said, is that Tibet cannot stand alone; that it must be subject to some influence; and that we cannot allow that influence to be other than British; and that British influence can only be maintained by a British agency in some form or other at the capital (Lhasa).

As far as the Tibetans were concerned, having thrown off the Chinese yoke they wanted to assert their independence and, if possible, following the Mongolian example, have no Chinese presence anywhere in Tibet proper. However, unlike the Russians, the British were not prepared to stick their neck out beyond a point. And that limit was the supply of arms, ammunition and military training to Tibet, but definitely not an armed intervention in support of the Tibetans. In fact, the British were keen that Tibet remain fully autonomous but under Chinese suzerainty.

The salient features of the British memorandum of 1912 relating to the status of Tibet and Chinese suzerain powers are as follows:

- While Chinese suzerainty over Tibet was acknowledged, active intervention by China in the internal affairs of Tibet beyond the scope of the Adhesion Agreement of 1906 had never been nor would be recognized.
- President Yuan Shih-k'ai's declaration of 21 April 1912 that Tibet was to be regarded as a proper province of China and the conduct of Chinese officials in Tibet were strongly objected to.
- Positioning of an Amban with an escort as an adviser to the Tibetan government on foreign relations was acceptable, whereas stationing of a large number of troops in Lhasa or elsewhere in Tibet was not acceptable.
- Recognition by the British government of the Chinese republic would be contingent on a written agreement on the above lines, up to which time all communications via India to Tibet would remain closed to the Chinese.

India considered Tibet as a strategic buffer, and consequent to the Younghusband mission, the Chinese woke up to the reality of Tibet being a strategic 'back-door'. As argued by Heather Spence:

… if the back-door was open and occupied by a foreign power, China would be exposed and vulnerable. The Chinese contention that the British in India coveted Tibet and would later use it as a base to attack China proper became an important ingredient in Anglo-Chinese relations. During the 1930s this matter, once again, became a major issue.[4]

Unstated and un-delimited formally till the second decade of the twentieth century, the boundary between Tibet and India, as it existed naturally, was in fact also the ethnic, cultural and traditional divide between the two neighbours. Portents of the future presence of the

Chinese at India's portals along the vast northern frontier began to grip the minds of British planners for the first time, bringing to the fore the vulnerability of British India's north-eastern frontiers and raising questions about the British policy of non-interference in Tibetan affairs. A militarily weak and pacific Tibet had posed no threat to the British Indian empire so far, but during 1905–11 the situation had changed radically. Ironically, it was the British who facilitated the re-emergence of Chinese power in Tibet by weakening the apparatus of the Tibetan state and lowering the stature of the Dalai Lama. Heather Spence has lucidly described the predicament of Britain in formulating afresh a policy on Tibet during 1912–13: 'The conceptual basis of Britain's new policy was flawed: *Britain wanted Tibet as a buffer but was not prepared to give the support necessary for it to remain independent* (emphasis added).' The predicament of the British was that 'on one hand they were committed by a promise to the Lhasa government to support Tibet in upholding her practical autonomy, which was of importance to the security of India, and, on the other hand, Britain's alliance with China made it difficult to give effective material support to Tibet'.[5]

According to Spence, 'What the British wanted was to create a balance. That is to say, give just enough support so that Tibet could protect India's Himalayan border without the British having to commit themselves to a major defensive initiative.'[6] It has then been reasoned by Spence that 'the ultimate objective was to get the Chinese to sign an agreement which would secure for the British stability in Central Asia. British tactics were impotent and the foreign office adopted a *wait-and-see* approach which dissolved into a *dormancy* policy.'[7]

The British imperialists found it expedient to follow a policy of carving out territories as informal assets or spheres of influence, where *power without responsibility* would be the underlying concept. To reinforce her argument, Spence has quoted from an article by Gallagher and Robinson, 'The Imperialism of Free Trade', *Economic History Review, 1953-54*: 'To consider imperialism only by the criterion of formal control was rather like judging the size and character of icebergs solely from the parts above the water-line.'[8]

Fundamentally, the British policy was to establish a stable environment in the heart of Asia, with an autonomous Tibet under the suzerainty of China, and at the same time ensure the security of India's northern borders. 'Such a conditional policy safeguarded British economic interest in China as well as the national security of the Indian Empire,' said D. Norbu in his book *The Europeanisation of Sino-Tibetan Relations*. And, as rightly deduced by Spence, that was 'the least expensive and most practical policy for Britain'.[9]

As far as Britain's relations with Tibet and China were concerned, the dilemma Whitehall faced was indeed very complex. It was an act of balancing on a tightrope. With Russia, it meant remaining within the bounds of the Anglo-Russian Convention of 1907 and bringing to an end the Great Game in Central Asia, and with China it was to safeguard British investments and trading interests. At the same time, implementation of the carefully nuanced British policy of 'Tibetan autonomy under Chinese suzerainty' posed a constant challenge to both the home government in London and the Government of India. The viceroy, in his farewell message to the Dalai Lama in 1912, who was then returning to Tibet from his exile in Darjeeling, categorically emphasized the British policy on the matter:

> ... the desire of the Government of India was to see the internal autonomy of Tibet under Chinese suzerainty, but without Chinese interference, so long as cordial relations were preserved between India and Tibet and treaty obligations were duly performed.[10]

As was borne out by subsequent events, the Chinese had no intentions of giving up their claim of sovereignty over the whole of Tibet. The declaration by President Yuan Shih-k'ai on 27 April 1912 making Tibet an integral part of China was a clear indicator, if any was needed, of the Chinese grand design to incorporate Tibet into its mainland.

Tibet had also now become the focus of attention of other world powers, namely, Japan, France and the USA. Britain did not display sufficient will to support the Tibetans all the way, as the Russians did with the Mongolians. Consequently, China was quick to discern Britain's predicament from the clauses of 'self-denial' in Britain's treaties with China and Russia of 1906 and 1907 respectively. China took full advantage of the situation to re-establish its hold on Tibet in a ruthless manner under the leadership of Chao Erh-feng and General Chung Ying. The Chinese addressed not just the bordering areas along the Marches and Amdo and Kham provinces, but gradually advanced to Tibet proper. Eventually, in 1910, this exercise took the Chinese invading forces, led by General Chung Ying, right up to Lhasa and the Potala Palace, compelling the hapless thirteenth Dalai Lama to flee once again, this time south to British India. The absence of the Grand Lama from the scene of action once again gave the Chinese an opportunity to usurp power and consolidate their authority over all of Tibet. During this period, the immeasurable contribution of the forceful and intrepid Chao Erh-feng in giving effect to the transformation of Chinese power in Tibet from 'a fictional suzerainty', as described by Curzon, to actual sovereignty by 1910–11 needs to be recognized. It is another matter that destiny ended the meteoric rise of Chao. The imperial decree by the Manchu court hastily deposing the Dalai Lama and ordering for his successor to be found was an ill-advised step not accepted by the Tibetans, and this resulted in huge embarrassment for the Chinese.

The imperial decree of 25 February 1910 also thoroughly denounced the conduct of the Dalai Lama since his return to Tibet (after his first exile) for its *'pride, extravagance, lewdness, sloth, vice, and perversity'*. It accused him of being *'violent and disorderly, disobedient to the Imperial Commands, and oppressive towards the Tibetans* (emphasis added)'.[11] Justifying the movement of Chinese troops up to Lhasa, the proclamation said:

> Szechuan troops have now been sent into Tibet for the special purpose of preserving order and protecting the Trade Marts. There was no reason for the Tibetans to be suspicious of their intentions. But the Dalai Lama spread rumours, became rebellious, defamed the Amban, refused supplies, and would not listen to reason ... He has been guilty of treachery, and has placed himself beyond the pale of Our Imperial favour.[12]

In fact, the decree commanded that wherever the Dalai Lama went, he should be treated as a 'commoner'. 'These powerful words, which left no doubt as to what the Chinese thought of the thirteenth Dalai Lama, were communicated on 26 February to the British Legation in Peking and to the Foreign Office in London.'[13]

This was the second instance of the Dalai Lama's deposition by the Chinese, the first having happened when he fled to Mongolia in 1904. These depositions were unsuccessful in diminishing the image of the Grand Lama amongst the people of Tibet and Mongolia, but they did dent the reputation of the Manchu emperor. It had become clear to the Chinese that the Dalai Lama would not dance to their tune. 'At the moment when his deposition was thus being announced by the Chinese, the Dalai Lama had taken up temporary residence in Darjeeling, and had informed Lord Minto that "I now look to you for protection, and I trust that the relation between the British Government and Tibet will be that of a father to his children".'[14]

After the First World War, the dynamics of power play by the important nations left no choice for Britain but to sacrifice Tibet in order to safeguard her 'wider commercial interests' in China. Slowly but surely, the decline of the British Empire began. Consequently, Britain chose to support the nationalistic Chinese regime.

10

Eastern Himalayan Frontier

For a clearer understanding of this frontier zone, it is necessary to have a good knowledge of the terrain and of the people inhabiting the Himalayan watershed east of Bhutan and right up to Burma. The eastern Himalayas are a continuation of the great Himalayan chain that stretches from Kashmir to Myanmar in an arc, forming the natural divide between the Tibetan plateau and India, Nepal, Bhutan and Myanmar. The historical, cultural and traditional boundary generally lay along the highest crest line of the Himalayas, broken here and there by some river valleys that cut across the Himalayas and whose waters flow into India. These river valleys facilitated interaction, and at times migration, of people and trade, from south to north, and vice versa. Religion, particularly Buddhism, was taken by Indian saints to Tibet, from where it seeped down in the reverse direction in certain areas. However, the major portion of this frontier lies along rocky and snow-covered mountains, 4,500 to 7,000 metres high. Glaciated areas too are found at a few places here. All this forms an impregnable barrier, except for a few high-altitude passes and rivers that cut across this mountain chain. This natural barrier has been aptly described by the historian John Lall: 'Perhaps nowhere else in the world has such a long frontier been unmistakably delineated by nature itself.'[1]

From Bhutan to Burma, the Himalayas stretch across 1,070 kilometres, most of which remained unexplored territory till the early twentieth century. Between the southern edge of the Tibetan plateau and the

Himalayan watershed is the Tsangpo Valley, which ascends gradually from its base at about 3,600 metres to the Himalayan watershed. This region, located north of the Himalayas and lying from west to east, comprises the areas of southern Tibet, namely Monyul, Takpo, Kongbo, Poyul or Pome/Pomed, Pemakoichen and Zayul. And to the south of the eastern Himalayan crest or watershed is the tribal belt, some 110–190 kilometres, going down to the Brahmaputra plains. These areas did not have precise geographical definitions or limits. This frontier zone stretching over 1,000 kilometres can be divided into two parts for ease of description and analysis. Going from west to east is, first, the region from Bhutan to the Siang Valley and then the region from Siang Valley to the Myanmar frontier.

Bhutan to Siang Valley

Monyul, the 'place of the Monpas', is spread over a large area. Tibetan texts and other local dialects have used the ethnic name Monpa (Monba) ever since the eighth century, referring to the people inhabiting this area south of the main Himalayan chain. It is not therefore surprising that one can find Monpas in Bhutan, Tibet and Arunachal Pradesh (going eastwards from Tawang up to Pachakshiri in the upper Siyom Valley and even Pemakoichen). Bordering eastern Bhutan, the people of Tawang, Dirang and Kalaktang in West Kameng district of Arunachal Pradesh are called Monpa[2] too, and are governed by the lamas of Tawang (Figure 10).

The northern slopes of the main Himalayas are mostly devoid of vegetation, except for the lower-altitude valleys, and are inhabited by Tibetans. The people who lived in the Pomed region were called 'Pobas', and were, for all practical purposes, almost independent under the nominal control of Lhasa. They were notorious for robbing travellers passing through their region, taking away their valuables and horses.

On the southern side there is a mountainous, hilly and densely forested tribal belt. Amongst the rainiest parts of the Indian subcontinent, this region has climate zones varying from the alpine to the subtropical. It has rainforests, and rivers and streams cascading down from about 6,000 metres to as low as 300 metres; it is perhaps the only part of the world with such geographical variation across such a small area. Besides the Monpas, Membas and other Buddhist clans, fierce tribes known as the Lao Kha,[3] also referred to as 'Lopas' by the Tibetans, live in this southern Himalayan region. They include the Miri, Aka, Dafla (Nyishi), Abor, Mishmi and other tribes, who were generally described as 'savage' or 'uncivilized' in the past. With their unique culture and traditions, they are distinct from both the Tibetans in the north and the plainsmen of Assam. As a policy, this tribal belt was loosely administered by the British. The tribal population zealously guarded their territories and way of life, and it was the Assamese they generally interacted with.

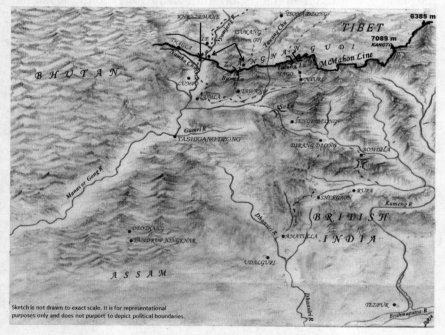

Figure 10: Evolution of the McMahon Line (1913–14)—The Monyul and Tawang frontier region

Some of the tribes living in the upper reaches of the Himalayas are Buddhists. They are ethnically different from the Tibetans, but because of their religion they are culturally closer to the peoples in eastern Bhutan and Tibet. Intercourse between the Monpas, Membas, the Sherdukpen highlander tribes and the Bhutanese and Tibetans was limited to barter trade, cultural and religious ties. The Tibetans and Chinese considered themselves culturally more evolved and therefore superior to these tribes inhabiting the southern slopes of the Himalayas. They have traditionally and culturally treated these tribes in an exploitative, shabby and often cruel way.

This part of the frontier along the Himalayan watershed stretches over 600 kilometres from the north-east of Bhutan and up to the famed 'Tsangpo bend' around Namcha Barwa. It is garlanded by the Tsangpo in the north and by the Brahmaputra in the south. On the Tibetan side are the areas of Takpo, Tsari, Kongbo, Pomed, Pemako and a part of Monyul. These southern areas of central Tibet are extremely remote, and are isolated from other areas by the Tsangpo, which is a major obstacle to movement in the region. As a result, traditionally, control of this region by Lhasa was nominal, and certain areas such as Pomed and Pemako were practically independent. The Great Fifth Dalai Lama had his origins in the Tsang region, the sixth belonged to Urgeling near Tawang, and the thirteenth Dalai Lama was born in a place called Trung Kang in the Takpo region.

The population of the Monyul region consists of Monpas (Monbas) and Tibetans. The Monpas are ethnically different from the Tibetans, and their language is also distinct from the Tibetan spoken in Lhasa, although there are some common words. There is, in fact, greater similarity between the languages spoken by the people of eastern Bhutan and the Monpas. The Tibetans are settled mostly in high-altitude areas, 3,000 metres and above, whereas the hardier Monpa people are found even at lower altitudes and warmer areas. Tsona Dzong and Tawang were the frontier towns and commercial hubs of the Monyul region. Three annual markets were held in Tsona Dzong, where merchants from Tibet and the lower Monyul area would congregate. The head lama, or abbot, of the famous Tawang monastery, along with the two Dzongpons of Tsona, were accorded high protocol in the Monyul area, the specific limits of which were undefined. Better known as 'Ganden Namgyel Lhatseling', the Tawang monastery houses about 500 monks. It was built between 1680 and 1681, under the supervision of Mera Lama, who had undertaken this mission on the urging of the fifth Dalai Lama.

Referring mainly to the Monpas inhabiting the Tawang area, Captain Bailey, who toured the area a century ago, said: 'Both in the nature of the country they inhabit, their customs, language, dress and method of building houses the Monbas are very distinct from the Tibetans, and resemble more the inhabitants of Bhutan and Sikkim. Their country is low lying and well wooded and their villages large and prosperous.'[4]

Looking eastwards from Point 6110 (20,045 feet, i.e., 6110 metres), the approximate tri-junction of Bhutan, Assam and Tibet is about 21 kilometres south of the Me La. For the first 50 kilometres or so, the geography has not presented a clearly definable and unbroken crest line. Here, therefore, the traditional boundary was evolved over the years, keeping in mind, relatively speaking, the most prominent ridge or watershed, the traditional and ethnic features of the population, and other factors. This region is loosely referred to as Monyul, the land of the Monpas. Tawang controls the southern part of Monyul, going down to Dirang Dzong and beyond. Western Monyul is the area around Tashigong Dzong in Bhutan. The high-altitude region between Tsona Dzong and Tawang is flanked by two rivers flowing in the north–south direction, making delineation of an east–west boundary an even more complex exercise. The first river that cuts across the Himalayas from Tibet is the Namjyang Chu, which is joined by two small tributaries, the Le Chu and Namka Chu flowing from the west, one to the north and the other to the south of the most prominent and dominating ridge, named Thagla. The last Tibetan settlements along the Namjyang Chu Valley are Le and Gordong, north of the Thagla ridge. Nine kilometres upstream of Le is 'Lepo Tsukang'—'custom house'—where traders had to pay 10 per cent tax to go further into Tibet, which indicated that they had entered Tibetan territory. Immediately to the north of Namka Chu is the Indian border outpost of Khinzemane, which lies at the foot of the Thagla ridge. There is a small Monpa settlement nearby, known as Pangchen. These landmarks became famous because of the fierce battle fought between the Chinese and Indian armies in October 1962. South of the Namka Chu is the Monpa village of Lumpo. Graziers of this village used to take their cattle to the Namka Chu Valley for grazing. The Namjyang Chu flows 20 kilometres west of Tawang. About 15 kilometres to the east of Tawang is the Tsona or Sho Chu (which later becomes the Tawang Chu), which too courses down in a parallel and southward direction from the Tsona Dzong area in Tibet. After making a loop around Tawang, it joins the Namjyang Chu before entering Bhutan, where it forms part of the Manas river. This river, along with the waters of its affluents originating in eastern Bhutan, eventually flows into the mighty Brahmaputra at Goalpara in Assam.

Hypothetically speaking, if one were to define a natural boundary applying the watershed principle between the Tsangpo Valley in Tibet and the Brahmaputra basin in Assam, the line would run far to the north of the present boundary alignment, known as the McMahon Line, particularly in this sector. Such an alignment encompassing Tsona Dzong was initially proposed by the General Staff at Simla in June 1912, but based on the timely inputs provided by Captains Bailey and Morshead in November 1913, McMahon decided to follow the watershed from Bum La along the traditional border about 25 kilometres north of Tawang. The line was extended westwards to the Namjyang Chu Valley and thence to the Bhutan border. Between Bumla and Tsona Dzong lay the Tibetan settlement of Nagdo, with a toll post, or Lepo Tsukang, nearby, where tax was collected from any trader going to Tsona Dzong from the Tawang side[5] along the well-established trade route from Tibet to Udalguri in Assam.

Proceeding eastwards from the frontier outpost of Bumla, located at an altitude of 4,430 metres, one descends 1,372 metres to the Sho Chu/ Tawang Chu gorge and then climbs up almost vertically about 3,000 metres to the crest of the highest and most formidable glaciated region of the eastern Himalayas, the Zanglang ridge, referred to as Zangnan Gudi in some maps (Figure 10). This 250-kilometre range follows a north-easterly alignment and has a number of virgin peaks ranging between 6,100 and 7,000 metres, including the Kangeddo, Gori Chen, Kangto and the revered Takpa Shiri, with several glaciers. This impassable high-altitude barrier makes for a natural divide and has three known passes, which generally remain open from May to October.

Tulung La, at 5,258 metres, is the most prominent pass of the three. It was crossed by Bailey during his path-breaking adventure on 3 October 1913. He recorded its height quite accurately as 5,259 metres! An amazing achievement, considering he had antiquated equipment such as the hypsometer, theodolite and plane table, which had to be lugged all over such terrain. Below this pass, one descends about 2,440 metres over 16 kilometres to Mago, a small village inhabited by a sub-tribe of the Monpas. Bailey noticed a lot of madder—a dark-red dye produced from the root of a plant which is used extensively in this region to colour monks' robes and other garments—being hauled to Mago by various tribesmen for trade. Apparently, Mago lies on an alternative, shorter but more difficult trade route to Tibet via the Tsona Dzong, Tsethang, Takpo and Kongbo regions, which are inhabited by southern Tibetans. Another reason for use of this route may have been to avoid the excessive taxation on the traditional trade route from Tawang to Tsona Dzong.

The Takpo, Kongbo and Pemako regions in the Tsangpo Valley north of the Himalayas are adjacent to the Monyul as one goes eastwards; they are predominantly inhabited by people of central Tibet. These regions constitute southern Tibet. The sacred area of Tsari and the venerated mountain of Takpa Shiri lie in this region. The well-known and revered monastery of Sangak Choling is also situated in this area. The Tsangpo Valley is the most productive of the valleys in this region because of its rich soil and its irrigation by the waters of the Tsangpo and many of its smaller tributaries and streams.

The next river that cuts across the Himalayas is the Subansiri, with its main tributaries, the Chayul or Loro Karpo Chu and the Tsari Chu (shown in Figure 11). Migyitun is the last Tibetan settlement on the Tsari Chu. These rivers cut through the main mountain chain at two points, 35 kilometres apart as the crow flies, and their confluence is approximately 40 kilometres downstream at a village called Murang, which is fairly deep into tribal territory. The Tsari area has been considered to be very sacred since ancient times. No animal, bird, fish or even insect can be killed in this holy land; even tilling of the land is a taboo. Pilgrims from all over Tibet and other parts of the world used to come to do a full *parikrama*, or circumambulatory trek, of about 190 kilometres along the Tsari Chu to the river junction at Murang, and return upstream along the Chayul or Loro Karpo Chu, ending the pilgrimage at Chozam. This pilgrimage, called *Ringkor,* took around sixteen days. It is performed once every twelve years, during the 'monkey' year. When entering tribal territory, the Tibetans paid an annual tax of 144 goats to the tribal chiefs and also gave salt, swords and *tsampa* as bribes in order to ensure their safety as pilgrims. And yet cases of theft, molestation and abduction for slavery had been taking place here occasionally. A shorter circuit involving a traverse of about 80 kilometres around a sacred peak called Dakpa Shelri (5,732 metres) was called *Kingkor*. This involves a week-long trek and is performed annually during the summer. There were rest houses along the pilgrim circuit, and they were manned throughout the period of the pilgrimage. A villager was stationed at each of these houses; his responsibility was to provide hot water and fuel to the travellers.[6] Also in this area are a cave and a sacred lake, the Tsari Tsokar, which lies about 15 kilometres north of Tsari and can be reached after crossing the Ja La (4,640 metres). These too are visited by a number of Buddhist pilgrims.

Figure 11: Evolution of the McMahon Line (1913–14)—The Subansiri Frontier

The Kongbo area lies on the northern side of the Tsangpo Valley and dominates the ancient road leading to Lhasa from the provinces of

Sichuan and Yunnan of China. To its east lies the Pomed region, which comprises the valley of Po Tsangpo, a major tributary of the Tsangpo, and includes the area where the mighty river almost hugs the main Himalayan chain, a distance of only 10–15 kilometres separating the two. It is here that the river cuts its way through the deepest gorge in the world and forms the 'Great Bend'—a geographical marvel (Figure 12). This wondrous area, circumscribed by the Tsangpo and its gorges around Namcha Barwa, is called Pemako. This 'land of promise' derived from 'ancient prophesies' is inhabited by Monpas and some Lopas, who are descendants of earlier settlers. Originally, this valley was inhabited by the Abors, who were pushed southwards by the Monpa or Drukpa immigrants during the eighteenth and nineteenth centuries. They had come in search of this land from Tawang and adjoining areas in eastern Bhutan. They continue to speak in a Monpa dialect, although they speak and dress like the Tibetans of this region. No definitive boundaries of this fabled area of Pemako exist.[7]

Figure 12: Evolution of the McMahon Line (1913–14)—Siang frontier region

In his book *Le Thibet Revolte*, published in 1910, M. Bacot, a French traveller, in a brief and striking narrative, describes this region as 'a land where rivers flowed with milk, where crops grew without the necessity of any labour, and whence their religion would spread over the whole world'. His Tibetan story said: 'When their religion was persecuted in Tibet, the people should go to Pemako.'

There is also the myth of a 'mountain of glass' to be found somewhere in the watershed area of the Dibang and Lohit rivers. Many Tibetans have travelled towards this region in the hope of finding this Shangri-La, but have failed to locate it because of the 'determined hostility of the Mishmis'. Most of those who migrated to the highlands near the sources of the Dibang river perished because of the unsustainability of the land, disease and the incessant hostile actions of the Mishmi tribes.[8]

The Pobas of Pomed were a mixed race of Chinese and Tibetan origin. It is believed that some Chinese soldiers had settled down in this area during the late eighteenth century.[9] Having intermarried with local Tibetan women, the Pobas speak in a Tibetan dialect akin to the dialect of the Khambas. Over the centuries they had acquired an autonomous status, which they were very averse to losing, and therefore were not easy to subdue.

East of the Tsari Chu tributary of the Subansiri, going all the way to Pemako and the great bend of the Tsangpo, is a continuous mountain range of about 230 kilometres. With heights of 4,000–6,100 metres, this chain forms a perfect watershed, with smaller rivers draining into the Tsangpo to the north, and the Siyom river and other affluents flowing southwards and joining the Siang, also known as the Dihang, which later becomes the Brahmaputra. This range ends abruptly with one of the highest peaks of the eastern Himalayas, a towering massif called Namcha Barwa (7,758 metres) before the Tsangpo cuts through the range. On the other side, to the north of the Tsangpo, is another formidable peak, Gyala Peri (7,294 metres). These peaks are as sentinels guarding the deepest gorge in the world (4,878 metres approximately), which hides the great bend and a mythical 'waterfall' in its bowels. Because of the inaccessibility of this region for centuries, the world could not unravel the mystery of the origin of the Tsangpo, which twisted, churned and cut its way through the Himalayas. Meandering so, the mighty river does a parikrama around Namcha Barwa and cascades down from a height of 2,896 metres to 1,494 metres over a distance of about 250 kilometres before it exits into the Abor Hills at Gelling. This segment of the river is undoubtedly a geographical marvel without parallel. Thereafter, the river winds its way downstream for another 300 kilometres to form the Brahmaputra.

The myth of the giant waterfall was busted authoritatively during the expedition of Captains Bailey and Morshead in 1912–13 and by Frank Kingdon-Ward in 1924, who reported the fall to be just about 9 metres high. This has been named the 'rainbow fall', as on a sunny day rainbows appear in the dense foam and spray thrown upwards to a height of about 15 metres by the volume and velocity of the water.[10] This phenomenon enhances the visual impact of this waterfall. Ending another mystery, Bailey's expedition also authoritatively confirmed that the Tsangpo, Siang and Dihang were names of the same river that became the Brahmaputra as it debouched from the hills near Pasighat and entered the Assam plains. Another waterfall of about 33 metres in the 'great bend' area is called the 'hidden fall', and was discovered near Tsangpo Badong in 1998.

Siang to Myanmar Border

East of the Siang river, the Tibet–Assam frontier traverses along a prominent mountain ridge for 150 kilometres to a peak called Kangri Karpo (5,335 metres), and then goes south-eastwards for another 310 kilometres till it hits the Lohit river at an altitude of about 2,744 metres between Rima and Kibithoo (Walong area). This ridge forms the natural watershed between the Dibang Valley on the southern side, the Chimdro Chu on the northern side and the Rong Thod/Gangri Karpo Chu on the north-eastern side. The Dibang and its numerous tributaries eventually join the Lohit at Sadiya, the well-known administrative centre of the north-eastern frontier of Assam. About 40 kilometres downstream, the confluence of these waters with the Siang or Tsangpo results, in the true sense, in the formation of the mighty Brahmaputra, one of the largest rivers in the world (see Figure 8).

Upstream of Walong, the Lohit river is joined by the Dichu stream. Along the northern bank of this stream there is a prominent spur that climbs steeply for about 45 kilometres and joins the main ridge about 8 kilometres north of the Diphu Pass where approximately lies the tri-junction of the frontiers of Assam, Tibet and Myanmar (Figure 9). This place is on the highest ridge going in the north–south direction, making it a distinct watershed between the Lohit and the Irrawaddy Valleys. On this divide also lies the highest peak of Myanmar, Hkakabo Razi, at 5,881 metres.

11

British Administration of Eastern Himalayan Region

Assam and the Tribal Areas

Since ancient times, Assam was an independent kingdom in the north-east of India. It has been home to a culturally rich and prosperous civilization in the fertile though flood-prone Brahmaputra Valley. Assam is divided and isolated to a large extent by the Brahmaputra, one of the largest rivers in the world. The great eastern Himalayan chain, extending slightly over 1,000 kilometres, forms this region's natural boundary to the north, and the densely forested Patkai range its natural boundaries to the east and south. The Assam region, including the hill states surrounding it, is considered a place of unique biodiversity and is one of the world's ecological hot spots. The Brahmaputra basin is over 712 kilometres in length and has a spread of 80 to 146 kilometres between Sadiya and Goalpara, where small hill ranges converge to isolate Assam from Bengal.

The original inhabitants of Assam were at some stage displaced by people of Aryan stock, who were in turn defeated and their territories conquered in AD 1226 by the Tibeto-Burman Ahoms, a Shan tribe of upper Burma. Over the years, the Ahoms adopted Hinduism and were assimilated by the indigenous races of the valley. The Ahom dynasty ruled for about 600 years, during which a rich, integrated yet distinct Assamese culture came into being. However, the declining Ahom Empire was defeated by the British in the first Anglo-Burman war of 1824–26, by the end of which the British annexed the Brahmaputra Valley and the hills adjoining it by the Treaty of Yandabo of 24 February 1826. Under this treaty, the king of Burma renounced his sovereign rights over all of Assam and its dependencies, and the British became their virtual masters. They placed Purandar Singh, an Ahom prince, on the throne of upper Assam. Singh concluded another treaty with the British on 2 March 1833. However, five years later, on the pretext of his having defaulted in paying the annual tribute, the British resumed his territory and brought it directly under their control by a proclamation of the Governor General in October 1838. The six districts that were then carved out in Assam were Lakhimpur, Sibsagar, Darrang, Nowgong, Kamrup and Goalpara.[1]

The hills surrounding the Brahmaputra Valley were very sparsely populated and were inhabited by fierce tribes who enjoyed a fairly autonomous existence. Living by their own rules, they had evolved their own identity. Since ancient times, these tribes have been mostly hunter-gatherers and believe in an indigenous form of worship of the sun and the moon, nature and animals. Extremely suspicious of outsiders—including Tibetans, the British and the plainsmen of Assam—they were fiercely possessive of their land and its resources.

Most of the cis-Himalayan rivers, and even those that originate in Tibet, flow from north to south and have, over the centuries, sliced the entire tribal belt into deep, longitudinal valleys. Densely vegetated with almost impenetrable forests, this area had almost no roads until recently. There existed very difficult tracks along the ridges or valleys, but none that laterally connected one valley with another. This secluded belt of hill territory is home to twenty-six major tribes and over 100 sub-tribes speaking different dialects. Only two have a script. The British classified these tribes into broad groups—Monpa, Aka, Miri, Dafla, Abor and Mishmi—primarily because they had little detailed knowledge of these indigenous peoples of the hills (see Figure 13 for a graphic depiction of the tribal areas in Arunachal Pradesh). Traditionally, the tribes used to interact and conduct trade with the people in the Assam plains. There were occasional raids by these tribes to settle disputes over land, forest produce and cattle with the plainsmen of Assam. They very rarely had any dealings with the Tibetans across the Himalayas, except with some

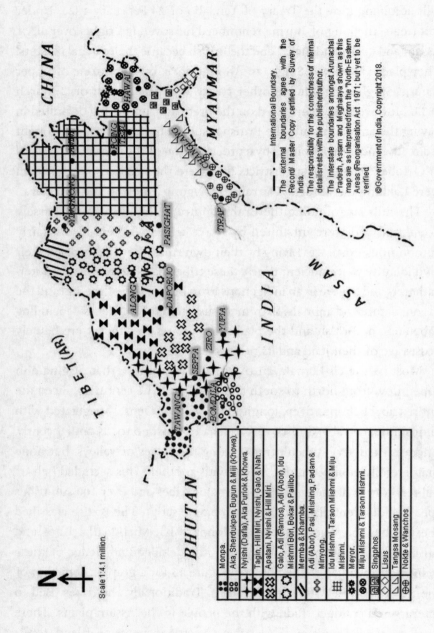

Figure 13: Demographic representation of the tribal areas of Arunachal Pradesh (NEFA)

northern tribes like the Monpas and Membas. Generally speaking, they zealously guarded their territory and were suspicious of outsiders. Entry either from Tibet in the north or from Assam in the south was strongly discouraged, if not forbidden.

According to Dalton, at the Udalguri fair in Assam in 1876, there were 3,600 tribesmen who came down from the hills, having trekked a number of days to reach the fair. The Sadiya fair attracted an equal number or more of tribal people comprising Abors, Miris, Mishmis, Singphos and Hkamtis.[2] In areas bordering Tibet, these tribals are called Lopa or Lao Kha by the Tibetans. They had some interaction and barter trade with the Tibetans. Also, there was some monastic and cultural influence of Lhasa over the Buddhist tribes like the Monpa, Sherdupken and Memba in the Tawang, Mechuka and Tuting areas. The Lopas were identified with the Aka, Nyishi (Dafla), Miri, Adi (Abor), Mishmi and other tribes. Historically, these semi-independent tribes were never under the influence or control of either the Tibetans or the Chinese.

Verrier Elwin's authoritative account of the north-eastern peoples makes a mention of the specific description of the tribes by the Mughal historian Shihabuddin Talish, who had accompanied the invading Mughal army led by Mir Jumla during its Assam campaign in 1662. Shihabuddin observed that the hills people greatly feared firearms and would say, 'The matchlock is a bad thing; it utters a cry and does not stir from its place, but a child comes out of its womb and kills men.' He also remarked that 'the Miri-Mishmi women surpassed in beauty and grace the women of Assam'.[3] This may not necessarily be factually correct, as the people of the entire north-east are simple, warm-hearted and good-looking.

The British administration had not reached out in a meaningful manner to the interior parts of this tribal territory till the first decade of the twentieth century, as they were content to have this buffer between India and Tibet. Yet the British were clear that the Assam Himalayas—although undefined—were the natural geopolitical divide between their Indian Empire and Tibet. However, before the British the Ahoms had been able to establish their sovereignty by a 'well organised system ... to control the tribal population'.[4] Shihabuddin noted, 'Although most of the inhabitants of the neighbouring hills paid no taxes to the Raja of Assam, they accepted his sovereignty and obeyed some of his commands.'[5] As it happens in every empire's sunset phase, the Ahom rulers had feeble control over the tribal peoples by the 1820s. In his account of the north-east frontier of India in 1883, the army officer-cum-historian Mitchell said: 'In 1820, before we took possession of Assam, the Mishmis were obedient to the orders of the Assam government, and paid tribute to the Sadiya Khowa Gohains.'[6] Remarking on the daredevil and ferocious spirit of the 'tribal legion of the Ahom army', the Assamese ambassador Madhabcharan Kataki, in an interaction with the Mughal commander Raja Ram Singh, had said: 'Their participation in this campaign has been directly sanctioned by His Majesty and they rush furiously against the enemy without waiting for the orders of the general. They are quick and sudden in their attacks, and their movements and actions cannot be presaged.'[7] These Gohains were chieftains of the northern Brahmaputra Valley under the vassalage of the raja of Assam.

The British had soon realized the immense potential of cultivating tea in the Dooars—the Terai region south of the Himalayas (the undulating and low hilly tracts of Assam lying between the flood plains of the Brahmaputra, the lower Himalayas and the Patkai range). Hundreds of acres were denuded of their lush vegetation and magnificent rainforests for plantation of tea. Commercial production of tea commenced in the upper Assam valley around 1840, with indentured labour brought in from the remote tribal areas in central India rather than from the tribal areas in the surrounding hills. As more and more areas came under tea, the British entrepreneurs' eyes fell on the high-quality timber in the region of the foothills here. The administration now felt the need to prevent the uncontrolled and reckless denudation of forests, both for expansion of the tea gardens or for timber and other forest produce, as also for hunting of wild elephants for ivory, as it was fraught with the risk of engendering conflicts with the tribal population.

Accordingly, in order to control man movement in the foothills, a law was framed. Known as the Bengal Eastern Frontier Regulation I of 1873, this recognized an *inner line*, drawn by the provincial government, beyond which entry was restricted and controlled by a system of permits. Sir E.

Gait, in his book *A History of Assam* (1926), says: 'The Inner Line was not the international boundary of the Indian Empire.' Alastair Lamb goes on to elaborate that 'it was a device to create a buffer zone, as it were, between the international boundary and regularly administered territory, a tract which marked the transition between the tribal hills and the Assamese plains'.[8] This line generally followed a west–east configuration along the foothills. Beyond it the pale of normal administration did not extend, no taxes were levied, and no proprietary rights could be acquired by outsiders.

Verrier Elwin, who had a deep knowledge of the north-eastern tribes, wrote about the 'patronising or scornful' attitude towards these tribal societies among many Europeans who interacted with them. An article by him, quoted in the *Pioneer* in 1965, has described the situation: 'The only idea which most men had, with reference to the hills and forests (of Assam), was that they were the habitat of savage tribes, whose bloody raids and thieving forays posed serious danger to the cause of tea.'[9]

Governance of the Tribal Belt

The British policy for governance of the tribal areas extending from the foothills to the Himalayan watershed took shape gradually over ninety years, from 1826 to 1916. The first phase of this policy evolution was from 1826 to 1873, during which the British found it neither expedient nor profitable to venture into the extremely difficult and densely forested hill areas rising up to the high Himalayas, and left the tribes alone. However, to ensure the safety of their subjects and the security of their assets and investments, they entered into a number of agreements, *kuboolyut*s (undertakings) and treaties with the chiefs of the tribes and with the petty rulers, commencing in 1826. During this phase, while the British hold over the Assam valley was being consolidated, British officials did not venture much into the tribal belt.

The exceptions to this hands-off policy, also referred to as Lord Minto's policy of 'non-interference', were a few punitive expeditions. These were launched to seek retribution for violent and barbarous acts such as raids, abduction, extortion and murders in the Assam plains, which the tribes had been indulging in from time to time since the Ahom rule of the region. These tribal depredations, at times for minor disputes, were more frequent during periods when the administration was ineffective. To preserve the peace in the region, the British officials found it expedient to compensate the tribal communities in cash and kind after taking a commitment and guarantee from them for ensuring peace. They were encouraged to carry out policing in areas of their jurisdiction, as per the agreements signed by the two sides. This compensation became locally known as *posa*, and would be withheld if any infringement took place. This action, coupled with blockades of tribal territory denying the tribals the opportunity to carry on their barter trade in the *haats* or markets, proved an effective punishment.

The next phase of the extension of British administration into the tribal areas commenced once the *inner line* was promulgated in 1873. It had emerged clearly that regulations and acts in force in the plains of Assam could not be applied to the 'unsophisticated tribes' of the hills, and at the same time exploitation of the forest resources by non-tribal peoples could not be arrested without delimiting the boundary between the tribal areas and the plains. Slightly to the north of the inner line came up the *outer line* that lay down the 'limits of loose administrative control. Yet to confuse it with the "international boundary of British India" or the "frontier of India" would be straining both the facts as well as imagination,'[10] as described in Parshotam Mehra's authoritative account, *The McMahon Line and After.*

Thus, rough rules were enacted under the Scheduled Districts Act of 1874, specifically for governance of these tribal areas. A rudimentary framework for administration of the inner line and the bordering tribal areas of Darrang and Lakhimpur districts came up under the authority of this Act, and became known as the Assam Frontier Tract Regulation of 1880. By the end of 1882, the post of assistant political officer at Sadiya was created under the deputy commissioner of Dibrugarh to look into all matters concerning the Abor, Mishmi and Singhpho frontiers. It was headed by Jack Francis Needham. Sadiya, once the capital of a small principality called Sutiya on the northern bank of the Brahmaputra, was the north-eastern-most administrative headquarters of the British administration in upper Assam.[11]

The frontier tracts and the tribes in the Siang (Dihang) or Tsangpo in Tibet, Dibang and Lohit Valleys thereby came under Needham's watch. During this period, 'the North-East Frontier as distinct from Assam began to emerge', as noted by Manilal Bose, a well-known historian. A good illustration of this development was the chief commissioner of Assam giving more teeth to the administrators entrusted with the governance of these unruly tribes by enacting rules for the administration of justice in the Lakhimpur Frontier Tract in 1886. These rules provided the fundamental framework of governance for the frontier tracts of Assam and were promulgated in all three sectors—Lakhimpur, Sadiya and Darrang (with its headquarters at Balipara) in 1914.[12] In these districts, the deputy commissioners or their assistants exercised both administrative and judicial powers within their areas of responsibility confined to the outer line. Beyond that line the policy of non-interference applied.

The third phase of British governance in the north-east frontier region began at the end of the first decade of the twentieth century, when the British decided to give effect to the 'forward policy', as recommended by Lord Minto prior to his departure from India at the end of 1910. The scare caused by Chinese presence on Tibet's south-eastern frontier spurred the British into activity. Consequently, at the General Headquarters (GHQ) in Simla, the military General Staff's appreciation was apparently sought. The Governor General was advised to authorize a systematic reconnaissance and survey of the entire tribal territory along the Assam Himalayas between Bhutan and Burma. In a private letter, Sir Arthur Hirtzl, secretary to the political and secret department at the India Office, commenting on the situation, wrote to Sir Richmond Ritchie, permanent undersecretary of state for India, on 12 January 1911:

> ... If anything goes wrong in Assam, there will be very voiceful public opinion against us ... in Lakhimpur District there are 70,000 acres of tea gardens turning out 30,000,000 pounds of tea annually, and employing over 200 Europeans and 100,000 Indians. The European capital risk in tea must be enormous, and there are other industries as well (e.g. coal, over ¼ million tons a year ...) Think of the howl the planters would let out, and the rise in the price of tea![13]

Punitive Expeditions, Reconnaissance and Surveys in Tribal Territories of Assam Himalayas

The enhanced activities of the Chinese in the Zayul and Pomed regions, and the physical presence of their officials and military force at Chikung, Rima (both places located well on the Tibetan side of the frontier) and the Pomed region of the Tsangpo Valley (also on the Tibetan side), led to the launch of exploratory missions by the British. Their aim was to survey the tribal territories along the eastern Himalayas and to ascertain the presence and influence of the Tibetans or Chinese along this frontier. As a matter of fact, the area familiarization, exploratory and reconnaissance missions carried out till the end of the nineteenth century were mostly along the Lohit Valley, whereas the other tribal areas to its west up to Bhutan were 'terra incognito'. Therefore, the need arose to ascertain and establish not only the natural frontier between Tibet and India but also the de facto southern limits of Tibet. These reconnaissance missions were expected to submit their recommendations for a viable and strategically sound boundary line extending from Bhutan to Burma, keeping in mind the imperial interests of the British Indian Empire. As with the Younghusband expedition, the unstated aim of these politico-military ventures was to demonstrate imperial Britain's power and reach. In the case of the cis-Himalayan areas, the British were determined to keep the presence or influence of both Chinese and Tibetans out of the tribal territories.

Almost ninety years after Assam had been annexed, British India formalized its de facto policy of 'loose political control' over the entire tribal belt along the southern side of the Himalayan watershed and created the North-East Frontier Tracts region—what has been known as the state of Arunachal Pradesh since 1987. Spurred by the aggressive forward policy adopted by the Chinese in the Marches of south-eastern Tibet from 1904 to 1910, and their unexpected presence in some strength in the northern Zayul and Pomed regions in 1910–12, not to mention some probing intrusions or forays by them into tribal territories south of the Himalayan watershed, the British were compelled to review their policy of governance of the Assam Himalayan region.

For the first time since the eighteenth century, the Chinese army had ventured to make their presence felt, or establish their writ, in the frontier regions of south-eastern Tibet. Their probes were made primarily into the upper Lohit or Zayul Valley, the Delei Valley to its west, and in the fringes of the Dibang Valley, where they did not transgress into Lopa territory. There was similar activity in the Siang Valley, where too they did not venture beyond a place called Rinchenpung, which is situated about two marches short of the frontier. Also, Chinese troops were neither seen in the valleys of the Char, Nye or Chayul (upper Subansiri) nor in Tawang or Monyul; but some visited Tsona (Dzong).[14] There was an uncorroborated report of four Chinese-looking strangers who reached the Aka territory through the Tawang tract in the summer of 1911. They were armed only with small knives and possibly were surveyors or explorers.[15]

Since the Chinese could not find any Tibetan administrative structures of even the most rudimentary level in the tribal areas during these missions, their intrusions lasted only for a day or two or, as in the case of the Delei Valley, for about a week, before their troops fell back to the Tibetan side of the frontier. On occasions, they coerced the Tibetans to convey their orders to the tribesmen, who were not readily amenable to such directives. Charles Bell, quoting from the report on Assam by the Indian General Staff about the 'serious implications' of Chinese forays in these 'undefended' tribal territories, said: 'That Assam would ever stand the slightest chance of being invaded by a civilized military power has never been contemplated, and consequently no strategic plan, no defences, no organisation whatsoever exists to repel a serious invasion.'[16]

Accordingly, Lord Hardinge forwarded a comprehensive assessment of the situation in the north-eastern frontier of India to the Marquess of Crewe, the Secretary of State for India, on 21 September 1911, effectively recommending a virtual turnabout of the existing policy of dealing with the tribal belt that lay south of the Tibetan frontier. Highlighting its justification for this, the assessment said:

Circumstances have thus forced us to revert practically to the original proposal of Lord Minto's government that endeavours should be made to secure, as soon as possible, a sound strategical boundary between China and Tibet and the tribal territory from Bhutan up to and including the Mishmi country ... [17]

Summing up the rationale for adoption of the new policy, the dispatch said:

> As long as such tribal territory lay between us and our peacefully dormant neighbour Tibet, an undefined mutual frontier presented neither inconvenience nor danger. With the recent change in conditions, the question of a boundary well-defined and at a safer distance from our administrative border admits of no delay. [18]

As was typical of the British, even in the face of China's brazenly assertive forward policy, Hardinge conveyed that once a reasonable boundary had been identified, China could be formally informed of the same.

The dastardly massacres of Mr Williamson, the assistant political officer based at Sadiya, and his friend Dr Gregorson, an adventurous doctor working in the tea estates of upper Assam, and most of the forty-odd members of his party, including the coolies (porters), by the fiercely independent, curious and suspicious Abor tribesmen of Kebang village at Komsing and Pangi in the Siang Valley during 30–31 March 1911 created an outcry that resonated throughout the British Empire. The official account of this gruesome tragedy, caused possibly by a grave misunderstanding and unfounded apprehensions, is contained in the *Abor Blue Book,* published at the end of 1911.[19]

When viewed against the backdrop of the Chinese activities on the south-eastern frontiers of Tibet, this incident triggered not only the launch of a punitive expedition but also exploratory surveys of the vast unexplored tribal territory along the Lohit, Dibang, Siang and Subansiri river valleys and the Tawang tract. Thus began a huge exercise by British India to reach out to the natural frontier and the Himalayan watershed to ascertain the southern limits of Tibet and the demography of the border region. Though there was general knowledge of this frontier, there were yet many dots that had to be joined to define it with greater authenticity and accuracy.

It needs to be highlighted that as late as 1910–11, it had not been authoritatively established that the Tsangpo and the Dihang or Siang were one and the same river, and the mystery of the gigantic waterfall in the gorge at the 'great bend' of the Tsangpo had yet to be unravelled. In order to fill the gaps in the existing knowledge of the terrain and of the people inhabiting the tribal region, specific guidelines were issued in 1911 by the military General Staff at Simla to the survey parties that accompanied every mission. The most important amongst them was, first, identification of a suitable watershed along the eastern Himalayas to form the border, keeping 'on our side' the tributaries of the lower Siang or Brahmaputra, the Dibang, Lohit and Irrawaddy rivers; and second, determination of the limits of the tribal areas.[20] This became imperative, as in Asiatic countries the frontiers were vaguely expressed and the boundaries not clearly defined, leaving great scope for misinterpretation.

It was a colossal task, with rather overambitious targets. Unsurprisingly, it only succeeded in partially achieving its objectives because of the extremely rugged and almost impassable forested tracts on the southern glacis of the Himalayas. This remote region was inhabited by fierce tribes, most of whom had never seen Europeans and were intrinsically suspicious of outsiders. On the other hand, approaching the Himalayan watershed and the few known passes over a 1,000-kilometre frontier was, in fact, considerably easier from the Tibetan side because of the relatively friendlier attitude of the people there as well as the gentler topography. Moreover, the absence of or reduced forest cover on the northern slopes of the Himalayas facilitated survey of the mountain ranges and triangulation of the prominent peaks.

Fortunately for the British, the intrepid adventurer Captain Bailey, accompanied by Morshead and a small support group, who were part of the Mishmi expedition led by Dundas, was able to cross over the Himalayan watershed through the Yongyap La in May 1913 into the Pomed region of Tibet by going northwards up the Dibang river. Apparently, this happened more by *accident rather than design*, as while reconnoitring the upper Dibang Valley, the team came across some Tibetan settlers at a village called Mipi who were familiar with the Pomed and Pemakoichen areas of Tibet. They had come to this area in the hope of finding the mythical 'holy mountain of glass', but the hostility of the Mishmis had prevented them from realizing their dream and thus they returned to Tibet.

Bailey's expedition was the first of its kind, and it was able to carry out a fairly systematic survey from the east to the west of the Tsangpo Valley in southern Tibet, the Pemakoichen, Pomed, Tsari, Mago, Monyul and eastern Bhutan areas. Amongst the most notable achievements of this expedition was its confirmation that Tsangpo, Siang and Dihang were the same river, and their proving that there was no spectacular waterfall in the Tsangpo gorge. This dispelled the myth of a 'gigantic' waterfall hidden in the bowels of the deepest gorge in the world. The only major waterfall recorded by the expedition was at Pemakoichen in the 'great bend' region, where the water cascaded through a deep gorge and fell with a great roar from a height of about 9 metres. The volume and velocity of the 'seething and boiling mass of water' were described as awesome. There was, in fact, another waterfall of over 30 metres in this area, at a place known as Shingche Chogye, where a smaller river falls into the Tsangpo. According to legend, 'a demon who gives his name to the falls' is seen only by the fortunate on certain occasions. He is believed to be chained to the cliffs behind the foaming and cascading torrent (Figure 14).[21]

Figure 14: The Waterfall and the Demon (sourced from Tibetan Thangka painting)

These were extremely valuable geographical findings that more or less confirmed the account of this area rendered by Kinthup, a British-trained spy and adventurer of Sikkimese origin, thirty years before. The findings of Bailey and Morshead were most timely, as well as the only reliably researched topographic account of the vast unsurveyed and virgin Himalayan range between the Tsangpo bend and the Subansiri, and westwards, between the Subansiri and the Nam Jyang Chu west of Tsona Dzong, and ascending up to the tri-junction of Tibet, Bhutan and India. Had this reconnaissance not been completed, there would have been no possibility of McMahon charting out the famous 'red line', demarcating the boundary between Tibet and the loosely administered tribal territories of British India, especially the frontier extending westwards from the Tsangpo or Siang gorge right up to Tawang and Bhutan. Although the frontier in the Lohit Valley was also fairly extensively reconnoitred by Dundas during the Mishmi expedition in 1911–12, by Bailey in 1910–11, and by O'Callaghan in early 1913, there remained a gap from Kangri Karpo peak at the head of the Chimdro river in the Pome region down to the Lohit Valley. In this gap, extending about 160 kilometres as the crow flies, the survey was apparently done from the southern side of the Dibang watershed, that too only partially, by a subsidiary exploration team led by Captain Hardcastle of the Mishmi expedition during 1911–12. This extremely rugged, densely forested and unapproachable area has the famous 'fish-tail segment' of the boundary, where the watershed could not be adequately surveyed and was therefore only loosely delimited by the General Staff and McMahon, based on inputs from the tribal people.

It may be pertinent to point out that prior to 1912 it was the deputy commissioner of Lakhimpur on whom devolved the responsibility of establishing a loose political control over the tribal areas. His span of control and responsibility for maintaining relations with the frontier tribes was reduced with effect from 1882 by the appointment at Sadiya of an assistant political officer for that area. The first such assistant was Mr Francis Jack Needham of the Bengal Police.[22] There is handsome praise and recognition of Needham's contribution in the preface to the *Sadiya Frontier Tract Gazeteer* of 1928: 'By his explorations and discoveries, Mr. Needham acquired an international reputation and his work from 1882 to 1905 laid the foundations of the modern North-East Frontier of Assam.'[23]

In a reorganization of the administrative set-up as a result of these expeditions, three frontier regions were created by mid-1912 to administer the Assam Himalayas; the Western at Balipara, the Central at Lakhimpur, and the Eastern at Sadiya, which had become a full-fledged district. S.N. Mackenzie, the first political officer of the newly created district of Sadiya had, in his first annual report, succinctly alluded to the fact that the reorganization of the administrative structure of the hilly north-east frontier region south of the Himalayan watershed took place as a consequence of the Abor expedition of 1911–12:

> The Dibrugarh Frontier Tract ceased to exist, and the district of Sadiya became a separate entity controlled by a Political Officer, working directly under the Chief Commissioner, with three Assistant Political Officers, one of whom was posted to Pasighat, and was, broadly speaking, in charge of the Abor Hills.[24]

The Abor expedition in the Siang Valley in 1911–12 was a major politico-military survey expedition under the overall command of Major General Hamilton Bower, the general officer commanding of Assam Brigade. This was launched in October 1911 to cover the Siang Valley, inhabited primarily by the Abor tribe. At the same time a series of exploratory subsidiary missions was also mounted, as part of the somewhat ambiguous policy of 'loose political control', to establish friendly relations with the Mishmi, Hill Miri, Dafla, Aka and Monpa tribesmen of the Lohit, Dibang, Subansiri, Tenga, Tawang and Namjyang Chu Valleys. Importantly, these missions were to also carry out surveys of all such untrodden territories so as to be able to propose 'a suitable frontier line between India and Tibet' in the north-east.[25]

The tasks of Major General Bower's *punitive and exploratory* mission during the winter season of 1911–12 were outlined by the viceroy, Lord Hardinge, in his communication to the Secretary of State in London on 29 June 1911. He emphasized that the basic aim of the expedition was to seek 'reparation for the murder of Mr Noel Williamson and party, and the establishment of our military superiority in the estimation of the Abor tribe'. He also underscored the fact that maximum advantage should be taken of this opportunity 'to carry out such surveys and exploration as may be possible, that we may obtain the knowledge requisite for the determination of a suitable boundary between India and China in this locality'.[26]

Elaborate instructions were issued by the commander-in-chief of the army as well as the Governor General in Council to Major General Bower with regard to the military, political and survey aspects of the special mission. With a force of about 2,350 of all ranks and a contingent of military police, Major General Bower, with A. Bentinck and Dundas as assistant political officers, was also given the responsibility of overseeing all subsidiary missions into the other largely uncharted tribal territories, besides the Abor area. A survey party comprising two British officers, four surveyors and thirty-six khalasis ('native helps') was provided to this expedition. Dundas, an officer who belonged to Bengal Police, rendered his services with great dedication in the north-eastern-most corner of British India as assistant political officer, and later as political officer, at Sadiya from 1911 to 1920.

With the exception of the Lohit Valley, all the other major river valleys were virgin territory. Most of the tribal peoples in these parts had never seen a white man with *yellow hair*, as access to the plains had been denied to the interior tribes by the Abors, the Mishmis and the Daflas of the lower valleys.

It is of interest to note that contingencies such as face-to-face meetings with Chinese officials or troops, just in case they happened, had been catered for even a century ago. The instructions to the British Indian expeditions were that in such an eventuality, *'endeavour should be made to maintain amicable relations. If however, such officials or troops be met within the territory of tribes on this side of recognized Tibetan-Chinese limits, they should be invited to withdraw into recognized Tibetan-Chinese limits, and, if necessary, should be compelled to do so* (emphasis added).'[27] However, there was no trace of any Chinese presence in these tribal areas, except for an odd Chinese foray in the Lohit and Dibang Valleys during 1910–11, that too confined to the close proximity of the customary boundary.

A fair amount of information about the Mishmi-inhabited Lohit Valley had already been obtained and collated based on the reconnaissance sorties carried out by Needham, Bailey and Williamson during the past two decades, but it was in the frontier areas of the Dibang, Siang, Subansiri, Kamala, Khru, Kameng, Tawang and Namjyang Chu Valleys that there were huge unsurveyed areas and considerable gaps in the topographical data. Many of the probes and reconnaissance missions into these valleys proved to be abortive or only partially successful. However, despite the total lack of background information on these areas and on the tribes residing in this territory, it was a great achievement to reconnoitre many of these valleys up to distances just three to four marches short of the passes on the main snow-covered Himalayan range. In the Miri-inhabited areas of the Subansiri and the adjacent Kamala river valley, the survey parties could not proceed beyond Mara and Tali, whereas in the Siang Valley they could go up to Sigging and in the Dibang Valley up to Mipi. At Tali there was an armed clash with the Miris, as a result of which Tali village, along with its granary huts, was torched.

However, the expedition was able to take the bearings and carry out rough surveys of the snow-covered main Himalayan range from the intermediate hills about 50–60 kilometres away as the crow flies, but could not go up to the major passes in these valleys from the south. West of the Kamala river there was a 70-kilometre-wide gap up to the Kameng river that remained unsurveyed. But the surveying team were able to observe a major snow-covered range, some of its peaks above 7,000 metres, extending about 200 kilometres westwards from the Subansiri to the Tawang Chu. This stretch has not been pierced by any river from the Tibetan side and has very few passes; in fact, only three were known (including Tunjun La, at 5,244 metres), and even these remained open only for a few months in the summer.

The British General Staff took stock of the information obtained by the Abor and affiliated exploratory missions and, by the collation, synthesis and analysis of these survey reports, were able to arrive at an outline boundary alignment between Tibet and India. But there remained some grey areas which needed to be addressed. The essence of the recommendations was to carry out further survey of the areas to fill the gaps.

The Aka promenade was accordingly planned during 1913–14 to obtain topographical details and explore the tribal territories of the Miris, Akas and Monpas. Led by Captain Nevill, it consisted of 1,032 of all ranks.[28] This expedition met with hostility from the Dafla tribe in Riang village, which the mission had to pass en route. The expedition had to fight its way through at a number of places.

This array of expeditions beyond the outer line was carried out with the least publicity so as to avoid any debate on it in British Parliament and the consequent hassle of responding to allegations of breach of the Government of India Act, 1858. Therefore, as described by Alastair Lamb in his authoritative account of the times, 'the press were kept as far away from the Abor Expedition as could be arranged, and an attempt was made to keep the Miri and Mishmi Mission secret'.[29] This was necessary not only to avoid possible hype in London over British India's forward push into the Himalayan watershed, but also to prevent the Chinese from raising an alarm. A Chinese newspaper, *Kuo-min Pao*, published from Chengdu, carried the news on 27 March 1912 that 'British activity up the Lohit was clearly directed towards Zayul and the *"Wild Men's Country"* (i.e., the Mishmi tribal tracts)'. If the British obtained control of Zayul, the paper declared, they could easily advance farther to the north-east to include both Batang and Chamdo within the sphere of influence of the Indian Empire. British influence in eastern Tibet would eventually lead to British domination of Szechuan province, it said.[30]

The British had of necessity to come out with the *Abor Blue Book* to support the official stand that 'neither the Mishmis nor the Abors were beyond the British external frontiers'.[31] This observation relating to the two major tribes of Arunachal Pradesh further reinforces the point that the tribal territories that lay to the south of the Himalayan watershed were within British territorial limits.

The only valley where the British were able to go across the known Tibet–India frontier was the Lohit—or Zayul, as it is called in the upper reaches—where the British missions reached up to Rima, a recognized Tibetan frontier outpost. Therefore, the reconnaissance carried out by Bailey and Morshead of the areas, mountains, rivers and passes from the Tibetan side during 1913 were of great value and helped to corroborate the findings of the exploratory missions launched from the southern glacis of the Himalayas under Major General Bower. I am of the opinion that drawing up the McMahon Line would have been impossible without the inputs provided by these two intrepid adventurers.

The Mishmi mission, led by Mr Dundas during the same winter, was divided into two parts; one force under Captain Bally, accompanied by Captain F.M. Bailey as political officer, tasked with exploring the 'completely unknown' Dibang Valley to ascertain the limits of Tibetan or Chinese influence, if any, and to discern the most appropriate boundary along the main Himalayan crest line; and the other (main) force under Dundas, accompanied by Captain Hardcastle and Captain Jeffery, a Chinese-language specialist, to survey and recommend the boundary as it traversed the Lohit Valley going from west to east up to the area north of the Diphu Pass on the tri-junction of India, Tibet and Burma. In the Walong sector, based on the reports filed by Captains Gunter and Morshead, who had mapped the area extensively, Dundas recommended a boundary alignment along the Tho Chu (Figure 9), which flows down from the Dibang–Lohit watershed into the Lohit river at a point midway between Rima and Walong (a mention of this has been made in his account of 26 January 1912).[32]

On his arrival at the Yepauk nala, that drains into the Lohit river near Walong, on 3 January 1912, Dundas found that the Chinese had 'put up fresh boundary markers besides the old ones of 1910', the new ones bearing a red flag with the image of a four-clawed dragon and a red placard bearing in Chinese and Tibetan the following inscription: 'Zayul, southern limit, boundary of Manchu Empire.' Dundas ignored these markers and advanced to Walong, camping there till 31 January 1912. Interestingly, the Chinese and Tibetan authorities at Rima with whom Dundas remained in touch never protested the British presence beyond their (Chinese) claimed area, but kept the latter in good humour by welcoming them with the traditional gifts of chicken, eggs and other local products.[33] Later, these Chinese activities were reconfirmed by the report of the Walong promenade led by T. P. M. O'Callaghan during early 1914. He recommended that the boundary going from the Lohit to the eastern tri-junction should be along the ridge just north of the Di Chu so that the Di Chu Valley and the track leading to Burma through the Diphu Pass would be under British control. He strongly advised occupation of a post at Walong, for reasons that he spelt out clearly:

> ... to assert our legitimate rights and claims ... A small force, operating from Walong, could occupy Rima and hold the Rong Thod Chu and Zayul valleys in 24-30 hours and vice versa, a force moving from Rima can unopposed be in position on Menilkrai at within 36 hours and effectually prevent any advance up the Lohit Valley.

He carried out his recce from January to March 1914, when the Simla Conference was in session and McMahon and Lonchen Shatra were in the process of finalizing the Tibet–India boundary alignment (the 'red line'). O'Callaghan's recommendations were indeed timely, and of immense help to McMahon in finalizing the eastern limit of the Himalayan boundary. O'Callaghan reportedly had the boundary markers *unilaterally* placed by the Chinese in the vicinity of Menilkrai, south of Walong, removed. He then proceeded to take them upstream to the border settlement of Kahao and disposed of them there. He thought leaving them at Menilkrai near Yepauk might, in later years, would be construed as a 'tacit admission' by the British of the southern limit of the Chinese or Tibetan frontier in the lower Zayul Valley.[34]

In addition to exploring the Lohit Valley, Dundas sent Captain Hardcastle to survey the extremely remote Delei (Dilli) river valley. Delei is a prominent tributary of the Lohit, and joins the main river at Hayuliang, about 70 kilometres from Tezu. This is an important settlement where the Lohit river debouches from the hills and spreads out into numerous channels. Hardcastle was also tasked to establish communications with the 'isolated' Mishmis in this godforsaken area. He was informed of a singular incidence of a Chinese incursion from the Glei Dakhru Pass in the north during the summer of 1911, which has been described in the previous chapter. The passes (with writing in Tibetan and Chinese script) handed over to the Mazanon villagers by the Chinese were collected by the patrol. On translating them, Captain Jeffery affirmed that the documents[35] corroborated the information provided by the headman. Other than this,

Hardcastle found no evidence of the presence or influence of the Tibetans or Chinese in this valley.

From Sadiya, the Dibang Valley rises steeply for about 200 kilometres to the crest line and then passes on to the snow-covered mountain range. Beyond that lies the Tibetan Pomed region. This valley, roughly 120 kilometres wide, is located to the west of the Lohit. It was largely an unexplored area until 1911. The subsidiary probes of the Mishmi mission in 1912–13 found evidence of Tibetan or Monpa people who had settled in the upper reaches of the Dibang and its tributaries such as the Dri and Adzon. They had come to this area during the first decade of the twentieth century in search of the 'sacred glass mountain' and also to save themselves from the rapacious Chinese soldiery. In the face of grave hostility shown by the Mishmis, many of these settlers perished in Mishmi raids or from disease, while the others returned to Tibet. Some of these settlers had come from the Pomed region after the devastating floods in the Yigrong-Pome Valley at the turn of the century (1899–1900), which swept away numerous villages. The bodies of the Pobas were carried away by the torrent all the way to Assam, along with trees of a kind not found in the southern slopes of the Himalayas. Hundreds were believed to have perished in this natural catastrophe.

As part of their imperial strategy, the British expanded their areas of 'control' and 'influence' from the plains up to the Himalayan watershed by entering into various treaties and agreements using persuasion and, at times, force. Starting from Ladakh and the hill states and principalities of Lahaul, Spiti, Kangra and Kulu, the British gained control of the western Himalayan frontier of India. Eastwards, by virtue of the Treaty of Sagauli (1816) with Nepal, the British got control of the Kumaon and Garhwal Hills. Thereafter came the acquisition of Darjeeling district from the raja of Sikkim in 1835, annexation of Assam in October 1838, and 'satisfactory settlements' with Sikkim in 1861 and with Bhutan in 1865. As a result of these actions, Kalimpong was also ceded to the British. East of Bhutan, the British entered into many 'agreements beginning in 1844 with the chiefs of little-known hill tribes living between the plains of Assam and the crest of the Himalaya, thereby secured the northern flank of the Brahmaputra Valley'.[36]

The British strategy was to see the emergence of a zone along the northern frontier of India that would act as a buffer between Tibet and India in the form of small and big kingdoms and estates dependent on the Indian government. Yet for centuries these states and their inhabitants have had religious ties and barter trade, and at some places shared grazing grounds with the Tibetans. Also, as observed by Richardson:

> The Government of the Dalai Lama did not exercise direct authority in Ladakh, Sikkim, Bhutan, or any area south of the Himalaya except for the Chumbi valley, nor was it represented in those countries by permanent envoys; but the ties of religious homage, trade, racial affinity and a degree of common interest had given Lhasa a special position and influence.[37]

Tibet's Turbulent Decade: 1904–1914

In every nation's history there are periods and phases of tranquility, peace and progress, as also of turbulence and strife. At the turn of the twentieth century, Tibet witnessed a phase of intense turmoil, uncertainty and unprecedented violence. This was a glorious period as far as the British Empire was concerned, and India was being presented as a jewel in its crown. In Central Asia, the Great Game was in full flow, with Tzarist Russia pushing southwards into Iran and the Pamirs. Great Britain was engaged in taking matching steps to contain this expansion. The Manchu Empire in China was on its last legs after its debilitating defeats in the Boxer Rebellion and its ruinous war with Japan. The Manchu court's hold over the far-flung dependencies like Xinjiang, Mongolia, Manchuria and Tibet was notional, or tenuous at best. Defeating the Russians both on land and at sea in the Russo-Japanese war of 1904–05, Japan had heralded its arrival as a major power in Asia. Most of the world powers, including France and Germany, were jockeying for control and spheres of influence, to get trading ports, concessions and other facilities in China. There was even this apprehension in Chinese minds that some parts of China might be sliced away to create European enclaves that would serve the purpose of trading bases along the Pacific rim. Despite its wobbly political hold over the outlying parts of the empire, the Manchu court did not give up, and continued to evolve organizations for more effective control of its frontier regions. In 1901 it set up the Boards of Territorial Development and of Frontier Defence, their oblique aim being to settle Chinese citizens in Mongolia and Tibet. It was hoped that with intermarriages and cultural exchanges over a period of time, the integration of these regions with the mainland would follow.[38] This scheme met with great resistance from people of both regions, and Sinification of the Mongolians and Tibetans failed to take root even later, despite the most vigorous measures adopted during the period of Chao Erh-feng.

In this environment, the hidden land of the lamas remained an enigma. Chinese control over Tibet was nominal, and more or less perfunctory. The thirteenth Dalai Lama was the God-king, with absolute spiritual and temporal powers. Born in the Takpo province of central Tibet, he was identified and 'brought to Lhasa when two years old, and kept in a hermitage until confirmation was received that the Emperor accepted him as the Dalai Lama'.[39]

He was enthroned at the age of three and brought up in the cocooned environment of the Potala palace. There, sheltered by the regent who managed the affairs of the state with the help of the cabinet or Kashag, comprising four ministers (Kalon), of whom one was a monk, and an ecclesiastical council that took care of religious matters, he grew up blissfully unaware of the outside world and without any female contacts. His formal religious training commenced when he turned six, and he gradually became proficient in spiritual and scriptural matters. The gifted and scholarly Russian Buriat monk Agvan Dorjieff was to become his guru and his only external influence and mentor. Besides his spiritual and religious instructional responsibilities, the tutor was also appointed by the Dalai Lama 'as "Work Washing Abbot", part of his duty being to sprinkle water, scented with saffron flowers, a little on the person of the Dalai Lama, but more on the walls of his room, on the altar, and on the books, as a symbol of cleansing. He was thus in a close relationship with the young god-king, now come into power.'[40]

The young Dalai Lama grew up with the belief that foreigners were not to be trusted, particularly the white man, and must therefore be kept away. The Russians were to be an exception, as a result of the 'Dorjieff factor'. The Tibetans had witnessed the amalgamation of Darjeeling and Kalimpong areas with British India by the employment of coercive tactics by the British against Sikkim and Bhutan. Further, the British making Sikkim a protectorate of the British Crown and taking it away from Tibetan control and influence did not do much to allay Lhasa's fears about invasion and possible colonization by the British. The armed expulsion of the Tibetan army in 1888 from an encroachment in an area near Jelep La, referred to as 'Natong' and 'Lungtur' (the areas are currently called Nathang and Lungthu), was the first military engagement between the British and the Tibetans. This one-sided and unequal skirmish led to the Sino-British Convention of 1890 that was signed in Calcutta on 17 March, settling matters relating to the Indo-Tibetan boundary in Sikkim and border trade. Significantly, the Himalayan watershed was agreed as the dividing line between Tibet and Sikkim. While accepting the status of Sikkim as a protectorate of Britain, the Convention spelt out that 'the boundary of Sikkim and Tibet shall be the crest of the mountain range separating the waters flowing into the Sikkim Teesta, and the affluents from the waters flowing into the Tibetan Mochu, and northwards into other rivers of Tibet (emphasis added)'.

However, the Tibetans had reservations about this Convention, as they were not a party to the agreement. Happenings in Mongolia had a collateral impact on the internal situation in Tibet. Both being Buddhist states, there was a fair amount of intercourse between them on religious and temporal matters. Theologically, Tibet and its monasteries had a higher standing, owing to the pre-eminent position of the Dalai Lama, the chief incarnation of the four-handed Chen-re-zi, the patron diety. At the same time, the Russians, considering Mongolia as a territory clearly within their sphere of influence, backed Mongolia's quest for independence and greater autonomy from China, unlike Britain in the case of Tibet.

The thirteenth Dalai Lama led an extraordinary life. He was forced into exile on two occasions, spending about eight years of the turbulent decade of 1904–14 away from his land and his people. It was but natural that his outlook was shaped by the environment he grew up in. Till the

Younghusband expedition, considered an 'invasion' by the Tibetans, the Dalai Lama had not ventured out of Tibet, and his only exposure to the outside world was through Dorjieff or through pilgrims from near and far Asia—Mongolians, Russian Buriats and Tibetans who sought his blessings. He was well aware of Tibetan history and had gained a profound knowledge of the Buddhist scriptures. Besides, he had read accounts of the famous king Songstan Gampo, the Tsong Khapa, the great scholar and founder of the Gelugpa School (the Yellow Hat tradition), and the 'Great Fifth' Dalai Lama. He was the first Dalai Lama to successfully graduate to the highest eccleisiastical level within the Gelugpa monastic tradition by qualifying for the degree of 'Geshe Lharampa' in 1899, when he was twenty-four. He survived what was considered a serious assassination attempt, through the medium of a tantric mantra embedded in the sole of his boots. On being discovered, the perpetrators of this devious plan were incarcerated, and they died in prison in 1900.

The turn of the century witnessed great turmoil in Central Asia. The situation in Asia, especially in China, Tibet, Mongolia and East Asia, had become very complicated because of the Ch'ing dynasty's downslide. Adding to this was the web of Russian intrigues with the Dalai Lama through Dorjieff, which strained relations between Tibet and British India. The fear of subjugation of Tibet or parts of it by Britain, and the inevitable commercial exploitation that might follow, made the Tibetans extremely suspicious of the British. This situation led to the Younghusband expedition, the flight to Mongolia of the Dalai Lama and his exile from 1904 to 1909. The Dalai Lama's exaggerated sense of mortification from his belief that the British would eliminate him made him flee at an unbelievable pace. The irony is that the British never even attempted a pursuit!

The reader already knows the story of the Dalai Lama's flight, which eventually ended in the Chinese Amban assuming temporal authority over Tibet and administering it with what remained of the Kashag, the Tsongdu and officials who were mainly Chinese. The Chinese 'fiction' of control over Tibet now became a reality, thanks to Younghusband's expedition and Britain's 'hands off' policy.

While the British were only prepared to accept Chinese suzerainty and not sovereignty over Tibet, for the Chinese it was only 'Chu Kuo' (sovereignty) as they did not believe in 'Shang Kuo' (suzerainty).[41]

The awestruck and bewildered population of Lhasa watched the alien forces moving around, indulging in hectic parleys during the brief occupation of Lhasa by the British. The amazing part was the mute witnessing of the proceedings by the Chinese Amban, Yu T'ai, and his guard, as if they had nothing to do with Tibet, the capital of a supposedly vassal state of the Chinese Empire. In fact, the Chinese Amban played a positive role in the parleys and discussions that took place in Lhasa, though he did not append his signatures on the Anglo-Tibetan Treaty of 1904. This continued till the signing of the Anglo-Tibetan Treaty, which took place with the pomp and show so typical of the British Raj on 7 September 1904 at the 'new Throne Room in the castle of Potala'.[42] The Tibetans, Chinese and others in Lhasa were equally bewildered and perplexed to notice that the British forces had no intention of remaining in occupation of Tibet and had begun preparations to leave Lhasa within two months. On 23 September, the British struck down their camp and commenced their journey back to Sikkim via Shigatse, where they were to establish a trade mart. Chumbi Valley was to remain under British occupation, as per the Lhasa treaty, initially enshrined for seventy-five years—up to 1979! Though, sadly for British India, this was watered down to three years by Whitehall, and the indemnity to be paid by Tibet reduced from Rs 75 lakh to one-third of that amount, to be paid in three annual instalments. This liability was taken over by the Chinese.

The immense loss of face and the rude shock delivered to the Chinese by the almost uncontested advance of Younghusband's force into the heart of Tibet woke them up from their slumber. The result was manifestation of an aggressive forward policy by the Manchu court as far as all its dependencies—Sinkiang, Mongolia, Tibet, the area of the Marches and northern Burma—were concerned. The Chinese army came down with a heavy hand on these regions, and the world witnessed the ruthless Sinification of all these regions from 1905 to 1910. This policy heralded the era of the 'butcher' Chao Erh-feng in the Marches, particularly along the frontiers of Amdo and Kham regions of Tibet. Encouraged by the weak 'hands off' policy of Britain, the Chinese began to consolidate their hold over eastern Tibet and gradually spread their power westwards to central and southern Tibet.

The Tibetans deluded themselves by believing the Chinese would not invade Tibet proper or advance up to Lhasa, and feverishly prayed that divine intervention or the incantations of the lamas would keep the Chinese away. It was too much to expect the ramshackle Tibetan army, badly mauled and demoralized as it was by the overwhelming fire power and tactics of a modern European army led by Brigadier Macdonald in 1903–04, to be able to contain the Chinese army along Tibet's traditional and time-worn eastern frontiers. The prolonged negotiations between the British and the Chinese, which were initiated in Calcutta and which concluded in Peking in 1906, on terms that were hugely advantageous to the Chinese, helped China to regain her prestige and power in Tibet. As a matter of fact, an enfeebled China could not have had a better deal!

The Russian bogey weighed so heavily on British thinking that the British preferred to have a stable northern border with Tibet under the suzerainty of a 'benign' China. They failed to see beyond the horizon. Rumours of construction of an off-shoot of the trans-Siberian railway line towards Sinkiang added to the exaggerated threat perception. Russo-phobia ran deep amongst the policymakers in London, so much so that they manoeuvred to have a disadvantageous self-denying agreement signed with Russia in 1907—a case of British imperial strategy superseding British India's interests. Though this convention largely contributed to ending the Great Game in Central Asia between the two powers, it tied their hands at the same time, as far as playing any role in Tibet was concerned. In fact, it offered Tibet on a platter to the Chinese, helping them secure the position they were desperately trying to wrest for themselves since 1720. In 1908, a fresh trade agreement, as decided during the Lhasa Convention of 1904 and the Adhesion Agreement of 1906, was signed between Britain and China, with a Tibetan representative acting under the Chinese commissioner, with the aim of reviewing and amending, where necessary, the Tibet Trade Regulations of 1893. This agreement was another example, if more proof was needed, of the pliability and spinelessness of British diplomacy regarding the safeguarding of British India's strategic interests along the Indo-Tibetan frontier.

With the signing of the Trade Agreement of 1908, the mandarins of the Manchu court had in one stroke gained many victories. The first was that Article III of the bipartite 1904 Lhasa Convention (Appendix 2) did not stipulate Chinese participation along with Britain and Tibet in future discussions on amendments to the trade regulations. This condition was given a quiet burial, to the detriment of Tibet's interests. The second victory for the Chinese was their being able to prevail on the British negotiators to make the Tibetan representative subordinate to the Chinese. The third was the unambiguous articulation of Chinese supremacy in the functioning of the trade marts in Tibet—the Chinese were given the final say in resolving local disputes. And, finally, the last lever of British influence in the region—the stationing of an armed escort for protection of British trading missions—was also sacrificed. Regulation 12 of the new agreement specified that these escorts would be withdrawn as soon as the Chinese were able to effectively police central Tibet. These regulations were not purely tools for streamlining border trade but, more significantly, for functioning 'as a means to secure political objectives' and gain moral ascendency.[43]

The eminent scholar Heather Spence, with reference to the Chinese 'forward policy' from 1905 to 1911, quoted from the *Saturday Review* of 5 March 1910, under the heading 'Chinese "Reforms" in Tibet':

The military occupation of Lhasa by the Chinese, with the deposition and flight of the Dalai Lama, is clearly the opening move in China's avowed policy of 'reform' in Tibet, in other words her annexation of that country. This movement, fraught with fresh danger to our Indian Empire, has unhappily been contributed to in no small measure by our *own blundering policy* (emphasis added) in Tibet.[44]

The Grand Lama had remained in exile from 1904 to 1909, at first escaping to Mongolia to avoid falling into British hands, and later prolonging his absence from Tibet on one pretext or the other, even though the Manchu court had granted him permission to return in 1908. All the while, the Chinese armies were subjugating the eastern frontier of Tibet—the Marches in Kham and Amdo and the contiguous areas of Pomed and Zayul in southern and south-eastern Tibet. The main reason for the Dalai Lama's refusal to return to Lhasa from his exile was his uncertainty about his own safety. He suspected the Chinese had an ulterior motive—a grand strategy to turn Tibet into a regular province of China. During the absence of the Dalai Lama in Lhasa, the Chinese had indeed gradually taken over the running of the state. Therefore, while at Urga, Kumbum and Wutai-Shan, the Dalai Lama desperately tried to seek the help of various foreign powers to restrain the Chinese from advancing into Tibet proper. Apparently, his pleas fell on deaf ears. He therefore sought an audience with the emperor and the dowager queen to have his titles and the status of Tibet restored before returning to Lhasa. His meetings with the royalty helped to buttress his standing amongst his people, and amongst the Chinese too.

During our visit to Beijing in 2014, I was keen to see the chamber in the vast summer palace where the Chinese emperor was imprisoned by his mother, the dowager queen. It was probably the place where he died in mysterious circumstances a day prior to the death of the queen herself. Ironically, it was to the humiliated Dalai Lama that the Manchu court had to turn for performing the final rites for both of them at the Yung-ho Kung. These tragic events cast a shadow over the last Ch'ing emperor's assumption of the throne, which was witnessed by the Dalai Lama. Realizing that it was futile to stay in Peking any longer, the avatar of Chen-re-zi decided to leave for Lhasa on 21 December 1908. He returned, not along the active and disturbed eastern road called the 'Janglam' that connected Peking to Lhasa via Chengdu and Batang, but by the more secure northern route via Sining, Kumbum and Nagchukha. He was given a warm farewell at the railway station and was seen off by the 'Manchu and Mongolian princes and other nobles'.[45] He travelled partly by train, and the rest of the journey on camel or horseback. Curious to learn more about this region, we travelled to Sining and also paid obeisance at the famous Kumbum monastery during this visit to China in 2014. (See Figure 15.)

Figure 15: The author at the Kumbum monastery near Sining, China, 2014

Unsure of the situation in Lhasa, the Grand Lama did not wish to make a dash to his destination. Accordingly, he moved deliberately from one monastery to the next while remaining in constant touch with developments in Peking and Lhasa. His sojourn in the sacred Kumbum monastery (Kumbum literally means 'one lakh images of Buddha') was a fairly long one, and he involved himself in setting right the administration and discipline there. As he moved on, he did the same at the other high-ranking monasteries he stayed in. The people of Tibet were eagerly looking forward to the Chen-re-zi's return to Lhasa after his absence of five years. As a mark of respect, the people contributed money to make a golden seal, which was presented to the Dalai Lama on his arrival at Lhasa. The inscription in Tibetan and Sanskrit on the seal read: 'Seal to Spokesman of Buddha's Words, Master in the Three Realms, Benevolent Leader of Buddhism, Knowledgeable Lama, Wish-fulfilling King Worshipped by All People.'

Very soon the Dalai Lama had to flee his palace again, this time to India, when Chao Erh-feng's best troops easily cut through the disorganized and confused resistance put up by the Tibetans, and the gates of Lhasa were once again forced open by an alien army. Having learnt the lesson that it was suicidal to leave the back door to Tibet open, the Chinese reaction of gearing up its administration and control over central Tibet was no surprise. The most direct and convenient route to the heart of Tibet was through the Chumbi Valley. Lhasa is much closer to Jelep La on the Sikkim border than is Kolkata. As a result of the Younghusband mission, the route from Kalimpong to Lhasa was transformed from a mule or yak track to a fairly good cart road, except for a few difficult patches. Even a disassembled mini Peugeot and a Clement car were physically carried across the Jelep La and assembled in the Chumbi Valley in 1907, to be driven the rest of the way to Shigatse for presentation to the Panchen Lama. (These were the first automobiles in Tibet!) Fortunately for the Chinese, the British themselves facilitated the Chinese consolidation in central Tibet by giving up the Chumbi Valley after receipt of the third and final instalment of the indemnity from the Chinese in 1908, a sum of 8,33,333 rupees, 5 annas and 4 pice.[46] Hypothetically speaking, had the period of the indemnity remained as originally decided in the Lhasa Agreement of 1904 and it was paid back in seventy-five instalments, India might have been in possession of the Chumbi Valley until 1979 or 1980! The impact of this even to this day on the geostrategic scenario along the boundary between Tibet and Sikkim, and on Bhutan, can be imagined, specially now with the Doklam stand-off of 2017 having taken place in the same area.

In 1906, without much loss of time after the return of the Younghusband mission, the Chinese sent an imperial commissioner, Chang Yin-tang, via Calcutta and the Chumbi Valley to take charge of the administration of Tibet and put it in order. He was also charged with the responsibility of investigating the allegations of mal-governance, corruption and treasonous conduct on the part of the Amban, Yu T'ai, who helped the Younghusband mission succeed in getting the Lhasa Treaty signed by all the parties concerned, although he did not sign it himself. Some reports suggest that Yu T'ai was enchained and humiliated, along with other Chinese and Tibetan collaborators, while under investigation by Chang and the new Amban, Lien Yu, and deported to China.

PART V

SIMLA CONFERENCE, 1913–14

Figure 16: The plenipotentiaries (L to R): Lonchen Shatra (Tibet),
Sir A.H. McMahon (British India) and Ivan Chen (China)

PART V

SIMLA CONFERENCE, 1914–15

12

The Prelude

Taking advantage of the October 1911 Revolution and the prevailing confusion in the Chinese government, the British, without losing any time, evolved a four-pronged strategy to resolve the many issues related to Tibet. The first step was to define the boundary and status of Tibet in consultation with China and Tibet; the second was to delineate the boundaries between Tibet and China, and between Tibet, north-east India and Burma; the third was to give an impetus to the emergence of a truly autonomous Tibet, albeit under Chinese suzerainty, thereby creating a buffer between the Chinese and British Indian empires; and the fourth was to keep Russian influence in Tibet at bay. Fundamentally, the British desired to have peace and quiet on India's northern frontiers, keeping inimical influences away, a clearly defined boundary between Tibet and China, and an end to hostilities. To achieve this, there could be nothing better than a harmless Tibet as a buffer state. However, for this it was imperative to establish a clear understanding of the *political status* of Tibet and have it accepted by China.

On 23 May 1913, the British wrote to the Chinese and Tibetan governments, inviting them to participate in a tripartite conference for settlement of the Tibet question. It was clarified at the outset that all three delegates would be on an equal footing, as had been made abundantly clear in the British Memorandum of August 1912 to the Chinese government. The Chinese demurred vehemently, but had to be reminded that the situation in Tibet had undergone a paradigm shift, as

163

by early 1913 not a single Chinese official or soldier was present in all of Tibet. The status and frontiers of Tibet, which comprised the main issues of the agenda, could not possibly have been discussed in a free and fair manner without a level playing field. Therefore the precedence of the trade negotiations of 1908, in which the Tibetan Shape (minister) was subordinate to the Chinese delegate, no longer held good. The British reminded the Chinese that the matter had already been settled and could not be raised again at this stage. The British hinted to the Chinese that a successful agreement would result in *Chinese suzerainty over a fully autonomous Tibet*, as otherwise they would have to achieve the same by conducting a long-drawn and costly military campaign.

Initially, this conference was scheduled to be held in Darjeeling. However, for reasons emphasized by the viceroy in a confidential note to the foreign secretary, the venue was changed to Simla. In his telegram, sent on 15 June 1913, announcing the change of venue, the viceroy wrote:

> It would greatly facilitate conduct of the negotiations and be in every-way more convenient if they could be held at Simla instead of Darjiling. At Simla we could exercise much more effective control over proceedings while Tibetan delegates would not be so exposed to Chinese intrigues as at Darjiling ...[1]

Not only was Simla the summer capital of the British Raj, the General Headquarters (GHQ) of the army being co-located there would also facilitate quicker decision making for the British. Besides these reasons, Darjeeling and Kalimpong had become notorious for espionage and subversive activities relating to Tibet, and the Chinese had developed a good network for generating intrigue and shady dealings. Lu Hsing-chi, a Chinese intelligence operative masquerading as the representative of a firm of furriers, Thinyik & Co., based at Calcutta, was the powerful mastermind behind these activities. The British endeavour was to keep such inimical influences at bay. Moreover, there were inquisitive powers like Japan and Russia, who had their own interests and would like to fish in troubled waters. Simla provided a more secure and conducive environment for such a conference.

As far as India was concerned, there couldn't have been a more important subject, or one that needed a more urgent solution, than this. The planning, conduct and analysis of the exploratory recces and geographical surveys in the northern frontiers was being done by the GHQ staff on a war footing, and maps were being constantly updated and revised. The geostrategic implications of the discoveries and other security issues had to be discussed, and advice offered to the viceroy.

The Chinese were apprehensive that Great Britain might follow the Russian precedent in Mongolia and support Tibet in its endeavour to achieve independence. This resulted in their mounting an offensive to regain territory in eastern Tibet in the Marches and beyond. In the spring of 1913, the situation had deteriorated to such an extent that a state of war existed between China and Tibet on the eastern frontier. The aim of the Chinese campaign was to recapture Litang, Batang and other areas subdued by Chao Erh-feng up to 1910, particularly those areas that, according to the Chinese, belonged to the newly planned province of Hsikang, extending to Chiangta (Giamda), just 200 kilometres east of Lhasa. The Chinese strategy was to also gain a hold over as much territory as possible so that during the ensuing conference in India their exaggerated claims would be substantiated. 'The Chinese claim to the Chiangta frontier appears to have been based on a recommendation by Chao Erh-feng in the spring of 1911, but even in the heyday of his advance, Chao never succeeded in securing any effective Chinese administration beyond a point between Derge and Chamdo,'[2] said the Memorandum on Tibet by Alston, the chargé d'affaires in the British Legation in Peking.

The Chinese president, Yuan Shih-k'ai, was therefore urged to issue orders asking his troops to maintain the status quo and refrain from further advances into Tibetan territory till the convention was over. Accordingly, he issued orders to this effect on 30 June 1913, also notifying therein the appointment of negotiators for the settlement of Tibetan affairs.[3]

The Sino-Tibet boundary shifted considerably between the eighteenth and twentieth centuries. The Chinese laid claims to a large part of greater Tibet, disregarding the fact that these areas were under the temporal control of the Dalai Lama and that their population was preponderantly Tibetan (Figure 8).

The Chinese were simultaneously and secretly looking at bilateral negotiations with the Tibetans, and in view of this wanted to delay the commencement of the tripartite conference in which they did not have their heart. Despite the Wai Chiao-pu (the Chinese Foreign Office) denials that China had made efforts to hold direct talks between Wang, the administrator of Lhasa and Tibet, and the Kalon Lama, the Tibetan administrator, at Chamdo, the situation on the ground was different. The Dalai Lama was being directly cajoled and threatened at the same time by the Chinese to resolve all issues with them. In May 1913, 'the Peking Government directed the Dalai Lama to send an officer to escort him (Lu Hsing-chi, the Chinese agent at Calcutta) thither (Lhasa), using threats of force unless the suggestion was carried out. The Lhasa Government refused to receive Lu on the plea that Chinese were behaving in an outrageous manner in Eastern Tibet.'[4]

Lu Hsing-chi was relentlessly pursuing his games of intrigue and was establishing a network of spies under a man named Tashi Wangdi. Tashi was tasked to 'win over officials' and 'induce' the Dalai Lama and his advisers to create a favourable environment for China. Despite Lu's best endeavours and the persistent efforts of the Chinese government, he was not permitted to proceed to Lhasa, even when he was nominated as the Amban designate, or 'Officiating Chinese Resident in Lhasa' or administrator of Tibet. The British soon put a stop to these attempts by the Chinese government to pressure the Dalai Lama through Lu: 'On July 30 His Majesty's Government approved a suggestion of Mr Alston's that Lu should be warned by the Government of India that any attempt to carry out the duties of his appointment as Amban would result in his deportation from India.'[5] This was duly acted upon and the warning was conveyed to Lu.

Though nominated on 14 June 1913, the formal appointment of Lieutenant Colonel Arthur Henry McMahon, secretary to the Government of India in the Foreign Department, as the British plenipotentiary for the Simla Convention was conveyed only on 13 August 1913 by a Royal Commission that addressed the affairs of Tibet.

It empowered him 'to sign any Convention, Agreement or Treaty which may be concluded at this Conference'.[6] As a young captain twenty years earlier, McMahon had accompanied Durand on his mission to Kabul and had spent two hard years demarcating the Durand Line. By 1914, McMahon had been knighted and was functioning as foreign secretary of the Indian government. He possessed remarkable moral strength, of the kind that Curzon must have had in mind when he spoke of the 'frontier school of character', where men were moulded 'in the furnace of responsibility and on the anvil of self-reliance'. McMahon relished the creation and laying down of boundaries, holding it to be not a science but an art as articulated by Lord Curzon. Further, while describing the process of boundary evolution, Curzon had remarked, 'so plastic and so malleable are its forms and manifestations'.[7]

Besides McMahon, the British side comprised a formidable team of China and Tibet experts who carried immense experience of frontiers and their demarcation. McMahon played a key role in demarcation of the boundary between Afghanistan and Baluchistan during 1894–96, and during 1903–05 had headed the Seistan Mission as commissioner.[8] Moreover, as foreign secretary, he was fully conversant with the Chinese forays in the Zayul and Pomed areas and had been also involved in the planning of all exploratory and survey missions along the Himalayan frontiers, along with the General Staff of the army. He had a deep understanding of the geopolitical and strategic issues that needed to be addressed while evolving the rationale for delineating an appropriate boundary. During the Simla Conference, he was accommodated in a wonderful cottage, called Knockdrin, on the Ridge in that town. This cottage is at present the Officer's Mess of Indian Army's Training Command.

Charles Bell, the political officer in Sikkim, and Archibald Rose, an experienced consular official working on Tibetan affairs at the Peking Legation, were appointed as McMahon's assistants. Bell, a noted Tibetologist, had been given the charge of looking after the thirteenth Dalai Lama during his exile in Darjeeling from 1910 to 1912, as we know. He was nominated for his 'requisite' local knowledge of Tibetan affairs[9] and, importantly, also because of his extremely close rapport with the

Grand Lama. Rose was endowed with a profound knowledge of China and the Chinese government. He had performed exceedingly well as British consul at Tengyueh near the Burma border from 1909 to 1911. Rose's selection was commented upon as an 'admirable one' by the India Office at London.

As a matter of fact, the Chinese would have preferred the talks to be held in London rather than in India, as they considered Whitehall to be more sympathetic to them than the Government of India. This view was dismissed, as it found no support on the British side.

The Chinese were extremely wary that the British and the Tibetans might go ahead with direct negotiations. Yuan Shih-k'ai told Jordan that he was considering nomination of Chang Yin-tang as the Chinese representative for these deliberations. However, Jordan was quick to object to this and suggested the name of Ivan Chen instead. Ivan was former counsellor of the Chinese mission in London and was currently commissioner for foreign affairs at Shanghai. Based on experiences of the recent past, Chang had not proved to be a success, and was therefore unacceptable, Jordan told Yuan.[10] After prevaricating and raising repeated objections to the tripartite nature of the conference on Tibet for a number of months, the Chinese president gave his assent to China's participation in it, and Ivan Chen was nominated as the Chinese plenipotentiary on 6 June 1913.[11]

Curiously, on 14 June 1913, a presidential order was issued appointing Ivan Chen and Hu Han-min, governor of Canton, as 'Pacificators' in Tibet. This measure was apparently a kind of red herring. The British questioned the Chinese motive for such a step while conveying their strong objection to Ivan Chen's appointment as negotiator while he held the title of pacificator, and also conveyed to them that Hu Han-min was not acceptable at the conference because of his antecedents. The Chinese responded saying their order could not be rescinded but would be superseded. They also assured the British that the title of pacificator 'carried no territorial powers'. It was at this juncture that the Chinese were cautioned that until the geographical limits of Tibet were determined in the conference, further advance of their army in eastern Tibet and the Marches was forbidden, and that hostilities must be suspended immediately. At the same time, the Chinese were also cautioned against further delay in dispatch of their plenipotentiary to the conference. They were told in no uncertain terms that the convention would commence on 6 October, with or without Ivan Chen.

Eventually, despite a lot of prodding, it was only on 2 August 1913 that a Chinese presidential order was signed formally appointing Ivan Chen as the special plenipotentiary for the Tibetan negotiations. The wording of the order is noteworthy:

It becomes the duty of this Government to order said plenipotentiary speedily to proceed to India, there to negotiate provisional treaty jointly with the plenipotentiary appointed by Great Britain and the Tibetan plenipotentiary, and to sign articles which may be agreed upon in order that all difficulties which have existed in the past may be dissolved.[12]

After a lot of dilly-dallying, Ivan Chen joined Archibald Rose for the voyage to India. They set sail from Shanghai for Calcutta on 3 September and arrived at Simla on 5 October 1913, in the nick of time for the convention.[13]

The Times, London, carried a report from Peking on 2 September 1913 on the departure of Ivan Chen for the Simla Conference. It said he was authorized to 'conclude an agreement which shall comply with the requirements stated in the British Note of August, 1912'.

The article went on to say: 'Naturally, China would now gladly accept any arrangement by which, through the good offices of Great Britain, her ancient position in Tibet would be restored.' The British maintained that 'we have done China a service in arranging the conference, but we have stipulated that the Tibetan and Chinese representatives shall meet on equal terms, and we are not likely to be guilty of tyrannically pressing upon Tibet the acceptance of any relationship with China that the Tibetans do not desire'.

In a report dated 30 August 1913 on the situation in Tibet, the British Legation in Peking said:

The question of the status of the Chinese and Tibetan delegates at the forthcoming conference continued to exercise the minds of the Chinese, and every effort was made to secure the subordination of the Tibetan representative. Finding that His Majesty's Government was firm on this point, however, the President eventually withdrew his objections, and on 7 August a note was received from the Wai Chiao-pu duly recording the appointment of Mr Ivan Chen as Chinese Plenipotentiary for the purpose of concluding an agreement with the British and Tibetan representatives thus *recognizing the tri-partite character* of the negotiations.[14]

It was learnt by Viceroy Lord Hardinge as early as 17 June 1913 that Lonchen Shatra had been earmarked by the Grand Lama to be his representative for the tripartite talks in India, but it was officially announced only some time in July. The Dalai Lama announced that his prime minister, Lonchen Shatra, would be the Tibetan delegate at the convention, and empowered him appropriately. '"The Chief Minister, Shatra Paljor Dorje, is hereby authorised to decide on all questions which may benefit Tibet, and to seal all documents relating thereto". He carried with him the seals of the three monasteries, of the National Assembly and of the Lonchens (ministers), and, on Bell's advice, received later that of the Dalai Lama.'[15] Lonchen Shatra had been part of the Dalai Lama's entourage during the period of his exile in India, and was thus known to McMahon, and more closely to Bell. He was, goes a description, 'a man of great ability and patriotism'; he had seldom travelled outside Tibet and was not a trained diplomat. But he had a charming and dignified presence and displayed 'knowledge of men and a grasp of political affairs that came as a surprise to many at the Conference'.[16] McMahon was highly impressed by the Tibetan plenipotentiary and spoke of his 'simplicity and charm', appreciating at the same time his 'very great shrewdness and capability'. McMahon noted in his final memorandum: 'The Lonchen proved quite his [Chen's] match in debate and political acumen.' These qualities 'endeared' him to all in Simla and Delhi.[17] He was assisted by 'Trimon, who had prepared detailed documentation on the legal status of Tibet, especially of the eastern border areas'.[18]

Both Ivan Chen and Lonchen Shatra were men of charming personality. The former had passed many years of his life in European chancelleries. Courteous and honourable, he did what he could to maintain the attitude of his Government, but remained on terms of personal friendship with us all.[19]

Unsure of the Chinese intentions in eastern Tibet, the Dalai Lama's regime was anxious to see early commencement of the tripartite negotiations. Also, the Tibetan delegation, which included monastic representatives, was more than enthused by the prospect of sitting at the high table as equals of the British and the Chinese. They had arrived in Simla well in time, and evidently were well prepared, armed with voluminous data and documents.

13

The Conference Proceedings

Picturesque Simla, summer capital of the British Indian Empire, has been described as the 'queen of hill stations' in India. Nestled in the south-western ranges of the Himalayas at an average height of 2,400 metres, Simla was in its glory during the first decade of the twentieth century. With the Viceregal Lodge and the GHQ of the British Indian Army co-located there, the Raj, as the British Indian Empire came to be known, was governed from Simla during the summer months. With the presence of the viceroy and his staff and the commander-in-chief of the army and the General Staff, Simla was the most appropriate venue for the historic tripartite conference of the British, Chinese and Tibetan plenipotentiaries in 1913–14. McMahon's task at the conference was facilitated immensely by the advice and guidance, as well as approvals, of the viceroy and the General Staff, who were readily forthcoming with help because of their proximity to the conference. Besides, assistance from the staff of the surveyor general, in terms of provision of constantly updated maps, was an invaluable contribution to the conference deliberations.

In anticipation of heightened political and diplomatic wranglings, Simla began to buzz with spies, efforts at subversion of delegates, intrigues and subterfuge. The main players in these matters were—besides, of course, British India—China, Russia and Japan. Russia wanted to have their consul general moved temporarily to Simla—but was discouraged from doing so on the pretext that he would be required in Calcutta by the Government of Bengal.[1] The Japanese consulate general had their people snooping on the goings-on at the conference. In fact, the plenipotentiaries of both Tibet and China complained to McMahon of the overbearing presence of the Japanese in Simla.

The Chinese were keeping a watch on the proceedings through the collaborators of their secret agent, Lu Hsing-chi, based in Calcutta, as has been explained earlier. He had been occupied with a series of intrigues with the Tibetans and had 'succeeded in introducing Tashi Wangdi as an intelligence officer into Lhasa'.[2] In addition, going by his messages to Wai Chiao-pu, which were intercepted by the British, he seemed to have even won over a member of the Tibetan delegation, thus planting his mole at the conference to keep himself abreast of the latest developments there. Lu Hsing-chi is reported to have advised the Chinese government in the spring of 1914 to send 'small forces' to show their flag in Pomed and Zayul to justify their claim of 'effective occupation' of these areas at the conference. This the Chinese were attempting to do, considering the strategic importance to them of a direct link between Tibet and Yunnan, as highlighted earlier. Reports emanating from the British Legation in Peking also alluded to continuation of the Chinese advance into the Marches, despite the formal denials. The Chinese were therefore warned not to disturb the status quo. At the same time, the Chinese complaints alleging aggressive actions by the Tibetans appeared to have been exaggerated, possibly to create grounds to resume their offensive when the opportunity presented itself.[3] The British, not to be left out, had also been keeping a close watch on the activities of the delegates and other foreigners in Simla. And of course they had been continuously and secretly monitoring all communications and other activities of Lu.

The Simla conference, described by Neville Maxwell, a journalist and a well-known author with a pro-China bias, as *'an exercise in diplomacy, power politics, and espionage* (emphasis added)',[4] commenced on 6 October 1913, although nothing more than introductions and the making of acquaintances occurred on that day. The schedule for the first formal meeting was finalized for 13 October. *'When Tibetan, Chinese and British delegations finally met in the palace of the Maharaja of Darbhanga in Simla on October 6, 1913, the question was who could get most out of whom* (emphasis added),'[5] observed Dorothy Woodman. This palace was the erstwhile 'Wheatfield' house. Today it is a well-known residential school, Tara Hall.

The three plenipotentiaries had been asked, well in advance, to assemble at Simla on 6 October and did in fact meet on that day. This was also the time when the Chinese National Assembly elected Yuan Shih-k'ai as their president and Britain's announcement of its recognition of the newly formed Republic of China was made (on 7 October). It was as if on cue that the British, along with a few other powers who had held back recognition of the Chinese republic as a lever all these days, were conceding it recognition. One can discern a pattern in these developments,[6] but whether this was deliberate or a coincidence is still a matter of conjecture.

First Meeting: Simla, 13 October 1913

The conference proper was set in motion on 13 October with the election of McMahon as president. He welcomed the other two plenipotentiaries and their delegations, and commenced the proceedings with 'interchange' of the appointment warrants issued by the governments concerned. An agreement on the rules and procedures to be followed during the conference was also signed by all the delegates.

Lonchen Shatra, the Tibetan plenipotentiary, then placed on the table the statement of Tibetan claims. This document was prefaced with a historical background of the centuries-old choe-yon (disciple and guru) relationship between the Manchu emperors and the Dalai Lamas. It also highlighted the recent Chinese acts of oppression in Tibet, specially the wanton killing of monks and the laity, and the razing of monasteries and destruction of religious scriptures. The conference then adjourned to study the documents.[7]

The essence of the Tibetan statement was that after the 'defeat' and subsequent 'eviction' of the Chinese from Tibet, *Tibet now had an independent status.* The document comprised six elements:

1. It sought 'Repudiation by Tibet of the Anglo-Chinese Convention, 1906, and recognition of Tibet as independent State'.[8] The material

change in the situation in Tibet and its relations with China after the Chinese Revolution of 1911 was highlighted.

2. The Tibetan claim of the boundary was elaborated. It was based on history, tradition and ethnicity, and comprised areas inhabited by Tibetans. Its alignment was described as follows, 'On the north of the Kuenlung range, the Altyn Tagh, the Tsedam range connecting the Altyn with the Ho Shili range, the Kakang Poto range ... to the border of Kanshu Province of China, then in a southerly and south-easterly direction, including country of ... Nyarong ... Dartsendo, thence in a southerly direction to junction of boundaries of Szechuan and Yunnan, and thence along the boundary of Tibet to Rima.'[9] In other words, this implied that Tibet was laying claim to territories and past revenues of Tibetan-inhabited areas such as the 'district of Kokonor and the March country as far east as Tachienlu'.[10] This issue consumed enormous time and created a fair bit of acrimony between the Tibetans and Chinese during the deliberations.

3. The document contained this statement: 'That Great Britain and Tibet will revise Trade Regulations of 1893 and 1908 in mutual agreement, China having no longer any concern with them.'[11]

4. It emphasized that 'in view of past troubles no Chinese Ambans or other officials and no Chinese soldiers or colonists would be allowed to enter or reside in Tibet, but that Chinese traders be admitted if authorised by Tibetan permits'.[12]

5. The document stipulated that the Dalai Lama should continue to exercise his present rights to 'select the incarnation of the ... Hutukhtu of Urga, and appoint his subordinate Lamas and officials', and the present practice, in which 'the people of Mongolia and Tibet send monks and pay large tribute to monasteries in Tibet and by which Buddhist monasteries and other religious institutions in Mongolia and Tibet recognise Dalai Lama as their religious head should continue'.[13]

6. The final clause related to compensation by China to Tibet 'for all recent forcible extractions of money and property taken from Tibetan Government, for the revenue of Nyarong and other districts, for the destruction of houses and property of monastery officials

and people of Tibet, and for damage done to persons and property of Nepalese and Ladakhis'.[14]

After his arrival in Simla around the beginning of October, and while awaiting commencement of the convention, Lonchen Shatra had probably sounded out or, more likely, taken the informal counsel of McMahon and his aide, Charles Bell, on his opening statement and the overall stand of the Tibetans. He had earlier consulted with Bell at Shigatse while on his way to India. Besides mentioning to Bell the terms the Dalai Lama wanted in the agreement, he had also also shown him letters sent by Chinese officials to the Dalai Lama, pressuring him to negotiate with them at Chamdo.[15] Accordingly, as was evident from his depositions, Shatra adopted a logical, albeit maximalist, approach keeping a reasonable cushion for subsequent bargaining.

The Chinese delegation, not as well prepared as the Tibetans as far as documentary evidence was concerned, responded on 30 October by presenting the Chinese counter-claims. Ivan Chen had rendered a background brief describing the historical ties between the two nations since the seventh century. The brief highlighted, among other things, the military aid provided by the Chinese to evict the Zungarians in 1717, and later the Nepalese, and their payment of the recent indemnity to India as a consequence of the British expedition to Lhasa. The Chinese laid the blame squarely on the Dalai Lama and on his 'intractability' and his 'ignorance of the international situation' for the current state of relations 'between the two peoples'.[16] Refuting the claims of the Tibetans, which Chen dismissed as 'inadmissable', he proceeded to lay down China's demands, stipulating that they were the 'only basis' for the deliberations on Tibet.[17]

The salient aspects of his document were:

1. First and foremost, that 'Tibet forms integral part of territory of the Republic of China. Tibet will respect and Great Britain recognise all existing rights of China due to above territorial integrity.' Also, in the preamble of this document, it had been emphasized that the Chinese

republic '*engages not to convert Tibet into a Chinese province, and Great Britain engages not to annex Tibet or any portion of it* (emphasis added)'.

2. China wanted to retain the right to station an Amban in Lhasa with all 'past privileges and rights, including escort of 2600 Chinese soldiers, of whom 1000 will be in Lhasa and remainder posted where Resident thinks fit'.[18]

3. As far as the 'foreign and military affairs' of Tibet were concerned, Tibet 'undertakes to be guided' by the Chinese and to 'not enter into negotiations with any foreign Powers except through intermediary of Chinese Government'.[19] This would not, it was clarified, apply to British commercial agents on 'matters as are provided for' by the Anglo-Tibetan Convention of 1904 and 'confirmed' by the Anglo-Chinese Convention of 1906.[20]

4. All Tibetans, including officials who had sided with the Chinese and who were facing the wrath of the Dalai Lama, were to be given amnesty, released from prison, and their properties restored.

5. The Chinese were prepared to discuss Clause 5 of the Tibetan claim relating to the Dalai Lama's spiritual authority and religious donations.

6. If required, the Trade Regulations of 1893 and 1908 may be revised by 'all parties concerned', based on 'Article III of Adhesion Convention 1906'.[21] That Convention effectively excluded the Tibetans.

7. Lastly, the Chinese defined the frontier between Tibet and China proper in an accompanying map to their document: 'From Kunlum going south-east to Giamda and then runs southwards to the Tsangpo and follows the river to Gyala, and thence runs roughly in straight line through Menilkrai to N'Maikha river (Burma).'[22] As one can appreciate, this boundary had been illogically and arbitrarily drawn, cutting across mountain ranges, rivers and valleys. This ridiculous and exaggerated claim was without much basis, except for vague assertions based on Chao Erh-feng's forays and escapades, which had perhaps only touched some points along this line. Evidently, McMahon had anticipated cartographic aggression from both sides, but not to such an extent. The east–west claim lines running through

Chiangta/Giamda (Chinese) and Tachienlu (Tibetan) were almost 1,600 kilometres apart (Figure 8)![23]

Second Meeting: Simla, 18 November 1913

After examining the claims of both sides, McMahon convened the second meeting of the conference on 18 November. However, he neither had an approved draft of the convention that he could place before the plenipotentiaries nor a clear idea of the southern limits of Tibet along the eastern Himalayas, as some of the important survey reports had not yet come in. The draft prepared earlier, in March 1913, by the India Office did not cater for a tripartite meeting, as initially the deliberations were envisaged to be bilateral, without the participation of the Tibetans.

Between the north-eastern corner of Bhutan and the tri-junction of India, Tibet and Burma, there remained many unsurveyed 'grey' areas along the frontier of over 1,000 kilometres. Often shrouded in mist or clouds, this area had virgin, snow-covered mountains, which neither afforded easy access nor allowed for their positions to be fixed, particularly from the south, using the rudimentary survey equipment carried by the explorers of those times. Reports of the latest reconnaissance and survey carried out by Captains Bailey and Morshead and other inputs were anxiously awaited so that the existing maps could be updated. So McMahon continued to put up appearances to avoid giving the impression that he was intentionally delaying the proceedings, while at the same time acting as an 'honest broker'.

McMahon opened the conference by sharing his dilemma with his colleagues. He laid on the table a skeleton map, on which the widely divergent boundary claims of both sides were marked. He was 'at a loss as to what was really Tibet'. He forthrightly conveyed to the Chinese and the Tibetans that it would not be possible to proceed further without an agreement on the 'limits of Tibet'. Lonchen Shatra agreed with him, but Ivan Chen insisted on discussing the first two clauses of the Chinese document—relating to the status of Tibet and positioning of their Amban with an escort at Lhasa. Besides, Chen had no desire to discuss areas east of Batang as those were, according to his contention, part of

China. He laboured hard on his position, stating that he was acting on specific instructions from his government. He also said he was under clear instructions not to discuss the issue of compensation at all.[24]

Eventually, McMahon ended the debate by suggesting that the two sides hold informal meetings, iron out their differences and submit their claims so that he could form an opinion on them. At that stage, Chen said he would have to refer back to Peking for directions. In the meanwhile, to save time, McMahon proposed that he would continue discussions on the 'limits of Tibet' with the Tibetan plenipotentiary, although he would have preferred to do so with the Chinese delegate too present. Lonchen urged McMahon to share the revised claims and additional evidence of Tibetan claims with Ivan Chen *at the same time as the latter communicated the Chinese evidence to him, and not before* (emphasis added)'. McMahon and Ivan Chen gave their assent to this request.[25] After this meeting had concluded, Chen claimed illness and took to bed! McMahon appreciated that China would be uncomfortable with the idea of Britain's bilateral parleys with the Tibetans, and would soon acquiesce to addressing the limits of Tibet. Not surprisingly, within a few days, on 23 November, the Chinese authorized Chen to enter into negotiations on the boundary.

Keeping in mind the severe Simla winter and the fact that life almost came to a standstill here because of the copious snow and near-freezing temperatures, the venue of the conference was shifted to Delhi after the second meeting on 18 November. During their stay in Simla, the Chinese delegation had been accommodated in a cottage named 'Oakover', and the Tibetan delegation housed in a bungalow named 'Mythe'.[26] As in Simla, where 'comfortable homes' had been provided to the delegations by the British government, suitable accommodation was arranged for them in Delhi too.

Informal Meetings: Delhi, December 1913

The month of December 1913 was largely spent on a series of informal discussions between the Chinese and Tibetan delegates, moderated by McMahon's able assistants, Bell and Rose, in the salubrious Delhi winter. McMahon believed that such discussions would allow the two plenipotentiaries to evolve the 'best method of dealing with the intricate question of the frontiers'[27] while helping him gain the much-needed time to finalize the memorandum in consultation with Whitehall.

The first of these informal meetings took place on 5 December in Delhi at the request of Ivan Chen, who suggested that these 'free and informal discussions' should not be minuted, and that the decisions arrived at not be considered binding, until they had been confirmed at a formal meeting of the conference. This was agreed to by all.[28] Thereafter, Chen proposed that the area under dispute between the Tibetan and Chinese claims should be discussed on 'broad and general lines'. After some discussion, both sides concurred on this. Lonchen Shatra then announced that he would ask for a meeting as soon as the Tibetan archives fetched up and he was ready with his brief.

Shatra called for the next meeting on 11 December, during which the two plenipotentiaries highlighted 'their general cases for the frontiers claimed by their respective Governments'.[29] It was clear that both sides had only reiterated their earlier stands and neither was prepared to concede any ground. Ivan Chen claimed that since the 'time of the Mongol Dynasty (13th century)' and until 1911, during the rule of the Manchus, China had 'maintained an effective occupation of the country'. This conferred on China a 'substantive right in international law'. The Chinese territorial claim extended 'as far west as Giamda (Chiangta), and included the districts of Pomed, Zayul, Markham, Derge, Draya and Gyade'.

Shatra countered Chen by saying: '*Tibet had always been an independent country* (emphasis added).' Tibet had fought wars with China, and on one occasion a Chinese princess was given in marriage to the Tibetan monarch. A pillar exists at Marugang near Kokonor marking the boundary line, which touches the well-known bend of the Yellow River and goes down to Chorten Karpo in the vicinity of Tachienlu. Though titles were given by the Chinese to some border princes, the administration and collection of revenues and taxes in the country was always in Tibetan hands. After Shatra had had his say, it was decided that deliberations on these issues should be scheduled for the next day and continued on subsequent days, whenever any side wished to present 'evidence in support of their claims'.[30]

On 12 December, as the meeting progressed, it became obvious that the focus had begun to shift from definition of the boundary to the 'political status' of the border region. Chen, quoting from a book authored by a Chinese Amban at Lhasa, emphasized that a boundary pillar had been erected along the Ching Ning range in 1727 about 125 miles (201 kilometres) west of Batang. It had an inscription in Chinese, saying, 'The country to the east is Chinese, the country to the west of it Tibetan.'[31] This was dismissed by Lonchen Shatra, who said he 'could not accept the evidence of a book which appeared to have no official authority'. He had proof that land titles of areas east of the pillar were granted by Lhasa authorities, who also administered the country inhabited by Tibetans extending to Tachienlu.[32] The dichotomy of the Chinese position was clearly discernible. On one hand, Chen was emphasizing that Batang was the historical boundary, and on the other advancing the Chinese frontier westwards to Giamda near Lhasa.

During the next meeting on 15 December, Ivan Chen, in order to buttress his claims, read out excerpts of John Jordan's statement in an interview at the Wai Chiao-pu (Chinese Foreign Office) on 30 January 1913, saying that, according to Sir Alexander Hosie, the boundary pillar had been placed in the vicinity of Batang during emperor Kang Hsi's rule.[33] Chen went on to emphasize that although this pillar was a 'historical boundary-mark' the Chinese claim did not rest at that, and in fact their territories had been extended further west by Chao Erh-feng. Chen was resting his case heavily on the account in General Fu Sung-mu's book highlighting the 'frontier campaigns' of Chao Erh-feng, and also on books by foreign authors like Thomas Holditch, an English geographer and author. To this, Lonchen retorted sharply that 'Chao's campaigns were rather in the nature of illegal raids than recognized conquests'.[34] He demanded that documentary evidence be furnished by Chen to admit the validity of his claim.

When Lonchen Shatra was asked by Rose to produce evidence in support of the frontier pillars at Marugong and Chorten Kaspo (sic) mentioned in his statement, he proceeded to lay on the table copies of the Tibetan inscriptions on the pillars signifying the Sino-Tibetan Treaty of AD 822. Besides, Lonchen also cited an 'original reference' to these inscriptions in a book compiled by the fifth Dalai Lama on the history of Tibet, titled 'The Golden Tree of the Index of the Sole Ornament of the World' (Dzo-dan-zhonui Gaton Serdang Dzamling Gyanchig-gyi Karchap).[35]

Lonchen Shatra agreed to provide translations of these inscriptions during the next meeting.

McMahon was content to allow these deliberations over a better part of December so that Whitehall had adequate time to consider his draft convention of 10 November. Besides, the vast spatial 'divergence' of the Chinese and Tibetan claims, which had been accompanied by a lot of wrangling and browbeating, did not offer much hope for resolution. This dead end, McMahon inferred, would allow both sides to get 'disheartened' with their respective stands and become more amenable to the 'inevitable compromise'.[36] The final informal meeting was called for on 19 December by the British representative. The discussions focused on the status of Nyarong and Derge, but Chen refused to discuss the subject as these places lay east of Batang. Instead, he was prepared to discuss Gyade and Gyamda, but Lonchen Shatra was not.

Since the discussions were not making much headway even after several meetings, Chen proposed that both sides should hand over their 'complete evidence' regarding the frontier to the British plenipotentiary at the next meeting of the full conference. After examination of all the evidence, McMahon could then convey his opinion to his colleagues for their consideration. Both sides agreed on this, much to the relief of McMahon, who was grappling with the impasse caused by the vastly exaggerated, uncompromising and unreasonable stands of the two parties. The British team also felt that agreement to the proposed Indo-Tibetan frontier (to cover as much of the frontier as time permitted) should be obtained from the Tibetans before McMahon gave his opinions on the Tibet–China boundary.[37]

The conference then adjourned and the plenipotentiaries took a break. Taking advantage of the Christmas holidays, Ivan Chen motored by road to Agra and other places of interest, and Lonchen Shatra decided to go on a pilgrimage to a Buddhist shrine. Both agreed to submit their comprehensive boundary claims in writing by 2 January, and with this the informal meetings came to an end.[38]

McMahon had a monumental challenge ahead of him. He had to work out a solution that would satisfy the two contending parties while also keeping the best interests of the British Empire and the recent international events uppermost in mind. He had to keep in mind the

Russo-Mongol Treaty of 1912, the Tibet–Mongol Treaty of 11 January 1913 (although not convincingly documented) and the Sino-Russia Treaty of 5 November 1913. He was aware that the Tibetan historical claims to Kokonor and other areas along the Marches down to Tachienlu were well substantiated with documentary evidence. However, the report dated 27 October 1913 of Louis King, the British intelligence officer positioned at Chengtu/Tachienlu to keep the Indian government informed of Chinese actions and other developments in the Marches, clearly indicated that Chinese presence and control in the Marches was more 'substantial' than what was accepted by the British.

Under these circumstances, McMahon, with his vast experience and deeper understanding of the strategic dimensions of such a dispute, came up with the brilliant idea of creating two zones in Tibet. The core area of Tibet proper, extending up to Chiamdo, which was both politically and geographically under greater control of Lhasa, was to be called *Outer Tibet*; this region would enjoy a large degree of autonomy. The remainder of extended Tibet, inhabited mostly by Tibetans and encompassed within the boundaries claimed by Lonchen Shatra, of areas up to Kokonor, Batang and Tachienlu, and matching with the frontiers of the Chinese provinces of Xinjiang, Szechuan and Yunnan, would comprise *Inner Tibet*. Not akin to a Chinese province, Inner Tibet would see the Dalai Lama and the principal monasteries being permitted to exercise only religious control, whereas the Chinese would be free to 'station officials, establish colonies and send troops there'.[39]

This idea was apparently modelled on the zoning done by Russia in the case of Mongolia during 1912–13. McMahon's reasoning and logic was sound and in consonance with the underlying British strategic thought. This step would *'perpetuate and safeguard Tibetan (and, indirectly, British) interests in Inner Tibet* (emphasis added)',[40] and also create a buffer around Tibet proper. Further, by including Chiamdo and Zayul in Outer Tibet, McMahon had endeavoured to secure an effective barrier between the frontier of north-east India and China. A tranquil border in north-east India with Tibet would prevent any friction between the British and Chinese Empires. However, the president of the conference did not share this idea of zoning with the other two plenipotentiaries till much later.

Chamdo assumes strategic importance not only because it is an important communication hub but also because this region controls the main road, known as 'Janglam', from Peking to Lhasa, and some other routes. This area also dominates a number of difficult high-altitude passes and, in McMahon's words, 'is of greatest strategic importance between the Chinese headquarters and Lhasa'. Therefore, it came as no surprise when Chamdo emerged as a serious bone of contention between the Tibetans and the Chinese as the convention progressed.

Third Meeting: Delhi, 12 January 1914

Having analysed the two detailed claims, McMahon called for a full conference. Accordingly, the third meeting was held at Delhi on 12 January 1914. The specific purpose of this event was to give an opportunity to the Chinese and Tibetan plenipotentiaries to produce and present 'statements of the evidence in regard to the respective frontiers claimed by them'.[41] That having been accomplished, copies of the documents were then exchanged. It must be admitted that (as recorded in the proceedings) the Tibetans had brought to the conference a huge lot of records and documents (over ninety), many of which were in their original form. Amongst the important documents were 'three original prints from the Lhasa Doring (stone pillar) showing both Chinese and Tibetan characters'.[42] These were supported by Chinese, English and Tibetan translations. Going by the Tibetan records presented at the conference, this pillar was erected 'about 1020 years ago', as a consequence of Tibetan victories during the reign of King Nga-dag Tri-ral. He had 'overrun several Chinese provinces and cities', and a peace treaty was finally concluded using the good offices of important Chinese Hoshangs (Buddhist priests) and Tibetan lamas. Another document contained an extract from the fifth Dalai Lama's book, *Dzo-dan Zhon-nui Ga-ton* ('Delightful Feast for the Youth'). It was in block print and described the 'setting up of the Doring (pillar)', and the defining of the Sino-Tibet boundary from Merugang near Sining, going southwards to the well-known bend of the 'Ma-chu (Huang Ho) river' and finally joining 'Chortenkarpo', which was in the close vicinity of 'Ya-chao in Szechuan'.[43]

The Chinese representative stated that he and Lonchen Shatra had had five informal meetings on the Tibetan boundary since the last time the conference met at Simla. Being unable to arrive at any definitive conclusion on the Sino-Tibet frontier, they had agreed to hand over their claims for Sir McMahon's 'consideration and decision'. On receipt of his decision, they would convey it to their respective governments and seek directions.[44]

Ivan Chen then placed on the table his statement of evidence to support the Chinese claims in Tibet. The areas claimed by the Chinese to the west of the historical boundary line that existed from 1727 to 1910, which ran in the north–south direction through Bum La on the Yangtze–Mekong watershed near Batang, were the areas where the short-lived raids (as the Tibetans referred to them) or 'conquests' of Chao Erh-feng were made during 1910–11. The prominent among these areas were Giamda (Chiangta), Shobando, Lhojong, Gyade, Dam, Pomed (Poyul), Pemakoi-chen, Zayul, Darge, Riwoche, Enta, Chamdo, Gartok, Draya, Markham, and Tenk'e, some of them being the newly proposed districts of Hsikang province, the brainchild of Chao. Providing only broad justification—and little by way of original documentary evidence—for including these areas in China, Ivan Chen mentioned the 'historic connections' and 'effective occupation' of all these places, which would sanctify Chinese claims by international law.

What he did not admit was that the Chinese had been evicted from most places west of Batang and the Mekong–Salween watershed by 1912 in the aftermath of the Revolution of 1911. The Chinese statement dealt with each region and advanced maximalist claims, some of them unsubstantiated or even incorrect. For example, it stated that Zayul was entirely 'outside the pale of Tibetan control', whereas in actual fact, on arrival for the first time in history at Rima in 1910, the Chinese had evicted the Tibetan Dzongpons who were till then controlling the villages near Rima extending to the southernmost limit—the Tibetan village of Sama. Beyond that lay the Mishmi tribal territory under the control of British India, its control exercised through the political officer based at Sadiya, Assam. The Chinese statement also recorded the passing of a bill by the National Assembly in Peking in 1912 making areas west of the historical

Sino-Tibet boundary the 'eighth division of the Parliamentary election districts of Szechuan'.[45]

The list of these districts, along with their Chinese names ending with Fu, Chow, Ting or Hien (also called Hsien), was appended to the statement. The bill's relevance is questionable, as by 1912 Chinese power and presence in Tibet had already begun to dissipate, and by early 1913 had almost disappeared; there were no Chinese left in Tibet proper for the first time in many centuries. It is significant that the Chinese side did not produce any authentic historical map (other than from the Tang dynasty period) that included the claimed territories or the claimed Sino-Tibet boundary, and relied heavily on a book by General Fu Sung-mu, Chao Erh-feng's successor, and a book on Tibet authored by the Chinese Amban, Sung of Lhasa. According to Sung, there existed a pillar at Nyin-jin Shan-lin, the mountain range that forms the Yangtze–Mekong divide. This had an inscription of eight characters defining the boundary; it read: *East of this is China, west of this is Tibet* (emphasis added).'[46]

In fact, the intercepted telegram of Lu Hsing-chi of 30 October 1913 to the military governor, Hu, and administrator Yin at Chengdu read: 'If you have any detailed maps of the Tibetan frontier or other documentary proof, please send them as soon as possible by insured post.'[47] This reveals the paucity of original documents with the Chinese to support their claims. Another secret telegram from Lu Hsing-chi to the Chinese cabinet on 13 November 1913 exposes the Chinese frontier strategy: 'As regards boundaries, if we can use as proof the map prepared by Fu Sung-mu, former Warden of the Marches, which shows Chiang-ta [Giamda] as the frontier, *not only shall we be able to include several thousand li extra but every important strategical point will come into our possession* (emphasis added).'[48]

Expectedly, there was a robust rejection of the Chinese claims in the Tibetan statement on 'Limits of Tibet' tabled by Lonchen Shatra. This consisted of a voluminous set of documents, some of them duly translated into English, as concrete and empirical evidence of the Tibetan claim to their historical boundary comprising areas inhabited by Tibetan people, who were Buddhists sharing the same culture, language and way of life, and comprising also certain tribal areas under Tibetan control. One of the documents says: 'These places formed part of Tibet during the reigns of the several successive righteous kings of the old dynasty, and after that of the Incarnate Chen-re-zi Drogon Phagpa and nineteen generations of the Sakya Hierarch's line, and after them Desrid Phagdru and ten successive rulers of his line, three generations of Rimpung Chogyal and three generations of Tsangpa Gyalpo.'[49] The line claimed by the Tibetans extended up to Tachienlu (Dartsendo) in the east.

The Tibetan statement had seven descriptive parts, each being a brief historical sketch providing details of the relevant areas, along with the original documents and records. All of this made out a strong case for Tibet and at the same time effectively rebutted the Chinese claims. Among the records were fifty-six different registers, containing details such as 'numbers of monasteries, houses or families, both religious and secular according to doorsteps and fireplaces, amount of income and expenditure, etc.'. In these areas, by and large, *the writ of the Dalai Lama was unquestioned* and it was His Holiness who appointed both the high lamas and the administrative officials and issued 'all the warrants, deeds, patents and orders'. Moreover, the people were obliged to provide free labour, transport and riding ponies to the Tibetan officials. Various monasteries were required to send 'noviciate monks to Sera, Drepung and Ganden monasteries and regular periodical money tributes to the Dalai Lama'. The Tibetan statement highlights the cruel, vengeful, high-handed, irreligious (anti-Buddhist) and unforgiving attitude of Chao Erh-feng and his 'scorched-earth, pillage and plunder' policy that earned him the nickname of 'butcher Chao'. He had destroyed several temples and villages by setting fire to them without any provocation and massacred many hundreds of Lamas and lay people. He plundered gold, silver, rare bronze images and many other priceless treasures and relics. He cast the bronze and copper offering vessels of worship into bullets and small coins. The most sacrilegious of all his acts of vandalism was to have paper soles for shoes made out of leaves of sacred Buddhist scriptures which contained the teachings of the Lord Buddha.[50]

Objectively viewed, however, Chao Erh-feng could be described as a ruthless but successful military leader who was a visionary in strategic terms. A strict disciplinarian, he is known to have executed a number of his own soldiers too for insubordination or for mutiny. With a relatively small force, his campaigns bore spectacular results, and his overall achievements are legendary. None of his successors came anywhere close to him, as leaders, tacticians or achievers.

The Tibetans emphatically rebutted the Chinese claims, particularly those based on Chao's so-called conquests, saying that

> Chao Erh-feng had been guilty of such glaring misdeeds and that even if he had a hundred lives he should forfeit every one of them to the law ... to base their claim on his raids as conquests and call it incontrovertible proof of just claim, it is like trying to swallow a living person—an impossible feat ...[51]

By the end of his examination of the hotly contested territorial claims by the two sides, McMahon was convinced that the best way to resolve the matter was to divide the 'enlarged Tibet'—based on history, culture, religion, tradition and the claims put forward by Lonchen Shatra—into two parts, *Outer Tibet* and *Inner Tibet*, as explained earlier (Figure 17).

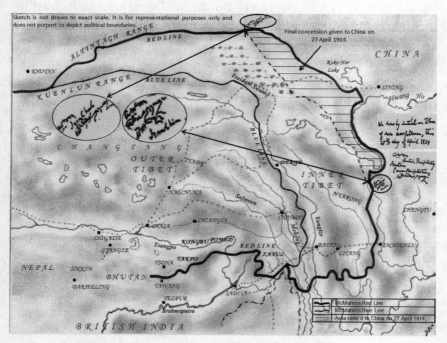

Figure 17: Proposed division into 'Inner' and 'Outer' Tibet:
McMahon's red and blue lines (1914)

Regarding their political status, McMahon had not been able to finalize the extent of autonomy to be accorded to Inner Tibet, whereas Outer Tibet would be fully autonomous and under temporal and spiritual control of the Dalai Lama, with minimal presence of the Chinese, although it too would remain under China's suzerainty. However, McMahon was clear that Inner Tibet *should not* be allowed to be converted into a regular Chinese province, and short of that the Chinese could do as they pleased. In his opinion, the Batang boundary pillar would be the most appropriate point on the Inner–Outer Tibet boundary line, which could follow the Yangtze–Mekong divide in the north–south direction. This would also ensure that the strategic node of Chamdo remained within autonomous Tibet. But this strategy would mean ceding the areas of Nyarong and Derge, two of the most productive districts of Tibet and Kokonor region, to Inner Tibet, in an effort to placate China. From a geopolitical and strategic point of view, McMahon had created the buffer of autonomous Outer Tibet between British India and the Chinese republic, particularly along the north-eastern frontier of India, as also between British India and the Russian Empire in the north-west. Evidently, this formula was based largely on the Mongolian model.

The British government did not have an issue with the division of Tibet into inner and outer zones. The viceroy proposed the division on 18 December 1913, and Whitehall gave its approval without loss of much time, on 6 January 1914.[52] While doing so, Whitehall's telegram from the secretary of state cautioned the viceroy: 'Tibetan position in non-autonomous zone will have to be clearly defined, and we should avoid incurring responsibility in respect of that area. Importance of including Zayul in autonomous zone will not be overlooked.'[53] However, the home government took its time to go through the draft convention. It was at this stage that McMahon decided to define the southern limits of Tibet, keeping in mind this boundary's impact on the security of the north-eastern frontier of British India, including north Burma. Having already received the valuable survey report of Captains Bailey and Morshead, McMahon asked Bell to carry out detailed discussions with Lonchen Shatra and his team to delineate this boundary on the map.

Fourth Meeting: Delhi, 17 February 1914

The British government's amendment to the draft convention dated 14 February 1914 was received by telegraph immediately before the fourth meeting of the conference on 17 February. McMahon conducted the discussions on the basis of the guidelines contained in it.[54] Having meticulously analysed the evidence produced by China and Tibet at the last conference, McMahon laid on the table the British understanding of the 'limits of Tibet', along with a skeleton map showing the 'historic Tibetan frontiers', indicated by a *red line,* and the supporting records made available by the Chinese and Tibetan sides. The British statement enunciated the rationale for division of Tibet into two zones, mentioning the Treaty of AD 822 and certain maps going back to the Chinese Tang dynasty period, and traced the historical events leading to the contemporary state of affairs at the time of the conference.[55]

To end the 'state of war' that existed between the two sides, the map also drew the proposed boundary between Tibet and China in a *blue line*; east of it lay the 'sphere of periodical Chinese intervention in Tibet', and west of it lay the 'sphere in which Chinese dictation was of a purely nominal nature' and the unquestionable writ of the Dalai Lama prevailed.[56] It was McMahon's design that greater Tibet retained to a reasonable degree its political and geographical identity, and that China was allowed to restore its 'historic position' in areas forming part of Inner Tibet. In this manner he put paid to the Chinese plans to incorporate eastern Tibet and the Marches into the new Hsikang province.

McMahon's dispensation of Inner and Outer Tibet and the boundary between them was vehemently opposed by both the Chinese and Tibetan delegates, and they conveyed their opposition to him in 'notes verbale' on 7 March. The Chinese were not prepared to accept the concept of Inner and Outer Tibet or to concede any areas brought under the Chinese yoke even briefly as a result of Chao Erh-feng's campaigns. The Chinese claim was ridiculously exaggerated and oblivious of ground reality; it extended to Chiangta (Giamda) near Lhasa. Further, the Chinese were only prepared to concede 'a limited Tibetan autonomy in a loosely defined area ... in the immediate vicinity of Lhasa'. On Tibet's part, it demanded inclusion of areas in eastern Tibet, such as Batang and Litang, on the basis of the clinching evidence furnished by their plenipotentiary, and also refused to accept many Tibetan-inhabited areas that were under no kind of control of the Chinese, as part of Inner Tibet.[57]

As communicated in Sir John Jordan's despatch number 131 of 2 April 1913:

The Chinese claim to the Chiangta frontier appears to have been based on a recommendation by Chao Erh-feng in the spring of 1911, but even in the heyday of his advance, Chao never succeeded in securing any effective Chinese administration beyond a point between Derge and Chamdo, as is shown by the Chinese evidence contained in General Fu Sung-mu's book on the Marches.[58]

This has been aptly elaborated on in Alston's memorandum of 30 August 1913:

The historic Chinese frontier, as marked by the boundary stone of A.D. 1727, follows the Ching Ning Range just west of Batang, and is shown by a red line on the accompanying map. The dotted red line is considered by the Government of India as the extreme limit to which the Chinese could be allowed to advance towards the West without serious prejudice to the territorial integrity of Tibet and the safety of the North-East frontier of India. The Chinese show a persistent tendency to secure the submission of Pomed and Zayul, but they can show no historical claim, nor any claim by conquest, to these two districts which are entirely beyond the bounds of their control.[59]

The Chinese intrigues in the Marches, at Chamdo, and in the Pomed region were aimed at scuttling the forthcoming conference in India by trying to reach some sort of an agreement with the Tibetans directly.

In a note to Earl of Crewe, the Secretary of State for India, on 3 June 1913, Viceroy Lord Hardinge emphasized:

I do not agree with Jordan's view that, by showing weakness to the Chinese, we have a better chance of getting mining and railway concessions. The experience of the Russians is just the reverse. They have bullied the Chinese over Mongolia, and they are getting all the railway concessions they want from there.[60]

Interestingly, while refuting the Tibetan claims based on tax collections from areas administered by Lhasa, the Chinese delegate stressed that the Dalai Lama's spiritual authority 'should not be confused' with the temporal; the taxes paid to the Tibetans by the various tribes in Hsikang were merely contributions to the monasteries, 'rather charity, than tax'.[61] On 9 March 1914, McMahon categorically rebutted Ivan Chen's statement and deputed Rose to convey his rationale in formulating the *blue line* in person to Chen. Yet it had become obvious to McMahon that the discussions had stalemated and that they were almost back to square one! Something needed to be done urgently. In the meanwhile, he had also received reports of armed clashes in the Marches between the Tibetans and the Chinese. Accordingly, he called for a meeting of the full conference on 11 March.

Fifth Meeting: Delhi, 11 March 1914

At the onset of this meeting, McMahon conveyed a warning to Ivan Chen and Lonchen Shatra of the grave consequences of the unabated hostilities and endeavours to change the 'status quo' along the frontier of eastern Tibet. The armistice was being violated by both sides and had to be put an end to. Neither side accepted the charges, but accusations flew back and forth. Thereafter, McMahon placed on the table the draft convention approved by Whitehall, with certain provisions ingeniously inserted to provide for leeway and bargaining space. He exhorted his colleagues to display statesmanship and an accommodative approach, stressing on the need for 'prompt and decisive action' to bring the onerous task entrusted to them to its culmination.

In keeping with the established Chinese strategem of protracted negotiations, Ivan Chen desired to know if it wasn't premature to discuss the draft convention before the broad principles had been accepted by all parties. He had not yet received assent from China, he said. McMahon dismissed this remark, insisting that, in view of the *grave situation* in the Marches, the matter had to be dealt with expeditiously, although acceptance of the general principles by all concerned was unexceptionable. It had come to the notice of the British government that Lu Hsing-chi, the Chinese intelligence operative at Calcutta, was behind the obstructive and non-cooperative attitude adopted by China during the proceedings. Unknown to him, all his secret communications from Calcutta to Peking and other places were being intercepted by the British, and a careful watch was being kept on his activities. On 10 July 1913, Lu Hsing-chi claimed that he had been appointed as 'Officiating Chinese Resident in Lhasa'. This was unacceptable to the British Indian government. In view of his intrigues and other subversive activities, he was administered a warning on 30 July that 'any attempt to carry out the duties of Amban would result in his deportation from India'.[62] Writing about Lu's role, McMahon said:

> Lu advised his government that McMahon felt that the internal situation in India made it impossible for us [India] to force upon China any agreement that was distasteful to her, and he [Lu] urged upon them a categorical refusal of our demands at Delhi and a direct appeal to His Majesty's Government.[63]

Peking did precisely as Lu advised, and on 20 March, McMahon was informed by Ivan Chen that his government had *virtually rejected* the entire draft convention. Simultaneously, representations were made both in London and Peking by the Chinese authorities demanding a better deal than the Simla conference was offering them. They were informed that the 'legitimate interests' of the three countries would be taken care of.

McMahon responded to Ivan Chen on 26 March, urging the Chinese to keep in mind the present ground realities in Tibet and work in a constructive manner towards a mutually acceptable solution. He warned that in the absence of such cooperation he would be compelled to 'withdraw' the draft convention and the 'accompanying map', and to 'lay before the Conference proposals of a different nature'.[64] This warning unnerved the Chinese to some extent, and they displayed unease at the prospect of the conference being called off, which might perhaps result in an Anglo-Tibetan accord to the exclusion of China. The upsurge of activities of the Chinese in the frontier region at this time could be ascribed to this apprehension.

Sixth Meeting: Simla, 7 April 1914

At the behest of Ivan Chen, a sixth meeting was called on 7 April 1914, during which the latest Chinese proposal was presented. Disregarding the actual conditions in Tibet, the Chinese again changed the goalposts, which they referred to as their final concessions: China's western boundary was now shifted back from Giamda to the Salween river; east of this river, all territory would be part of China to all intents and purposes. China further claimed that all of Tibet 'west of the Salween shall be within the limits of the autonomy of Tibet, provided it is agreed that Tibet forms a portion of the territory of the Republic of China just the same as Outer Mongolia'.[65]

Succinctly summed up, the Chinese version of the boundary would hive off a large part of greater Tibet comprising Kokonor region, parts of Amdo, Gyade, Derge, Nyarong and Chamdo regions, Markham, Batang and areas east of it up to Tachienlu, and eastern Kham, in favour of China. It was evident that this dispensation would not be acceptable to the other two parties. At the end of another frustrating round of discussions, McMahon had a private tête-à-tête with Ivan Chen. After covering the course of the deliberations of the past six months and once again emphasizing the need for a mature understanding of the challenges involved in arriving at a 'settlement which would prove equitable to the three countries concerned', McMahon in no uncertain terms blamed the Chinese for the breakdown of the convention. Thereupon he decided to 'suspend' all interaction with Chen till such time as the Chinese side adopted a more reasonable stand. McMahon asked Rose to try and convince Chen as best he could, and also convey to him that the final meeting of the conference was being scheduled for 14 April, and would be of a 'conclusive nature'.[66]

In Peking too, Jordan exhorted the Wai Chiao-pu to see reason and 'show the same magnanimity' that the British had displayed in Lhasa in 1904, particularly in view of confirmation that had been recently received from Louis King, an intelligence officer who had been stationed in the Marches, that 'the Chinese had never at any time received any revenues from the districts west of Chiamdo',[67] implying that the Chinese claims to those areas were baseless.

However, one day prior to the final meeting, Ivan Chen appealed to the Foreign Office to postpone the meeting by a few days so that he could obtain further directions from Peking. His request was granted, with a clear understanding that at the next meeting on 22 April, the draft convention, along with the map that was presented on 17 February, would be placed before the conference for final approval and acceptance by the three delegates. A warning was also conveyed to Ivan Chen that if he failed to initial the above-mentioned documents, the entire proposal would be withdrawn. Ivan again requested for some concessions regarding the boundary, and McMahon, in an effort to take the proceedings forward, indicated he was prepared to offer 'exclusion from Tibet of the Lake of Kokonor and the towns of Tachienlu and Atuntze'.[68]

Soon the Chinese appeared to have had a change of heart, and their attitude suddenly became more purposeful as they did not want a 'rupture' of the conference. Chen spent about ten hours at the Foreign Office in serious deliberations, going over the draft convention 'clause by clause'. Besides deletion of the indemnity clause, there was only some minor rephrasing of the text to make it sound more acceptable to the Wai Chiao-pu, and save face for China amongst the international community.[69]

Despite these back-breaking efforts, at the last minute the Chinese put another spanner in the works by making *five new demands*. These related to the proposed Sino-Tibetan boundary, specifically the limits and status of Tibet, which continued to be the main 'stumbling block'. The Chinese, giving in incrementally, were now prepared to accept the Salween as their boundary with Tibet, but made some other vague and unreasonable demands. These, in brief, were:

- Areas west of the Salween up to Giamda to have a level of autonomy that is different from the autonomy recognized for the core of Tibet around Lhasa (another red herring);
- East of Salween, as well as Kokonor region, to be sovereign China;
- Lastly, the Amdo region of thirty-nine tribes to remain autonomous but under loose Chinese control.

Despite McMahon's (and others') patience having been stretched to breaking point, McMahon acted maturely, agreeing to put these conditions on the agenda for the next day's meeting.

Seventh Meeting: Simla, 22–27 April 1914

Although McMahon was clear in his mind that the conference was heading towards a dead end, he put up a brave front, believing that they were entering a decisive phase of the deliberations. Beginning with a résumé of the proceedings thus far, he drew the attention of the other two plenipotentiaries to the draft convention and the attached map, and asked them if they were prepared to initial them. Ivan Chen gave a negative response, on the grounds that the fresh demands made by his government were yet to be discussed. Lonchen Shatra replied that, considering the Chinese attitude, he could not be a party to an accord that would make Tibet sacrifice the prosperous districts of Derge and Nyarong and reinstate the Chinese Amban at Lhasa. The theatricals culminated in McMahon ordering the draft convention to be 'withdrawn'. And, to the consternation of the other two colleagues, '*it was removed from the table with as much ceremony as possible* (emphasis added)'.[70]

Ivan Chen realized that he had probably made a miscalculation and that McMahon had not been making idle threats after all. However, much to the relief of the participants, McMahon announced that the conference was being adjourned for a day as he desired to give them one final chance to reconsider their stand. He also clarified that '*the withdrawal of the Convention would not be absolute till the meeting actually terminated* (emphasis added)'.[71]

Considering the fervent appeal by Ivan Chen to be provided another opportunity for consultations with the Wai Chiao-pu, McMahon agreed to reschedule the meeting after five days. The discussions were renewed on 27 April. The Chinese government's latest instructions had been received by Ivan Chen only the previous evening. The Chinese had *generally accepted* the articles of the draft convention and the principles enunciated in it, *but for Article IX relating to the boundary* (China-Tibet). On this issue they insisted that their new demands be met, and Ivan

Chen refused to initial the documents. He was then asked to retire to an adjacent room while McMahon, in a last-ditch attempt, asked Lonchen Shatra if a tract in the region of Kokonor lake could be excluded from Inner Tibet and made a part of China proper, and if it was acceptable that representation of Tibetans in the Chinese National Assembly would not apply to Outer Tibet. On getting Lonchen Shatra's nod, both the draft convention and the accompanying map were duly modified and initialled by McMahon and Lonchen Shatra. On a closer examination of the map, one cannot fail to notice that a large strip of land in the vicinity of Kokonor lake and adjacent areas of Amdo and upper Huang Ho Valley had been sliced from Inner Tibet and made a part of China proper. This amendment of the boundary line was apparently carried out on 27 April itself, and had been initialled/signed and authenticated at both ends by the three plenipotentiaries, as shown in Figure 16 (in the case of Ivan Chen and Lonchen Shatra, one can notice their full signatures, which have been circled for emphasis). This area included the famous monastery of Kumbum near Sining, and was a substantial *final concession* given to China, in the hope that it would induce the Chinese plenipotentiary to come on board. That concession ploy indeed worked as intended.

Rose was then assigned the task of explaining to Chen the latest concessions offered by the Tibetans, as also the ramifications of China not initialling the convention. Most importantly, Rose told him, there was a distinct possibility of China losing its place in the tripartite conference and an Anglo-Tibetan accord being signed, excluding the Chinese. Thereafter, he left Ivan alone to contemplate what he had said and to deliberate over the documents already initialled by McMahon and Lonchen Shatra. Eventually, Ivan made up his mind to initial both the draft and the map. He re-entered the conference chamber and, much to the relief of all who were present, proceeded to complete the formalities. But not without a cautionary statement, according to an account: 'He would feel bound to await definite authority from his Government before the Convention was formally signed and sealed.'[72] (It needs to be pointed out that even on the documents which had to be initialled, the full signatures of Ivan Chen and Lonchen Shatra are clearly discernible.) At last, without any doubt, the concurrence of all three plenipotentiaries was obtained, on both the convention and the attached map.

Earlier, on 24–25 March, the Indo-Tibet boundary had been delineated and sanctified by signature and seal on large-scale maps by the British and Tibetan plenipotentiaries and ratified by the two countries. This historic boundary has later acquired fame as the 'McMahon Line'. This boundary was part of the 'red line', even though it was incorporated into a small-scale map, which formed an important adjunct of the Simla convention. A small-scale map condenses distance whereas in a large-scale map, it is zoomed in and hence contains more details.

McMahon thanked his colleagues and also felicitated them for the successful conclusion of the convention, saying it would be in *the best interests of our three countries* (emphasis added)'.[73]

Alas, this was not to be, for on 29 April, Chen informed the foreign office that the Chinese government had *'repudiated'* his signing of the convention! Though this announcement was not entirely unexpected, McMahon felt frustrated that the Chinese had disavowed a fair and just dispensation, completely unmindful of their current status in Tibet. This, according to him, displayed 'their proverbial inability to recognise finality in any issue'.[74] After repeated last-minute postponements of meetings to accommodate the Chinese plenipotentiary's requests, having conceded most of the Chinese demands for changes in the wording of the convention, and after the territorial concessions granted to the Chinese side, this was extremely disappointing and ungracious on the part of the Wai Chiao-pu. The conniving role played by Lu Hsing-chi became well known by this time. Apparently, he was able to prevail upon the Wai Chiao-pu, not only to repudiate any agreement but to take other actions also. In one of his communications to the Chinese cabinet, dated 13 November 1913, he had counselled them to say: 'I think that if, at the present conference, we can show some strength and can hold out for a short time, we may reap the fruit of success.'[75] Besides, he had reassured Peking that the British had 'no intention of usurping Tibet'.[76] One British account says that Lu, in a note on 5 March 1914 to Peking, urged the Chinese 'to hold fast to their present military position in Eastern Tibet, to meet our [British] proposals with a categorical refusal in Delhi, and a protest in London; to seize Pomed and Gyade, and, if possible, to make a forced march on Lhasa'. The 'result of this Conference will have a far-reaching effect on China's relations with other powers', Lu assured Peking. His concluding remark on the situation was: 'It will be impossible for the British to force upon China any agreement which is distasteful to her.'[77]

In the event, the Chinese, acting as advised by Lu, raised the Tibet issue in Peking on 30 April through Dr Wellington Koo, deputed by Wai Chiao-pu, and on the next day in London through the Chinese minister, Lew Yuk-lin, who recommended that the venue of the conference should 'forthwith' be shifted to either Peking or London. In fact, Dr Koo had even alluded to Ivan Chen having been forced to agree to the convention. He held out a threat: *'If the Indian Government tried to insist on the validity of this agreement ... British commercial interests in the Yangtze valley might suffer* (emphasis added).'[78]

Britain's freedom of action during the Simla conference was restrained by its self-denying agreement of 1907 with Russia. It was now obliged to keep Russia informed of the essentials of the convention, particularly those aspects impinging on the agreed parameters of the 1907 Anglo-Russian Convention. In view of many important developments since that accord—such as changes in Russo-Mongolian and Mongol-Tibet relations and the changed status of Tibet—the need to make necessary modifications in that agreement became unavoidable. The British policymakers at Whitehall were fully aware that the Russians, while acceding to their demands on Tibet, would definitely seek concessions in Persia, Afghanistan and perhaps Sinkiang too.[79]

During May 1914, parleys took place at St Petersburg, but Sazanov, the Russian foreign minister, proved to be a difficult negotiator. He made it clear that the 'Tibetan and Mongolian question could not be related, because Mongolia had not been dealt with in the 1907 Convention'.[80] As Russia had been assured that it would be apprised of the proceedings of the Simla Conference, the draft convention and the map showing the boundaries of Inner and Outer Tibet, the draft text of the new trade regulations, and the notes exchanged with respect to the Indo-Tibetan boundary (without the maps) were shared with the Russians on 4 May.[81]

Negotiations between Britain and Russia, specially with respect to three articles of the Simla Convention, consumed the whole of May 1914. The Russians wanted equal commercial and mining rights as would accrue to Britain, as contained in Article VI. The right granted to the British trade agent to visit Lhasa along with his escort to resolve issues which could not be settled by 'correspondence or otherwise', vide Article VIII, was requested to be offered to Russian trade agents too. Thirdly, Article X was unacceptable to the Russians, as its wording conveyed the sense that Tibet was a protectorate of Britain. The Russians said they would readily agree with the British if, 'in case of any difference of opinion', instead of the British being called upon to make an 'equitable adjustment', the article was rephrased to conclude 'that the English text of the convention be deemed authoritative'.[82]

Compared with Russia's unabashed involvement in Mongolia, the British appeared to be overly cautious and defensive in dealing with Tibetan affairs, even though the security of India's north-eastern frontiers and the huge British investments in upper Assam were at stake. Moreover, China's aggressive intent had become quite clear, right at the outset of the negotiations at Simla. Additionally, as a price for its concurrence, Russia wanted to secure some more concessions, such as the occasional visits by Russian agents to Herat, recognition of Russia's 'predominant interest' in northern Persia, and an undertaking that British subjects' demands for irrigation works, railways or industrial enterprises in northern Afghanistan would not receive any support from the British government. The Russians also demanded unhindered access for Russian subjects to Lhasa through India for pilgrimage purposes, which had been denied in some cases in the past.[83]

The Chinese attitude was dichotomous, intended to drag on negotiations interminably to avoid committing to a final decision. But the Chinese did not want to be seen as the party that broke off the negotiations. So they made allegations suggesting that their plenipotentiary had been pressured to initial the convention and that McMahon had been 'partial' to Tibet. It appears from the disavowal of their plenipotentiary's signing of the convention that the Chinese doubted both the sincerity of McMahon and the capability or commitment of their plenipotentiary to safeguard

China's interests. This was why they sought to change the venue of the conference. Not being able to succeed in taking the parleys to London or Peking, the Chinese came up with a memorandum on 13 June, which was marginally different from their earlier position, but again quite unreasonable and unacceptable to the Tibetan and British sides.

Besides other reasons brought out forcefully by the Tibetan plenipotentiary, from the geostrategic perspective, the British too considered it essential that Outer Tibet should include both Gyade and Chamdo regions, as they dominated the northern and eastern roads to Lhasa and the difficult passes in their proximity.

On 25 June, Jordan was asked to hand over to the Wai Chiao-pu the British response to the Chinese memorandum of 13 June. In their memorandum, which rejected the Chinese claims, the British firmly conveyed a *final concession*, which, presumably, McMahon would be able to extract from the Tibetans. This was to consider the Kunlun, instead of the Altyn Tagh range, as the boundary between Tibet and China. With that the British memorandum went on to emphatically convey that the Chinese must withdraw all other claims and sign the convention without further delay, failing which, as they had cautioned earlier, Britain and Tibet would proceed to do so independently.[84] The Chinese responded promptly on 30 June but their reply, in McMahon's words, was 'vague in its terms and unintelligible in its practical application', and hence 'entirely unacceptable'.[85]

Final Meeting: Simla, 3 July 1914

After almost nine months of gruelling and mostly frustrating discussions, presentations, diplomatic manoeuvring and the inevitable procrastination on China's part, the final meeting was held on 3 July 1914, at 11:15 p.m. Amidst a lot of drama, McMahon, as a special gesture, had delayed the meeting to accommodate the Chinese envoy's request for more time as he was awaiting a response to his latest recommendation to Peking. It would be no exaggeration to say that McMahon had yielded to the utmost to satisfy Chinese demands, even at the cost of Tibetan interests at times, in the hope that China would eventually sign the convention. Alas, all his efforts proved to be in vain. Realizing that the Chinese plenipotentiary was unable to append his signature on the document, McMahon then asked Lonchen Shatra whether he was prepared to initial the convention. His response was that having accepted the agreement on 27 April he would sign it, as instructed by his government. He remarked pointedly that it was despite some reservations about the agreement that his government had given the go-ahead to him. The British and Tibetan plenipotentiaries proceeded to initial and seal the convention, and to safeguard their national interests they also signed a *'declaration that the Convention was binding on them and that so long as the Chinese Government withheld its signature it would be barred from the enjoyment of privileges accruing from the agreement* (emphasis added)'.[86] (See Appendix 4 for text.)

Ivan Chen made it known then that *'the Chinese Government would not recognise any treaty or similar document that might now or hereafter be signed between Great Britain and Tibet* (emphasis added)'.[87] It may be of interest to note that notice of this final meeting, along with the draft of the convention, was intimated to the Chinese government well in advance. It was also conveyed to them that in the absence of accord from the Chinese, the British and the Tibetan plenipotentiaries would proceed to conclude the agreement 'in the form (tri-partite) in which it had been communicated to the Chinese Government at Peking'.[88] During the signing of the documents by Britain and Tibet, Ivan Chen retired to another room. However, he rejoined his contemporaries in the conference chamber for the closing event. A sombre McMahon delivered his concluding remarks, whose sentiment was shared by Lonchen Shatra too. McMahon acknowledged that the work of the conference had been arduous and trying for them all, and that in spite of the fact that their Chinese colleague had found it necessary to maintain an attitude of opposition and to meet their proposals in an uncompromising spirit, his courtesy throughout had been unfailing, and their personal relations had been unimpaired.[89]

As has been described above, every effort was made till the very end to persuade the Chinese plenipotentiary to obtain the approval of his government. As a matter of fact, McMahon conveyed to Ivan

Chen through Rose the benefits China would derive by adhering to the convention. Briefly, they were:

- Tibet would be under Chinese suzerainty, thereby implying that it may give up its claim to independence.
- Tibetans would be prevailed upon to continue to accept the validity of the Anglo-Chinese Adhesion Convention of 1906, much against their will.
- Acceptance of Tibet as a part of China was conveyed in an accompanying note, and not as a part of the text of the convention.
- Posting of a high-ranking Chinese official at Lhasa with an escort of not more than 300 soldiers.
- A say in the appointment of the Dalai Lama.
- Possession of the rich and prosperous regions of Nyarong and Derge, although at the same time loss of the strategically located town of Chamdo, which at that moment was under Chinese control.
- An end to the costly, exhausting and unending conflict in the eastern Kham region and peace and prosperity in the region—the principal reason for initiating the tripartite conference.
- An opportunity to restore China's lost prestige among the Tibetans.

In case the Chinese demurred, the field would be left open for Britain to operate freely in Tibet, without any restrictions on the size of their military escorts.[90]

Consequently, a window of a few days was kept open for Ivan Chen to consult with his government and endeavour to change their mind so that he could append his signature to the Simla Convention before the departure of the other two plenipotentiaries. The convention even indicated readiness to reassemble on 6 July should Ivan Chen by then be 'in a position to sign the convention'.[91]

Chen said he would communicate the final day's proceedings to Peking and assured his colleagues that he would revert to them immediately if reassembling of the conference was necessary. He then conveyed his 'grateful thanks' to the British government and to McMahon for their kind hospitality, and also to Bell and Rose, in particular, for their kind services. He also had a special word of praise for Waugh, the secretary of the conference.

Lonchen Shatra ended his remarks by saying he would stay on for a few days more in the hope that his Chinese colleague would sign the convention.[92]

This brought the Simla Conference to an end. Within a month, the First World War was unleashed on the world, and it overshadowed all matters that had been otherwise engaging the attention of the world powers—Tibet being one of them. Despite the war raging in many parts of the world, the Himalayan region and Tibet remained comparatively peaceful for the next four decades.

While forwarding McMahon's final memorandum of the conference, dated 8 July 1914, to the Earl of Crewe, the Secretary of State for India, Viceroy Lord Hardinge in Council expressed their appreciation of the services of Sir McMahon and his team:

> We wish to take this opportunity of placing on record our appreciation of the services of Sir Henry McMahon and his assistants in the conduct of these prolonged and troubled negotiations. Sir Henry has shown throughout good judgement, tact and perseverance in most trying circumstances. The fact that the negotiations here have been concluded without the signature of the Chinese Representative to the Convention is no reflection whatever on the able diplomacy of the British Plenipotentiary. Indeed, it says much for Sir Henry's conduct of the negotiations that he was able to obtain in April the Chinese Representative's initials to the Convention; while the arrangements made with his Tibetan Colleague, particularly in regard to the settlement of the Indo-Tibet frontier and the Trade Regulations, are most creditable to our Plenipotentiary. As regards the services of Mr. Bell and Mr. Rose, we desire cordially to endorse what is said of them in the enclosed Memorandum.[93]

Although the Simla Convention was seen by most analysts of the time as a failure, or as an inconclusive tripartite conference, the import and significance of the 'red line' defining the Indo-Tibetan boundary was substantially underestimated by the policymakers of imperial Britain. The fact that China was totally sidelined (till such time as it would come on board, if it ever did), the boundary agreement—which concretized and initialled on two large-scale map sheets the north-east frontier of India, (provisional, scale 1 inch: 8 miles)—and the Indo-Tibetan trade treaty were great achievements. These agreements were perhaps underplayed at that time because of the international political power play then happening and the war clouds on the horizon, not to mention the self-denying (for Britain) Anglo-Russian Convention of 1907 (see Appendix 3). The Simla agreement was, as a result, not accurately recorded in Aitchison's treaties soon afterwards.

For independent India, the McMahon Line, as it is referred to now, has proved to be a boon; it is cartographically accepted and shown as the boundary in maps worldwide. In retrospect, it would be fair to conclude that Sir A.H. McMahon, in drawing up the Simla Convention, added an invaluable feather in his cap, one that would also be remembered by India forever.

14

Defining and Delineating the McMahon Line

'... of all these natural features, a definite line of watershed carried by a conspicuous mountain ridge, or range, is undoubtedly the most lasting, the most unmistakable, and the most efficient as a barrier.'[1]

One of the principal British objectives of the Simla Conference, although unstated, was to identify, concretize and delimit the frontier between Tibet and the British Empire in the north-eastern region of India and northern Burma. Chao Erh-feng's advance into central Tibet and Lhasa, his forays into the Himalayan frontier during 1910–11 and the flutter it created amongst the British administration and the European community in the tea gardens and oilfields of Assam, resulted in a U-turn of the British policy of 'non-involvement', not only in Tibetan affairs but also in the affairs of the indigenous tribes living in the densely forested and unpenetrated hills up to the Himalayan crest line. It would be correct to say that until 1910, not much was known of the tribal territory in this region, apart from the Lohit Valley and the trade route coming down from Tawang to Udalguri along the Bhutan border. The rest was 'terra incognito', and this information void could have been a costly lapse and a source of huge embarrassment to the British Empire.

In a September 1911 note to Whitehall, Viceroy Lord Hardinge was clear about what British policy on these matters would be. He said:

206

Circumstances have thus forced us to revert practically to the original proposal of Lord Minto's government that endeavours should be made to secure, as soon as possible, a sound strategical boundary between China and Tibet and the tribal territory from Bhutan up to and including the Mishmi country, and this should, we consider now, be the main object of our policy.

As long as there existed a tribal belt between India and a 'peacefully dormant neighbour' like Tibet, there was no threat, went his rationale; but 'with the recent change in conditions, the question of a boundary well-defined and at a safer distance from our administrative border admits of no delay'.[2]

The viceroy then tasked the chief of General Staff with carrying out an appreciation of the Himalayan border and submitting a report suggesting a 'suitable frontier line', keeping in mind the geostrategic imperatives and factors such as the historical background, *traditional frontiers and ethnicity* of the region. It is remarkable that even a century ago the British policymakers gave so much importance to *custom, tradition and ethnicity* while deciding the boundaries of their empire.

Accordingly, survey missions were launched during the campaigning seasons from September to April of 1911–12, 1912–13 and 1913–14. These were the *Mishmi mission* that explored the Lohit and Dibang Valleys; the *Abor mission* that endeavoured to penetrate the hitherto untrodden Siang or Tsangpo Valley (as a matter of fact, this was a punitive expedition to avenge the murder of Williamson) and the Siyom Valley to its west; the *Miri mission* that had been given the task of venturing into the unknown Subansiri, Kamala and Khru Valleys, where no white man had been seen before; and finally the *Aka mission*, which was given the responsibility of exploring the Kameng Valley and the Tawang Chu and Namjyang Chu Valleys, where, again, no Westerner had entered until 1910.

However, it needs to be borne in mind that some kind of agreements had already been made with these tribal people by the Upper Assam administrative authorities through their political officers. Besides gaining knowledge of the topography of the land, the aim of these military–civil ventures was to establish friendly relations with the tribes, to institute a system of *loose political control*, and to demonstrate the *superiority* of British military power.

The British General Staff in Simla, the Military Department in the Government of India and the surveyor general began working feverishly during the period 1910–14 to carry out fresh strategic analyses and assessments based on the numerous reconnaissance reports and tour diaries as they arrived. At the same time, the sketchy and incomplete topographical information available on maps was revised without delay. The same sense of urgency was transmitted to the frontier officials and the field force of the army. As of 1910, geographical information about the region was grossly inadequate. This was emphasized in the memorandum of 8 July 1914 summarizing the events from 1911 to 1914, which was appended to the final memorandum of the Simla Conference. On the inadequacy of the empire's knowledge of the terrain at the frontier up to 1910, McMahon had said in the memorandum:

> We had practically no geographical knowledge in regard to the configuration of the country, the position of the frontier was undefined and unknown, and the Government of India was well content to leave the tribesmen to their own devices, so long as they confined themselves to the hills, and respected the lives and property of British subjects in the cultivated and administered plains which lie just to the south of the mountainous tribal belt.[3]

Traditional age-old boundaries did exist, though not defined formally, along the natural divide formed by the highest mountain ranges, the passes and river valleys in the region. However, these kept changing over the centuries as migration of peoples kept taking place. Even though there were no settled populations along the seemingly impassable high-altitude areas, the indigenous tribes referred to as 'Lopas' by the Tibetans and others exercised their rights for hunting, grazing, and collection of medicinal herbs and rare edible rock algae up to their side of the high Himalayas. The Lopas fiercely defended their territories against intrusion by aliens.

The remoteness and inaccessibility of this region resulted in its appellation of 'Shangri-La'. The course of the Tsangpo in the area of the famous bend in the Himalayan gorge was unknown to both the Western world and to the people in India, even to those living in the plains of Assam. Myths abounded, of a river descending from the heavens and of a mammoth waterfall in this region. The lack of geographical information on this area was in fact astounding; whether the Tsangpo and the Siang, Dihang and Brahmaputra were one and the same river had till then not been conclusively proved. The upper reaches of many other rivers flowing through the tribal areas, some of them cutting through the Himalayas— such as the Namjyang Chu, Tawang Chu, Kameng, Subansiri, Kamala, Siyom, Siang, Dibang and Lohit—were 'unknown territory'. Access to the Himalayan watershed from the south was barred to outsiders by the tribal peoples in the area. The sole exception was the Lohit Valley, which had been penetrated by a Westerner; it had been entered from the Tibetan side by Captain Bailey in early 1911 and a few times from Sadiya, a frontier administrative base in Assam. In those days, a white man with 'yellow hair' was viewed with immense curiosity and suspicion by the native tribes.

It was McMahon's design that this boundary should, first of all, define the southern limit of Tibet by being drawn as a red line, eastwards from the north-eastern corner of Bhutan to the tri-junction of Tibet, India and Burma north of the Diphu Pass. Beyond that it would then continue eastwards along the Irrawaddy watershed and then southwards to the Isu Razi Pass in the Taraon Valley. Delineation of this boundary would also result in delimitation of the northern frontiers of Assam and Burma. From there the red line was to be drawn in a loop going upwards and westwards, marching along the historical and traditional boundary of Tibet with the Chinese Szechuan and Xinjiang provinces, to end near the Karakash river in western Tibet, thereby encompassing the whole of Tibet and delimiting its frontiers with India's north-east and with the Yunnan, Szechuan and Xinjiang provinces of China. This red line eventually came to be known as the McMahon Line (see Figure 17).

At the second meeting of the Simla Conference on 18 November 1913, McMahon had emphasized that it was imperative to decide on the geographical and political limits of Tibet as an entity before any discussion could take place on its status with respect to China. Both Tibet and China had adopted maximalist positions as far as their boundaries were concerned; their claims stretched to such an extent that Tibet claimed territory as far east as Tachienlu and Kokonor lake, and the Chinese felt they were entitled to extend theirs westwards to include Chiangta (Giamda), about 200 kilometres from Lhasa. Understandably, both sides had catered for some latitude for bargaining, but there was an amazing and ludicrous spatial gap of over 1,600 kilometres between the two claim lines (Figure 17). This proved to be a major hurdle during the negotiations and was the principal reason for refusal by the Chinese to be a party to the agreement. Whereas McMahon's proposal received the Tibetan delegation's assent, the Chinese plenipotentiary continued to demur and procrastinate. Despite this, McMahon decided to continue discussions independently with the Tibetans till such time as Ivan Chen received the go-ahead to join in. As a matter of fact, instructions to that effect were indeed received by Chen soon after these independent discussions, thus proving the efficacy of the British threat and indicating the degree of Chinese sensitivity to direct Anglo-Tibetan talks.

During the Simla Conference, the British and Tibetans commenced serious parleys for a month, starting in mid-January 1914, to arrive at a mutually acceptable boundary between Tibet and the north-east frontier of the British Empire, including northern Burma. By then the most crucial and important geopolitical inputs, significantly from the Tibetan side, based on the first-ever surveys done by any European after traversing and surveying about 600 kilometres of an important and previously unsurveyed part of the Himalayan frontier, from the mystical Tsangpo gorge up to Bhutan, had also been obtained. This vital survey report was submitted to McMahon by Captains Bailey and Morshead in November 1913 at Simla. All these reports helped fill vital voids and grey areas, not only in the geographical knowledge of that particular region but also in what was known about the ethnic composition of the peoples inhabiting the frontier region on both sides of the Himalayan divide. The surveyors were also able to discern to a fair degree of accuracy the southern border of Tibet and the area controlled and inhabited by the indigenous tribes or the Lopas.

The identification of and correlation between the various peaks of the highest Himalayan chain in the region, which had now been surveyed from both sides—from a closer proximity and greater accuracy from the Tibetan side—proved to be a boon for McMahon. His team was able to come up with a fairly accurate boundary in the nick of time. Details about the local conditions and ethnicities gained by them, particularly of the Tawang region, proved to be of vital importance. It needs to be borne in mind that this particular reconnaissance by the two outstanding adventurers was the first by any European along this route. To have covered 2,700 kilometres in a period of about six months (15 May to 14 November 1913), averaging 15 kilometres daily, was a stupendous feat by any standard. This arduous journey was made mostly on foot, and at other times on horseback, wherever the terrain and the track permitted.

It bears highlighting that many studies of the Indo-Tibetan boundary have not adequately analysed the interrelationship between the Burma–Tibet and India–Tibet boundaries. As has been mentioned earlier, the Chinese design was to carve out a new province of Hsikang by including in it Amdo, Kham and the Marches, along with areas of Tibet proper as far west as Chiangta / Gyamda, the south-eastern districts of Pomed and Zayul, and the upper Irrawaddy region in Hkamti Long. Possession of a direct route between Yunnan province of China and Lhasa through the Zayul and Pomed districts was a *core strategic objective* for the Chinese, although, according to the British Legation at Peking, the Chinese could 'show no historical claim, nor any claim by conquest, to these two districts which are entirely beyond the bounds of their control'.[4] For the Chinese, this vital artery would avoid not only the difficult terrain comprising deep gorges formed by the Yangtze, Mekong, Salween and their tributaries, as well as numerous high-altitude and snow-covered passes, but also the ungovernable tribes of the southern Kham region. Besides, the existing southern route was prone to heavy snowfall and massive landslides, remaining generally closed during winter.

The British were quick to realize the dangerous portents of this new link, even if their primary concern at that time was only to ensure the security of the tea plantations and the oilfields and coalfields of upper Assam, and other European investments. So they took steps to ensure that no encroachments by the Chinese were allowed in northern Burma and in the Taraon Valley.

From the Isu Razi Pass, the alignment of the boundary followed the Irrawaddy watershed up to the tri-junction between Burma, Tibet and India, slightly north of the Diphu Pass. As part of their strategy, the British also established firm control over this region by developing Myitkyina as a railhead and road terminus, and thrust ahead with their flag to the watershed of the Irrawaddy north of Putao, where they established a frontier outpost, naming it Fort Hertz. This was to honour the services of William Hertz, a civil service officer, towards consolidation of the British Empire in north Burma between 1888 and 1913. By these measures, China's quest for a secure, all-weather and direct (shortest) route from Yunnan to Lhasa was given a quiet burial.

Going westwards from the tri-junction of Burma, Tibet and India, the boundary descended into the Lohit Valley along the northern shoulder of the Dichu stream, cutting across the Lohit river upstream of Walong and north of a hamlet called Kahao. The last Tibetan settlement is at Sama, which is just across the boundary. From there the boundary continued westwards to the source of the Tho Chu and followed the watershed of the Rong Thod Chu and the Dibang and its numerous tributaries. The alignment of this stretch of the proposed boundary, up to a peak named Kangri Karpo, which was the fount of three valleys—Rong Thod Chu to the east, Chimdro to the north and Dibang in the south—was based on sketchy information obtained from the locals. Even though Kangri Karpo peak, which is of a height of over 5,000 metres, had been fixed by the survey parties of Dundas's Mishmi mission in 1912 with a fair degree of accuracy, no exploration teams could have penetrated the thickly forested slopes and extremely challenging terrain leading to the south-eastern part of the Dibang watershed. Perhaps because of this, an approximate alignment based on oral evidence supplied by the indigenous peoples was accepted for this section of the frontier, from the Kangri Karpo peak to the Glei Dakhru Pass and eastwards to Lohit river. The extent of inadequacy or incompleteness of such a survey probably explains the creation of two prominent salients nicknamed the 'Fish Tails'. Based on information provided by the Mishmi tribals, these wedges were supposed to define the watershed by following the shoulders of the valleys formed by the tributaries of the Rong Thod Chu, as incorrectly marked in the map of that period that accompanied McMahon's memorandum of 8 July 1914. These tributaries do not actually exist as confirmed by modern surveys and even tourist maps!

Unlike in 1913, when it would have been possible to enter Tibet and survey the territory along the Rong Thod Chu valley to determine the alignment from the Tibetan side of the range rising to the Kangri Karpo peak, the short-lived Chinese presence in the Zayul region had prevented such an endeavour during 1911–12. There is a stretch of unbroken ridge dividing the Dibang and Zayul Valleys going in the north-west–south-east direction along the entire length of the Rong Thod Chu, from its source at the foot of Kangri Karpo to its confluence with Zayul Chu near Rima, from where it is known as the Lohit. Had an explorative venture eastwards, akin to Bailey's and Morshead's, from across the Kangri Karpo Pass been undertaken during 1913, it would have definitely helped McMahon draw his line with greater accuracy along the crest of the Kangri Karpo's south-eastern ridge and down to the Glei Dakhru Pass, and eventually to the Lohit Valley, a distance of approximately 195 kilometres. That an anomaly was created by inaccurate or incomplete surveys is apparent. Based on the watershed principle, this inaccuracy could be easily rectified, as such small corrections and modifications on the basis of later surveys had been provided for in the Simla Convention.

It needs to be pointed out that in his confidential note written on 1 June 1912, the chief of General Staff had categorically said:

Although the survey and exploration work of the past season (October–May 1911–12) has not been so fruitful in results as might have been hoped for, yet much remains to be done before we shall be in a position accurately to define our frontier with China, much useful geographical and political information has been gained from which an indication can be given of the line the frontier should take.[5]

He recommended the following actions:

An exploring party, accompanied by a survey party, should proceed up the Delei valley to the top of the Glei Dakhru Pass. Last season the Mission only penetrated as far as Tajobum in this valley and the position of the Glei Dakhru Pass does not appear to have been correctly fixed, according to tribal evidence. It is necessary to determine the configuration of the watershed proposed as a frontier line in this region...[6]

An exploring and survey party should proceed up the Dibang valley to determine the course of the main river and configuration of the main ranges.[7]

This explains why the need to make minor variations in the agreement based on information or facts subsequently discovered was accepted by both India and Tibet in March 1914 at the time of their signing of the maps showing the Indo-Tibetan boundary. Basically, the McMahon Line followed the watershed alignment of the eastern Himalayas comprising three segments—the Zangnan Gudi range, including the glacial region of Gorichen and its knot of snow-covered peaks and glaciers; the range between the Subansiri and the Tsangpo/Siang, which rises gradually to end at the towering massif of Namcha Barwa (Figure 12); and the ridge that climbs sharply from the eastern edge of the Tsangpo gorge to the Kangri Karpo and then continues in the south-eastern direction to the Lohit Valley south of Rima. These three ranges formed the basis of the McMahon Line along the eastern Himalayas.

The western extremity of the line was decided by McMahon after very careful and detailed deliberations between him and Charles Bell and consultations with Bailey and Morshead. From the south of Mela Pass, moving eastwards along the most prominent ridge, the red line was fixed referencing the village of Pangchen on the Indian side and Le in Tibet. As described by Bailey, the people of Le were dressed differently from the people on the Pangchen side. Even though there were Monpa villages up to Trimo, which lay 16 kilometres upstream along the Namjyang Chu, the people here looked 'very Tibetan in their appearance'. Halfway between Le and Trimo there was a Tsukang or custom collection point, where tax was collected on all goods, people and animals moving up into Tibet. As recorded by Bailey and Morshead, the tax was 10 per cent of the cost of the merchandise; and half a tanka per person and one tanka per animal (four tankas equalled one Indian rupee). The official who collected the tax was an agent of the Dzongpon of Tsona Dzong, the district headquarters, located about 40 kilometres to the north-east. There was another Tsukang on the eastern trade route to Tsona Dzong from Tawang (passing through the area referred to as the Bumla Pass). Interestingly, no taxes were levied for 'goods going down from Tsona', whereas the Monpas and other tribal people going up from Tawang area had to pay the same.[8] Keeping all this in mind, McMahon concluded, with a fair degree of accuracy, that the alignment of the boundary should lie on the southern side of the two custom houses (Figure 10). As highlighted by McMahon in his memorandum of 28 March 1914:

> ... the boundary line in the west follows the crest of the mountain range [Zangnan Gudi] which runs from peak 21431 [Gori Chen] through Tu Lung La and Menlakathong La to the Bhutan border. This is the highest mountain range in this tract of country. To the north of it are people of Tibetan descent; to the south the inhabitants are of Bhutanese and Aka extraction. It is unquestionably the correct boundary.[9]

It may be of interest to note that Desideri, a Jesuit missionary who lived in Lhasa for several years during the second and third decades of the eighteenth century, had written of Tsari as a place lying on the extreme borders of Tibet. He writes that further east of Tsari lay Congbo, which marched with the 'people called Lhoba, which means southern people ... Not even the Tibetans, who are close neighbours and have many dealings with them, are allowed to enter their country, but are obliged to stop on the frontier to barter goods.'[10]

China was not directly involved when these deliberations were taking place, but once this boundary was formalized it formed an intrinsic part of the tripartite discussions on delimitation of the frontiers of Tibet. The boundary was clearly indicated with a thick red line on the maps, but on a small scale (1 inch=60 miles). This line, when transposed on modern maps, could mean a band about 2 kilometres wide. A discerning Wai Chiao-pu could not possibly have missed the boundary alignment showing the southern limits of Tibet in the Kongbo, Pomed, Zayul and Taraon Valley areas along the Himalayan watershed, particularly when the Chinese themselves had designs to create their new province, Hsikang, which would encompass some of these areas as well as the Marches along the Kham region. At no stage of the deliberations did the Chinese raise any objections or make observations on the McMahon Line as it appeared in the maps in question, right from 17 February 1914—when Tibet's limits as a geographical and political entity were laid on the table for the first time during the fourth meeting of the conference held at Delhi—till the final meeting on 3 July 1914, when the conference terminated in Simla.

As a matter of fact, during Chao Erh-feng's campaign in 1910–11, the Chinese had planned (though never executed) an extensive survey of their projected boundary running eastwards from Chiangta (Gyamda) in Kongbo to Pomed and then in an absurd southward thrust to Mebo near Pasighat along the Brahmaputra, then continuing further eastwards to Sama in the Rong Thod Chu Valley and thereafter crossing over the Irrawaddy headwaters to Sung-t'a on the Salween (the southern boundary of Hsikang). This survey team was to be led by the chief of the survey section at Chengtu, Fu Hsieh-ch'en, who had two other members, Ch'u Cen-hsieng and Chao Chuang-hsuan. The team was asked 'to map the frontiers adjacent to Assam and northern Burma, in order that the diplomatic blunders in the Kachin Hills of Yunnan may be avoided when negotiations are begun for the delimitation of this part of the border'.[11]

At about the same time, another team under Chiang Feng-ch'i, accompanied by an English-speaking interpreter, Chao Yang-yun, and a guide, Shu Chin-liang, was sent from Chengtu straight to Zayul to parley (chiao-she) with an English forces, as the Chinese had learnt that 'English troops were furtively entering' the Zayul area.[12] It is therefore difficult to believe that the Chinese were not aware of the alignment of McMahon's red line, which delineated Tibet's southern boundary with north-east India. That China had at no stage raised any objection to this part of the boundary is also a known fact.

As mentioned earlier, the Indo-Tibetan boundary along the eastern Himalayas was delineated on a set of fairly large-scale maps (1 inch: 8 miles) that were formally signed and sealed on 24–25 March 1914.

McMahon's formal note of 24 March 1914 to Lonchen Shatra, the Tibetan plenipotentiary, said:

> In February last you accepted the India–Tibet frontier from the Isu Razi Pass to the Bhutan frontier, as given in the map (two sheets), of which two copies are herewith attached, subject to the confirmation of your Government and the undermentioned conditions:
>
> a. The Tibetan ownership in private estates on the British side of the frontier will not be disturbed.
>
> b. If the sacred places of Tso Karpo and Tsari Sarpa fall within a day's march of the British side of the frontier, they will be included in Tibetan territory and the frontier modified accordingly.
>
> I understand that your Government has now agreed to this frontier subject to the above two conditions. I shall be glad to learn definitely from you that this is the case.
>
> You wished to know whether certain dues now collected by the Tibetan Government at Tsona Jong and in Kongbu and Kham from the Monpas and Lopas for articles sold may still be collected. Mr. Bell has informed you that such details will be settled in a friendly spirit, when you have furnished him the further information, which you have promised.
>
> The final settlement of this India–Tibet frontier will help to prevent causes of future dispute and thus cannot fail to be of great advantage to both Governments.
>
> Delhi, 24th March 1914, A.H. McMahon.

Lonchen Shatra had already received approval for this from the Dalai Lama's government, and he replied to McMahon the next day. A translated version of his reply says:

> As it was feared that there might be friction in future unless the boundary between India and Tibet is clearly defined, I submitted the map, which you sent to me in February last, to the Tibetan Government at Lhasa for orders. I have now received orders from Lhasa, and I accordingly agree to the boundary as marked in red in

the two copies of the maps signed by you, subject to the conditions
mentioned in your letter, dated the 24th March, sent to me through
Mr. Bell. I have signed and sealed the two copies of the maps. I have
kept one copy here and return herewith the other.[13]

Sent on the 29th day of the 1st Month of the Wood-Tiger year (25th
March 1914) by Lonchen Shatra, the Tibetan Plenipotentiary.

Seal of Lonchen Shatra.

These historical documents have not merely been signed by the
plenipotentiaries of Tibet and British India but have the approval of the
two governments too. The Indo-Tibetan boundary shown in the two
map sheets on a fairly large scale, duly signed by both plenipotentiaries,
has thus acquired a high standing and sanctity. It needs to be appreciated
that in those times dispatch of dak by courier from Simla to Lhasa and
back would have involved travel by train to Siliguri, thereafter by pony,
then by yak and on foot to Lhasa via the Chumbi Valley. The whole
process could easily take three to four weeks by the fastest means! It is
to the credit of Charles Bell and Lonchen Shatra that these vital inputs
were obtained in time for the convention to be signed. What has not
received the desired recognition and acclaim was the delimitation of the
Indo-Tibetan boundary by McMahon on a large-scale map-set, which was
indeed a far-sighted and visionary idea. It has been aptly described that
his 'object in obtaining this detailed mutual agreement with the Tibetan
Government regarding this section of the India–Tibet boundary has been
to minimise as far as possible the chances of future misunderstanding
and dispute on the subject. This section of frontier in question, although
over 1,280 kilometres in length, has hitherto been absolutely undefined.'[14]

PART VI

POST-SIMLA, WORLD WAR I AND AFTER

'Unless we learn how to protect our land, the Dalai Lama and the Panchen Lama, the Father and the Son, the upholders of the Buddhist faith, the glorious incarnations, all will go under and leave no trace behind.'[1]

The Thirteenth Dalai Lama

15

Dalai Lama's Temporal, Spiritual Rule Reinstated

The Simla Convention failed to conclude on a tripartite basis. However, it was fairly successful from the point of view of British India and Tibet, and both countries benefited from it. Having refused to sign the convention, China was deprived of the benefits the convention would have fetched it, such as having suzerainty over Tibet, almost total control (save ecclesiastical) over Inner Tibet, and a presence at Lhasa after reinstatement of its Amban with an escort. However, the Tibet issue was overtaken by events in Europe, as the First World War started within a month of the Simla Conference ending. The fate of an orphan-like Tibet was thus consigned to the sidelines of history for the next four decades.

The somewhat inconclusive and abrupt ending of the Simla Conference should not be seen as a failure, as some scholars have held it to be. Though it was given no publicity, as the British wanted to keep the Tibetan issue low-key, the outcome of the deliberations from October 1913 to July 1914 was significant in many ways. Britain, China and Tibet, the three protagonists, were impacted geopolitically, strategically and economically. While Britain played the role of an 'honest broker', there were in this exercise huge stakes for the British Indian Empire, which McMahon never lost sight of. Foremost among them was the security of India's northern frontier, the north-eastern segment in particular. As far as the Chinese were concerned, their continued procrastination and reluctance to conclude any agreement except on unreasonably favourable terms to themselves, which were totally out of tune with reality, deprived them of a number of advantages. Their loss from not signing the convention was Tibet's gain, and the British Empire's too.

Tibet's new-found independence from the Chinese yoke made it yearn for international recognition. That is why the Dalai Lama had readily agreed, from the outset, to be part of the tripartite convention to discuss the Sino-Tibetan situation. And now Tibet found the convention an excellent opportunity with which to consolidate its status, which was analogous to that achieved recently by Mongolia. Tibet did not have to accept being 'a part of China' which, much against its wishes, adherence of China to the convention would have implied. Besides, the division of Tibet into 'Inner Tibet' and 'Outer Tibet' was avoided, and the prestige and authority of the Dalai Lama as its spiritual and temporal ruler, as the Chen-re-zi and avatar of Buddha, were restored.

Tibet also gained the reassurance and support of a world power (Great Britain) that had no aspirations of making her a protectorate or acquiring her territory. This support was not completely wholehearted, and was carefully nuanced by Britain, keeping in mind its larger imperial interests. That was why, in spite of the obdurate and uncooperative attitude of China during the entire period of the Simla Conference, Britain had continued to maintain that Tibet should be 'fully autonomous' yet remain under Chinese 'suzerainty', notwithstanding the ambiguous interpretation of these terms in the Asiatic context.

Although Tibet felt secure from the south, its eastern flank continued to be inflamed because of the border war with China. Also, threat of a Chinese invasion from Szechuan, like the one led by Chao Erh-feng, loomed large. But this time the Tibetans were determined to resist any Chinese advance; their resolve was somewhat strengthened by the supply of British arms, ammunition and military training.

Significantly, during the Simla Conference, Britain and Tibet formalized, with signatures and seals, the Indo-Tibetan boundary, the now-famous McMahon Line, delineated from the north-eastern corner of Bhutan to Isu Razi Pass in northern Burma on a set of two large-scale maps as mentioned earlier.

The British were always cognizant of the natural geographical divide running along the Himalayan watershed, although they restricted their administrative boundary to the foothills. Though the Chinese were not co-opted in the boundary discussions between the Tibetans and the British team led by Charles Bell, they were provided the map, although one on a much smaller scale (1 inch: 60 miles), which was part of the draft convention which was initialled or signed by all the three plenipotentiaries on 27 April 1914. The prominently marked red line outlining the limits of Tibet, commencing from the north-eastern tip of Bhutan to Isu Razi Pass on the Mekong–Salween divide, following the traditional frontiers with Yunnan, Szechuan and Xinjiang provinces and terminating near the western extremity of the Kunlun range, was definitely scrutinized by the Chinese delegation prior to the signing of the document. The map, despite its small scale, had the latitude and longitude grids as well as prominent place names in English, Tibetan and Chinese, leaving little ground for misinterpretation.

The Chinese did accept the boundary delineated by the 'red line' (McMahon's alignment) from the tri-junction of India, China and Burma to the Isu Razi Pass, but they have not agreed to the validity of this very line up to the present day, as far as settling their boundary with India is concerned. Incidentally, near its western extremity, this line runs between Tsona Dzong and Tawang (both marked on the map), showing Tawang well on the Indian side of the boundary. In fact, there was a much lesser known but equally prominent 'blue line' marked on the same map, defining the boundary between Tibet and China. This was vehemently opposed by the Chinese, and this was the reason why the Simla Convention eventually failed to fetch their adherence. But the Chinese had no problem with the red line and McMahon's alignment of the Indo-Tibetan boundary, either during the conference or even later. In light of this, their objection to this line in the present times is difficult to reconcile with.

The Military General Staff and survey teams attached to the politico-military British expeditions provided extremely valuable inputs and reports to McMahon for formulation of the boundary. But for these timely inputs, including vital information on the geography, geopolitics, Tibet's southern limits, the country's administrative reach and the ethnicity of peoples on both sides of the Himalayan divide gathered by the intrepid adventurers Captains Bailey and Morshead, McMahon would not have been in a position to draw up the Indo-Tibetan boundary.

'The McMahon Line confirmed an obvious geographical frontier to the south of which live a number of tribes most of whom have no close affinity with either Tibetans or Chinese,' emphasized Hugh Richardson.[2] This was undoubtedly one of the most significant achievements of the Simla Conference, although it was underplayed in a big way by Britain at that time. This achievement enhanced the prestige of the British manifold; not only did they gain unrestricted access to Lhasa and a conducive trade environment in Tibet, but also a 'special position' and exclusivity as far as 'political influence' and Tibet's dealing with other nations was concerned.[3] A decade after 1904, Britain's relations with Tibet had undergone a paradigm shift. From being once snubbed by the Dalai Lama (before the Younghusband expedition), Britain was, by 1914, in a close embrace with Tibet, to the exclusion of China. The northern boundary of British India, from Kashmir to Burma, was secured against both Russian and Chinese intrusions and intrigues. Inclusion of Tibet in Britain's sphere of influence was the safest bet for the security of India and the other cis-Himalayan states—Nepal, erstwhile Sikkim and Bhutan.

Britain was by far the biggest beneficiary of the historic but controversial tripartite conference. The north-eastern frontier was secured from Chinese penetration or influence. The agreement provided British trade agents free access to Lhasa, and Great Britain gained a predominant influence on 'autonomous Tibet'. And with the signing of the new Anglo-Tibet Trade Regulation accord on 3 July 1914 superseding the earlier agreements of 1893 and 1908, a fair amount of commercial benefits accrued to British India, to the exclusion of China and other powers.

The policy of 'non-interference' and of leaving the indigenous tribes to their own devices was a conscious decision of the British so that there would exist a loosely administered buffer territory between a peaceful Tibet and India. Britain did not want to extend its administrative reach right up to the Himalayan crest line, as the huge cost of setting up infrastructure there and manning it was disproportionate to the insignificant commercial benefits that would accrue to them. Other than getting forest produce, there was no attraction in venturing into remote and inaccessible frontier areas, whose mineral wealth was yet to be explored. Timber was plentiful in Assam, and the inner line was a device to prevent uncontrolled exploitation of this resource. One also had to contend with the fiercely independent tribes of this region who were profoundly suspicious of outsiders, the inhospitable climate, and a host of pestilential fauna, including mosquitoes, leeches and 'dim-dam' flies, whose bite left a painful itch for days.

However, because of Chinese non-acceptance of the Simla Convention, the undeclared war between Tibet and China continued to rage in the Marches in eastern Tibet. This, in a way, defeated one of the principal aims of the tripartite conference—of bringing peace in the Sino-Tibetan frontier region. Peking was not in a position to effectively enforce China's 'Tibet strategy' while it had to also deal with the two frontier provinces of Szechuan and Yunnan, which were determined to follow whatever policies suited them. Despite all this, upon termination of the Great War and even a little prior to that, China took the initiative to restart negotiations with the British, hoping it could secure a better deal for itself. At the same time, China also tried to engage the Dalai Lama in direct talks, using aggressive posturing and threats. The Dalai Lama held his ground, with the tacit support of the British, and advised the Chinese to sign the Simla Convention. On 28 June 1915, the Chinese president conveyed to Jordan that he was prepared to concede Chamdo to Tibet, with the caveat that the phrase 'Tibet is a part of China' be mentioned in the text of the convention proper rather than as a note.[4] But accepting such changes would portray weakness on the part of the British, and also could not be done without the concurrence of Tibet, so this proposal was rejected. In the meanwhile, Yuan Shih-k'ai's endeavours to start a new dynasty ended in failure, consuming him too in the bargain. His passing away in 1916 ushered in an era of extreme instability and a state of civil war in Szechuan and Yunnan, in which Tibet got embroiled too. On 23 May 1917, yet another fruitless attempt to reopen talks was made by the Chinese foreign minister.

With some British help in terms of military training, supply of arms and munitions, the Tibetans soon got the upper hand and were able to throw back General Peng Jih-sheng's forces from Chamdo, Markham, Derge and other areas along the Marches. They were, in fact, able to capture a large number of prisoners, including General Peng, the governor of Szechuan. Although stretched, the Tibetans were poised to take Nyarang and Batang, and even threaten Tachienlu. The situation of the Chinese was so precarious that, to quote Teichmann, 'another month or two would possibly have seen several thousand more Chinese prisoners in Tibetan hands, and the Lhasa forces in possession of all the country up to Tachienlu'.[5]

Surprisingly, the Chinese government, though on the back foot, still did not show eagerness to settle their frontier with Tibet. Undoubtedly, they were more concerned with regaining control of the rebellious provinces of Szechuan and Yunnan. The Tibetans, on the other hand, wanted to capitalize on the favourable ground situation consequent to the victories of Kalon Lama's forces, and thus repeatedly sought the intervention of Sir Eric Teichmann, the British consular official at Tachienlu. They, as also the local Chinese officials and the people of the area, were looking to working out a permanent solution of the boundary issue with China. Teichmann mediated between Kalon Chamba Tendar, the Tibetan general, and Liu Tsan-ting, the Chinese general. On 19 August 1918, an agreement was signed by the three at Chamdo.

The boundary corresponded roughly with the course of the upper Yangtze [and further down along its watershed with Mekong—more or less following the historic frontier during the Manchu period] with China retaining the regions to the east of it, excepting the areas of Derge and Beyul. [This alignment was almost akin to the Blue Line drawn by McMahon in 1914.] The Tibetans, however, retained control of all the monasteries in the areas that passed to the Chinese.[6]

About two months later, at Rongbatsa, a supplementary agreement was orchestrated by Teichmann, after a lot of behind-the-scenes manoeuvrings. It was signed on 10 October 1918, in the presence of Teichmann, by 'Han Kuang-chun and the Chakla Gyalpo for the Chinese, and Khenchung Lozang Dondup, Dapon Khyungram, and Dapon Tethong for Tibet'. It called for a ceasefire, withdrawal of troops and a truce for one year, effective from 31 October.[7] According to the Rongbatsa truce, 'China remained in control of Batang, Litang, Nyarong, Kanze and the area to the east of Kanze, while the Tibetans retained Chamdo, Draya, Markham and Derge.'[8] Sadly, but unsurprisingly, these agreements were not ratified by the Chinese government, despite the best endeavours of both Jordan and Teichmann, who, in particular, was at this point of time 'deeply upset by the duplicity and chicanery' of the Chinese frontier officials.[9]

16

Tibet: A Political Chessboard; Panchen Lama; Death of Dalai Lama

The First World War came to an end with the signing of the armistice on 11 November 1918. This resulted in the demise of some empires, the redrawing of some boundaries and the creation of new nation states. Great Britain, like most of the other major powers, was reeling under the economic burden of the war. Issues such as Tibet, which had been shoved to the sidelines, once again began to receive attention. The British and the Tibetans were keen to resolve the Sino-Tibet boundary dispute before the Rongbatsa truce expired in October 1919. The Chinese, whose aim appeared to be resumption of negotiations on the basis of the Simla Convention, with some changes, lacked the determination or political cohesion to take the Tibet issue to its logical conclusion. They raised the subject repeatedly almost every year since 1915. In view of the attitude of proctrastination on Peking's part, Whitehall even advised Lhasa to 'claim self-determination at the forthcoming Peace Conference at Paris'. Finally, as a result of repeated urging to commence negotiations, the Chinese put forward a proposal in May 1919. This proposal contained four basic demands:

- Insertion in the main text, and not in the attached note, of a statement to the effect that 'Tibet formed a part of China'.
- Acknowledgement of Chinese suzerainty over autonomous Tibet in a separate clause.

- Chinese commissioners to be positioned at various trade marts in Tibet.
- A revised Sino-Tibet boundary that would cede Batang, Litang and Tachienlu to Szechuan, creation of Inner Tibet under greater control of China and to include Derge, Nyarong and southern Kokonor; and the rest of the regions, including Chamdo, Markham, Draya and Gonjo to comprise autonomous Tibet.[1]

Though this boundary proposal would have benefited China considerably, that too at Tibet's expense, the British found it acceptable as a starting point. Besides, nowhere was the Chinese frontier marching along north-east India, so the British investments and tea industry in Assam appeared secured. This proposal represented the final stance of the Chinese government on the boundary issue. As can be seen, it did not contain any objection as far as the Indo-Tibetan boundary east of Bhutan was concerned. However, despite some progress, this attempt to 'renegotiate' the Simla Convention was abruptly ended by the Chinese themselves. Jordan learnt later that this step was taken under intense pressure from Japan, and possibly also because of the adverse reaction of the Chinese people and likely 'opposition' to the proposal from some of the provinces like Yunnan and Szechuan.

It may not be out of place to mention here that Tibet too would most likely have rejected the terms proposed by China. As a matter of fact, on learning of these direct parleys between Britain and China, the Tsongdu (National Assembly) adopted a resolution that was conveyed to the British, in which they categorically 'rejected the Peking negotiations and the four points raised by China'.[2] The Tibetans also insisted that they should be part of any future talks. Fortunately, as we have seen, such a situation did not arise! Summing up his understanding of Chinese negotiating tactics, Jordan told Curzon: 'The whole history of the Chinese on Tibet and on the Tibetan border ... has been one of alternate bullying, chicanery, and intrigue.'[3] Nonetheless, the humiliation of the British by the unprecedented termination of these talks led to the recall of Jordan, who, 'for well-nigh a quarter century, was the most powerful, and influential, man in Peking's diplomatic corps'.[4]

In line with their strategy of directly negotiating with the Tibetans and keeping the British out, the Chinese worked behind the scenes to get an unofficial delegation from Kansu to visit Lhasa, to prevail upon the Dalai Lama to have direct talks with Peking. This group, led by Chu Hsien, comprised Kansu officials and important lamas from the famous Kumbum monastery. Although formally not invited by Lhasa, they were given a more than traditional welcome. The mission stayed in Lhasa from January to April of 1920.[5] However, the outcome of negotiations was anything but fruitful, as the Dalai Lama felt the Chinese could not be trusted, and desired to conclude no agreement 'without the presence and cooperation of a British representative'.[6]

In a face-saving measure, China then disowned this mission and its proposals. The Kansu mission, however, set alarm bells ringing in both New Delhi and London. The British policy on Tibet went through a reappraisal. The British did not want to see a Chinese-controlled Tibet, and with the collapse of the Tsarist Russian Empire, the obstacle to an 'open door' policy towards Tibet had disappeared. In a note to Curzon dated 27 April 1920, Alston, the Secretary of State for India, said, 'The previous policy of sterilising Tibet had merely played into China's hands. In fact, an open Tibet would mean a Tibet strengthened and developed under British patronage.'[7] Britain thus had to take some concrete steps to shore up its 'prestige' in Tibet.

Charles Bell's mission to Lhasa was the consequence of this new Tibet policy. It was egged on by Bell himself through a series of notes and other correspondence. But it was not before the middle of October 1920 that Whitehall finally gave the go-ahead to Bell to proceed to Lhasa. This order, typical of the British ambivalence on Tibet, contained a number of conditions, and the visit's duration of one month proved to be unimaginative and woefully inadequate to the task the mission had set out to do. In the event, Bell stayed in Lhasa for almost a year.

Bell was entrusted with rebuilding the close ties fostered between Tibet and British India during the Dalai Lama's exile in Darjeeling. However, while he was asked to display utmost 'sympathy' towards the Tibetans' pleas for assistance, Bell wasn't empowered to promise them supply of arms or ammunition. His close personal relations with the Grand Lama and his presence in Lhasa helped re-establish British influence over Tibet, keeping an obdurate China in its place. Bell also obtained intelligence on the direct Sino-Tibetan negotiations, particularly on the outcome of the Kansu mission, and was able to advise British India on their Tibet policy accordingly.

While Bell was welcomed in Tibet, there was a conservative element, incited by the lamas of Drepung, who saw danger in Tibet being opened up to the outer world, and her religion, culture and traditions being influenced adversely. This element preferred that Tibet arrive at an accord with China 'in order to salvage Tibet's traditional autonomous state and hopefully, Chinese patronage of Buddhism'.[8]

At the same time there were also many people in the country who felt the British should assume the role of Tibet's patron in place of the Chinese, a role the British were clearly unwilling to play. As the Chinese continued to ignore proposals to enter into negotiations with Britain on Tibet on some pretext or the other, the supply of British arms and ammunition to Tibet was resumed on the advice of Bell. The arms came with the stipulation that they would not be used for purposes other than for 'self-defence', and an undertaking to this effect was obtained in writing from the Dalai Lama. Bell recommended that in addition to ammunition, 10,000 rifles, twenty machine guns and ten mountain guns be given to Tibet.[9] These were to be paid for in instalments in certain cases. Besides this, military training too was imparted to some Tibetan officers and soldiers at Gyantse, and the technique of making gunpowder was taught to them. The British also helped the Tibetans construct a telegraph line from Gyantse to Lhasa. Geological surveys were conducted by Sir Henry Hayden prospecting for minerals in central Tibet, and assistance was provided to the Tibetans for construction of a small hydroelectric plant at Lhasa. Laden La, an experienced officer of the Darjeeling police, who was of Sikkimese origin, was deputed to Lhasa to form a small police force on modern lines. Lastly, a proposal was made to start an English school at Gyantse for the children of the nobility and the elite. This school started in 1924.[10] Tibet had to bear the expenses of these development schemes.

The Dalai Lama's efforts to see that Tibet was modernized were hampered by the resistance offered by the lamas. 'The richest monasteries were to be found in Lhasa—Drepung, Sera and Ganden—and there were others like Kumbum at Sining and the Panchen Lama's Tashilhumpo at Shigatse. Without exception, all were unwilling to contribute financially to modernising Tibet.'[11] Besides the financial angle, the lamas did not want to help create another power centre comprising the army and the newly reorganized police that could 'challenge the traditional lamaist theocracy'.[12] Nonetheless, the Grand Lama was able to prevail, and overcame the opposition with a heavy hand.

Bell was firmly convinced that a stable, strong and free Tibet was in the best interests of British India, as that would intrinsically provide it a secure northern frontier. In January 1921, Bell cautioned the Indian government that if the British did not come to the help of the Tibetans, they 'will certainly regard us as having betrayed them, and the influence and power of China on the northern and eastern frontiers of India will in time become greater than ever before'.[13] This advice proved to be quite visionary. It was also felt that this rekindling of Anglo-Tibetan ties would spur China to return to the negotiating table. Unfortunately, the unhappy state of affairs in China's internal administration and its lack of effective control over the outlying provinces of Szechuan and Yunnan did not allow any talks to take place.

Commenting on British aid to Tibet, Heather Spence has said: 'When China was weak the deficiency in British support was not important, but as China increased in military strength in the inter-war years of the 1920s and 1930s, the Tibetan government was forced to take the view that there was no alternative but a policy of accommodation with the "New China". Ultimately, this obliged the Dalai Lama to follow a non-alignment policy.' Spence had rightly analysed the situation: 'To encourage Tibet to claim full independence from China would have undercut Britain's own position in many parts of the world—Egypt, Africa and India.'[14] This aspect has had a major influence in the formulation of British imperial policies, particularly during the third and fourth decades of the twentieth century.

During the thirteenth Dalai Lama's rule, currency notes on handmade paper and, later, postage stamps, were introduced in Tibet for the first time. This was followed by the minting of gold and silver coins. These measures, along with other developments, were indicative of the 'de facto' independence of Tibet.[15] Describing the Dalai Lama, W.W. Rockhill, the American ambassador to China, said, 'He is a man of undoubted intelligence and ability, of quick understanding and of force of character. He is broad-minded, possibly as a result of his varied experiences during the last few years, and of great natural dignity.'[16]

Choskyi Nima, the Panchen Lama, was against the Dalai Lama's policy of modernization and opening up (even if selectively) of Tibet. His main grouse was that the Tashilhunpo monastery would have to carry forward the Dalai Lama's initiatives, particularly the maintenance of a larger and better equipped army. Citing Melvyn Goldstein, Warren W. Smith Jr, a scholar of Tibetan history, described how relations between the two lamas 'were further exacerbated by the requirement placed on Tashilhunpo to bear a quarter of the total financial burden of the army',[17] somewhat like the precedent of the bearing of one-fourth of the expenses incurred during the Sino-Tibetan campaign to throw out the Nepalese from Shigatse and other districts bordering Nepal in 1791. The Panchen Lama appealed to the British government to intervene, but the latter declined to interfere in what was considered an 'internal' matter.

Although on the surface relations between the two Great Lamas were cordial, the undercurrents spoke a different language. En route from India to Lhasa in June 1912, the Dalai Lama was welcomed by the Tashi Lama and his officials at Ralung, where they apparently discussed various matters, which might probably have included the Panchen Lama's justification of his conduct during the period of the Dalai Lama's sojourn in Mongolia and China, and later, during his exile in India. The Dalai Lama believed the Tashi Lama had acquiesced to the Chinese to some extent, going along with their government and administration during the period of his exiles, even though the Tashi Lama had refused to occupy the Dalai Lama's seat or participate in the ill-advised search and appointment of a successor to the Dalai Lama, as demanded by the Chinese. As a matter of fact, some of the lamas from Tashilhunpo had bent over backwards to please their Chinese overlords. The Dalai Lama was also furious with the followers of the Panchen Lama who, along with some monks of Loseling and Drepung monasteries, failed to reinforce the efforts of the Tibetan volunteer army to throw out the Chinese during 1912–13. The pro-Chinese monastery at Tengyeling gave shelter to the Chinese soldiers, and this led to a long Tibetan siege of the monastery before the soldiers' eventual capitulation.

His monastery unable to meet the financial demands of Lhasa and already in arrears, because of which some of his representatives were imprisoned at Lhasa in 1922, the Panchen Lama decided to flee to Mongolia and China with his key followers. The pretext he used to move northwards towards Kumbum in December 1923 was ingenious: to collect donations from his adherents. The Dalai Lama wasn't able to prevent him from doing this, and the true intentions of the Tashi Lama dawned on him much later.

After a brief sojourn in Mongolia, the Panchen Lama showed up at Peking in February 1924. The Chinese bestowed on him honours such as the title of 'Complete Lord of the Religion of the Conqueror' (the Buddhist religion),[18] and exploited his presence in Peking to the hilt by indulging in political intrigues and power play with him. Meanwhile, the Dalai Lama, having decried the Panchen Lama's 'selfishness', made alternative arrangements for administration of Tashilhunpo monastery without replacing the incumbent Lama.[19] The Tibetan culture, though medieval in many respects, permitted a wonderful practice of public criticism or satire in poetic form. An example of this was the street song aimed at the Panchen Lama's 'duplicitous' conduct during the Dalai Lama's exile:

The bird known as magpie (the Panchen Lama)
Has a body that is half black and half white.
After the great cuckoo bird (the Dalai Lama) arrives,
we will slowly be able to have discussions.[20]

The absence of the Panchen Lama, the second most revered reincarnated lama of Tibet, certainly had its impact on the Tibetan people at large. The conservative elements of Tibetan society, mainly the leading monks, found fault with the modernizing policies of the Dalai Lama. This growing resentment, a fair amount of which was directed against the British for their imperialistic tendencies, nearly led to an armed confrontation between the military hierarchy and the lamas in Lhasa and a mini-revolt in the Pomed region, because of which the local ruler, the Kanam Deba, fled to Assam. The Dalai Lama was thus confronted with one of his greatest challenges. He overcame the crisis by demoting key military and civil officials and reversing most of the recent irksome and unpopular policy changes[21]. The English school being run at Gyantse under the tutelage of Frank Ludlow was shut down in 1926. Upon his dismissal on 28 October that year, he (Ludlow) wrote in his diary:

> It seems that the Indian govt can do nothing right for Tibet. We lend them Laden La to train their police and they allow all his good work in Lhasa to rot. We train officers for their army and they are dismissed wholesale. We try to run a school for them and they throw it to the dogs... They will regret their decision one day when they are Chinese slaves once more as they assuredly will be.[22]

At one stage, when the Chiang Kai-shek regime had taken control in China in 1929 the Panchen Lama went to the extent of exhorting the Chinese 'to take charge of affairs in Tibet. To the chagrin of the Dalai Lama, the Chinese hosted the Panchen Lama for well over a decade till his death at Jyekundo on 1 December 1937.'[23]

As mentioned earlier, the Chinese, British, Russians, and to some extent the Japanese too, indulged in political games and intrigue with the two lamas. The British invited the Tashi Lama to India during 1904–06 when the Dalai Lama had fled to Mongolia. He was given lavish presents and hosted extravagantly during his visits to religious and other places in India. The Russians intrigued with the Dalai Lama during his exile at Urga in Mongolia. Dorjieff was the conduit through which the Lama kept in touch with the Kremlin. The Chinese, not to be left behind, received the Dalai Lama warmly, although they granted him a status that was a couple of notches below the recognition awarded to the Great Fifth, taking advantage of his helplessness as an exile. The mandarins at Peking tried their best to win him over by other inducements. However, when the Chinese army under Chao Erh-feng invaded Lhasa in 1910, the Dalai Lama was literally driven into the arms of the British. Over the next two years and thereafter, the Dalai Lama gained the trust and support of the British. During this time, the Panchen Lama was given greater prominence by the Chinese but ignored by the British, who relegated him to the sidelines. On the Grand Lama's jubilant return in 1913 to Lhasa— when, for the first time after 1727, Tibet was rid of Chinese power and presence from its soil—Dorjieff was back to his Russian intrigues and the Japanese had found a niche in Tibet by providing one or two military advisers and material help. One of them, Yajima Yasujiro, was a veteran of the Russo-Japanese War of 1904, and helped train the Tibetan army from 1913 to 1919. Another, Aoki Bunkyo, a monk, 'translated Japanese army manuals into Tibetan'.[24] The third was Togan Tada, a Japanese monk who stayed for eleven years in the Sera monastery. Besides studying, he could have been politicking too, as surmised by Bell in a note to the Indian government on 6 February 1921: 'Japanese, as a rule, find it difficult to abstain from politics.'[25]

The internal strife and schisms in the Chinese polity after Yuan Shih-kai's downfall, Tibet's dependence on the British, and the British Empire's geographical proximity and ease of access to Tibet made Britain the paramount power and wielder of influence in Tibet for the next four decades (that too without its assumption of any responsibility). This was despite the power play and intrigues by other powers. With a faction-ridden power like China held at bay and a benign and peaceful Tibet as neighbour, India's northern border remained secure. Now a complacency set in, to the extent that there were hardly any efforts made by the British to penetrate the densely forested wildernesses of the tribal areas and to change or modify their policy of 'loose political control' of the north-eastern frontier tracts south of the Himalayas.

The situation along the Sino-Tibet frontier, though largely peaceful, remained tense, and there was skirmishing in some of the disputed areas in eastern Tibet. The absence of a mutually acceptable and well-defined boundary between China and Tibet was the root cause of this violence. The Dalai Lama continued to press for ratification of the McMahon Convention and its 'blue line', with certain changes, but to no avail. He also wished that the Panchen Lama should return to Tashilhunpo. However, the Tibetans had made it clear that the Panchen Lama would not be allowed to enter Tibet accompanied by a Chinese escort, as was insisted on by the Panchen Lama himself and his hosts. The Tibetans even suggested that he could return by the sea route, enter Tibet through India and proceed directly to Shigatse. The Dalai Lama had laid down two conditions for the Panchen Lama's return: first, that he would have to pay the normal tax dues as well as the 'new tax' to finance the 'national defence programme'; and second, that he would be allowed entry into Tibet accompanied by his Tibetan retinue alone, and not with an armed Chinese escort.[26] The Panchen Lama was unable to have his terms for return to Tashilhunpo accepted by the Tsongdu, despite much effort. He passed away at Jyekundo in November 1937, 'to the mingled sorrow and relief of the Tibetan people'.[27]

The Chiang Kai-shek government made many overtures to engage with the Dalai Lama directly, as they considered Tibet an integral part of China and believed it was unnecessary to involve the British in Sino-Tibetan matters. In this regard, two delegations were sent to Lhasa during 1929–30. One was led by Liu Man-ch'ing, a half-Chinese born in Lhasa of a Tibetan mother, who was tasked to convey the message of Chiang Kai-shek that Tibetans should 'rejoin the family of the Republic as brothers'.[28] The second mission arrived at Lhasa on 16 January 1930. This one was empowered to engage in a dialogue for direct settlement of Tibetan issues and was led by a Tibetan, Yungon Dzasa, the head abbot of the Yung-ho Kung temple at Peking. He had been appointed head abbot by the Dalai Lama himself. These delegations and initiatives were well received, but the Dalai Lama was not prepared to accept the terms offered by Chiang Kai-shek. According to Bell, the Dalai Lama 'was determined to free Tibet as far as possible from the Chinese rule' and believed that the 'majority of the Tibetan race were with him'. Bell has recounted the words of the Dalai Lama describing the way of Chinese strategic thinking:

> The Chinese way ... is to say or do something mild at first, then to wait a bit, and, if it passes without objection, to say or do something stronger. If this is objected to, they reply that what they said or did has been misinterpreted and really meant nothing.[29]

This observation perhaps holds good to this day!

With his understanding of the Chinese mind, the Grand Lama was able to keep Tibet free of Chinese presence 'by creating a balance of power between China and India', in the process being 'able to maintain Tibet's independence'.[30] It would not be an exaggeration to say that during the last two decades (1913–1933) of his life, Tibet was *de facto an independent kingdom.*

Tibet witnessed a period of relative peace and stability after the Simla Conference, if one did not consider the skirmishes on its eastern frontiers with China. Peace was elusive in the Kham and southern Amdo regions, as there did not appear to be much central control over the provinces of Szechuan and Yunnan, where only the writ of the regional warlords and generals could run. There were many warring factions among them which did not see eye to eye with Chiang Kai-shek, and before him with President Yuan Shih-k'ai, and waged internecine wars for petty gains. Because of their expansionist tendencies they posed a constant security threat to the eastern frontiers of Tibet. The thirteenth Dalai Lama therefore had no choice but to strengthen and modernize his army. He was able to do this in a fairly satisfactory manner, primarily because of the help provided by the British. Ironically, at the same time, Great Britain did not want to make Tibet so strong that it could stake a claim for total independence from China.

During the final phase of his reign, the Dalai Lama had a team of three powerful confidants—Kunphela, Lungshar, and Tsarong—apart from his young prime minister, Silon Langdun, who was also his nephew. Though the three confidants worked closely, there was a deep undercurrent of rivalry among them. Tsarong, though at one time very powerful, had been removed from the position of commander-in-chief of the army in the purge of British-trained leadership from the modernized Tibetan army. He had also been demoted from the Kashag. Lungshar, given the rank of Tsepon (finance minister), was made responsible for the military in Tsarong's place. Although he too was removed from that position for nearly starting a war with Nepal over the arrest of Sherpa Gyalpo for illegal commercial activity from the precincts of the Nepalese resident in Lhasa without the approval of the Dalai Lama, he retained his power and status, being a Tsepon. Kunphela, holding the rank of Khenche (senior abbot), was the powerful chief of the mint and had the responsibility of 'importation and distribution of arms and ammunition'. As a means of gaining more power, he created a new regiment called Drong Drak Makhar, comprising the sons of the elite. Lungshar believed Kunphela was instrumental in his dismissal and nursed a grudge against him.[31]

The era of the thirteenth Dalai Lama ended on 17 December 1933, when he left for the 'honorable field'. A Tibetan proverb aptly sums up the predicament of the Tibetans, now that the British were not holding their hand firmly:

Sheep that trusted in the pasture
O'er the precipice were hurled.[32]

Two years before his death, the Dalai Lama wrote a testament for his people. This was published in a small book of nine pages, known amongst Tibetans as the 'Precious Protector's Ka Chem'. First, the Dalai Lama described his personal life and experiences, including the hardships he suffered during his two periods of exile from his country. Then he articulated his concern about the future threat to the Tibetan religion, culture and way of life from communism, both from without and within. The communists were destroying monasteries in Mongolia, he wrote, and the search for the reincarnation of Jetsun Dampa of Urga had been 'disallowed'.[33] He advised Tibetans to 'maintain friendly relations with Britain and China, both of which have powerful armies'.[34] He said in warning: 'Unless we can guard our own country, it will now happen that the Dalai Lama and the Panchen Lamas, the Father and the Son, the holders of the Buddhist faith, the glorious rebirths will be broken down and left without a name.'[35] He exhorted young and vigorous Tibetans to enlist in the army to defend the nation: 'High officials, low officials, and peasants must all act in harmony to bring happiness to Tibet.'[36]

His passing away created a leadership void and a state of instability and uncertainty in Tibet. A struggle for power instantly ensued. According to Tibetan tradition, a regent had to be selected. At the same time, the search had begun for the Dalai Lama's reincarnated successor. Within two months, the Tsongdu, probably influenced by Lungshar, nominated the young and inexperienced incarnate Lama of Reting as the regent.[37] The scheming and vengeful Lungshar wanted to discredit Kunphela, and as a first step towards this called for the mass resignation of the entire Drong Drak Makhar regiment. With the backing of the important monasteries, it did not take long for Lungshar to become the power centre. Sidelining the Kashag (council of ministers), Lungshar was able to win over the support of the Tsongdu, whose members were promised an important role in the future political dispensation that he planned for Tibet. He was able to completely overshadow Kunphela by laying the blame on him for not informing anybody of the Dalai Lama's illness and for the inadequate medical attention that the Dalai Lama got. As a punishment, the Tsongdu was possibly prevailed upon by Lungshar to exile Kunphela to Kongbo in south Tibet.[38] Thereafter, till his dramatic downfall, Lungshar was one of most powerful men in Lhasa.

As these events unfolded, Lungshar's ambitious plan to overthrow the present government by arresting the regent and ministers and to create a republic, wherein the council or Kashag was subordinated to the Tsongdu, was exposed. His diabolical plan of assassinating Kalon Trimon, an important minister and a respected conservative (who was also Lonchen Shatra's principal guide at the Simla Conference), whom he considered a major obstacle in his chosen path, was also simultaneously unravelled. Lungshar was arrested and, having been found guilty of treason, was blinded[39] and sentenced to life imprisonment. His lust for power ended his regal dreams within a brief span of four months. Tibet emerged from this quagmire quite unnerved, but was kept afloat by the state institutions such as the Kashag and the Tsongdu, who functioned along the guidelines contained in the Dalai Lama's testament. During this period, the irksome shadow of the Panchen Lama, which was ensconced in China, loomed large over the political horizon in Tibet. The Panchen Lama spent his time engineering clever plots against the Lhasa regime till his passing away in 1937 in Jyekundo on the Chinese-held western frontier. As prophesied, he never returned to Tashilhunpo.[40]

This situation in Tibet continued for more than a decade and a half, till the Chinese military takeover in 1951 snatched the country's autonomous existence of near freedom. The Chinese violated all the existing agreements and promises it had made with Tibet and Britain by this invasion.

The death of the Dalai Lama was just the kind of opportunity the Chinese republic was waiting for to re-establish its presence in Tibet proper. The Tibetan government had not permitted any Chinese to enter Tibet for official or other purposes since 1912. Chinese traders and merchants were perhaps the only exceptions. Trying to take advantage of the special circumstances, the Chinese government sought permission to send a mission to 'offer religious tribute and condolences for the late Dalai Lama'. Given the religious and ceremonious tenor of the request, it was difficult for the Tibetans to refuse them. Accordingly, in April 1934, a high-powered delegation led by General Huang Mu-sung arrived in Lhasa. Having gone through the formalities that protocol demanded, Huang got down to his real mission of making the Tibetans acknowledge the overlordship of China and become an equal member of the republic under the ambit of the 'five races' policy.

Despite his intense cajoling and lavish inducements, he was unable to get any worthwhile commitment or concessions from the Tibetans. It is to the credit of the Kashag and the Tsongdu that the Tibetans held on to the conditions stipulated in the Simla Convention of 1914, making it clear that they were not prepared to forsake their fully auotonomous character. They also emphasized that the 'British Government should be a party to any agreement reached between Tibet and China'.[41] Despite the numerous discussions he had with the Tibetans, General Huang was unable to secure any commitment from them beyond what was in the 1914 Convention, be it concessions on the Sino-Tibet boundary or status of Tibet. Taking no chances, Williamson, the political officer in Sikkim, sent his representative, Rai Bahadur Norbu Dhondup, to keep a close watch on the activities of the Chinese mission at Lhasa.

As far as the Panchen Lama's return was concerned, the Tibetan officials conveyed to the Chinese that an early return of the Tashi Lama was desirable, but unaccompanied by any Chinese military escort. A disappointed General Huang eventually left for China after a few months, but left behind two liaison officers and a Chinese official from Kansu, along with a wireless set. This ad hoc establishment slowly firmed in, assuming the shape of a 'regular diplomatic mission'. For the first time since 1912, there was a small yet credible Chinese presence at Lhasa. This was undoubtedly the most significant achievement of Huang's mission.[42] The visit of Huang was followed by a high-level delegation led by Basil Gould, the new political officer in Sikkim. The aim of this visit was to reassure the incumbent Tibetan government of British support against Chinese pressure and help them reconcile matters relating to the Panchen Lama's return. Like the Chinese, the British too stationed their representative, Richardson, along with a wireless operator, in Tibet to facilitate speedy communications when Gould returned to India[43].

Meanwhile, the process of discovering the reincarnation of the thirteenth Dalai Lama had commenced. Guidance and help was sought through the medium of oracles, the high lamas, prophecies and tests. The young candidate was found in the village of Takse in the Amdo region in 1937. He was brought to Lhasa, and the necessary formalities were conducted for training him for the temporal and spiritual responsibilities that would be his on his assuming eighteen years of age. Until that time, the regent, with the authority of the Tsongdu and the Kashag, would run the affairs of the state. It was at this juncture that the McMahon Line was resurrected, on the initiative and commitment of Sir Olaf Caroe, the deputy secretary in the foreign department. This happened as a consequence of the Tibet visit of the adventurer and botanist F. Kingdon Ward, who entered the Pome and Kongbo areas north of the Tsangpo without the sanction of the Tibetan government. He had crossed the red line (the McMahon Line), which continued to be the de jure boundary as agreed on in 1914. Because of the sensitive nature of the negotiations carried out during the Simla Conference, coupled with the fact that the text of the convention had not been communicated to either the Assam government or to the political officer in Sikkim, there was considerable lack of awareness with regard to the McMahon Line. This was how Ward was allowed to cross the red line from the Assam side, where the administration had little knowledge of the red line. This was not the case in Tibet, where the powers that be were aware of McMahon's red line.

This deficiency on the British side was set right by Olaf Caroe, who had the map of the McMahon Line and the '1914 Convention with Tibet and connected agreements' published in the Aitchison's Treaty series, Vol. XIV in 1936 as well as the depiction of the McMahon Line boundary done by Survey of India, even though both actions were done without much publicity. The older, 1929 version of the Aitchison's Treaty series was withdrawn and discretely replaced with the revised version. After this, Captain G.S. Lightfoot was assigned the task of touring the Tawang area in April 1938 and to report on the situation along the McMahon Line. He was instructed to convey to 'all concerned that Tawang is by treaty Indian'.[44] However, his recommendation of positioning a small administrative set-up was turned down, mainly on account of the financial commitment that it would entail.

Soon, the Second World War broke out, and once again Tibet was consigned to the sidelines of history. In fact, China consolidated her ties with the USA and the Allies by helping in the war effort and in containment of the Japanese. However, at the same time, Tibet continued to exist as a practically independent nation and maintained a neutral posture, unlike during the First World War when it had volunteered its support to Britain. Unfortunately, an independent Tibet did not offer any strategic advantages to any major power, because of which none of them showed interest in lending it a helping hand, as that might be at the cost of strained relations with a stronger China. Besides having its own army since 1923, Tibet had its own flag, currency and passports, and maintained a de-facto independent existence. Tibet's unenviable position during the inter-war years has been brilliantly described in the words of an Australian scholar and researcher, Heather Spence: 'It was Tibet's particular misfortune to be caught in the clutch of two powerful neighbours, Britain and China, who used her as a pawn in the compassionless game of political intrigue and diplomacy.'[45]

At the time of transfer of power to India in 1947, the Tsongdu in Lhasa, 'after the fullest deliberation, placed on record its tacit acceptance of the Simla Convention and the Trade Regulations of 1914, albeit, it was of the view that these should be revised in due course of time'.[46]

PART VII

BOUNDARY ISSUE BETWEEN INDEPENDENT INDIA AND PEOPLE'S REPUBLIC OF CHINA

'Even Brahma cannot see the end of a well-devised deceit.'[1]

Panchatantra

17

Bonhomie, Appeasement, Imprudence, Deception

India and China represent two ancient civilizations, separated by a high-altitude desert plateau and a grand mountain chain, one of the most spectacular in the world. These two great nations were not neighbours in the real sense, as Tibet formed the buffer between them. Geography has largely prevented the two nations from close interaction, trade and commerce, or, for that matter, from being a military threat to each other. For centuries, therefore, these two civilizations coexisted peacefully, although the two empires—their core areas set apart by a few thousand kilometres—waxed and waned in their power and domination of the peripheral states within reach of their respective spheres of influence. At times, as borne out by history, these areas of interest overlapped, as has been described by John W. Garver in his masterly analysis[2] of the challenges in Sino-Indian relations. Yet, on the whole, two distinct and profound cultures evolved over time in the Indus and Gangetic plains in South Asia and in the Huang Ho and the Yangtze basins in East Asia with some overlap.

Even though both nations had to face numerous invasions and even suffer foreign rule, the profundity and innate strength of their cultures absorbed the outsiders, who ended up adapting to the civilizations of their subordinated nations. At the zenith of the Mughal and Manchu empires in India and China respectively, about 40 per cent of world trade was generated by these populous and prosperous nations. This period was

247

followed by the Industrial Revolution in Europe during the seventeenth century, and an era of colonization of Africa and Asia for about three centuries by the Western powers. India had to endure over two centuries of British rule. In the case of China, which was not colonized except for a few parts, it was forced by the world powers to be subservient to them and made to comply with a number of 'unequal treaties'. It suffered a century or more of this 'humiliation'. China also went through two revolutions and a civil war, all of which resulted in intense internal strife. The first revolution overthrew the Manchu Empire in 1911 and proclaimed a new republic. The second resulted in the creation of People's Republic of China (PRC) in 1949, having pushed the defeated Chiang Kai-shek's regime into Taiwan. The end of the Second World War heralded a new era, and both these great nations emerged as sovereign and independent countries, one embracing a parliamentary democratic system of governance and the other following the path of communism.

When India announced its recognition of PRC on 30 December 1949, within three months of the republic's formation, it became the second non-communist country to do so after Burma.

As India took its first strides as an independent nation, the undefined and undemarcated portions of its northern boundary with the Tibet region of China, which were inherited from the British, needed to be addressed as a priority. After the inconclusive war initiated by Pakistan over Kashmir in 1947–48 ended with a ceasefire, the India–Tibet Autonomous Region (TAR) boundary question emerged as the next major challenge for India. The Chinese takeover of Tibet by force during 1950–51 exposed the northern borders of India to potential Chinese threat for the first time, highlighting our vulnerability.

The British strategy of over half a century, of having an autonomous Tibet as a buffer, was put to rest as India looked on passively. The geostrategic implications of this event were, surprisingly, not given due consideration and were hardly debated by the Indian policymakers of the time. In a muted protest, the Government of India conveyed 'deep regret' about the Chinese resolution of the Tibetan problem by use of force. During that time, the war in Korea diverted world attention and had now assumed international proportions. It sucked in the US and its allies, who were arrayed against Soviet-backed North Korea and China. It was the first major conflict of the 'cold war'. As the rest of the world looked on, China blatantly crushed under its army boots its repeated assurances to Tibet and British India that it would respect Tibetan autonomy and not turn Tibet into a regular province of China. The tragedy of Tibet has been poignantly described in Amar Kaur's authoritative account of Tibetan history: 'The political chessboard had finally yielded "the smallest of pawns" and Tibet, faced with a neighbour unwilling to guarantee her independence, fell victim to her own weakness and in the face of imperialist expansionism.'[3]

India's first prime minister, Jawaharlal Nehru, was given sagacious advice by eminent leaders like his home minister, Sardar Vallabhbhai Patel, and the secretary general in the external affairs ministry, Girija Shankar Bajpai, on settling the boundary matter with China. In an elaborate letter to Nehru on 7 November 1950, soon after the capture of Chamdo by the Chinese army, which threw open to them the gates to Lhasa, Patel, the visionary that he was, said in no uncertain terms:

The Chinese Government has tried to delude us by professions of peaceful intention... The final action of the Chinese [invasion of Tibet], in my judgement, is little short of perfidy ... we have to consider what new situation now faces us as a result of the disappearance of Tibet, as we know it, and the expansion of China almost up to our gates ... We seem to have regarded Tibetan autonomy as extending to independent treaty relationship. Presumably all that was required was Chinese countersignature (referring to the Simla convention of 1914 and the McMahon Line). The Chinese interpretation of suzerainty seems to be different. We can therefore safely assume that very soon they will disown all the stipulations that Tibet has entered into with us in the past.[4]

Patel went on to highlight the challenges posed to our security in the light of the new threat and suggested measures to meet them. Unfortunately, his strategic advice fetched a tepid response from Nehru, and Patel too passed away soon afterwards. There was no one left in India to challenge Nehru's views. A former diplomat and China expert has commented: 'No official had the temerity to raise it (the impact of China overlooking the southern slopes of the Himalayas) anymore.'[5] Any such views were brushed aside with disdain.

Had these recommendations been acted on, the history of Sino-Indian relations might have been different. Ignoring Patel's sound advice, Nehru and his close advisers in foreign policymaking, Ambassador K.M. Panikkar in particular, believed a close friendship with China would be in India's long-term interests even if, in the bargain, Tibet's autonomous existence of near-independence had to be forsaken. On 18 November 1950, Nehru responded to his home minister, Patel: 'It is exceedingly unlikely that we may have to face any real military invasion from the Chinese side, whether in peace or in war, in the foreseeable future.'[6] It is clear that Nehru did not seriously consider a threat to India from China across the Himalayan frontier till about 1956. In fact, when the first commander-in-chief of the Indian armed forces, General Sir Robert Lockhart, presented an elaborate plan for expansion of the Indian Army to Nehru, the prime minister peremptorily dismissed the idea. Nehru said: 'We foresee no military threats. You can scrap the army. The police are good enough to meet our security needs.' Yet there was gross ambivalence on Nehru's part when, addressing the Lok Sabha on 20 November 1950, he said:

> ... the frontier from Ladakh to Nepal is defined chiefly by long usage and custom ... Our maps show that the McMahon Line is our boundary and that is our boundary—map or no map. That fact remains and we stand by that boundary, and we will not allow anybody to come across that boundary.[7]

This was a reassuring statement as far as our nation was concerned, but it did not encourage any discussion or discourse on the boundary issue, as all appeared to be well on the Himalayan frontier; *tout va bien*!

It could not escape the attention of any rational strategic mind that to honour such a commitment to the nation India would need appropriate military muscle—a capable army, navy and air force. How did Nehru fail to see this logic or, for that matter, fail to seek professional military advice? At that critical juncture in India's history, who was responsible for the national security strategy? The unilateral desire of a nation to live in peace cannot be a guarantee of its peaceful existence. The ignoring of this axiom led to our nation paying a heavy price eventually.

Nehru was unquestionably a visionary statesman, but he was as much an idealist too. Ranged against him were committed communist leaders like Mao Zedong and Zhou Enlai—pragmatic and earthy veterans of People's Republic of China. They were sworn proponents of a geopolitical strategy to regain all the 'lost' Chinese territories and avenge the 'century of humiliation' of China by the world powers. They had envisioned a policy for the consolidation of Tibet and other outer dependencies to create a strong nation of five races, the Han, Manchu, Mongol, Tibetan and Muslim (Hui). The Chinese believe 'they are and have always been of one race, that they share a common origin, and that those who occupy what is China today have always enjoyed a natural affinity with each other as one big family'.[8]

Moreover, China is a 'civilization-state', whose historians are convinced that the process of 'territorial expansion' has to be considered as one of 'unification' rather than 'conquest', and who have alluded to such expansion as 'a progressive evolution towards a preordained and inevitable unity'.[9] The Chinese takeover or 'liberation' of Tibet had, in one stroke, made their intentions very clear, throwing overboard any semblance of vacillation, indecisiveness or weakness that China may have displayed in the first half of the twentieth century.

At this point in history, unlike the Russo-phobia of the British Empire, which prompted it to prefer a weak China as a buffer country, India's security interests would have been best served by an autonomous Tibet instead. This buffer vanished, leaving India with two options to counter China's action. The first was to render assistance to Tibet by all means, including use of force if the need arose, and the second was to sympathize with the Tibetans and protest diplomatically while accepting the situation as a fait accompli. Viewing the scenario in a realistic manner, the Indian government found itself left with no choice but the latter option. Unarguably, at that point, dispatch of an expeditionary force into Tibet was, militarily speaking, out of the question. Besides, there were other equally, if not more, pressing demands for use of the military for consolidation of the Indian republic, such as integration of Hyderabad and Junagarh, and liberation of Goa, Daman and Diu, besides, of course, the new commitment of defending the ceasefire line in Jammu and Kashmir.

Speaking in support of the decision his government had to make, Nehru, who was also the foreign minister during his entire seventeen-year tenure as prime minister, said: 'The only result of such a course (firm stand) might be a flare-up on our border or more oppression, more cruelty against the Tibetans. I do not believe in making empty gestures—it is of no use unless I have the power and strength to implement any decision that I take.'[10] There was a certain amount of dichotomy and ambivalence in the above statement when viewed in the context of Nehru's earlier statement on the inviolability of the McMahon Line, because that was based on a false sense of bravado rather than on India's actual military capability. Further, nothing much was done to enhance our defence preparedness during the decade of the 1950s. Anything Nehru said, wrote or approved on foreign affairs became our policy, such was the aura of his persona. And his views became so sacrosanct that his policies were very seldom questioned.

This remained the case at least during the first decade of our nationhood. Wing Commander R.V. Parasnis has emphasized the lack of a comprehensive approach to foreign policy evolution. He recorded that, 'According to B.K. Nehru, he alone among the politicians, other than Jawaharlal Nehru, had any understanding of foreign affairs in those early years after Independence. (Among the bureaucrats the only knowledgeable person was Girija Shankar Bajpai.)'[11] Subsequently, it was the 'Nehru-Menon combine' that gave directions to the bureaucracy on foreign policy issues. 'Keeping the defence services out resulted in a lame Indian foreign policy, without the backing of the required military muscle,' said Parasnis.[12] Reflecting on Nehru, a former foreign secretary and an old China hand, Jagat S. Mehta, commented, 'We shall never again have the likes of Nehru and we, the professionals, lacked the courage to offer him timely corrective counsel … His bark was frightening but his bite was not vicious.'[13]

Sadly, emphasis on national security strategy was conspicuous by its absence at the highest level, and the military leadership was snubbed into silence or indifference. The Nehru–Menon combine played havoc with the military leadership, literally forcing them to accept militarily unsound commitments. Giving more than due importance to the assessments of the intelligence chief, B.N. Mullik, Nehru and Menon were able to persuade the acquiescing generals like Thapar and Kaul to agree to their 'forward policy' of showing our flag in remote frontier areas along our boundary.

Kaul said, '(Since China was unlikely to wage war with India) there was no reason why we should not play a game of chess and a battle of wits with them, so far as the question of establishing posts was concerned.'[14] In a caustic remark in an article he wrote for the *Tribune* published in March 2013, Inder Malhotra, a reputed journalist, said: 'If, instead of interfering with the making of policy, he [the director, IB] had done his job of gathering intelligence on China, India would not have been taken by surprise and might even have escaped the humiliation.' He was equally critical of the other key personalities of the time, including Nehru.

The subjugation of Tibet was proving to be a bigger challenge than China had earlier imagined. India's efforts to mediate and render advice to them to resolve the Tibetan problem peacefully were snubbed. The Chinese response to India was curt and unambiguous: 'Tibet is an integral part of Chinese territory. The problem of Tibet is entirely the domestic problem of China on which no foreign interference will be tolerated.'[15] Mao's advancing armies homed in on Lhasa from all directions in a multipronged invasion. To overcome the logistic nightmare of supporting his army in the vast desert expanse of resource-starved Tibet, road communications were vital. Mao's strategy to liberate Tibet was to 'advance while building roads', goes one narrative. An excerpt from an account of the invasion talks about how the Chinese were unmindful 'of the thousands of workers who died due to the exacting work and living conditions in the oxygen-less high altitude terrain'.

Fearing the Chinese onslaught, on 17 November 1950, the young Dalai Lama fled to Yatung in the Chumbi Valley, a stone's throw from the Indian border. Thereafter, on India's urging he returned to Lhasa.

Conscious of the fact that there was 'lack of American and British support' too to the Tibetan cause, he sent his delegates to Peking to 'seek a peaceful settlement with Peking which safeguarded Tibetan autonomy'.[16] A seventeen-point Sino-Tibetan Agreement on Measures for the Peaceful Liberation of Tibet was signed between the two sides in Peking on 23 May 1951. Not unexpectedly, China was able to coerce the Tibetans into securing in Article I itself an admission by Tibet that it was a part of China and that 'the Tibetan people shall return to the big family of the Motherland—the People's Republic of China', thus legalizing its subjugation of Tibet. Other articles in the agreement referred to 'the centralised handling of all external affairs of the area of Tibet', 'integration' of the Tibetan army with the People's Liberation Army, and establishment of a 'Military Area HQ' in Tibet. This signalled the end of Tibet's de facto independence and China-free existence that it had enjoyed for four decades since 1912. This treaty also allowed China to station its troops in Tibet, bringing both India and China face to face for the first time.

At this stage, India's China policy faltered. We failed to see through the Chinese game plan and overall strategy. In an endeavour to create a peaceful neighbourhood and to smooth ruffled feathers, Nehru decided to placate China by unreservedly accepting Tibet as a part of China and by endorsing the Panchsheel agreement on 29 April 1954. This agreement laid down guidelines for peaceful relations between the two countries, the salient ones being:

- Mutual respect for each other's territorial integrity and sovereignty,
- Mutual non-aggression,
- Mutual non-interference in each other's internal affairs,
- Equality and mutual benefits, and
- Peaceful coexistence.

Granting accord to these 'five principles' enshrined in the agreement, India also gave up its inherited rights in Tibet, which had been gained after painstaking and costly ventures undertaken by the British since the first decade of the twentieth century. These were the Younghusband expedition, the Anglo-Tibetan Treaty of 1904, the establishment and functioning of trade agencies in Yatung and Gyantse, military escorts, telegraph lines and rest houses along the road from Sikkim, and the legacy of the Chumbi Valley, which could have been in British India's possession for seventy-five years from 1915, as originally conceived by Younghusband, and therefore could have been under Indian control up to 1990, theoretically!

The intangible loss of India's stature and its perceived role in these developments in the eyes of the Tibetans was not insignificant either. An account paraphrasing a letter written to Zhou Enlai by Nehru, the idealist and moralist, says, '(Nehru) insisted that dislike of imperialists' mores had never been more evident than when he agreed to sign away these extra-territorial privileges from India to China.'[17] As borne out by later events, the Panchsheel agreement did not stand the test of time, and the two nations went to war over the boundary issue in 1962.

It is difficult to comprehend why India did not seek any quid pro quo for this one-sided political and diplomatic largesse. We could have, for example, demanded or insisted on Chinese acceptance of the Indo-Tibetan boundary of 1914, the McMahon Line, or more favourable terms for trade, and other concessions. As a matter of fact, as has already been highlighted earlier, the Chinese had never raised any reservations or objections about the Indo-Tibetan portion of the famous 'red line' drawn during the Simla Conference. During Prime Minister Nehru's visit to China in 1954, he raised the issue of the major cartographic error in Chinese maps 'showing the whole of N.E.F.A. (North East Frontier Agency) in China', a matter that had been brought to his notice by Dr S.P. Mookerjee in Parliament. 'Zhou En-lai replied that they were reproductions of old pre-liberation maps. Nehru gracefully said that he could well understand how the "many and heavy pre-occupations" [sic] of the Chinese Government led to the postponement of more up-to-date cartography.'[18] The Chinese continued to show NEFA in the same manner in their maps published in 1956 too. That was the era of bonhomie, albeit short-lived, between India and China, summed up in the slogan 'Hindi Chini bhai bhai' (India–China brotherhood). It is a fact that later, in 1963, Nehru admitted in Parliament that it was 'foolish' of him to have assumed that 'there was nothing to discuss' about the boundary with the Chinese leadership.[19]

Between 1954 and 1959, there were a number of Chinese intrusions into Indian territory, despite the apparent state of bonhomie and well-being on both sides. As a matter of fact, during this period the Chinese were discreetly carrying out their first-ever surveys of the border areas with the help of Tibetan villagers inhabiting the northern glacis of the Himalayas to ascertain the southern limits of Tibet. The locals made out maximalist claims that included some pastures south of the Himalayan watershed such as Shipki La.

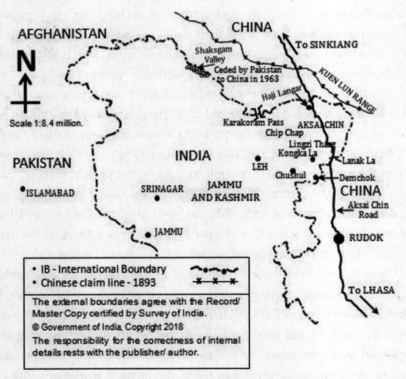

Figure 18: Chinese claims on boundary in Ladakh

In 1955, Chinese troops entered Barahoti and Danzan in erstwhile United Provinces (present Uttar Pradesh); and in 1956, the Shipki La was crossed a number of times. In 1957, they entered Walong in NEFA. Members of an Indian police patrol were arrested in Aksai Chin and kept as prisoners in custody for five weeks. The Chinese had unilaterally altered the traditional boundary in the western sector, as was evident from their 1956 claim line which lay approximately 60-100 kilometres to the west of the Aksai Chin road (Figure 18). Commenting on Nehru's policy of diplomatic appeasement of China, Jagat Mehta, a former foreign secretary, said:

> There was the beginning of a suspicion that 'south of the Himalayas' was not accepted in China as part of India's outer strategic and cultural frontier. For the sake of promoting a climate of peace, it was considered prudent not to raise these controversial questions [the boundary with China], which could dilute the solidarity of anti-imperialism. India was inclined to be indulgent and suppress the differences. The dominant credo was that non-alignment must assuage fears aroused by containment.[20]

Unfortunately, with the passing away of Sardar Patel, who was not only an erudite political personality but also endowed with the strategic wisdom to advise Nehru in balancing national security interests with building an international image for India or buying our peace, there was no one left of that stature in the country. The unresolved Sino-Indian boundary, spanning a distance of 4,057 kilometres of high-altitude mountainous terrain, has today become the subject of the most complex and intractable border disputes in the world.

Three months after the signing of the Panchsheel agreement in 1954, Nehru decided that India's maps should show properly defined frontiers based on the historical, geographical, ethnic and cultural divide between India and China, and also taking into account earlier agreements, tradition and usage. The existing maps, where the boundary was either shown by a colour wash accompanied by the words 'boundary undefined' on the outer extremity or, in the case of the McMahon Line, where it was printed 'boundary undemarcated', would be withdrawn. A careful examination of the Survey of India maps of that period shows that the words 'BOUNDARY UNDEFINED' and the colour wash were not randomly printed, but that the upper line formed by the letters defined approximately the silhouette of our northern boundary. This outline roughly included the Aksai Chin area and was synonymous with our traditional and customary boundary. On Prime Minister Nehru's directions, our northern boundary was thereafter firmly and unambiguously marked on Survey of India maps.

By this time Nehru was fully aware of the incorrect depiction of the Sino-Indian frontier on Chinese maps of that period drawn up unilaterally by China. Both nations were thus guilty of unilateral actions that were highly vulnerable to misinterpretation, and potentially conflictual. Unfortunately, neither the elite nor the lay people of either country were informed of the real situation before these unilateral steps were implemented. The seeds of the showdown between the two nations were sown between 1954 and 1956.

In the case of China, the fault was of greater significance, as it began construction of a motorable road from Sinkiang to western Tibet passing through Indian territory, even though this territory was undefined or undemarcated until 1954. This activity was done with great secrecy and sans media publicity, even in their country. But whatever doubts may have existed before the new maps were issued by the Indian government in 1954, they no longer remained after this action by the Indians. The Chinese had no grounds to blatantly go ahead with the project without a dialogue with India. And it was particularly surprising that this was done when the Chinese were talking of peaceful coexistence and goodwill with India.

China definitely knew where the alignment of the road infringed the boundary shown on these Indian maps. But the plans for its strategic road from Sinkiang to Lhasa had been consciously decided on, as geography did not permit an eastern alignment over the Kunlun range skirting Aksai Chin, although there is another very difficult track that goes over the Keria Pass at an altitude of about 5,515 metres. On the other hand, although the Indian side was perhaps not totally ignorant of China's road project, India decided to lodge a formal complaint only in August 1958, drawing attention to the wrongly depicted Sino-Indian boundary published in *China Pictorial Magazine*, Issue No. 95, of July 1958.[21]

Verification that the road ran through Indian territory was also physically carried out by our patrols later, and existence of the road was confirmed. According to Mullik, director of the Intelligence Bureau, his agency had been regularly sending the government confidential reports about China's construction of the Sinkiang–Tibet road (Figure 18) since November 1952. He said a jeepable road between Sinkiang and Rudok in western Tibet had become operational in 1953. However, he assumed that the alignment of this road was across the Kunlum and not through Aksai Chin, the ancient and traditional caravan route which traversed through Indian territory. This fact could have been verified without much difficulty with the help of smugglers, traders or just one or two aerial photographic sorties by the Canberra aircraft that our air force possessed in 1954–55. Surprisingly, during my research on the subject, I did not come across any comment by well-known strategic experts on Sino-Indian boundary on this course of action, which was eminently 'doable', till end-1958.

It would be fair to assume that the Chinese knew that Nehru and his advisers were likely aware of their construction of the Aksai Chin road but chose not to acknowledge its significance and decided to play it down. The Chinese leadership were smart enough to keep this game going for as long as it suited them! Besides the inputs the IB had been giving to the government about this road, even the military attaché in the Indian embassy at Peking, Brigadier Mallick, had sent a special report on this project to the Ministry of External Affairs (MEA) in 1956. Despite this the Indian government did not take a serious view of the development. It has been remarked that the ambassador was diffident about dispatching his report, lest it should displease Nehru![22]

Once the new Indian maps were published in 1954 by the Survey of India, showing a well-defined boundary based on the advice of China experts in the MEA, the stakeholders of India's national security ought to leave no stone unturned to ensure that no violation of India's territory took place unchallenged. The publication of these maps meant that positioning of border control posts at important locations manned by the respective state armed police and IB personnel had become mandatory. But this was not done in an effective manner, and the Chinese exploited this failure to the hilt. Across a frontage of over 4,000 kilometres, only twenty-one IB and/or armed police check-posts were established initially, a highly inadequate number. Later, when the situation worsened in 1959–60, these posts were increased to about sixty.

Mullik mentions in his book *The Chinese Betrayal* that information regarding construction of the Aksai Chin road had been regularly reported by the IB to all concerned (the Prime Minister's Office; the ministries of external affairs, defence and home; as also the army headquarters) since October 1952.[23] If this is true, the question of culpability on the part of several key people of the time arises. Worse still, the nation was kept in the dark about all this till 1958. No strategic analysis of these developments appeared to have been made between 1954 and 1958, as there are no records in the public domain of discussions on it at the level of the prime minister, secretary general of the MEA, chief of army staff, home secretary or director of IB, at least until 1958. Even at that stage, the foreign secretary, during a conference in June 1958—which he presided over and which was attended by the chief of General Staff of army HQ and the director of IB—was of the view that there was no point in lodging a protest without conclusive proof that the Chinese had violated Indian territory.

It is incomprehensible why aerial reconnaissance was still not ordered by the government when Indian Air Force had Canberra aircraft with excellent photo-recce capability. One or two sorties would have been adequate to photograph the alignment of the road passing through the Aksai Chin area. In fact, the IB director, the MEA and army HQ should have demanded aerial photo cover as early as 1954 (when our maps showing a definite boundary were published). That they did not is nothing short of bizarre, particularly when the director of IB had claimed that his sources had been providing inputs on construction of the road from 1952 onwards. But he claimed he was not sure which alignment the road traversed; he presumed it was the Keriya Pass route! In this regard, purely from the historical perspective, the truth must be discerned and recorded, and the lessons from it learnt.

Moreover, Mullik's assessment that the People's Liberation Army (PLA) troops had used a circuitous and much more difficult and hazardous track over the Kunlun and had come across the 5,515-metre (18,090 feet) Keriya Pass during the 'liberation' of Tibet in 1950–51 was perhaps faulty, as it contradicted Zhou Enlai's statement that Chinese troops used the traditional route from Sinkiang during this 'liberation' (invasion), though it would be unwise to take the Chinese leader's statement at face value too. It would have been most likely that a small Chinese infantry force with a complement of horsed cavalry, with logistic support in the form of animal transport comprising yaks and mules, could indeed have followed the centuries-old caravan route from Sinkiang across Aksai Chin, developing the same alignment into a motorable road subsequently. In terrain like in Ladakh or Tibet, where there is no cover, the road would have stood out prominently in aerial photographs, and their interpretation would have provided the proof the foreign secretary was seeking.

Our bright and ingenious intelligence czar should have been able to see through the Chinese game, and it is surprising that he did not present a more accurate assessment to the policymakers at the national level. Failure to get this vital information verified by ground or air surveillance for a period of six whole years, from 1952 to 1958, is inexcusable. Mullik, on whose shoulders rested the responsibility of external intelligence, failed to join the dots and synthesize the many inputs he received on Chinese activities. As a matter of fact, in his book he has admitted he 'made a serious mistake in not taking up the question of the road [Sinkiang] with the Prime Minister directly … My talk would have induced the Prime Minister to order a high-level study of the implications of this road and this would have resulted in our taking more vigorous preventive measures to stop the further extensive encroachments which occurred in the next few years.'[24] To send long-range patrols during the autumn of 1958 to confirm whether the Sinkiang road traversed across Indian territory in the Aksai Chin area was action taken that was absurd and too late. We ought to have taken appropriate steps in 1954–55 itself.

Significantly, in 1956, China published new maps which not only repeated their previous claims but also included areas west of the Aksai Chin road, which had actually already been occupied by them in Ladakh.[25] This should have injected a certain amount of suspicion in the minds of our leadership and policymakers, raising questions about what the Chinese were really intending to do while overtly professing friendship with India. In fact, after the Trade Agreement of 1954 between India and China, India's border trade in Ladakh declined because of closure of Sinkiang and other restrictive measures taken by the Chinese. In all probability, China wanted to throw a cloak of secrecy over its construction of the Aksai Chin road. It is intriguing how India failed to piece together these indications and to analyse Chinese strategy correctly. In view of India's unquestionable good intentions demonstrated towards China ever since the birth of People's Republic of China, nothing should have stopped India from seeking a clarification from that country once reports were received concerning this strategic project that went on from 1952 to 1957. India's inexplicable and ostrich-like inertia was shameful. All this resulted in India being presented with a 'fait accompli' that was impossible to undo, and which became another major cause of its subsequent conflict with China.

In July 1954, Nehru addressed a secret memorandum on the Sino-Indian border to the secretary general in the MEA, the foreign secretary, the defence secretary and the Ministry of Commerce and Industry, describing the Tibet treaty as 'a new starting point of our relations with China and Tibet'.[26] Nehru's misplaced confidence that China would continue to be a peaceful neighbour remained only a cherished hope, as China had its own agenda and national interest to take care of. Moreover, China had no hesitation in employing subterfuge or deceit to achieve its goals.

Nehru had also said: 'Both as flowing from our policy and as a consequence of our agreement with China, this frontier should be considered a firm and definite one, which is not open to discussion with anybody. A system of check-posts should be spread along this entire frontier. More especially, we should have check-posts in such places as might be considered disputed areas.'[27]

Ashok Karnik, a distinguished officer of the Intelligence Bureau, wrote: 'Pandit Nehru and IB Chief B.N. Mullik evolved what was later termed as the "Forward Policy".' As the border check-posts necessarily had to be manned by the border guards or the police, 'Mullik offered to establish the posts through the IB staff'.[28]

According to Karnik's version of the situation, 'The Army refused to man the posts as it was essentially a civilian job and the posts were militarily indefensible.' Apparently, Nehru and Mullik decided to go ahead with their strategy, which consisted of showing the flag, hoping such an action would prevent the Chinese from encroaching into unoccupied Indian territory, as had been the case in Aksai Chin. Nowhere has it been recorded that Nehru ever sought professional military advice (until 1959) while evolving and implementing this forward policy. The boundary matter, including issues related to the tribal territory in the region, evolved into a domain that was exclusively handled by the MEA and the IB under the direct guidance and supervision of Nehru, the prime minister (also holding charge as minister of external affairs). There was an element of high secrecy in this enterprise, and even the cabinet was not kept in the loop.

The administrative affairs of the north-eastern frontier tracts were the responsibility of the state administration of Assam and the MEA. In 1951, the North-East Frontier Agency (NEFA) was created to include these tribal areas. Keeping in view the sensitivity and strategic importance of NEFA, it was placed directly under the MEA (although constitutionally it remained a part of Assam), with the governor of Assam acting as the agent of the president. The Indian Frontier Administrative Service was raised in 1956 for administration of these tribal areas. As described by Verrier Elwin, they were a 'body of senior officers' with a 'special aptitude for serving in the frontier areas'.[29]

The 'forward policy' was IB's strategy of establishing isolated posts in the Aksai Chin area to 'fill the vacuum'.[30] Obviously, the Indian appreciation of Chinese reactions to its own moves was flawed. At the same time, taking advantage of favourable terrain, the Chinese were building roads, moving up and deploying troops and munitions, and establishing logistic bases. While proffering friendship and extending the hand of peace to India, the PLA was also getting ready to teach India a lesson if and when the necessity arose. With a more astute and deeper understanding of China, we might have been able to see through this charade and perhaps been better prepared to face its onslaught when it came. Instead we indulged in wishful thinking.

18

Disputed Areas in the Ladakh and Central Sectors

The Indian subcontinent, which starts from the Hindu Kush and lies south of the Pamirs, the Karakoram, Kunlun and Himalayan ranges, jutting into the Indian Ocean, has been historically, and by custom and tradition, known as *Hindustan*. The Sino-Indian boundary, from the Pamirs to the Gya peak north of the Spiti river, covering a distance of about 1,500 kilometres, represents in actuality the boundary between the state of Jammu and Kashmir and the erstwhile Chinese Turkestan (Sinkiang) in the north, and Tibet in the north-east. Kashmir has for ages been an intrinsic part of India, whereas Ladakh, also called 'little Tibet', was a small Buddhist kingdom which had close ties with Tibet. It was amalgamated with the rest of Kashmir during the Mughal period in the seventeenth century.

At times between the eleventh and sixteenth centuries, Ladakh was independent or semi-autonomous, but during the expansion of the Sikh empire under Ranjit Singh in the nineteenth century, it was brought firmly into the ambit of the Lahore Durbar and made a part of Punjab. Thereafter, once the British were victorious in the Anglo-Sikh wars, this region passed on to Jammu and Kashmir under the Treaty of Amritsar in 1846, and remains so till date.

Buttressing the Karakoram from the east, the Kunlun range encloses a desolate and almost uninhabited area of high plateau, where Buddhist Ladakh merges with Sinkiang in the north and Tibet in the east. It is this very sparsely populated region where the boundaries of British India, Tibet and China kept changing as three factors played out—the Russian threat, the waxing and waning Chinese hold over Tibet, and the British policy of retaining a buffer between Russia and its Indian Empire that would be cost-effective too. The boundary in this sector remained fluid and fluctuating (Figure 18). This flexibility and lack of finality to it was also a direct result of China's stated policy of avoiding a boundary settlement with the British from a position of weakness. It believed the consequences of doing so would be akin to giving the 'imperialists blades with which Chinese territory could be pared away'. This logic was also helpful to the Chinese in warding off the criticism they fetched for their proverbial 'procrastination and lack of finality' in dealing with boundary matters.

Karakoram–Aksai Chin region

The northern part of this sector, from the tri-junction of the boundaries of India, China and Afghanistan along the Qara Tagh range up to the Kunlun mountains, was historically controlled by the ruler of Hunza, the northernmost region of Pakistan Occupied Kashmir (POK) bordering China. Its limits were only vaguely known. In the absence of a distinct and continuous watershed line, there does not appear to exist any clear-cut traditional or historical boundary in this region. The only historical records (including maps) available of this part of the boundary are from the British period, beginning from about the middle of the nineteenth century, when Kashmir came under control of Britain as a dividend from the Sikh wars.

There were two distinct strands of British thinking which dictated the limits of Jammu and Kashmir in this region: (i) the forward alignment, advocated by W.H.Johnson, who was part of the Great Trignometric Survey (GST) of British India, and Major General Sir John Ardagh, director of intelligence at the war office; and (ii) the moderate and pragmatic boundary proposed by George Macartney, a civil servant who was the British consul in Sinkiang for over two decades up to 1918, and Claude MacDonald, a British soldier-diplomat posted as a minister at the legation in Peking. The forward alignment had projected British India's frontiers to the north of the Karakoram range, going eastwards up to the Kunlun mountains, thereby including within India the Aksai Chin plateau and the upper courses of the Yarkand and Karakash river systems too. This proposal was put forth after the defeat of the Chinese at the hands of Japanese in 1895.

At this stage, it was expected that the Chinese would not be able to maintain their control over the Xinjiang region and that Russia could take advantage of the vacuum thus created. In order to forestall this possibility, it was suggested by Sir John Ardagh in 1897 that the British should include the whole of uninhabited Aksai Chin within their territory as China may no longer be able to function as a buffer region. The British aim was to keep the northern approaches to the passes in their possession. The proposed line ran along the crest of the Kunlun range and came to be called the Johnson–Ardagh Line. The western terminus of McMahon's 'red line' drawn in 1913–14 coincided with the Ardagh alignment at the north-western corner of India.

However, Viceroy Elgin and his advisers rejected the 'forward policy' as being impractical and unnecessary, and recommended acceptance of the Macartney/MacDonald line. Consequently, the British made an offer based on this line to the Chinese government in 1899.[1] This moderate solution saw the line follow the northern side of the Karakoram range, cut across the Aksai Chin plateau and join the Lanak La. This gave to China the whole of Karakash Valley, a trade route and almost all of Aksai Chin proper, except the Lingzi Thang salt plains and the whole Changchenmo Valley (Figure 18). Colonial empire building and consolidation required the making of such compromises, as colonial powers were not impinged by nationalistic impulses. However, since this boundary never received formal recognition and acceptance by the Chinese, and on account of another bout of 'Russo-phobia', the British frontier policy reverted to inclusion of Aksai Chin within British territories during the term of Lord Hardinge in the early part of the twentieth century.[2]

In 1927, the Government of India appears to have again looked into the matter and decided that the boundary from Afghanistan to the Karakoram Pass (where the Chinese had created a boundary pillar in 1892), should run along the northern side of the main Karakoram range, encompassing the Shaksgam Valley comprising an area of 5,180 square kilometres (a region illegally ceded by Pakistan to China in 1963). Eastwards of the Karakoram Pass and to the south of the Kunlun range lay the Aksai Chin and Lingzi Thang plains claimed by the Chinese. However, till 1951 there was no semblance of Tibetan, let alone Chinese, administration in this area. On the other hand, during the official talks in 1960, the Indian side produced evidence of revenue collection from this area belonging to Tangtse in Ladakh district (tehsil), whereas the Chinese were unable to provide credible evidence to prove that the area south of the Kunlun mountains was ever a part of Sinkiang.[3]

However, the status and precise definition of the boundary east of the Karakoram Pass to the Kunlun range is not well recorded. Nevertheless, at the time of India's independence, the boundary, as indicated in maps by the colour wash and the silhouette formed by the letters of the words 'boundary undefined', more or less followed the watershed between the Shyok and the Yarkand rivers, and then ran along the Qara Tagh range till it reached the Kunlun mountains. It then ran along that range, from where it took a southward direction till it reached the Lanak La.

The words 'boundary undefined', it must be noted, were not printed on the maps in a random manner. It would be incorrect to assume that there was no boundary inherited by India at the northern frontier, even if the boundary wasn't precisely marked. The Chinese position on the issue of alignment of the boundary in the Ladakh region was on shaky ground, and the goalposts shifted historically from 1890 onwards and up to the mid-twentieth century. Further, the westward shift of the 1956 line to the 1960 line, and subsequently to the line after the 1962 war with India, was achieved by aggression on the part of the Chinese.

Border Region of Eastern Ladakh

The eastern boundary of Ladakh with Tibet offers an example of a traditional boundary modified by political changes, unlike in the case of its bleak and remote northern boundary with Sinkiang. This region, comprising the frontier from Lanak La up to the Spiti river, includes the Indus basin, the traditional trade route from Ladakh to Tibet (Lhasa), and also the pilgrimage routes to Manasarovar and Mount Kailash. Before the tenth century AD, 'Ngari Khorsum', or western Tibet, formed a part of the Ladakhi kingdom, and its boundary with the rest of Tibet lay at the Mayum Pass. This included the entire Indus–Sutlej basins within Ladakh, which gave the kingdom a perfect watershed boundary with Tibet.

Two significant treaties confirmed Ladakh's frontier as 'anciently established', though without further definition. The first treaty dates back to 1684, when Ladakh was a major Himalayan kingdom. It was drawn up between the king of Ladakh, Skyid-Ida-Ngeema-Gon, and the Tibetan plenipotentiary, Mee-Pham-Wang-Po. The agreement said, 'The boundaries fixed in the beginning when King Skyid-Ida-Ngeema-Gon gave kingdom to each of his three sons shall still be maintained. Besides the sanctity of the frontier, this agreement stipulated conditions for wool trade between the Ngari and the Khorsum regions.[4] This emphasized that a clear understanding between the Ladakhis and the Tibetans did exist on the question of the boundary between them. It also illustrates the legal standing of both kingdoms, especially Tibet, to sign treaties.

The second treaty was signed in September 1842 by Ladakh after its annexation by Gulab Singh, himself a feudatory of the Sikh empire. It was signed by the plenipotentiaries of Kashmir, the Dalai Lama of the time and the emperor of China. Making references to the boundary in the region, the treaty said, 'We shall neither at present nor in future have anything to do or interfere at all with boundaries of Ladakh and its surroundings as fixed from ancient times.'[5] (See Appendix 1 for excerpts of the text.) The treaty further reinforced the fact that the traditional boundaries of Ladakh and Tibet had been fixed for centuries.

In this context, a note sent by the British government to the Chinese imperial commissioner at Canton on 13 January 1847 reads: 'Respecting the frontiers, I beg to remark that the borders of these territories have been sufficiently and distinctly fixed so that it will be best to adhere to this ancient arrangement.'[6] The Chinese response of silence to this note may have been considered as their tacit agreement to it.

In making over the state of Kashmir to Gulab Singh and his heirs in 1846, the British India authorities hoped at the same time to negotiate a fixed frontier with Tibet and the Chinese Empire in this area, and to create conditions for peaceful trade. When it proved impossible to draw Tibet and China into discussions, frontier survey and definition were carried out by British officers, who adopted for this purpose a principle of 'watershed lines between the drainages of different rivers'. Geographical details of the natural features of the inaccessible northern plateau (Aksai Chin) lacked accuracy; but southwards from the Lanak La and through the Pangong lake area, a year of careful survey culminated in a well-authenticated boundary, which held good until the Chinese communist takeover of Tibet in 1951.

In fact, the treaty of 1842 gave renewed sanction to the customary and traditional frontier in this region. This treaty too did not define the frontier because it was already well defined by custom, usage and tradition. Actually, the Chinese government informed the British authorities in India that since this sector of the India–Tibet boundary was already well known and well defined, additional measures in respect of it would be unnecessary.[7]

However, the Chinese now argue that though these treaties do mention a traditional boundary, none of them actually specifies the boundary. 'The Indian government holds that the boundary line was fixed by a treaty concluded between Tibet and Kashmir in 1842. As a matter of fact, the treaty was a non-aggression pact which bound each to respect the territory of the other. It did not specify where "the old, established frontiers" lay between them,' as narrated by Xuecheng Liu, a Chinese scholar.[8]

To the west of the Karakoram Pass the Chinese claimed the Shaksgam Valley, an area of nearly 5,180 square kilometres, lying north of the Karakoram range. In their agreement reached in 1963 over this part of the boundary with Pakistan (in whose control this region is at present), the Chinese were successful in securing their territorial claims from Pakistan. However, a proviso has been made integral to this treaty in Article 6, stipulating that 'the two parties have agreed that after the settlement of the Kashmir dispute between Pakistan and India, the sovereign authority concerned will reopen negotiations with the Government of the People's

Republic of China on the boundary as described in this Article'. In this manner, China has kept the door open for negotiations with India, which rightfully is the sovereign nation of which the entire state of Jammu and Kashmir (including the Shaksgam Valley) is de jure an inalienable part, the state having formally acceded to India in October 1947. When viewed in the context of the sinister and illegal extension of the LoC from NJ 9842 eastwards to the Karakoram Pass by Pakistan on their maps, thereby claiming the Siachen glacier region, and the publication of this alignment in some international maps, the 'Sino-Pak game' becomes evident. Sadly for Pakistan, the Indian occupation of Siachen glacier put paid to their plans for a link-up with China in this region.

The Chinese have laid a claim to approximately 38,000 square kilometres of territory comprising the entire Aksai Chin plateau, part of the Lingzi Thang plains and the area around Demchok. They claim that from the Karakoram Pass, the frontier between Sinkiang and Ladakh ran its entire length along the Karakoram range, although there is no credible proof in contemporary Indian or British documents to support it.[9] 'Some twentieth century Chinese maps have shown the Karakoram range as its boundary in the western sector. Unfortunately the British authorities had not settled this matter with the Tibetan or Chinese governments before they left India in 1947.[10] However, there appears to be no historical or traditional background, or jurisdictional evidence for this unilateral claim. The Chinese boundary has been creeping southwards from the Kunlun range during the period 1890–1960 (Figure 18). The final alignment of the 1960 Chinese claim line really makes no geographical sense, in that from the Karakoram Pass it comes southwards up to Pangong lake, cutting across the Chip Chap and Chang Chenmo river valleys, including also the area around and including Demchok in China, before it joins the traditional eastern boundary between Ladakh and Tibet at Imis Pass.

An examination of the southern frontier of Sinkiang in Chinese maps of the eighteenth and nineteenth centuries, as depicted in geographical and historical works such as *Hsi yu tu chih* (1762) and *Hsin chiang chi lueh* (1821), reveals that China's southern boundary was along the Nanshan or the Kunlun range right through history, from the Han to the Ch'ing dynasties. This was corroborated later by Chinese postal maps of 1917, 1919 and 1933 too.[11] While there may be claims and counterclaims on both sides, it is apparent that the boundary in this sector was recognized more through traditional and historical understanding rather than through physical demarcation on the ground. This was acknowledged as such by the Indian prime minister, in his address to Parliament on 12 September 1959:

> This place, Aksai Chin area, is in our maps undoubtedly. But I distinguish it completely from other areas. It is a matter for argument as to what part of it belongs to us and what part of it belongs to somebody else. It is not at all a dead clear matter. However, I have to be clear with the House. It is not clear.[12]

While for India, Aksai Chin was not critically important to hold, for the Chinese it was. As emphasized by Garver, not only was it 'essential to Chinese control of *western* Tibet' but also 'very important to its control over *all* of Tibet (emphasis added)'.

The Central Sector

The frontier of the states of Uttar Pradesh, Himachal Pradesh and Uttarakhand with Tibet forms the central section of the Indo-Tibetan border. This region, unlike Aksai Chin and certain parts of Arunachal Pradesh, is inhabited on both sides of the border. Therefore, although the area has very high mountains, there are well-known passes and routes used since ancient times by pilgrims, travellers and traders, as well as by herdsmen seeking pastures. The boundaries here evolved by tradition, custom and usage, and there is enough documentary evidence to establish the historic and de jure writ of either side. The Chinese have laid claim to four areas along the Himalayas in the central sector—at Spiti, Shipkila Pass, Nilang–Jadhang and Barahoti–Sangcha Malla–Lapthal, as shown in Figure 19.

The boundary between Uttar Pradesh and Tibet follows the watershed between the Sutlej and the Ganga or Ganges (Kali, Alaknanda and

Dudhganga). Revenue records and other evidence with the Government of India are said to establish the fact that in this part of the boundary, the high Himalayan range, with passes at elevations of up to 5,183 metres, forms the traditional and well-known boundary. The boundary here too follows the watershed principle. Authentic Chinese maps, even as late as 1958, showed this as the boundary. The Nilang–Jadhang and the Barahoti–Sangcha Malla–Lapthal areas, according to the contention of the Chinese government, lie within the limits of Tibet, but are in fact well on the Indian side of the watershed. The boundary between Himachal and Tibet is the water parting between the eastern and western tributaries of the Sutlej. The border between the erstwhile Punjab and Tibet is the major watershed between the Pare Chu and Spiti river systems.

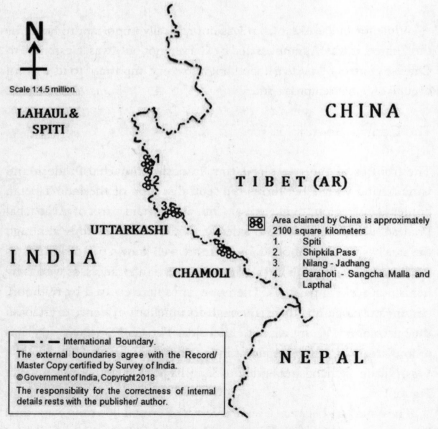

Figure 19: Chinese claims in central sector

Geography, as is usually the case, makes the task of the map-maker most challenging. In this frontier region, the first complication comprises the groups of awesome peaks such as those of the Nanda Devi, Trishul, Badrinath, Kedarnath, Gangotri and Bandarpunch (all above 6,000 metres) which lie south of the main Himalayan watershed and form a parallel range. Also, all the rivers here flow southwards, and none into Tibet. Secondly, the area where the Sutlej cuts across the mountains through a deep gorge and where many of its tributaries join it from both east and west makes precise delimitation of the boundary here tough. These factors have led to differing perceptions of the boundary in this region, even though the areas under contention are small. This area has well-known border passes like the Shipkila, Mana, Niti, Tunjun and Taklakot, which have been used for centuries by traders—particularly those dealing in pashmina, wool and yak tails—to access Tibet. Most importantly for Indians, these passes have been used to access the famous Hindu pilgrimage sites of Manasarovar and Kailash Parbat. And besides these factors, there is the issue of common pasturage in some areas.

The mention of these border passes in the 1954 Sino-Indian agreement was done with the intention of using them as markers while delimiting the boundary, as has been the case with numerous passes such as the Karakoram, Lanak La and Jelep La. These were, in fact, portals for entry into Tibet from India, and vice versa. For these reasons, resolution of the boundary in this region should not pose insurmountable problems.

The southern glacis of the Great Himalayan range in the middle sector has historically been the domain of small Hindu chieftaincies or hill rulers ('Pahari Rajas'), who went by the titles of 'Sena', 'Rana' or 'Thakur'. They considered themselves to be rulers but were actually vassals of the stronger amongst them or the monarch at Delhi. However, sensing their vulnerabilities, fractiousness and lack of unity, the ruler of Nepal expanded his kingdom to include all the sub-Himalayan territory from Kangra in the west to Bhutan in the east, between 1803 and 1814. He also brought under his fold the fiefdoms in the hills of Punjab up to the Jamuna.

However, nothing can arrest the vicissitudes of time, and the Anglo-Nepalese war of 1814–15 put an end to these dreams of a Nepalese empire in this region. After the Gurkhas were defeated, as per the Treaty of Sagauli of 1815, they had to surrender all territory to the west of the Kali river, the Kumaon hills, Garhwal and the Punjab hilly areas to the British. These territories were either annexed to the dominion of India or under some form of protectorate. The treaty also provided for a British resident to be stationed in Kathmandu for recruitment of Gurkha soldiers to the British Indian Army and deportation of all American and European officers who had been employed to train the Nepalese army. During the next three years, agreements or *sanads* were signed with the large number of chiefs, Pahari Rajas and Thakurs, who were given various titles and were made to pay tributes or *nazaranah* 'for defraying the expenses of protection by British troops'. There were other stipulated terms. Undoubtedly, 'according to the terms of the *sanads*, the British regarded their boundaries as traditionally fixed and in the aggregate extending to the borders of Tibet'.

After the defeat of the formidable Sikh army by the British in the Anglo-Sikh wars—more as a result of treachery, sabotage and the treasonable conduct of a few of the generals of the Khalsa army than to any superior stratagem of the British on the battlefield—the kingdom of Jammu and Kashmir—the hilly area between rivers Indus and Ravi, and Ladakh—was founded under Gulab Singh. The British cleverly did not commit their resources and efforts to the unremunerative Ladakh and hill areas of Jammu region, but retained Kulu and Spiti Valley in order to have an access to the 'wool producing districts of western Tibet'. Thus, from the mid-nineteenth century onwards, British India and Tibet shared a frontier from Gya peak south of Demchok in Ladakh to the border of Nepal.

Lord Curzon has described the situation in 1907 after Nepal, Sikkim and Bhutan had been converted into a chain of protectorates. He said the British were 'content to rest their boundary there comfortably beneath the foothills'. In 1890, China signed with Britain a convention recognizing Sikkim as a British protectorate and delimiting the Sikkim–Tibet boundary; in 1910, over the protests of China, the British signed a treaty with Bhutan, in which that kingdom bound itself to be guided by Britain in her foreign relations. This situation was ideal for the British, so long as the approaches to India could be guarded by obedient feudatories as securely as British power itself could, and far more cheaply too.

In the central sector, the Chinese claimed approximately 2,100 square kilometres of Indian territory, specifically in the areas of Spiti, Shipkila Pass, Nilang–Jadhang (Sang and Tsungha) and Barahoti–Sangcha Malla–Lapthal, as shown in Figure 19.

Spiti was a Hindu kingdom since ancient times, as per historical records. Its kings bore the surname or suffix of 'Sena'. It was annexed in the tenth century by Ladakh, and eventually brought under British rule in 1846, along with Kulu. During this latter period, its boundary with Tibet was demarcated by Captain A. Cunningham and Vans Agnew, and subsequently a detailed survey of Spiti was undertaken during 1850–51 by J. Peyton. This survey placed the Indo-Tibetan boundary on the 'watershed between Spiti and Pare rivers'. Moreover, examination of the revenue records of these areas shows adequate evidence of their having formed part of the small Indian fiefdoms mentioned earlier, thus reinforcing the 'validity of the Indian alignment along the east of Spiti'.[13]

In the area of the Shipkila Pass, contrary to the Indian stand, the Chinese regard as theirs 'not merely the pass but also the pastures on its west upto Hupsang Khud'. Various historical accounts, revenue and travellers' records indicate that the area up to the pass was part of India. In fact, the pass itself is known in Tibetan as 'Pimala' (meaning 'common pass') and hence has always been regarded as such.[14]

Similarly, in the Nilang–Jadhang, Barahoti and Sangcha–Malla–Lapthal areas, the claims of the Chinese are not based on convincing facts. 'From times immemorial, this region as a whole has been regarded as one of special sanctity by the Hindus. It has been described as "Kedara Kshetra" in ancient Sanskrit Literature.'[15] The sacred temples at Gangotri, Kedarnath and Badrinath are visited by pilgrims from the entire subcontinent, who trek for days in these forbidding higher altitudes in their thousands even to this day. In our scriptures, this region is referred to as 'Deva Bhoomi'.

The first incident hinting at a boundary problem here happened in 1954, when the Chinese border guards transgressed across the Niti Pass and came to the Barahoti plains. This was an area where for centuries the local inhabitants had been bringing their cattle and yaks for grazing. Some of these graziers used to come from the Tibetan side and might have spurred their new Chinese masters to claim these pastures. Taking an expansionist and maximalist stand, the Chinese proffered a claim to the Barahoti plains in 1954; and subsequently, after a gap of a few years, in a clandestine manner, occupied Sangcha Malla and Lapthal in close vicinity of the border on the Indian side, in 1958. Not only that, in 1960 the Chinese also laid claim to the adjacent areas of this remote and unpopulated region. This approach, not atypical of the Chinese, was also reflective of the lack of clarity in their own claims; or else they were taking advantage of geography and advancing their claims southwards because there are higher peaks and a parallel range here, but they forgot (or chose to forget) that the watershed is along the northern Himalayan range.

A striking fact that stands out and goes against the Chinese logic is that none of the rivers in this region flows northwards into Tibet. However, as mentioned earlier, the differences between the claims of India and China in this region are the least complicated of their disputes and involve much smaller parcels of territory. Moreover, the region being populated on both sides of the Himalayas, there is enough historical, political and customary evidence to find a mutually acceptable solution. For resolution of the long-standing Sino-Indian boundary problem, this could be the crucial first stepping stone.

Finally, at the time of India's independence in 1947, Nepal too became an independent country, and fresh treaties were signed between the two countries in 1950.

19

Hurtling Towards the Border War

The geostrategic importance of Tibet in eastern Asia, particularly for India and China, cannot be underestimated. 'He who holds Tibet dominates the Himalayan piedmont; he who dominates the Himalayan piedmont threatens the Indian sub-continent; and he who threatens the Indian sub-continent may well have all of Southeast Asia within its reach, and all of Asia,' said George Ginsburg, in his study *Communist China and Tibet: The First Dozen Years*.[1] While the British had come to such a conclusion more than a century ago, presumably Mao was aware of it too. It was the British Empire's grand design to retain Tibet as an 'autonomous buffer state' and thereby keep at bay potential adversaries like Russia or China.

As emphasized by Kissinger, Sun Tzu's *The Art of War* advocates attacking the opponent's 'strategy' and 'alliances', and that would 'involve psychology and perception'. Sun Tzu 'places considerable emphasis on the use of subterfuge and misinformation. When able, feign inability, when deploying troops, appear not to be. When near, appear far, when far, appear near.' This precept 'remains a central text of Chinese military thought'.[2]

During the so-called 'liberation' of Tibet in 1950–51, one prong of the PLA's thrust into Tibet was from the north-west. The Chinese sent troops, though not substantial in number, from Sinkiang; they took the ancient caravan route to reach Rudok and Gartok in western Tibet, travelling on horseback and on foot. Later, the Chinese used this route for maintenance of their troops in western Tibet. Yaks were extensively used for transportation of resources and as 'meat on hoof'. While developing the other vital routes connecting Sining, Chengdu and Kunming to Lhasa, the Chinese also decided to develop this strategic communication artery as early as 1951. In fact, Mao's command to his advancing armies was to build motorable roads as they penetrated into Tibet. These roads took four to six years to be completed, and entailed a huge cost of human life and resources. However, while the other roads passed through Chinese territory, the Sinkiang route traversed partly over the disputable Aksai Chin area.

It is reasonable to presume that China, at the time of Indian independence, had access to Indian maps in which the Aksai Chin area had been depicted by a colour wash, with the qualification 'boundary undefined'. This colour wash indicated that it was Indian territory whose precise limits were not determined. As the terrain, particularly the Kunlun mountain range, precluded a viable alternative alignment for this strategic artery, the Chinese decided to go ahead with laying the road through this area, doing it as secretively as possible, to present a fait accompli to the world. To keep prying Indian eyes at bay they abruptly forced closure of the Indian consulate at Kashgar. This should have been contested strongly, but India simply acquiesced to it without a murmur. Ambassador K.M. Panikkar failed to appreciate the Chinese design. The forthright words of Zhou Enlai to our ambassador were: 'The privileges which were being enjoyed by the Government of India as a result of the unequal treaties forced by the British did not any longer exist.' The Chinese leader also suggested that 'fresh negotiations' would be necessary to resolve trade and other issues with respect to Tibet.[3] This led to the talks at Peking from December 1953 onwards, which concluded in the famous 'Hindi Chini bhai bhai' slogan and the Panchsheel and Trade Agreement of 1954. On the altar of peaceful coexistence and brotherhood, Nehru sacrificed all rights and privileges of India with respect to Tibet—privileges the British had acquired over half a century and had bequeathed to India without a quid pro quo.

Once the Aksai Chin highway was presented as an achievement to the world in 1957, the PLA began to flex its muscles and expand westwards.

The principal Chinese objective in Ladakh was to acquire real estate to provide depth to their strategic artery and keep it beyond the reach of long-range artillery and surveillance from ground patrols. In this way, the Chinese kept all the dominating heights on their side of their claim lines. They moved their 1956 claim line further west by 1960, taking advantage of the easier topography of this area to push their troops to assume control of the vacant spaces up to the new claim line wherever feasible.

With the publication of the new Survey of India maps, as directed by Nehru in 1954, India's frontiers were clearly and unambiguously defined, although unilaterally. But this was the case with the Chinese maps too. In a policy note issued to all the relevant ministries in July 1954, Nehru directed that this boundary issue 'is not open to discussion with anybody' and that the frontier should be safeguarded by a 'system of checkposts', especially in those areas 'which might be disputed'.[4] As a result of this directive, a few frontier posts manned by civil police and the Intelligence Bureau were established by the Indian government.

In 1954, Zhou Enlai had assured Nehru, when the latter raised the issue of faulty depiction of the Sino (Tibet)-Indian boundary in Chinese maps, that China had not had the time to 'revise' their old Kuomintang maps. Not surprisingly, the Chinese, following their grand design, published new maps in 1956. These maps, besides not making any corrections to the old maps, incorporated within China even more areas of Ladakh. This development should have sounded alarm bells among the Indian civilian and military leadership, but elicited only an apathetic response.

In the Kongka Pass incident, an Indian patrol was ambushed by the Chinese and nine Indian soldiers were killed and ten were captured in October 1959. According to Jagat Mehta, Nehru wrote to Zhou Enlai expressing his dismay at what had happened, but he still nursed the naive hope 'that China would be frank, and his ideas of non-alignment would not be exposed as hollow and wishful. It should have been clear that both sides were on different wavelengths and neither understood the other.'[5] This aspect will be discussed in the following chapter.

The simmering unrest in Tibet came to a boil in 1959 when the Khampa rebels had fierce clashes with the Chinese army in the eastern Marches. It was only a matter of time before this revolt spread to central and southern Tibet. This did happen, and it led to a regime of severe repression by the Chinese government. Many Tibetan institutions and monasteries were destroyed and thousands of Tibetans killed or arrested. The country was laid to waste once again. The Tibetans began fleeing in hordes. The only secure direction and destination was southwards across the Himalayas to India—the land of the Buddha. In order to avoid detection by the Chinese army, most of them took to hazardous mountain trails and many perished en route. Those who succeeded in reaching India sought refuge here and were accorded asylum, as per international norms.

Fearing his apprehension and deportation to China, the young Dalai Lama, on 17 March 1959, decided to make good his escape to India along with eight of his close aides and advisers. Deliberately, he chose a route different from the one taken by his predecessor and fled to the south. Like the thirteenth Dalai Lama almost half a century ago, he too successfully evaded his Chinese pursuers and made it to India. He crossed the border in the Khinzemane area of Tawang district on 31 March 1959. He was received warmly, and he and his followers were granted asylum.[6] Respecting Chinese sentiments, India advised him to refrain from political activities while in India.

However, the Chinese were deeply angered by the response of the people, press and Parliament in India and the widespread expression of sympathy with the Tibetan cause. They did not hesitate to convey their displeasure at this. In response to this, the foreign secretary of India sent a demarche on 23 May 1959 to the Chinese government, saying, 'In India, unlike China, the law recognises many parties, and gives protection to the expression of differing opinions ... and this freedom of expression, free press and civil liberties in India are not fully appreciated by the Government of China.'[7] Defending the strong reactions of Indian parliamentarians to the harsh suppression of the Tibetans, the Chinese were apprised of the fact that Indian lawmakers belonged to 'a sovereign parliament of a sovereign country and it does not submit to any dictation from any outside authority'.[8]

As the situation along the disputed frontier was spinning out of control during 1958–59, one of the most important meetings on the boundary dispute between the prime ministers of India and China took place in April

1960 at New Delhi. After the politburo decision taken on 8 September 1959—a decision later confirmed by Mao—authorizing Zhou Enlai to hold talks with Nehru, the former proposed a meeting to discuss ways to resolve the complex boundary issue. The Chinese felt they were being isolated, as India seemed to have received support from both the USSR and the USA, and 'world opinion, particularly within Afro-Asian nations, was turning against China'.[9] The political scientist M. Taylor Fravel observed that China 'was willing to settle border disputes with neighbours through a compromise when it was internationally isolated and internally weak'. In his masterly analysis of the Sino-Soviet split, Lorenz Luthi highlighted the severe Chinese famine in 1960 and the intense leadership struggle internally, indicating that 'the Chinese state itself was in the process of collapse'.[10] That was when Mao decided to fight the war in the Himalayas (1959–60). Henry Kissinger made this observation of the decision: 'When Mao felt the national interest challenged, in the midst of all its self-inflicted travail, China needed to stand up.'[11]

The Delhi meeting was ostensibly at the behest of Zhou Enlai, and Nehru, although reluctant initially, eventually agreed to it, as both wanted to avoid an armed conflict and neither wanted to be seen in a poor light internationally. However, Nehru had doubts about the outcome of any talks when there was such a vast variance between the claims put forward by the two countries. Was Zhou setting up a trap was the question. At the same time, Nehru had his back against the wall because of the public outcry against occupation of Indian territory by China and the casualties suffered by our troops while patrolling in their own territory, as happened during the armed clashes at Kongka La and Longju during 1959. Any latitude shown by him towards the Chinese would have amounted to political harakiri. During an earlier internal meeting, Nehru, summing up the discussions concerning the 'barter' proposal of the Chinese (India to concede Chinese claim in Ladakh and in return, the Chinese could give up their claim in the north-east of India), said, 'If I give them that I shall no longer be Prime Minister of India—I will not do it.'[12]

To project a neighbour-friendly approach, China reached a 'non-aggression' accord with Burma in January 1960, signing a liberal border agreement that adhered to the McMahon Line alignment. This was followed by a border agreement with Nepal in March 1960. Soon afterwards the Chinese said, 'What has happened between China and Burma can take place between China and other countries.'[13] These initiatives were intended to impress and indirectly pressure the Indian leadership to accept the Chinese proposal for the boundary settlement. In the next three years China signed border agreements with Mongolia, North Korea, Afghanistan and Pakistan.

The Chinese prime minister arrived in Delhi on 19 April 1960 at the head of a huge delegation, including his foreign minister, Chen Yi, in three special aircraft. Premier Zhou Enlai's delegation had apparently come well prepared for substantive discussions extending for a few days, whereas the Indian side thought the deliberations would at best go on for two days. The Chinese delegation received a cold though protocol-wise appropriate welcome. This event took place under the shadow of the insurrection in Tibet, particularly in the Kham region, which had been going on since 1956. By 1959, the insurrection had spread to other regions, including Lhasa proper. The same year, in March, the Dalai Lama made his dramatic escape from Lhasa to Tawang. The Chinese chose to believe that India, along with the CIA, had a hand in fomenting the uprisings in Tibet. They felt India had connived with the Americans in this matter. The fallout of these developments on the Chinese psyche was profoundly negative.

The two prime ministers, who represented one-third of humanity, had seven tête-à-têtes, with Paranjpe and Chieh acting as interpreters for Nehru and Zhou Enlai respectively. In order to keep the proceedings highly confidential and away from the public gaze, the venue chosen was Teen Murti House, the prime minister's residence. Neither the foreign secretary, M.J. Desai, nor Jagat S. Mehta and Sarvepalli Gopal, although present throughout the week-long confabulations, were ever called into the meetings to provide any inputs.[14] Since there were no formal minutes made of the meetings, there were discrepancies in the records maintained by the two sides. These have been highlighted in the succeeding paragraphs.

The Chinese prime minister put forward six points which he felt could form the basis for a friendly dialogue. The Chinese intention was to somehow make India agree to their viewpoint. The first point was that 'disputes' exist with regard to the boundary between the two countries. An unbiased analysis would suggest that if an undelimited boundary exists between two neighbours and conflicting claims have been put forward by both sides for the same area, it becomes a 'disputed territory'. It is an accepted fact that India inherited an undefined northern boundary up to Nepal, which was depicted on Survey of India maps simply by a colour wash and the words 'boundary undefined' printed on the outer limit of the colour-washed area. These maps continued to be used till 1954, when Nehru ordered that our maps must have well-defined boundaries showing territory that is ours and that old maps be replaced by new ones. The validity of this unilateral delineation is something that is being questioned by China, although China itself is equally or more guilty of unilaterally depicting Indian territories as part of China, even earlier than India did so with its claimed areas.

The second point of the Chinese was that 'there exists a line of actual control up to which each side exercises administrative jurisdiction'. This was only partially true, as there were many 'unheld gaps' and some disputed areas that were forcibly occupied. This statement's acceptance by India would confer legitimacy to China's aggressive and expansionist policy.

The third point stipulated that 'certain geographical principles, such as watersheds, river valleys and mountain passes, should be equally applicable to all sectors' while determining the boundary. The Chinese had probably intended to have the boundary delineated in the Ladakh sector along the Karakoram watershed and enclose most of Aksai Chin within their territory using the ploy of holding the watershed as a guideline.

Their fourth issue highlighted the importance of taking into account 'the national feelings of the two peoples towards the Himalayas and the Karakoram Mountains' while arriving at a settlement of the boundary. The reference to the Himalayas is justified and undisputable, but from the Chinese point of view Tibet was far too remote, and the eastern Karakoram even more so. For the Chinese civilization, the Kunlun range was the outer limit of the 'middle kingdom'. Seldom if ever were either the Himalayas or the Karakoram ranges mentioned in ancient Chinese texts or scriptures. But the Chinese cleverly crafted this line to justify their claim to Aksai Chin as it lay on the northern slopes of the Karakoram range. By no stretch of imagination could one compare the influence of the Himalayas on Indian civilization with that of the Karakoram range on the Chinese psyche—the Karakorams hardly impacted the average Chinese mind.

The fifth point that Zhao Enlai put forward related to maintenance of the status quo along the Line of Actual Control—in other words, the Chinese wanted to make sure that their occupation of Aksai Chin got indirectly sanctified and its consolidation continued unhindered.

The sixth suggestion of the Chinese was, 'Both sides should continue to refrain from patrolling along all sectors of the boundary.'[15] The Indian parliamentarians thereupon questioned Nehru, demanding to know whether our soldiers could not patrol our own territory. Nehru responded that he did not agree to this condition of the Chinese.

The major point of contention was whether or not Zhou Enlai had proposed a 'package deal' to Nehru that implied India's acceptance of the Chinese claim to Aksai Chin in return for China's recognition of the McMahon Line. Chinese accounts of the discussion claim that Zhou Enlai said at the outset that 'although the area south of the McMahon Line was once part of Tibet, yet China would be "practical" and not raise new demands'. In a subsequent discussion, Zhou said (according to the Chinese account) that 'the customary "Line of Actual Control" be treated as the basis of a settlement ... that in the Eastern sector we recognize the line reached by India's administrative jurisdiction and in the Western sector, India should recognize the line of China's administrative jurisdiction'. This has also been alluded to in Garver's authoritative account highlighting the Chinese proposal of 'reciprocal acceptance of present realities in both sectors'.[16]

On the contrary, the Indian account of the discussions, according to Gopal, who was heading the historical division of the Ministry of External Affairs (MEA), had concluded that there was no concrete offer of 'swapping' territorial claims or a 'package deal' made by Zhou Enlai.[17] According to a declassified US study on this subject, a message regarding these talks sent to Indian missions on 27 April said, 'Throughout the discussions [the Chinese] had invariably linked Ladakh with NEFA and stressed that the same principles of settling the boundary must govern both areas.' Therefore, based on various accounts and statements made on this matter, and also from interpreting the six-point proposal and reading between the lines, the Chinese account of the package deal cannot be dismissed. This view has also been endorsed by Kissinger.[18] Although Zhou Enlai appeared ready to accept the McMahon Line alignment, as China did in the case of Burma, in return it expected India to agree to the Chinese claim in Aksai Chin. Unfortunately, at this stage Nehru was in no position to accept any 'barter deal'. Thus it would be reasonable to surmise that he might have played down Zhou's offer.

Nehru had planned meetings of important personages like the vice-president and some of his senior cabinet colleagues with Zhou Enlai during this visit. It is appreciated that perhaps Nehru wanted Zhou Enlai to get a first-hand feel of their views and also to enable his cabinet members to convey their opinions to the Chinese prime minister directly. This was done also because Nehru's position was weakening by the day, and any leeway he had to accept any compromise on the boundary issue had been seriously constricted. He wanted the burden of a possible failure of the talks to be shared, and at the same time for Zhou Enlai to know the political pulse of the nation.

Natwar Singh has, in a revealing account, described the meetings Zhou Enlai had with Vice-President Radhakrishnan, Home Minister G.B. Pant and Finance Minister Morarji Desai. 'When an exasperated Zhou said to Desai, "You have said enough," Morarji's boorish rejoinder was, "You have said more than enough."' The Chinese prime minister was livid the next day to see himself caricatured as a 'cobra' in a cartoon in the *Indian Express*. Natwar cooled him down a bit by saying the media would not spare Nehru either.[19]

As expected, the talks were an abject failure and resulted in a curt joint communiqué that said, 'The talks did not result in resolving the differences that had arisen.' Yet, in order to continue the engagement to resolve the boundary problem, the prime ministers agreed to have a time-bound report submitted by the officials of the two sides, who 'should meet and examine, check and study all historical documents, records, accounts, maps and other material relevant to the boundary question, on which each side relied in support of its stand'.[20] The communiqué also said that while the officials were engaged in the examination of factual material, 'every effort should be made by the parties to avoid friction and clashes in the border areas'.[21] However, the officials of the two sides were neither empowered nor assigned the responsibility to recommend solutions to the problem. The official teams were led by Jagat Mehta on the Indian side and by Chang Wen-chin on the Chinese side. The intention of this exercise was to discern areas of agreement and areas of discord in order to help the governments to carry out a logical analysis of the situation and find solutions acceptable to both sides.

These talks took place for over six months commencing June 1960. The two sides handed over their reports to their respective governments in February 1961. Both sides more or less justified their respective alignments of the Sino-Indian boundary based on factual evidence, logic and reasoning. At one stage, says Jagat Mehta, he coerced the Chinese into parting with a map showing their claimed boundary, failing which, he had told them, it would be assumed they desired to end the negotiations:

At times it may be necessary to risk rupture and try brinkmanship in negotiations but it has to be carefully calibrated and never overplayed. I hinted at stopping the talks in Peking when China showed reluctance to provide her own certified maps of what the Chinese delegation considered to be the frontiers of China. (Of course, I wanted to undercut the untenable Chinese contention that boundaries are not valid unless formally delimited.)[22]

Nehru presented the report to Parliament in February 1961.[23] The report further hardened the stance of the Indian people and eliminated any scope for concessions or bargaining, something inevitable in boundary negotiations, historically speaking.

Zhou Enlai left India feeling angry and bitter. He made no bones about his disappointment with the 'arrogant' Nehru. He also held a midnight press conference at Delhi before leaving India, trying to impress upon the media that his efforts to get India to accept his six-point proposal for further dialogue to resolve the boundary dispute sadly proved to be in vain.

Nationalistic fervour was palpable by now, and people expressed their anger in a public rally in the proximity of the prime minister's house 'demanding that the Government of India should not truckle under Zhou En-lai's personal pressure. Nehru came out and addressed the crowd and assured them that not an inch of Indian soil would be yielded to China.'[24]

Unfortunately, Nehru had by then boxed himself into a corner where any give or take, adjustments or exchange of territory would be seen as a sell-out. At the same time, the Chinese were aware that the Indian armed forces were ill-prepared for anything beyond minor skirmishing along the northern frontier. The Indian Army brass were given to understand that there would be no war with China, and a state of 'guarded complacency' had begun to creep in among them. There appeared to be no urgency to modernize the armed forces. Defence Minister Krishna Menon was focused on indigenization and setting up ordnance factories and defence infrastructure, but prioritization was conspicuous by its absence, affecting the operational readiness of the army. Time criticality was least understood, either by the minister or by the bureaucrats in the Ministry of Defence! As the two ministers, Krishna Menon and Morarji Desai, did not see eye to eye, money for acquisitions was not forthcoming, particularly the foreign exchange element. As a result, modernization and the making up of deficiencies in our defence capabilities took a back seat, and the appeals of the armed forces for the same remained unheeded.

The armed border clashes in Ladakh and the north-eastern frontier regions in 1958–59, where India lost many more soldiers than China, made Parliament sit up and question the government strategy to free Indian territory from Chinese occupation. What was not articulated or amplified adequately to the people of India was that Britain had bequeathed to India no defined political boundary from Shaksgam and Karakoram right up to Nepal. That the Indian armed forces were not capable of facing the PLA in an all-out war was also not shared by Nehru, neither with Parliament nor, definitely, with the people of the country.

Nehru was under the wrong impression that he would be able to prevail upon the Chinese to vacate Aksai Chin. He perhaps never truly comprehended or was correctly advised that for China the road alignment through Aksai Chin was a geostrategic imperative. Because of the Kunlun range, there was no other feasible route that could connect Sinkiang with western Tibet. An alternative route would be a circuitous one, a few thousand kilometres longer. Under no circumstances could China contemplate giving up the Aksai Chin region. This was not adequately appreciated by Nehru and his advisers. The Indian Foreign Service officers and the intelligence agencies were unable to join the dots and establish that China must have had some grand design in closing down the Indian trade agency in Gartok and preventing the Indian consulate from functioning from Kashgar. As reasoned by me earlier, the Chinese wished to conceal the building of their road through Aksai Chin from the Indians. They even stopped traders from using that route during the 1950s.

Unfortunately, India's national strategic planners, if they were at all considering possible threats from the northern frontier, were unable to see through the Chinese bluff and bluster and to come to the right conclusions. Although the director of the Intelligence Bureau, Mullik, has claimed that he kept the ministries concerned informed about the construction of the Sinkiang road, no effort was made to ascertain whether its alignment violated Indian territories. In fact, Mullik has gone on to state there were two possible alignments of the road from Kashgar to Rudok in western Tibet. This argument is manifestly incorrect, as there was only one historical trade route joining the two towns, and it went through Saidulla and Haji Langar in Aksai Chin. The other possible route was through the Keriya Shankou Pass (5,599 metres) across the Kunlun range, which was a difficult fair-weather foot track at best. Mullik should have known this, or endeavoured to find this out using all possible means.

As I have mentioned earlier, India possessed the capabilities of aerial photography using the Canberra aircraft, and one or two sorties would have given us the status of road construction by the Chinese in the open wilderness of Aksai Chin. It is difficult to imagine why this was not done. Alternatively, we could have sought the help of any other friendly power. Waiting till 1958—when the Chinese had completed construction of the motorable road and announced it to the world—to ascertain whether it traversed Indian territory by physical patrolling the Aksai Chin area was too late, and displayed a total lack of ingenuity on the part of the Indians.

Or was it that the unpalatable truth was being deliberately pushed under the carpet? I believe this to be the case! Even today, the route over the Kunlun range has not been developed into a road by China because of the very high altitudes here (between 6,500 metres and 7,000 metres) and extremely difficult terrain.

What followed thereafter was a clumsy and pussilanimous act by our foreign office—in that we lodged a protest with China for having constructed a road through our territory without seeking our permission or even informing us! As we considered it as our territory, how could the question of our permitting the Chinese to construct a road across it arise in the first place? The Chinese must have had a hearty laugh at our foolishness. The note verbale sent on 18 October 1958 by the foreign secretary read:

> It is a matter of surprise and regret that the Chinese Government should have constructed a road through indisputably Indian Territory without first obtaining the permission of the Government of India and without even informing the Government of India.[25]

Adding to this absurdity, the note also complained that Chinese personnel working on the road, as also travellers using the road, had not applied for visas from the Government of India! How much more ridiculous could our handling of such serious matters be? First, we displayed our ignorance of such a massive road project traversing approximately 160 kilometres through Indian territory, and which had commenced in 1951 and was inaugurated with much fanfare in October 1957, and next we sought Chinese help to secure information on the whereabouts of our missing patrol in our own territory! In fact, taking advantage of the fait accompli and our ignorance, the Chinese had the gall to invite the Indian ambassador and defence attache for the event, thereby rubbing salt into our wounds. The embarassment was all the more heightened by the ignorance of these developments on the part of Parliament, and, of course, the people of the country.

The true face of the Chinese was on display towards the close of the decade of the 1950s. Accoding to the account of Jagat Mehta,

> The Chinese insensitivity to and disregard of Indian territorial integrity, as publicly notified, came only in September 1959. Nehru's

chief concern was still not to get deflected from non-alignment, but due to being generally misled, or even deliberately deceived, he was put on the defensive in the Parliament. Without prior consultations, he committed himself to the release of all correspondence and notes exchanged with China since 1954 in 'White' papers.[26]

It appears that by 1959 Nehru was torn between two strands of thought as far as the Aksai Chin frontier was concerned. On the one hand, he believed that the northern boundary, as shown on our maps since 1954, was historically and traditionally a part of Jammu and Kashmir and that Aksai Chin was therefore undoubtedly Indian. On the other hand, as mentioned earlier, he introduced an element of ambiguity when he made a vague statement relating to Aksai Chin in the Parliament on 12 September 1959 stating that 'the matter has been challeneged for a hundred years. There has never been delimitation there.'[27]

He could have boldly told the nation that since China was asserting her claim to Aksai Chin the two nations could examine records, carry out a joint survey and delimit this frontier. There might have been at least a slim chance of finding an acceptable solution if the nation had been taken into confidence earlier. Unfortunately, that not being the case, our 'misinformed polity' had by then taken an extremely hard stance and Nehru was helplessly stuck. Vulnerable to a vitriolic opposition, he had no option but to let this opportunity pass.

A very interesting and almost incredible story has been recounted by Jagat Mehta, the chargé d'affaires in the Indian embassy at Peking from 1964 to 1966:

On the file I found a letter, written some months before [the border war in 1962], with a specific warning that the Chinese were planning an attack on the Indian frontier. I felt this was explosive and so I removed it from the file and took it with me when I went home for consultation in 1964 and showed it to Foreign Secretary Gundevia. He recognized that it could be dynamite in its implications, as it should have been transmitted to Delhi instantaneously. Without much ado, he promptly tore it into shreds![28]

Obviously, Nehru and his policymakers were not looking at the strategic or tactical implications of the Sinkiang road and its vital importance from China's point of view, otherwise they would have called for a detailed appreciation of the threat such a development held, besides, of course, understanding the improbability of China ever vacating the Aksai Chin and adjacent areas to the west of this strategic artery so as to provide tactical depth to it.

The Chinese, in contrast, had a well-considered strategy to ensure the security of this road, which was why they drew their 1956 claim line to the west of and more or less parallel to the road alignment, thus keeping the Indians at bay. Besides, as borne out by their 1960 claim line, it kept creeping westwards to create an effective buffer zone between the road and the boundary (a distance of 35–45 kilometres, so as to deny possible firm bases to launch offensive action against the Aksai Chin road and effectively keep it out of the long-range artillery of the Indian Army of that time, and also out of reach of ground-based observation and surveillance). To meet this requirement, the line was drawn arbitrarily, and did not follow any well-defined geographical features of the region. Surprisingly, this aspect has seldom been commented on before. This reasoning may not have occurred to a civilian, but it definitely should have made sense to a military strategist. Perhaps the two seldom sat together to carry out in-depth analyses of such developments. And to top it all, the policymakers kept many issues under wraps or as closely guarded secrets.

As if all this was not bad enough, Nehru apparently misinformed the Parliament when he made this statement there in November 1959:

> ... at no time since our Independence, and of course before it, were our defence forces in better condition, in finer fettle ... I am quite confident that our defence forces are well capable of looking after our security.[29]

This was after operational contol of the border had been handed over to the army in November 1959, consequent to the severe mauling of one of our patrols in the Kongka Pass and the earlier detention of another under Lieutenant Iyengar, when it was reconnoitring the northern areas of Aksai Chin. This patrol was released at the Karakoram Pass in October 1958 after a month in Chinese custody.

In April 1961, Krishna Menon, the defence minister, went one step ahead of Nehru, assuring Parliament that the morale of the defence services had 'never been higher'. He went on to say that the armed forces had 'vastly improved their logistics capacity ... there had been a great improvement in training, provisioning and manufacture of arms ... Our equipment are of a better character: our troops are in advanced positions.'[30] Major General D.K. Palit, director of military operations at the time, remarked that even though there were political compulsions for such statements to be made, it was 'difficult to reconcile these pronouncements in Parliament with what Army HQ had been telling the government during the past year. Kaul had personally apprised the PM of the shortages in our order of battle, in arms and equipment and in our logistical potential. There could have been no room for a misunderstanding.'[31]

The sound advice to Army HQ in mid-August 1962 from Lieutenant General Daulet Singh, the general officer commanding-in-chief, Western Command, responsible for the Ladakh frontier, recommending suspension of the forward policy till such time as his force levels were adequately built up, went unheeded. He anticipated that the Chinese would retaliate with force if their strategic Aksai Chin artery was even remotely threatened. The General Staff at Army HQ did not take his frank professional advice as seriously as it should have. Lt General Daulet Singh concluded his advice with great sagacity:

It is imperative that political direction is based on military means. If the two are not coordinated there is a danger of creating a situation where we may lose both in the material and moral sense much more than we already have. Thus, there is no short cut to military preparedness to enable us to pursue objectively our present policy aimed at refuting the illegal Chinese claim over our territory.[32]

The lieutenant general conveyed to the establishment in no uncertain terms that he was not prepared to take on the Chinese unless he was given the additional force of a division with all the supporting elements.

Presumably, this was not relayed by Army HQ to the Ministry of Defence (MoD). It cannot be denied that there couldn't have been more honest and profound professional advice the government could get than this.

However, at an MoD conference as late as 22 September, the army chief, General P.N. Thapar, did express his opinion—in the context of the government's directive to evict the intruding Chinese across the Thagla Ridge along the McMahon Line—that the Chinese would 'retaliate against the Indian forward posts in the western sector, perhaps overrunning all of them east of the Chinese claim line'. This military assessment, conveying a starkly dismal prognosis, was emphatically ruled out by the civilian policymakers with the stock phrase that 'China would not launch any general attack'.[33] Although General Thapar acquiesced in their request, he insisted that the order be given to the army in writing. The directions of the government, signed by H.C. Sarin, a joint secretary in the MoD, and cleared by Defence Minister Menon, who was attending the General Assembly session of the United Nations in New York, read:

> The decision throughout has been as discussed in previous meetings, that the Army should prepare and throw out the Chinese as soon as possible. The Chief of Army Staff was accordingly directed to take action for the eviction of the Chinese in the Kameng Frontier Division of NEFA as soon as he is ready.

This highly confidential order was reported by the *Times*, London, on 23 September and also carried by the *Times of India* four days later: 'The Government of India took the political decision ten days ago to use force if necessary to throw the Chinese intruders out.'[34] This gave the Chinese advance notice of our operational plans at the national level. These events speak volumes of our security consciousness during that period.

As mentioned in the account written by Lieutenant General B.M. Kaul, when Nehru was conveyed the same misgivings earlier by General Thapar, he brushed them aside. Kaul writes, 'He (Nehru) had good reasons to believe that the Chinese would not take any strong action against us.'[35] In his narrative of the border war in the Indian north-east frontier, Brigadier John Dalvi, commander of the ill-fated 7 Infantry

Brigade, recounts the words of Lieutenant General B. M. Kaul on 10 October 1962, when the first major skirmish between the Chinese and the Indian Army took place: 'Unbelievable but amazing was the fact that the Corps Commander had come to the Namka Chu area to exhort and pep-up his frontline divisional, brigade and battalion commanders, and to witness the launch of "Operation Leghorn" to evict the Chinese from the Thagla Ridge.'

Pushed into battle for political expediency, a hastily assembled, ill-equipped and inadequately supported force of company strength was ordered to occupy a position on the Thagla Ridge to challenge the vastly superior Chinese force. On 10 October, the Chinese attacked the hapless and unsupported Indian Company of 9 Punjab at Tseng Jong and forced them to fall back. The attack by an overwhelming enemy force supported by artillery and mortar fire shattered the make-believe world of Lieutenant General Kaul, who was watching the event unfold as from a grandstand akin to a peacetime manoeuvre. Dalvi records that Kaul's 'first reaction was one of disbelief, shock and disillusionment. "Oh my God," he cried, "You are right, they mean business." This disastrously ended his moment of challenging grandeur.'[36]

Leaving Dalvi to handle the battle thrust on him by the cabal of reckless leadership comprising politicians, military brass, diplomats and bureaucrats as best he could, Kaul made an ungraceful exit and rushed to Delhi to apprise the prime minister of the stark reality of the operational situation. He bypassed the Command and Army HQs while doing so. This is not the normal practice but Kaul could have his say because of his proximity to Nehru and weakness of his superior, Lieutenant General L.P. Sen, the army commander, and the army chief, General P.N. Thapar. He cursorily kept the Command and Army HQs in the loop while doing so. Furthermore, a few days after his return to Tezpur, a sickly Kaul had to be flown back to Delhi because of severe chest pain. Surprisingly, he continued to command his corps from his sick bed even as the Chinese launched their major offensives on 20 October 1962, not only in NEFA but also in Ladakh. It was perhaps the first time in our history that a corps was being commanded in war by remote control by a recuperating commander located 1,500 kilometres away from his sick bed. This shameful episode exposed the manner in which decisions on national war strategy were being taken during that period.

If military modernization and border infrastructure development had commenced in a planned manner in India from the mid-1950s, the narrative of the Sino-Indian border discord would have been different. While the Chinese were fully engaged in building roads from mainland China into Tibet from all directions, the Indian leadership was focusing primarily on development, the economy and enhancement of its image among the developing and non-aligned countries. Upgradation of our defence capabilities had been given a back seat, on the assumption that there was no threat from the northern border.

To cite an example, the renowned 4 Infantry Division, also called the Fighting Fourth of the Second World War fame, was employed in constructing the housing project 'Amar' at Ambala during that period, and was in 1959 abruptly moved to NEFA to face the Chinese threat. This formation was expected to fight in the high Himalayas with weapons of Second World War vintage, and in clothing and equipment designed for the hot and dusty plains of north India on man-pack basis, as there were hardly any roads. Moreover, the political and military leadership failed to provide higher direction during the war. It was hardly surprising that the war was an unequal fight between India and China.

The interplay of international power politics of the time—the Cuban Missile Crisis, the threat from Taiwan, the Sino-Soviet ideological and boundary disputes, India's grant of asylum to the Dalai Lama, the establishment of his government-in-exile in India, coupled with internal compulsions within China—had a major bearing on Mao's decision to launch a limited war in Ladakh and the north-eastern frontier regions of India during 1962. His aim was to teach India a lesson, lower its image and cut Nehru to size. October–November 1962 was assessed to be the most suitable period for the campaign. The Chinese offensives were strategically timed, exploiting the three-month window available between the end of the monsoon and the snowy winter in the high-Himalayan region—a fact not adequately appreciated by most researchers. The decision and consequent preparations for such a contingency was perhaps taken during 1959–60, as it would give the Chinese army adequate time to build the roads and stock the required levels of munitions and supplies. The Indian Army's forward push into disputed pockets played into Chinese hands, offering the Chinese an ideal pretext to launch their sudden onslaughts.

However, the world, including the Soviet Union, was not fooled, and condemned China as the aggressor. When it came to fighting a war, China's strategic thought process and its planning at the national, operational and tactical level outclassed the personality-oriented, uncoordinated and knee-jerk reactions of the Indians. The Indian actions did not flow from a mature national security strategy, and often appeared to consist of amateurish steps based on gut feeling or wishful thinking. Pragmatism and the logic of realpolitik were absent.

Unfortunately, Indian policymakers were deluded by the outward air of bonhomie between the two sides from 1954 to 1958 and tended to downplay if not ignore the threat perception, particularly from the northern borders. On the contrary, the Chinese were following a clear-headed strategy to ensure that their hold over Tibet was strengthened and that the Sinkiang–Tibet highway remained securely in their possession. To this end they deployed military posts with the required infrastructure to the west of this road, creating a buffer zone of 'Chinese-occupied' territory to ward off any threats from India at that time or in the future. The western limit of this zone, now known as the 'Line of Actual Control' (LAC), follows no geographical or topographical features and cuts across the grain of the country.

The unilaterally drawn LAC does follow one unstated principle—that of providing tactical depth to the Aksai Chin road besides strategically connecting the western perimeter of China. This particular road follows the alignment of an ancient trade route through Aksai Chin, linking Kashgar in Chinese Turkestan with Kashmir and Tibet, and has been historically referred to as the 'graveyard of caravans'. The strategic relevance of this communication artery gets magnified manifold as there is no feasible alternative route to its east because of the impassability of the Gobi Desert, the Kunlun range and the uninhabited, trackless and waterless Changthang region of Tibet, whose average altitude is 4,500 metres.

In pursuance of Nehru's directive, the Indian civil administration and police began to establish border check-posts during 1954–56. Perhaps at the functional and lower levels, their endeavour was to reach up to or close to the watershed or the well-known passes in the region, but they were careful to remain on the Indian side. At the same time, following an ambiguous policy of both profferring a hand of friendship and asserting their claims to not only Aksai Chin but to other areas of India in the central and eastern Himalayas too, in particular a vast stretch of tribal territory in the north-eastern frontier region of India, then known as North-East Frontier Agency (NEFA), the Chinese began a process of surveying the border areas and asserting their claims.

For the first time in history, as mentioned earlier in this book, Chinese presence was seen in the central Himalayas west of Nepal, in areas such as Nilang–Jadhang, the Barahoti plains, the Shipkila Pass, Kaurik and other places. In most cases they withdrew to the Tibetan side on being cautioned by the Indians about their trespass into Indian territory. Passes like Niti and Shipkila found specific mention in the 1954 Trade Agreement, which sanctified their status as boundary passes, leaving little scope for misinterpretation. Surprisingly, the Chinese displayed a lack of awareness of such historical facts.

From 1956 to 1959, the border issue began its ferment, which found illustration in a flurry of diplomatic protests, claims and counterclaims. It became almost a ritual for both sides to blame each other for acts of aggression or intrusion, and for both sides to also deny them, claiming they were operating in their own territories. This pattern continued until the stage of armed clashes began. Mostly, it was the Chinese with their superiority in numbers and weaponry who used force and caused casualties to Indian border police or Assam Rifles, or manhandled, and at times even illegally detained, Indian paramilitary personnel. Their response to formal Indian protests was that their soldiers had acted in self-defence, under provocation by the Indian border troops. The prominent incidents of such border skirmishes and armed encounters during 1958–59 were at Longju in the Subansiri sector, and at Khinzemane in the Tawang sector. There were incidents at Chang Chenmo and Kongka Pass in the Ladakh sector too.

On 9 September 1962, during a meeting at the MoD held by Defence Minister V.K. Krishna Menon and attended by General Thapar, Chief of

Army Staff, Lieutenant General Sen, GOC-in-C of Eastern Command, S.S. Khera, cabinet secretary, Mullik, director of the Intelligence Bureau, S.C. Sarin, a joint secretary in the defence ministry, and some other officials, it was decided that 'the Chinese must be evicted immediately and forcefully'. Dhola post and Thagla Ridge were Indian territory, as per the Indian understanding. The Chinese, of course, have a different perception regarding Thagla Ridge. Importantly, the pastures to the north of Namka Chu and on the Thagla Ridge belonged to the Indian village of Pangchen (acknowledged by the Chinese too), as had been jointly clarified in a meeting of local officials of both sides in 1953. At that time it had been agreed that the villagers on the Tibetan side of Thagla could continue to use these pastures, as they were willing to pay for the same.[37] Over time, Thagla Ridge being the most prominent watershed in the west–east direction, was understood to be the boundary. The Khinzemane border outpost of India was located at the foot of this range, along the Namjyang Chu.

The central sector of the Indo-Tibetan border is comparatively more accessible and populated, and has a clear ethnic, religious and cultural divide. Moreover, in this region, commonly known as the Uttar Pradesh–Tibet border, a historical, traditional and customary boundary exists, leaving little scope for dispute, except in the case of some pastural areas. Thus, the few petty territorial claims involving 540-odd square kilometres in this area would be the easiest to resolve during the process of boundary resolution between India and China.

Chinese maps released in 1954 showed Aksai Chin and small parts of both the Uttar Pradesh–Tibet border and the NEFA within China. Nehru and his advisers had apparently not taken a serious note of these blatant acts of cartographic aggression. And even if they had done so, why did it evoke only a mild protest from our side? It appears that this serious matter was neither raised formally with the Chinese during the first decade of our Independence nor analysed in depth. This is inexplicable! Nehru should have been appropriately counselled by the mandarins of our foreign service and his other key advisers. Instead of being overawed by the personality of the colossus that Nehru was, it was their duty to tell him the hard facts, the sensitive nuances and the harsh ground reality of the northern borders we had inherited from the British. 'We professionals must share the blame for there being not a single word of dissenting caution,' admitted Mehta a few years later. He was a former foreign secretary and a hands-on China expert.[38]

The Chinese leadership were not lacking in clarity at all. They were clear they would not rake up the issue until their strategic communication arteries and other basic elements of infrastructure were completed, particularly the road linking Sinkiang and Western Tibet. Until these objectives were achieved, their leadership kept misleading India on one pretext or the other. Zhou Enlai said the maps of the Koumintang era were old and China had had no time to 'revise' them. On another occasion he is reported to have said that the time 'was not ripe' to discuss China's boundary with north-east India.

Unfortunately, India has proved to be only too willing to be beguiled. It is not that there were no indications of the devious intentions of the Chinese, but we failed to follow the leads or to join the dots. Moreover, as a sequel to China's arbitrary and unilateral cartographic aggression by including in their maps Aksai Chin and NEFA in China, Nehru's decision to unilaterally define and delimit our northern boundary on Survey of India maps and replace the existing maps in 1954—even though in our case the boundary had been drawn based on historical facts, custom and usage—did not help matters. Both countries should have entered into dialogue and resolved the matter peacefully. In the eighteenth and nineteenth centuries it had been possible for powerful nations to change boundaries and expand empires or acquire colonies by conquest or coercion, but in the mid-twentieth century the world was unlikely to accept such actions.

In Asia, where the concept of precisely defined and demarcated boundaries between nations did not exist, there were frontier zones and traditional boundaries in areas that were populated. In the regions that were uninhabited or were home to nomadic and shifting populations, boundaries remained vague and undefined. Therefore, in the post-colonial period, most nations in Asia inherited some boundary dispute or the other with their neighbours. It was then not unusual that the entire length of the 4,057-kilometre frontier between India and the Sinkiang and Tibet regions had not been defined unambiguously, particularly the segment from the tri-junction of India, Afghanistan and China to the Karakoram Pass and onwards to Nepal. The British, during their rule of India, were unable to get the Chinese to commit to an agreed boundary line in this region, and ended up bequeathing to independent India this 'hot potato' of a vague frontier. The internal situation in India during 1961 is described by Jagat Mehta as follows:

> The overriding political fact was that the Prime Minister of India was boxed in by Parliament and the aroused public opinion in the country. It should be emphasized that in April 1960 there was not the remotest apprehension of a major conflict ahead between the armed forces of China and India.[39]

Under a mistaken belief that the Chinese would not retaliate with force against our setting up posts in territory we believed was ours, a decision was taken by India in early November 1961 to establish posts to fill the vacuums where they existed and to show our flag in areas which we perceived as belonging to us. This chess game–like exercise was indulged in by both sides. But while the Chinese had a clear-cut aim and long-term vision of what they wanted to achieve, the Indians displayed incredible naivety, failing to register, on account of their ostrich-like attitude, the gravity of the boundary problem. The other possibility is they did not want to face the reality. Nehru and his close advisers had a firm conviction till the very end that the situation would remain limited to border skirmishing and not result in a major conflagration. Their overwhelming belief, which was shared widely in India till mid-1962, was that China with all her problems would never resort to war against peace-loving India. As revealed in a book on G. Parthasarathy, a renowned diplomat and scholar, Professor Ashok Parthasarathi says, 'Nehru cautioned GP (G. Parthasarathy) on 18 March 1958, a day before his departure as ambassador to Peking, to always remain vigilant. He said, "I don't trust the Chinese one bit ... They are an arrogant, untrustworthy, devious and hegemonistic lot." Further, Nehru directed him not to keep anyone else in the loop on "important matters" and to deal directly with him; not even Krishna Menon, the defence minister.' It is unfortunate that Nehru neither advised his army or other top functionaries of such an assessment of China, nor ordered steps to be taken to prepare militarily for a major confrontation. Our leadership seems to have been living in a world of make-believe and wishful thinking, hoping they could ride out the storm! In the words of Lieutenant General S.K. Sinha, 'The political and military leaderships appeared tailor-made to lead the nation to disaster.'[40]

The Chinese consciously did not pursue extension of the 1954 Panchsheel agreement beyond its eight-year limit, which ended in 1962. They did not want to be constrained or tied down by any commitment that would come in their way in case use of force became necessary to assert their boundary claims. It is telling that Deng Xiaoping's statement that the Indian government, and Nehru in particular, were supporting the uprising in Tibet, concluded with the remarks, '*and, when the time comes, we certainly will settle accounts with them [Indians]* (emphasis added)'.

China's decision to exercise the war option in the Himalayas was carefully and deliberately taken after assuring itself of the security of the eastern seaboard and also of the support of the Russians, who hoped to have the Chinese on their side during the then ongoing Cuban Missile Crisis as a quid pro quo. Chinese apprehensions of a US-abetted and supported offensive by Taiwan were allayed when the US ambassador in Warsaw, on being questioned by Wang Bingnan, the Chinese ambassador, as to whether preparations were being made for an amphibious assault by the Nationalist forces in Taiwan, replied that 'the United States desired peace and "under present circumstances" would not support a Nationalist offensive'. According to Ambassador Bingnan, this input 'played a "very big role" in Beijing's final decision to proceed with operations in the Himalayas'.[41]

By early October 1962, the Chinese were fully prepared to strike Indian positions along the disputed border. They were simply looking for an opportunity that would allow them to colour their premeditated onslaught as a '*counter-attack*', and used Nehru's ill-advised outburst—'*Throw out the Chinese*'—to the hilt to achieve their aim.

At a key meeting on 6 October 1962 on the outskirts of Beijing, after having taken the decision to go to war with India, Chairman Mao Tse

Tung said the possible isolation of China on the world stage would not be a '... *decisive factor ... as long as the frontline troops fight well we will be in an advantageous position ... It's better to die standing, than to die kneeling. If China fought successfully, in an awe-inspiring way, this will guarantee at least thirty years of peace* (emphasis added).'[42]

As far as India was concerned, the people were ignorant of the harsh reality of their country's lack of preparedness for war, the adverse relative strength of our forces vis-à-vis the Chinese, and the poor logistical backup for our army and paramilitary forces deployed on the borders. On our side, there were no roads in most places. On the other hand, the Chinese had given top priority to construction of a network of roads and infrastructure in preparation for any future conflict. Supply of equipment by air in these parts has its limitations and is dependent on weather conditions. In the north-east, the monsoon lasts from June through September, and it rains copiously, definitely more than in Cherrapunji! Despite the warnings given by many Indian military commanders, the political leadership, the powerful head of the IB and key foreign office functionaries, including the ambassador, continued to misread Chinese intentions. So convinced were they that China would never launch an all-out offensive in Ladakh or NEFA that they prevailed upon or silenced saner advice, and continued to meddle in the military aspects of external challenges and the guarding of our borders. Unfortunately, they were eventually able to get key military commanders also to tow their line. Generals like Kaul, the chief of General Staff, and Thapar, the army chief, went along with the faulty strategy of the political leadership and their advisers. In fact, Lieutenant General Kaul pushed the policy of showing the flag as far forward as possible by ordering establishment of section (ten men) or platoon (thirty men) piquets all along the frontier, with no mutual support or reserves to reinforce them in an emergency.

Since the national leadership under Nehru did not expect a war, they were prepared to lose a few soldiers in skirmishes here and there, as had happened in Kongka La or Longju during 1958–59. Not surprisingly, when war was about to break out, the prime minister was abroad on some visit and the defence minister was engaged in a conference at the

United Nations. Not to be left behind in the wishful thinking that 'all is well' on the borders, even the chief of the General Staff was cooling off in Kashmir that September, and the director of military operations, the man whose responsibility it was to help the army chief evolve military strategy and coordinate its execution, was on a cruise on an aircraft carrier with a parliamentary delegation! A strong army chief would have recalled them. Incredible as these events were, it would have been of immense value if General Thapar's perspective of this period had been penned by him. He must have had an interesting albeit sad story to recount.

On the dawn of 20 October, the nation and its political and military leadership got a rude jolt as its military disaster began to unravel in a deadly spiral. Deployed in a linear formation on tactically unsound positions in the valley of Namka Chu, 7 Infantry Brigade was overrun in a couple of hours, and the brigade disintegrated, losing a large number of officers and men, who were killed, wounded or captured as prisoners of war. Brigadier J.P. Dalvi, whose brigade faced the major brunt of the Chinese attack, has recalled in his touching account a conversation with Lieutenant Colonel Rikh, one of his commanding officers, on the night of 19 October, just before the Chinese offensive began. The Lt Col's last words were:

> Don't worry, Sir, despite the Chinese superiority, the Rajputs will not let you or the country down. We will fight till we have nothing more to fight with. If you get back please see that the culprits who landed us in this mess get their just punishment.[43]

Had the reality of the undelineated and, in some cases, unilaterally drawn boundary, and of the unequal and inadequate fighting capabilities of our forces been shared with the people in general and with parliamentarians in particular, perhaps the clamour of the nation to nudge the government to throw out the ingressing Chinese would have been checked. *If only the people of both countries had been told the truth from the beginning, the war could possibly have been averted.*

The Chinese onslaught across India's northern border in October–November 1962 resulted in a shameful politico-military defeat for India and its military. The conflict was confined to the disputed areas along the Sino-Indian boundary. There had been no formal declaration of war by either side. This border war nonetheless shocked the leadership as well as the people of India, making them feel as if they had been stabbed in the back.

Having more or less advanced up to the maximalistic claim line by 21 November 1962, the Chinese unilaterally declared a ceasefire and announced that their forces would fall back to positions 20 kilometres behind the Line of Actual Control (as on 7 November 1962) in Ladakh area and the McMahon Line in NEFA. This they completed by 1 March 1963.

However, the world did not get fooled. It unhesitatingly branded the Chinese as the aggressor. In his book, Mehta writes: 'I told him (Chang Wen-chin, Chinese team leader during the official talks in 1960) that the Sino-Indian War was a tragedy born of mutual misjudgements.' We probably did not know that the Chinese would consider our Forward Policy provocative, but the Chinese had made a big blunder by accusing Nehru by name as responsible for the 'revolt in Tibet'. Surprisingly, he did not demur.[44]

What surprised not only India but the world at large was the well-orchestrated and publicized unilateral declaration of ceasefire by the Chinese across the entire front and the withdrawal of its forces from there. This decision of the Chinese was communicated to the world media almost at the same time as it was conveyed to the Indian ambassador in Beijing. A rational analysis of this episode leads one to the conclusion that China, having achieved its strategic goals of cutting India down to size and securing its own communication artery from Kashgar to Lhasa, must have attempted an image-building exercise so that it was not adversely publicized as an expansionist state. It also wanted to avoid the huge logistical effort of sustaining its army during the ensuing winter, when most passes would have closed.

PART VIII

THE ENIGMATIC DRAGON

The Chinese style of dealing with strategic decisions: thorough analysis; careful preparation; attention to psychological and political factors; quest for surprise; and rapid conclusion.

—Henry Kissinger[1]

20

Understanding the Middle Kingdom and the Dragon

While dealing with China, it is vital to gain an in-depth knowledge of its history, geography, culture, strategic thought process and systems; something that independent India's leadership and their advisers ought to have seriously done. It appears that this was not the case, at least in the first decade and a half of our Independence. Even in the present day, we do not have an adequate number of China experts of the desired level of knowledge of the country, its demographics, its political systems and philosophy, its strengths and vulnerabilities, and its languages. This inadequacy has to be overcome, and our leadership must get itself thoroughly acquainted with the nuances and finer points of Chinese strategy. Our leaders need to be competent enough in China matters to effectively engage with China to resolve the variety of issues that confronts the two nations, the boundary dispute being the foremost. Prof. Srinath Kondapalli, a noted China expert, estimates the number of Chinese experts in India at not more than 100. 'It is quite shameful that very few Indians focus on China. For 1.1 billion people looking at 1.4 billion people, we are actually understaffed to understand the other side,' he has remarked. And whatever 'experts' there are, not all of them are able to speak and write Chinese.[2]

This chapter endeavours to address the important aspects that have a bearing on Sino-Indian relations to facilitate a more realistic understanding of the Dragon. Indian policymakers need to study Chinese philosophy and strategic thinking, their culture and characteristics as a people, their leadership and way of doing things—all of which go to make up the strengths and weaknesses of their civilization. Unless we understand the Chinese mind, how can we successfully negotiate with them? If independent India had been doing this right from the time the People's Republic of China was born in 1949, we might not have made the grievous errors in our Tibet policy that we did, for which we continue to pay the price to this day. Jagat Mehta has said: 'One cannot help but conclude that we have yet to fully and unsentimentally understand the "otherness" of China.' He went on to say, 'China is able to wait out strategically and improvise tactically. This stumps democracies like India which have no comparable patience or sustained policy spread over decades, leave alone centuries.'[3]

However, despite China's 'historical self-confidence' that is 'unique', it may or may not be able to handle the Tiananmen-type of spontaneous public outbursts or simmering unrest in Uighur province of the present era, where information technology and social media have made it difficult for a nation to conceal facts or suppress public opinion. 'Just as China never bothered to understand the working of a democracy, India never followed carefully the impact of domestic debate inside China.'[4]

Mao's forceful ideological drive at the Lushan plenum in 1959 and his subsequent actions led to the disastrous 'Great Leap Forward', which resulted in a severe famine in China in which thirty million people died. But despite China's internal problems, Mao did not hesitate to plan and to give the go-ahead for the country's border war with India when he thought 'the time was ripe'—to use the oft-quoted Chinese metaphor. The leadership of both countries faced the monumental challenges of their agrarian economies, burgeoning populations, poverty and lack of infrastructure. In the case of India, most of the arable land was heavily dependent on the monsoon, whose failure often resulted in famine. In the case of China, it had large tracts of unproductive land, such as the Tibetan plateau, the Gobi Desert and some areas of Inner Mongolia and Manchuria. 'And with 0.08 hectares per capita compared to a world average of 0.24, China falls just above Bangladesh and Egypt.' China was positioned twelfth from bottom in this respect.[5] Both countries paid great attention to agricultural reforms, as large-scale industrialization was a long way off at their nascent stage of nationhood. Mao Zedong's first major policy initiative was aimed at freeing the poor and landless peasants from the rich landlords through a programme that came to be known as *fanshen*, which has been wonderfully described by Rebecca Cairns, in her article 'Agrarian Reform', in which she quotes Mao defining the process of agrarian reforms in June 1950 thus:

> Land reform in a population of over 300 million people is a vicious war. It is more arduous, more complex, more troublesome than crossing the Yangzi, because our troops are 260 million peasant soldiers. This is a war for land reform, this is the most hideous class war between peasants and landlords. It is a battle to the death.[6]

Fanshen resulted in the execution of over a million landlords or rich peasants, and redistribution of lands among the poor farmers and landless cultivators. In democratic India, land reforms did not take off as intended, as many provinces did not enact or enforce the reforms with the required zeal. Besides, India did not exploit its higher threshold of industrialization and its advantage of familiarity with English. Moreover, both India and China got deeply immersed in regional conflicts, India with the Indo-Pakistan war of 1947–48 over Jammu and Kashmir, and China with the war in Korea. Internal strife and territorial consolidation too consumed the attention of the leadership and resources of both countries. Mao assigned the 'liberation' of Tibet to the People's Liberation Army (PLA) during 1950 as a top-priority objective, besides the subjugation of recalcitrant and warring factions in the country, particularly in the southern and western frontier regions of China. The Indian leadership was occupied with assimilation of Hyderabad and Junagarh states into India, and later with liberation of Goa, Daman and Diu from Portuguese rule.

Socio-economic development, infrastructure and industrialization were the other vital result areas for both nations, which embarked on five-year plans to achieve their targeted growth. In the case of India, one can say with certainty that the defence sector received less than the desired importance or attention. Being a democratic, peace-loving and development-oriented nation, India had no security threats—this was the impression and belief of both India's first prime minister, Jawaharlal Nehru, and many other national leaders of the time. They naively considered the Himalayas in the north and the seas along the peninsula as sentinels that would ensure the security of India's vast frontiers.

But the Chinese had a fairly evolved national security strategy, and their leaders were battle-experienced veterans who understood the need to secure the country's frontier regions and the necessity and importance of being militarily strong. So while India did not accord the Sino-Indian boundary the attention it deserved, particularly in view of the undemarcated nature of a large part of this boundary, China deliberately did not want to raise this issue of its demarcation until the 'time was ripe'—a characteristic Chinese strategy deployed effectively even during the Simla Conference of 1913–14 over a century ago! India, since Independence, has neither displayed extraterritorial ambitions nor endeavoured to export any ideology, although the country was proud of its democratic moorings. But Mao never concealed his unambiguous objective of reclaiming territory that at some point of time had belonged to China. This expansionist policy, along with the 'hard-core' communist ideology that China not only imposed on her far-flung dependencies like Tibet, Xinjiang and Mongolia, but also urged its neighbours to adopt, made for a precipitous combination loaded with potential for conflict.

The Chinese believe that any territory that was once invaded by their army belongs to China and that they can assert their rights to such areas forever afterwards. For example, China's now extinct claim to Nepal was based on a single Sino-Tibetan expedition across the Himalayas in the nineteenth century. The Chinese believe their nation is the 'Middle Kingdom', an ancient and rich civilization of a superior race. They are a proud people and tend to look down on others as less cultured or civilized. Though they too had been ruled by outsiders—the Mongols and the Manchus, as India had been by the Mughals—these rulers were eventually assimilated into their civilization and culture. Since the days of the Manchu Empire, the Chinese have given great importance to their minorities, assuring them of equal status and referring to them as a family of five races—the Han, Manchu, Mongol, Muslim and Tibetan—represented by the stars of their national flag.

In fact, the Chinese can never forget the 200 years of their subjugation from 1749 to 1949 by Western powers and by Japan, and avenging this at an opportune moment in the future is always on their mind. They are not in a hurry, though, as they believe time is on their side. The Chinese display enormous patience; when the world talks of decades, the Chinese talk of centuries. In their negotiations, they often achieve their goal by exhausting the tolerance of the other side or by exploiting their haste. 'Procrastinate to frustrate' seems to be their aim. They do not hasten to finalize any agreement, particularly if it relates to the boundary, unless it is on their terms. When required, they can be evasive and vague, and can resort to obfuscation with uncanny ease.

Chinese procrastination was not accidental, but a well-orchestrated strategy to extract the best deal and not be hustled into arriving at decisions not most favourable to themselves. They demonstrated a proclivity to prolong negotiations and wear out the other side, thereby securing the best possible deal for themselves. Time has never been a major determinant for them in arriving at a conclusive decision. In July 1914, the Chinese kept Viceroy Lord Hardinge and Arthur Henry McMahon hanging on the slim hope that British India would eventually succeed in getting the Simla Convention accepted, only to dissappoint them.

Another characteristic of the proud Chinese race is non-acceptance of 'loss of face'. The British Empire in its heyday had also taken prudent decisions keeping in mind the threshold of China's ability to accept those decisions. The leaders of communist China were clear that they had to avenge the 'century of humiliation' that was inflicted on their country when it was weak. China was also wary of the British Empire expanding to gain control of southern Tibet, including the Chumbi Valley, Shigatse, Gyantse and the contiguous areas south of the Tsangpo. After the Younghusband expedition, the Chinese realized that Tibet was the vulnerable western flank of their empire, the security of which had to be ensured. Moreover, that vulnerability was accentuated by the non-acceptability of Chinese rule to the Tibetans, resulting in the 'back-door threat' syndrome. Many Chinese analysts have read a lot into India's Tibet agenda, and India's proximity to southern Tibet is a factor that weighs heavily on the Chinese mind. During his visit to India in April 1960, Zhou Enlai is reported to have said: 'The developments in Tibet have a direct bearing on the border problem.' Further commenting on the 'unfortunate' skirmishes along the border in 1959, he believed that 'it was a logical outcome of the revolt in Tibet and the coming of the Dalai Lama to India'.[7]

Prime Minister Nehru's visit to Peking in October 1954 was the first landmark visit of any Indian national leader to China. The Indian prime minister was given a rousing reception and the visit was high on ceremonials. The 'Hindi Chini bhai bhai' slogan resounded everywhere. During this visit, Nehru pointed out the inaccuracy of the boundaries on Chinese maps. Zhou Enlai's explanation was that these maps were reproductions of the old Kuomintang maps and that the present government had not had the time to revise them.[8] When the new Chinese maps published in 1956 still showed large parts of India within the Chinese boundary, Nehru again flagged the matter with Zhou En-lai during the Chinese leader's visit to India that year. As said by Neville Maxwell in India's China War, the Chinese premier spoke only about the McMahon Line in response. 'This line, established by the British imperialists, was not fair ... it was an accomplished fact and because of the friendly relations which existed between China and the countries concerned, India and Burma, the Chinese Government were of the opinion that they should give recognition to this McMahon Line.'[9]

However, unlike in the case of Burma, the Chinese did not honour their word to India. Zhou Enlai remained consciously guarded as far as revealing the Chinese strategy on the boundary issue in the western sector was concerned, not wishing to discuss that until completion of the Aksai Chin highway, which was one or two years away! Describing one of the fundamental features of Chinese strategy more than a century ago, the thirteenth Dalai Lama told Charles Bell, his biographer:

The Chinese way ... is to do something rather mild at first; then to wait a bit, and if it passes without objection, to say or do something stronger. But if we take objection to the first statement or action, they urge that it has been misinterpreted, and cease, for a time at any rate, from troubling us further. The British should keep China busy in Tibet, holding her back there. Otherwise, when the Chinese obtain a complete hold over Tibet, they will molest Nepal and Bhutan also.[10]

These are precisely the tactics the Chinese have been applying in Ladakh, Arunachal Pradesh, the South China Sea islands and other places. It is sad that our policy planners failed to register this historical Chinese pattern of the past. However, in June–July 2017, when the Chinese tried to ingress into the Doklam plateau (in Bhutan) near the tri-junction and build a road there, they were stopped in their tracks by the Indian Army on the request of Bhutan. This was the first time such an action was taken by the Indian government, and the Chinese were taken by surprise. The tense stand-off continued for over two months and has been resolved peacefully for the present by diplomacy. However, it must be noted that diplomacy works best when it is backed by military strength, as it is in this case. Both sides agreed to retreat from the eyeball-to-eyeball confrontation. The imminence of the ninenteeth National Congress of the Communist Party of China also prompted the Chinese to avoid an armed clash, which could cast a shadow on the conference. The de-escalation of this situation was accomplished with great finesse so that neither side lost face.

Referring to a Sino-Soviet polemic in a pamphlet published in 1964–65, Jagat Mehta explains what peaceful coexistence meant to the Chinese: 'Peaceful co-existence was temporary tactics: it was not an article of faith. This fits in well with the Chinese leadership's strategy that justified the advancing of national interest by improvisation, including postponing the resolution of problems considered not ripe for solution.'[11] It can be recalled that even though in 1954 the Chinese were quite aware of the boundary alignment shown on Indian maps, they did not raise the matter and instead chose to conceal information regarding their construction of the Aksai Chin road. As far as the McMahon Line was concerned, they kept their cards close to their chest. They did not reciprocate in equal measure the goodwill and many acts of solidarity and support undertaken by India.

In addition, there was an undercurrent of rivalry between the leaders of China and India with regard to who held the pole position amongst the Afro-Asian community. These two emerging giants were aiming at socio-economic development, but were evolving along different trajectories. One was following the path of communism, now labelled as 'socialism with Chinese characteristics', and the other was an adherent of parliamentary democracy. Because of their opposing ideologies, there were bound to be contradictions and differences in their approach to the same goals. 'A successful and democratic India, which rises fast and eliminates its poverty in a reasonable period, is the biggest challenge to the legitimacy of China … The competition between India and China is, therefore, an ideological one,' argued K. Subrahmanyam, a noted strategic thinker and author.[12]

By the mid-1950s, Nehru had succeeded to a large extent in acquiring a niche position as a statesman and important leader of the developing countries and the non-aligned world. Sometimes unabashedly displaying his position as prime minister of the largest democracy of the world, he would adopt a chaperoning attitude towards other leaders. Carlos Romulo, representative of the Philippines at the Afro-Asian Bandung Conference in 1955, has described how Nehru deftly played 'mother hen' to Zhou Enlai, then prime minister and foreign minister of China. 'Nehru arranged a number of private gatherings calculated to bring Zhou into closer contact with other delegates.'[13] Nehru's tendency to display a 'dogmatic, impatient, irascible and unyielding' attitude conveyed a sense of 'the affectation of cultural superiority induced by a conscious identification with an ancient civilization',[14] which many delegates found off-putting. On the other hand, Zhou Enlai greatly impressed the delegates with his 'apparent humility and reasonableness'.[15]

In a candid comparison of the two leaders, Jagat Mehta, who played a key role during the official-level talks in 1960 between the two countries and was an observer during the extensive discussions held between the two prime ministers prior to the talks, said: 'Zhou Enlai was an ace diplomat, in total command of details and able to weave these into a plausible conceptual framework. Nehru understood international affairs in depth and combined it with the transparent sincerity of an idealist, but did not have the matching capacity of marshalling facts.'[16]

The adulation received by Zhou did not escape the attention of Nehru. In order to diminish China's influence on the developing Afro-Asian nations and other 'take aways' [sic] from the Bandung Conference, Nehru ardently began to promote the Non-aligned Movement (NAM). The spadework done by Nehru, Nasser and Tito yielded results, and in September 1961, the non-aligned nations held their first convention at Belgrade. 'It provided a high-minded, moralistic formulation for Indian foreign policy, differentiating India's morality-based leadership from the supposedly amoral power politics of the two Cold War camps, while giving India an arena within which it could play an independent, major role in the world.'[17] Undoubtedly, though Nehru placed a huge premium on friendly relations with China and undertook many initiatives to help China establish itself in the comity of nations and gain recognition by the United Nations, China was not prepared to play second fiddle to India in Asian affairs. It must not be forgotten that the newly forged People's Republic of China had appeared on the world stage after winning a decisive 'people's war' against the Nationalists, who were pushed across the Taiwan Strait into Taiwan, and a fairly successful campaign in the Korean War.

China, at that point, was a poor, populous, underdeveloped yet proud and victorious nation led by clear-headed, battle-hardened, pragmatic leaders, an enthusiastic communist party and a war-experienced army that was thoroughly committed to the party's ideology. What is significant is that the Chinese leadership carried no moralistic baggage and were not afraid to change their goalposts when it suited them. They had developed a strategy of making vague and complex assertions, delaying finite conclusions until they had achieved their objectives. For example, Mao Zedong's comment on the overall situation was that 'the East wind prevails over the West wind'. He used to say it was China's 'sacred duty' to liberate Tibet, as it was 'the final goal' and of 'supreme importance', and the cost or means mattered less ... The question arose as to whom the Tibetans were being 'liberated' from! The Chinese leaders described the boundary dispute as a 'complicated question left over by history', and, as to why they never raised the boundary issue before 1956, the reply was, 'the time was not ripe then'. These typically Chinese expressions—vague, noncommittal, or capable of being variously interpreted—have been developed into a fine art as weapons of realpolitik. Claiming to be the 'sovereign' of Tibet, how could China fail to notice major variations in the delineation of its empire's southern limits?

When India had published new maps in 1954 delineating its boundary with Tibet Autonomous Region, clearly showing the Aksai Chin as part of India and the McMahon Line as the international border in the east, the Chinese had not protested. They very well knew their western highway from Sinkiang to Lhasa via Rudok was transgressing through Indian territory. But they chose to lie low as it was not the appropriate time to raise the matter. Later, in December 1958, when Zhou Enlai was asked to comment on the McMahon Line, he replied that it was British imperialism that had established the line, but that since it was an accomplished fact and beceause of the friendly relations that existed between India and China, he was prepared to give provisional recognition to the line.

Zhou said they had not consulted the Tibetan authorities on the matter yet but proposed to do so.[18] This was another instance of the Chinese taking our leadership up the garden path.

When the Chinese completed the road connecting Sinkiang with Tibet, they broadcast the news to the world with much fanfare on 6 October 1957. As soon as weather conditions permitted, Indian patrols were dispatched during the summer of 1958 to verify whether the highway traversed Indian territory. They encountered Chinese frontier guards. A patrol of ours, overwhelmingly outnumbered, was forcibly detained. A second Indian patrol was able to return safely on completion of its mission. The existence of the road, and that it traversed about 160 kilometres through Indian territory in the Aksai Chin area, was confirmed by the patrols. They reported that the area itself appeared to be under Chinese control. The mystery as to why our mission in Peking and the Government of India remained unaware of the planning and construction of this strategic road over a period of four to five years, from 1952 to 1957, remains unresolved. Quite a few key personages of the time, including B.N. Mullik, then director of the Intelligence Bureau, and S.S. Khera, then cabinet secretary, have written about China's construction activity of this road being known to the Indian government and other agencies concerned from 1952 onwards. Clearly, adequate concern was not shown by the decision makers, and this information was kept under wraps.

As a matter of fact, D.R. Mankekar has stated that the Indian defence attache in Peking, Brigadier S.S. Mallick, had forwarded a special report on the construction of the road through a reluctant ambassador, R.K. Nehru (who perhaps did not wish to displease the prime minister!), in April 1956,[19] in addition to a routine report he had made five months earlier. This report did create some alarm in the corridors of power in New Delhi, but only for some time. In fact, the response of the stakeholders to this strategic development was grossly lackadaisical and irresponsible. This road was undoubtedly a vital north–south artery along the western periphery of the extended Chinese Empire. The new republic sorely needed the ancient caravan route to be upgraded into a motorable road in order to transport the military resources, men and material from Sinkiang to Rudok to consolidate their hold on western Tibet. How many more reports may have met with a similar fate or may have been concealed from the public gaze so that certain individuals or organizations could save face is the question. How, then, can we expect to learn the right lessons from history?

It was reasonable to expect that India could at the very least have demanded a strategic quid pro quo. China should have been made to pay a price, but instead it managed to stage a fait accompli and get away with it. On China's completion of the road, all India did was to lodge a diplomatic protest! Without any doubt this was a serious breach of faith on the part of the Chinese, who chose to unilaterally and secretively execute the project and claim the territory over which the road lay. The Chinese were definitely aware that the road traversed about 160 kilometres of territory claimed by India. That is perhaps why they had not agreed to an Indian trading outpost at Rudok.

Surprisingly, Nehru did not inform Parliament until 28 August 1959 about this Chinese road-building activity, their physical occupation of our territory, the patrol clashes and other incidents. 'Without our knowledge they (the Chinese) have made a road,' said Nehru—which, as mentioned earlier, is not entirely true. Unquestionably, the spirit behind the Panchsheel agreement and the 'Hindi Chini bhai bhai' slogan were thrown overboard by the Chinese, and a trust deficit was injected between the two nations. This quiet acceptance of the state of affairs by India certainly emboldened the Chinese and exposed Indian weakness. In view of the situation, it should have been clearly realized by our leadership that the armed forces needed to be beefed up and their capability to defend the border raised many notches, commensurate with the emerging threat. Unfortunately, this did not happen, as Nehru and Krishna Menon did not heed professional military advice. They chose to be guided by the miscalculations of some diplomats, bureaucrats and intelligence agencies, or went by hunch or gut feeling, or, as they did later, by the advice of pliant and incompetent generals.

From 1959 to 1964, covert support in terms of training and provision of arms and equipment was provided by the CIA to the Khampa rebels. Training camps were located in remote areas like Mustang in Nepal, among other places. Despite India's vehement denials, the Chinese believed the Tibetan rebels were secretly operating from a control centre in Kalimpong with India's support or tacit approval. However, it is well known that the Chinese had established guerrilla training camps in the Kunming area along the Kachin border to arm, train and equip the Naga and Mizo underground rebels during the 1950s and 1960s. When I was serving as a captain in 9 Maratha Light Infantry during 1965–68 in the Tuensang district of Nagaland, we participated in one of the finest counter-insurgency operations done by India. During 1967–68 we intercepted, trapped and captured the entire gang of over 200 Naga rebels led by the self-styled general Mowu Angami who were returning after their training in China. They were carrying a huge consignment of Chinese-made small arms, machine guns, grenades, rocket launchers and ammunition. And significantly, each member had a small red pocket book on Mao's thoughts!

On reaching China after an arduous trek of two months through leech-infested, jungle-covered mountains (according to one young insurgent captured by us), the famished Nagas were herded into thatched huts. They were urged to pray to their god to give them food, which most of them, being good Christians, did. As no food appeared, they were then asked to beseech Chairman Mao, and their prayer was fulfilled within minutes! One hopes all that remains as something belonging to the past.

To achieve their objectives the Chinese work within the framework of a strategy that is carefully evolved. They do not accept any deviations at the functional level. The originator of the strategy alone can revise plans or change the goalposts, something the Chinese have been doing so often. Subordinates are seldom given such authority. They simply have to accomplish their assigned duties or tasks. As narrated by Bertil Lintner, 'Old treaties that China doesn't like are branded "unequal treaties" and therefore there is no reason to honour them. More recent international decisions that have not been in China's favour are branded as an "interference in China's internal affairs".'[20] The Chinese psyche is best illustrated by the manner in which Mao Zedong held a meeting with Nikita Khrushchev in his private pool in 1958, at a time when Sino-Soviet relations were on the rocks. Mao, an accomplished swimmer who had once swum across the Pearl river, made his guest, who didn't know how to swim, wear water wings and enter the pool, just to embarrass Khrushchev and keep himself in an advantageous position. While the two statesmen conversed, their interpreters swam or moved alongside. While Mao got even with his ideological adversary, Khrushchev was not amused.[21] There couldn't have been a more ingenious and effective way to convey to the mighty Soviet Union that China was no pushover. The Chinese message was understood.

In its dealings with bilateral issues—the boundary dispute in particular—China continues to enjoy a distinct advantage over India. Whereas China's internal strategic thinking and discussions on all sensitive issues remain a secret and are very rarely publicized, everything is an open book in a noisy and 'argumentative' democratic polity like India. Issues that get debated or raised in Parliament are broadcast in the public domain, and that is what gives China its edge. The Chinese know our strengths and weaknesses, and what our next step is going to be. On the other hand, there is nothing open about the Chinese system, which carefully vets information before it is released for public consumption. The Chinese governments have thus mastered the art of exploiting the transparency of parliamentary democracies and their free press. In fact, as mentioned earlier in this work, they have been doing this in the case of both the UK and the US, as well as with other nations, perhaps for more than a century. They definitely did this during the Younghusband expedition, the two world wars, the Korea and Vietnam wars, and thereafter. India therefore is no exception to their scheme of things!

In 1959 or a bit earlier, China's leadership had decided in principle to 'teach India a lesson'. They wanted to achieve a number of objectives: to reduce the prestige of India amongst the Afro-Asian nations; to humiliate Nehru; to assume leadership of the developing world; and to make the world powers, the US and the Soviet Union in particular, aware of China's capabilities. This campaign also included securing territory in Aksai Chin, ensuring that there would be no impediment or threat to the strategic artery connecting Sinkiang province with western Tibet. Mao Zedong and Zhou Enlai also saw this conflict as an ideological clash as much as a military challenge. It had to be won decisively so as to ensure peace for China for a few decades at the very least. Mao bluntly articulated this when he said, 'I think the characteristic of the current situation is that the east wind prevails over the west wind; that is, the strength of socialism exceeds the strength of imperialism.'[22] China's victory would leave a lasting impression on the Tibetan people and possibly hasten Tibet's amalgamation into China.

The Chinese then set about systematically preparing their army and civilian administrative machinery to achieve their national objective. And, while the preparations for an armed conflict—the gradual and unobtrusive build-up of troops, weapon systems, munitions, construction of roads and logistics infrastructure—were taking place, the leadership of China kept sending signals to the Indians that the dispute could be resolved by peaceful diplomatic measures. Their deliberate acts of deception succeeded in making the Indian leadership, the country's intelligence agencies and diplomats, and a few politically influenced high-level military leaders believe that skirmishes along the disputed areas could take place but an all-out war was a remote possibility. This they almost ruled out! At the same time there were a few perceptive, visionary and pragmatic political leaders and high-ranking military and civil service officers in

India who did sense the lurking Chinese threat to our borders. But their counsel went unheeded. The Chinese were also successful in misleading the international community to a large extent.

In September–October 1962, while the Chinese army was settling into their launch pads and battle positions, their leadership was closely monitoring the situation, calibrating their military actions along the border. The level of their preparedness can be gauged from the fact that they had Chinese personnel fluent in several regional Indian languages positioned at the front and used them for propaganda purposes prior to and during the war of 1962. Such expertise couldn't have been achieved overnight! The Chinese leaders were now on the lookout for an excuse that would function as the trigger to commence the border war. The Indian leadership, both civil and military, was of course blissfully ignorant of the impending Chinese military onslaught. Claude Arpi aptly wrote: 'Nehru, Panikkar and their followers were philosophers, dreamers, and idealists, but, for Mao or Deng, only action and if necessary violent action could bring the change they were aiming at.' Arpi quoted Deng in this context: 'It does not matter if a cat is black or white as long it catches mice.'[23] Hard-nosed pragmatism, coupled with deft cunning, characterized Chinese leadership. As Kissinger has incisively pointed out, having just overcome a famine, China ventured into a conflict with India, where the adversary underestimated its strength and capabilities and made 'grave errors in grasping how China interprets its security environment and how it reacts to military threats'.[24] For the Chinese, surprise, deception and shock effect were the cardinal principles to focus on in their preparations for the 1962 border war. They had practised this strategy earlier in Korea and had taught to the Vietcong for use in Vietnam. As a matter of fact, the Chinese were hugely successful in ensuring that till the very end the Indians had their guard down, and when the Indians did realize the Chinese meant business, it was already too late!

Even to this day, the Chinese create unsettling or unexpected situations to mentally pressure the leadership of nations whose leaders might be visiting, or when there are key events relating to them. For example, China conducted a nuclear test during President R. Venkataraman's visit to that country in 1992, made an intrusion in the Daulat Beg Oldi area before Prime Minister Manmohan Singh's China visit in 2013, and created a military stand-off in the Chumar and Demchok areas of Ladakh during President Xi Jinping's visit to India in 2014. It is hard to imagine that these events were merely coincidental and could have taken place without the nod of the political bosses! As noted by Teresita and Howard Schaffer in their book *India at the Global High Table*: 'During the period from 1988 to 2015, China's practice of negotiating with signals and facts [actions] on the ground continued.'[25]

The Chinese have become adept at the strategy of psychologically exploiting the vulnerabilities of their adversaries or of weaker nations, in what constitutes a kind of 'psychological imperialism'. They have been quite successful in using the free media in India to its advantage for conveying alarmist news or to broadcast confusing signals to the lay citizens, whether they relate to territorial claims, intrusions across the LAC or diversion of river waters. Sensational, amateurish and poorly researched stories have been carried by some sections of the Indian media as a result of this. Misreporting 'bridges' over the Tsangpo river as 'dams' is just one example of this. The Chinese make no efforts to correct such misperceptions or false impressions, as news items of this kind admirably serve their purpose. The diversion of the waters of the Tsangpo to the mainland across a series of mountain chains over more than 1,000 kilometres is such a geographical challenge that it should have been questioned, both logically and from the point of view of feasibility and financial viability. But this is a subject that has been overplayed by some of our analysts and media. Here again, the issue did not evoke a clear response from the Chinese side, very likely deliberately. The net result is an alarmed Indian public that is even more antagonistic towards China. Kissinger has quoted Sun Tzu in his book *On China*, highlighting another important principle which the Chinese have deployed successfully: to focus on 'the means of building a dominant political and psychological position, such that the outcome of a conflict becomes a foregone conclusion'.[26]

As the China war was creeping upon India, quite unknown to its leaders, Prime Minister Nehru and Defence Minister Krishna Menon were abroad during the autumn in 1962 on considerably long official visits; and General Kaul, Chief of General Staff, and Brigadier D.K. Palit, the Director of Military Operations, were out of Delhi too, as described earlier. On the front, the military commanders were made to believe till as late as August 1962 that the Chinese would not be in any position to launch a major attack for another year or two, and that skirmishes in the disputed areas of the frontier might be the only challenge. A front-line commander like Brigadier John Dalvi had been granted leave for September–October that year, despite the ominous forebodings of war whose signals the Indian side did not pick up. His brigade had been given the unenviable task of defending the disputed Thagla Ridge sector. All these developments—which the Chinese were well aware of, courtesy of our media and our democratic polity—could not be construed, by any stretch of the imagination, as indicators of a nation that was planning to start a war shortly, as propagated by China! Thus the Chinese allegation that India attacked first, compelling it to 'counter-attack in self defence', is absurd and illogical. As China's entire leadership was at their duty stations, the cover was blown off their lie; the ludicrous Chinese theory did not cut much ice with the rest of the world, and most countries saw through the clever game that China had played.

Today's China is following an entirely different path, one that Deng Xiaoping charted out in 1978–79, of 'peaceful rise' and of greater emphasis on economic development. The scholar Zheng Bijian, chair of China Reform Forum, has said that unlike the historic rise of Germany and Japan leading to the two world wars in the twentieth century, China 'will transcend ideological differences to strive for peace, development, and cooperation with all countries of the world'.[27]

We are currently witnessing a new era of India–China relations, with two strong nationalistic leaders, Prime Minister Narendra Modi and President Xi Jinping, at the helm of affairs in the two countries. With the rise of the two Asian giants under a new generation of leadership, the paradigm shift in the balance of power is definitely going to impact the world order. Modi has a massive mandate behind him, and in case he is re-elected he would remain in power till 2024. He has injected a new approach, one of greater confidence and robustness, in our relations with our neighbours. The guiding philosophy adopted by the Modi regime is for India to achieve a key position in the region while retaining 'strategic autonomy' and adopting a more understanding approach. This shift has been demonstrated in the accommodative streamlining of India's border with Bangladesh by the exchange of irksome enclaves, and, on a contrasting note, by the firm stand taken against the Chinese intrusion at Doklam. India is now an acknowledged regional power. At the same time, we see in President Xi Jinping a colossus riding the landscape of China as the unchallenged leader of the republic, the Communist Party of China and the People's Liberation Army (PLA). At the nineteenth National Congress of the Communist Party of China (CPC) held in 2017, his position as the 'core' leader of China was sanctified and his 'key thoughts' on 'socialism with Chinese characteristics for a new era' statuted in the Constitution of the CPC, alongside the thoughts of Mao Zedong and Deng Xiaoping. Xi waxed eloquent on the 'Chinese dream', on 'rejuvenation' of the nation, and spelt out the two ambitious centenary goals being nursed by China. The first, to build a moderately prosperous society by 2020, and the second, to transform China by 2049, the republic's hundredth anniversary, into a 'great modern socialist country that is prosperous, strong, democratic, culturally advanced, harmonious, and beautiful', and also into 'a global leader in terms of composite national strength and international influence'. He emphasized that to ensure effective governance, the 'party must be both politically strong and highly competent'.

Xi has emerged as the most powerful leader of China, and perhaps the world too, after the US president. Xi exhorted the PLA to 'obey the Party's command' and 'maintain excellent conduct'. At the same time he made a commitment to 'build a powerful and modernised army, navy, air force, rocket force, and strategic support force ... and create a modern combat system with distinctive Chinese characteristics. The PLA would continue to focus upon integrated joint war fighting characterised by short duration regional wars under hi-tech informatised conditions.' Xi also said at the National Congress that China is 'closer, more confident and more capable than ever before of making the goal of national rejuvenation a reality'. He went on to say: 'No one should expect China to swallow anything that undermines its interests.' Allaying the fears of its neighbours, President Xi said, 'China's development does not pose a threat to any other country. No matter what stage of development it reaches, China will never seek hegemony or engage in expansion.' Importantly, he did not fail to mention the challenges of unequal development, and of corruption and contradictions in China's system of governance, and the unstoppable tsunami of the Internet and social media, the aspirations of the people at large and of the gen-next in particular, and of acceptance of dissent by the government.

Xi's era has begun with his consolidation of power and strengthening of the party's hold over the polity and the military. He has deftly weeded out those whom he could not trust, those out of sync with his ideology, and the non-performers or functionaries past their prime. His new civilian and military team comprises capable and proven men, mostly in their early sixties, who are loyal (to him as well as to the party) and will strengthen his hand in the Chinese march towards the centre stage of the globe and realization of the 'Chinese dream'. It is apparent that he wants to have a firm grip over the military and ensure that its political orientation is made more solid. It is reckoned that Xi Jinping today wields much more power than the earlier two iconic Chinese leaders. On 25 February 2018, the Central Committee of the CPC did away with the stipulation of restricting the tenure of the president and the vice president to two terms of five years, thus paving the way for Xi Jinping's presidency to continue indefinitely. This amendment of the constitution was overwhelmingly endorsed by the party hierarchy and instituted accordingly. Xi can therefore take bold political and diplomatic initiatives backed by military and economic muscle power as never before.[28]

In *Inside the Mind of Xi Jinping*, China expert Francois Bougon has pointed out that 'Xi Jinping is also a *hong er dai*', literally a 'Second-Generation Red', and has an impressive revolutionary lineage. 'It is his turn to make history, and hereditary legitimacy is not without significance for a leader who intends to fight on the ideological front,' underscores Bougon.[29] The high pedestal on which Xi stands today could therefore be argued as eminently justifiable.

In order to match China's growth, India's current and future leadership would need to understand and learn how to deal with the Dragon's new avatar, and work with dedication to ensure India's rise too.

The Chinese view of the new global order after the nineteenth National Congress of the CPC was articulated in a positive and optimistic statement by the Chinese ambassador to India, Luo Zhaohui. He said, 'The "New India" initiative proposed by Prime Minister Narendra Modi and the "Chinese Dream" are closely connected and can be synergised as well.' He went on to emphasize that 'China attaches great inspiration to China–India relations. There will be series of institutional dialogues between the two countries.' Ambassador Luo then commented on the need to have 'long-term goals for our relations' on global issues, a 'treaty of good neighbourliness and Friendly Cooperation', 'early harvest' on the boundary issue and 'alignment of the Belt and Road Initiative with India's development strategies'. He concluded by saying that India and China need to enhance mutual trust and focus on cooperation while properly managing differences, in a bid to promote China–India relations to a new level.[30]

Prudence and rationality demand that we take such statements with an element of caution and avoid complacency. Yet, keeping in mind the matrix of global security and economic dynamics of the twenty-first century and the growing interconnectedness of the multipolar world, a Sino-Indian conflict is neither a viable nor a wise option, making its likelihood remote.

PART IX

TOWARDS RESOLUTION OF THE BOUNDARY DISPUTE

'Cooperation between India and China is essential to maintain peace and stability around the world.'

—Narendra Modi, Prime Minister of India

'China and India are both important engines for global growth and we are central pillars for promoting a multi-polar and globalised world. A good China–India relationship is an important and positive factor for maintaining peace and stability in the world.'

—Xi Jinping, President of China[1]

21

India–China Boundary Negotiations

'Boundary mountains or hills are such natural elevations from the common level of the ground as separate the territories of two or more states from each other. Failing special treaty arrangements, the boundary line runs on the mountain ridge along with the watershed.'[2] The rationale of following the broad principle of the watershed while determining the boundary in the absence of any treaty, as defined by a world acclaimed geographer like L. Oppenheim, is sound and has stood the test of time. This principle has been applied to determine the boundaries in the case of European nations, between Spain and France, and between Chile and Argentina in South America, on the basis of the watershed formed by the Alps, Pyrenees and the Andes respectively.

Undoubtedly, in the case of India and China, a 4,057-kilometre-long frontier can very well be delineated on this principle too, with some exceptions where geography and traditional and customary usage make it necessary. As explained earlier, the focus of this work relates mainly to the frontier of north-east India and the Tibet Autonomous Region of China. I have primarily focussed on the complexities of this boundary dispute and the measures taken by both India and China to resolve it. The geographical, historical, political and geostrategic aspects of this frontier zone have been covered in the earlier parts of this book. I believe that the lay people of both countries are ignorant or have inadequate knowledge of this Himalayan frontier, which has resulted in pressuring the decision makers in both India and China to adopt a rigid approach, with neither side ready to accommodate the other's position on the boundary issue. This has led to the stalemate we see even to this day.

Our nations have inherited their boundary or frontier problems from the earlier regimes, the Indians from the British in 1947 and the Chinese from the Chiang Kai-shek–led Kuomintang government in 1949. At the height of the Great Game being played out in the Pamirs, the British were not very concerned about the north-eastern part of India's frontiers because of the absence of any external threats and the ruggedness of the terrain enhancing the inaccessibility of the region. Their attention was glued to India's north-western frontier that was exposed to the intrigues and expansionist designs of the Russian Empire. As a result, the British were content to govern the tribal belts on the Indian side of the Himalayas under a loose form of political control, establishing 'inner' and 'outer' lines to demarcate the areas that were left to be administered by the tribes themselves. Many of the tribes had signed treaties of sorts with the British administration in Assam.

However, an energetic projection of power by China began to take place in southern and south-eastern Tibet as a consequence of the 1904 Younghusband expedition to Lhasa. As a chain reaction, Chinese forces under General Chao Erh-feng started to assert themselves through aggressive probes in the region and made attempts to establish their hold there. Some exploratory forays were made during 1910–11 by the Chinese for the first time in history in the areas bordering the tribal territories in India's north-east, which set alarm bells ringing in the tea gardens of Assam. Fortunately for the Tibetans, as has been brought out earlier, the Chinese Revolution of 1911 extinguished these forays and ended the process of subjugation of Tibet. The Chinese hold on Tibet during 1912–13 was almost non-existent because of the decline of the Manchu Empire and the outbreak of civil war among the emerging Nationalist regime, the Manchu loyalists and independent regional warlords. In 1913, a 'China-free' Tibet under the thirteenth Dalai Lama, who had just returned from his second exile, declared its independence in a subtle and indirect manner even though the conditions in parts of Amdo and Kham region were not peaceful, sans recognition by any world power. This unstable situation encouraged the British to convene a conference with

Chinese, Tibetan and British plenipotentiaries to discuss the status of Tibet and its boundaries with China and India, and other matters relating mainly to the geopolitics, economy and security of the Tibet region. Consequently, under the aegis of the British, a tripartite conference was held at Simla and Delhi, stretching from October 1913 to July 1914.

The key players of this now historic conference were Sir Arthur Henry McMahon, the foreign secretary to the Government of India, and Lonchen Shatra and Ivan Chen, representing British India, Tibet and China respectively. McMahon was born in Simla in 1862 and had grown up in an environment that helped him understand the complicated dynamics of the South Asian frontiers and of empire building of that period. During this conference, a number of parleys, discussions, deliberations and study of historical records, including documents, maps and oral presentations, took place in eight recorded formal tripartite sessions, as described in Chapter 13. There were also many informal and secret meetings between the key players conducted in the bipartite format. Although McMahon was able to obtain the signatures or initials of the three plenipotentiaries as a token of their acceptance of the memorandum and the accompanying maps on 27 April 1914, as is evident from a close examination of the relevant documents, this agreement was, unfortunately, repudiated by the Chinese a few days later. The next two months were spent in hectic negotiations, and a concluding session of the conference was called on 3 July.

A final agreement with maps and associated documents was signed and sealed on 3 July 1914 by McMahon and Lonchen Shatra, whereas Ivan Chen declined to be a signatory to the accord as the Chinese government refused to give their consent to it. It is remarkable that McMahon was able to draw his line with a reasonable degree of precision. This was possible thanks to the surveying and mapping done in the tribal territories during the preceding two years. Considering the difficult terrain, the lack of modern survey instruments and technology, it must be conceded that McMahon and his team did a fine job. In a memorandum signed on 28 March 1914, McMahon stated that 'the Tibetan Government at Lhasa has fully considered this frontier question and agrees with the Tibetan plenipotentiary in recognising the line now defined as the correct boundary between Tibet and India'.

However, during the discussions it was accepted by both the British and the Tibetan plenipotentiaries that 'in the light of the more detailed knowledge' that either side 'may acquire in the future' the same would be looked at positively, although 'no obligation to do so has been mentioned in the agreement'.[3] The implication of this clause was that small adjustments and corrections would be acceptable to both nations in future. This agreement between British India and Tibet in 1914 established the international boundary known as the McMahon Line from Bhutan to Burma and provided it legal sanctity.

It bears emphasis that the present-day Tawang district was clearly shown well to the south of the McMahon Line and accepted by both sides. The Chinese delegate never protested or demurred on this issue. On the basis of such an authoritative boundary agreement and other reasons, India's claim to the tribal territory on the southern side of the natural Himalayan divide is unexceptionable. At the same time, it is worth keeping in mind that neither the Chinese nor the Tibetans were at any time in history in occupation of any part of Lopa territory south of the Himalayan watershed (present Arunachal Pradesh), nor were they able to produce any old Tibetan map that showed the southern boundary of Tibet that included the above-mentioned areas. However, when we talk of Tibet's southern neighbours, the views of the tribal people who are non-Tibetan and inhabit the southern slopes of the Himalayas in the Indian state of Arunachal Pradesh assume great importance.

On many occasions during my gubernatorial visits to remote frontier areas during 2008–13, I was told by the tribals that even their forebears had never seen the Chinese. At quite a few places they told me that their ancestors used to grant grazing rights to the Tibetan people who came across from the northern side of the passes, receiving payment for this in coins or in kind. Without their permission no Tibetans could enter their territories. In all the surveys carried out in recent years including that by *India Today* magazine, the people of Arunachal Pradesh have overwhelmingly voted to remain a part of India, and have emphasized that, historically, China had neither been in contact with them nor had anything to do with their state. They acknowledge Tibetans as their neighbours, but they had very little interaction with them.

Underscoring the patriotic fervour of the people of Arunachal, the chief minister of Arunachal Pradesh, Pema Khandu, commented in an April 2017 interview in *India Today* that the border dispute should be settled soon. However, he added unequivocally: 'Whatever the solution, Arunachal Pradesh's geography [political limits] must not be compromised in the bargain.' The chief minister, himself a Monpa and a committed nationalist, belongs to Mago village, located a few kilometres from the border (McMahon Line) in Tawang district. On the fiftieth anniversary of the India–China war of 1962, the chief minister of Arunachal Pradesh paid rich tributes to the martyrs of this war, emphasizing again that 'Arunachal Pradesh is an integral part of India and its citizens are very proud Indians'.[4]

At the end of the First World War, the British economy (as well as other world economies) was shattered. For Britain, therefore, rebuilding its economy took precedence over other matters. It is no surprise then that Whitehall quite forgot they had a frontier issue to resolve in one of their colonies, in this case the Indo-Tibetan boundary so painstakingly evolved by McMahon in 1914. The hands of the Indian government were tied, and an ambiguous policy with respect to the British Indian Empire's area of influence along the frontiers did not help in deciding the limits of its reach. Financial constraints were a serious handicap; most importantly, the law that no expenses be incurred on expeditions beyond the administered areas of British India without the approval of Parliament was a serious impediment. British commercial interests in China and the British investments in the Yangtze Valley, in Shanghai in particular, had an overwhelming influence on British policymaking as far as Tibet was concerned. In some respects, one could say that Great Britain had to forsake Tibet on financial considerations, besides other reasons.

An overview of the boundary issue between India and China reveals that India's northern boundary is essentially the end result of the impact over centuries of factors like geography, history and environment. Although most parts of the boundary had acquired traditional and customary sanctity before the subcontinent's colonization by Britain, the rest evolved under the influence of new concepts of security introduced by the British to ward off potential threats to their empire from Central Asia (Russia) and, later, from China. Consequently, the outcome was the emergence of political boundaries largely based on the principle of the highest crest line or watershed of the northern mountain system. This principle was reinforced by the invariable congruence of the traditional boundary with the watershed. 'The idea of a demarcated frontier is itself an essentially modern conception, and finds little or no place in the ancient world,' Lord Curzon observed, at the beginning of the twentieth century. Until then, he pointed out, 'it would be true to say that demarcation has never taken place in Asiatic countries except under European pressure'.[5]

The vague and ambiguous manner of description—or rather, the established norms for definition of boundaries in the oriental system of governance—can be gauged from the inscriptions on the famous stone pillar of Lhasa, which say: 'Downward from the place where the Chinese are met will be China and upward from the place where the Tibetans are met will be Tibet.'[6] Similarly, as presented by the Tibetan plenipotentiary at the Simla Conference, 'They (Tibetans) fixed upon a stone pillar at Merugang (North of Sining), bend of the Ma-chu (Huang ho) river and Chortenkarpo (near Ya-chao in Szechuan) as boundaries.'[7] Pillars akin to the one at Meru 'had been set up both at Lhasa and Xian, the Chinese capital (about 1,020 years ago)'. The Tibetans produced in support of their claims 'tomes of delicate manuscripts bound in richly embroidered covers … also with the official history of Tibet, compiled by the 5th Dalai Lama and known as the "Golden tree of the Index of the sole ornament of the World", a work of great scope and colossal dimensions'.[8]

As has been described earlier, in Chapter 20, after a period of warm and cordial relations in the early 1950s, the complicated dimension and contours of the boundary dispute between India and China began to emerge from 1957 onwards. This happened as China failed to keep its word on revising the old Kuomintang (KMT) period maps which showed large parts of Indian territory in China. To top it all, in 1957, the Chinese announced with great fanfare the formal inauguration of the Aksai Chin highway, which passed through Indian lands. China was clearly in control of the situation, having sensed the discomfiture of India's leadership when these facts emerged in the public domain. The presence of the Chinese army in Aksai Chin began to be monitored and challenged by Indian patrols, leading to ugly situations and aggressive face-offs. These incidents were handled at the highest political and diplomatic levels by the two nations, but unfortunately the boundary problem and these events were not debated in Indian Parliament and were kept outside the public domain. The Chinese maps of 1956 included Aksai Chin and Arunachal Pradesh as part of China. In an official magazine, *China Pictorial*, published in July 1958, there was a map of China 'which showed the whole of NEFA [except present-day Tirap district], large areas of Ladakh, considerable areas in Uttar Pradesh and Himachal Pradesh ... as part of China'.[9] There was a flurry of diplomatic demarches and correspondence between the two countries' foreign offices, and protests lodged against the growing number of intrusions and air violations in the region, particularly since 1956, but these were not talked about until 1959.

Beginning 14 December 1958, Nehru decided to confront Zhou Enlai and display serious concern and surprise at the depiction of parts of India as Chinese territory even after nine years of China's becoming a republic. At least nine letters were exchanged during the following year between the two prime ministers on the boundary dispute. Eventually, they agreed to meet in 1960, even though the vast perceptional variation in the two countries' boundary claims made chances of a positive outcome extremely remote. The proceedings of this meeting have been covered in Chapter 19. In those days the media were not so alert, and the nation to a large extent was unaware of Chinese activities along the northern frontier and of China's territorial claims in Aksai Chin and the north-east. Friction and tension caused by contradictory perceptions of the boundary led to armed clashes and face-offs between the two sides in the late 1950s.

Eventually, acting under pressure from all quarters, including the Congress party, and to show transparency, Nehru decided to put India's entire correspondence with China relating to the boundary dispute in the public domain in the shape of White Papers. The first of these was laid before Parliament on 7 September 1959.[10] However, upon receipt of this information, an alarmed nation, media and Parliament raised the political stakes so high that any compromise was ruled out. It was not the same in the case of China, where the CPC leadership was kept well informed but their media was muffled and the people were only exposed to heavily edited and biased information. There was no question of any overt opposition to Mao's decisions, even if it meant China's going to war to resolve the border dispute. Eventually, despite serious internal problems, Mao decided to go to war with India in 1962.

Before we examine the progress and current status of India's boundary negotiations with China, it would be prudent to review the resolution of such disputes by China with some of its other neighbours. 'Any consideration of Beijing's boundary policy must include a discussion of "unequal treaties" because of the pivotal role they play in nearly all of China's boundary disputes and settlements. The PRC's definition of an unequal treaty is neither clear nor consistent.' Additionally, the list of such treaties has undergone changes based on 'political expediency'.[11] An endeavour has been made here to discuss the status of China's frontier disputes and the Chinese modus operandi of resolving them.

China has one of the largest land frontiers of any country in the world, extending over 22,000 kilometres with fourteen neighbouring countries. It has more or less settled its land boundaries with all its neighbours except India and Bhutan. Its boundary agreements were often timed keeping in mind the dynamics of the international situation and maintenance of balance of power in the region. However, as far as its maritime frontiers are concerned, China has continuing problems with quite a few countries in the South China Sea and East China Sea region as well.

The first challenge for the People's Republic of China was to secure its place as an independent and sovereign nation. This process took a few years. India was one of the first non-communist nations to recognize the new republic. At the Conference of Afro-Asian Nations at Bandung in 1955, Zhou Enlai, the Chinese prime minister, extended a friendly hand to other nations and said China would like to peacefully settle its boundaries with its neighbours. China realized that the world hadn't failed to notice that its 'liberalization' of Tibet wasn't peaceful at all, and had also noted the duress under which the seventeen-point agreement was signed by the Tibetans. Moreover, by the late 1950s, as China's relations with India and the Soviet Union began to deteriorate and US involvement in South Asia increased, China decided to resolve its boundary disputes with its smaller neighbours. Most of these nations had an innate fear of an expansionist China.

In the early 1960s, apprehending castigation by the non-communist world, China began an endeavour at image building. Thus a 'reasonable and accommodative' China settled its boundaries peacefully with Burma (Myanmar), Nepal, Pakistan, Afghanistan and Mongolia. It would not be out of place to mention that wherever the Chinese conceded their claimed territories in favour of the countries mentioned above, the areas in question were not of critical significance to them. Also, 'the settlement of the disputes served larger important strategic objectives', noted Eric Hyer in *The Pragmatic Dragon: China's Grand Strategy and Boundary Settlements*. In the case of Nepal, with tension building up along the Sino-Indian border, Zhou Enlai displayed a spirit of conciliation and concluded a boundary settlement with B.P. Koirala, the prime minister of Nepal, on 20 March 1960, based on the watershed principle and the five principles of peaceful coexistence (Panchsheel). Similarly, the Chinese also signed an accord with Burma (Myanmar) in 1961, again basically adopting the watershed principle as well as the line drawn by McMahon in 1914. This was also done to project to the world the 'reasonableness' of their approach to boundary resolution with its neighbours.

China's largest land frontier, of about 4,250 kilometres, was with the erstwhile Soviet Union (Russia); here it had serious boundary disputes that led to many armed clashes in the 1960s. Ideological differences between the two had precipitated their boundary dispute. In 1969, there was a major incident in the disputed island of Zhenbao on the Ussuri river, in which heavy casualties were taken by a Soviet army patrol. The Chinese strategy is best described by Kissinger in *On China*: the Chinese 'laid a trap' so as to decimate the Russian patrol and 'deal him [Russia] a psychological blow to cause him to desist'. However, this strategy did not work and the Soviets reacted violently, literally wiping out a Chinese battalion at the Xinjiang border. With the deterioration of relations between the two countries, there was a massive build-up of opposing forces. It was feared that a major Soviet offensive was imminent. The possibility of an attack on China's nuclear facilities was also not ruled out. This is when the US intervened and warned both sides that it would not, as narrated by Kissinger, 'remain indifferent' and 'that it would act according to its strategic interests'. It remains unclear whether it was this warning that prevented the situation from escalating into war or whether it was the 'Cold War dynamics' that settled the matter, as noted by Kissinger in *On China*.[12]

However, the Sino-Soviet boundary problem over the disputed islands along the Amur and Ussuri rivers, and over some areas along the western borders, simmered until boundary treaties were signed in 1991 and 1994 for these regions, as the cold war had ended with the disintegration of the Soviet Union. The final resolution of this boundary dispute was achieved by involvement of the political leadership, who displayed high statesmanship and strong political will. Both sides understood the changed international power matrix, and negotiations were now pegged on earlier treaties and negotiations and on non-insistence of preconditions by either side. While delimiting the boundaries, the status quo was maintained, by and large, with small adjustments, with both sides conceding some of their claims. Importantly, the Chinese were able to retain the Zhenbao Island, and the Heixiazi or Bolshoi Ussurysky Island was made into an 'eco-tourism zone' shared by Russia and China, each getting 50 per cent of the island territory.

The Chinese believed their policy of standing firm, based on the principle of mutual understanding and accommodation, even against a stronger nation, eventually yielded dividends. The Chinese are convinced that from the eighteenth to the twentieth centuries, they were subjected to unequal treaties and humiliation by the world powers. China shares a frontier of about 1,350 kilometres with Vietnam, and its disputed frontier with that nation dates back centuries. Although it had been an independent nation for most of its history, Vietnam had been a vassal state of China for a few centuries before its colonization by the French in the nineteenth century. Eventually, Vietnam became independent in September 1945. China decided to forcibly settle the festering boundary problem with Vietnam, despite its being a communist country.

One needs to analyse the reasons that prompted China to launch a massive offensive across the northern border of Vietnam with about twenty infantry divisions supported by armour and artillery in the spring of 1979. As it did with India, China attacked a militarily unprepared adversary, in Deng's words 'to teach the Vietnamese a lesson'. China wanted Vietnam to first 'tow its line' on the boundary dispute. Second, the close relationship between Vietnam and the Soviet Union was like a red rag to China, and it wanted to settle scores with the Soviet Union because of its ballooning ideological differences with that nation. Third, the Chinese took umbrage at the Vietnamese invasion of Cambodia and its harsh and unfair treatment of the minorities, including the ethnic Chinese, living in northern Vietnam.

Curiously, one more reason put forward by some analysts was that Deng wanted to expose and weed out some of the dead wood from the senior ranks of the PLA, which as a matter of fact he did. Another factor that influenced the Chinese decision was the unlikelihood of intervention in this conflict by the West, particularly the US. Though both China and Vietnam claimed to have won, this war resulted in a victory for neither side but ended in a colossal loss of life and destruction of property. Northern Vietnam was laid waste and thousands of innocent civilians were killed. The Chinese were reported to have lost 7,000 to 9,000 soldiers. A greater number were wounded. The Vietnamese casualties were even higher. As was the case in its border war with India in the north-east, the Chinese withdrew unilaterally from the captured areas in Vietnam, asserting that they had achieved their aim. This war reinforces the Tibetan adage mentioned earlier in this work: 'Lion fights dog; even though victorious, lion defeated.' Eventually the Chinese lost face in the bargain.

China offered many concessions to the Central Asian states after the break-up of the Soviet Union in order to get their support, and was thus able to settle its boundaries with them easily. The Chinese offered them favourable terms, as they had with India's smaller neighbours in the 1960s. Thus, by the 1990s, China had been able to resolve most of the boundary disputes with its neighbours, except for India and Bhutan. When viewed in the context of China's recent trillion dollars' worth One Belt One Road (OBOR) and the China–Pakistan Economic Corridor (CPEC) initiative, which would connect most of these Central Asian states with China to the east and Europe to the west, and to the warm waters of the Arabian Sea through Pakistan, these boundary agreements make eminent sense, and reflect the far-sightedness of the Chinese leadership.

Dr Wenwen Shen, an Asia expert and visiting fellow at Australian National University, in *China and Its Neighbours: Troubled Relations*, writes: 'It is, however, the maritime borders that have caused most trouble … with China being accused of increasingly assertive behaviour towards its neighbours … (China has) to assure its neighbours that it is not a bully … The last thing that China needs in its current situation is an armed conflict with any of its neighbours. In an era of growing political and economic interdependence such a development could only impact negatively on China. This analysis is exceptional.'[13]

Relations between the two Asian giants had nosedived after the undeclared border war. Although diplomatic relations were not broken, the missions had been scaled down to that of chargé d'affaires on both sides. India insisted that relations with China would be normalized only once the boundary issue was resolved. The thaw began in 1976, when the Mao era subsided and ambassador-level representation was restored.

Deng Xiaoping met with India's foreign minister, A.B. Vajpayee, in 1979 and proposed a solution to the boundary dispute based on a 'package' deal. If that was not possible at an early date, said Deng, he was recommending cooperation in other domains. Talks on the boundary problem commenced at the official level from 1980 onwards, but hardly made much progress. It needs to be recalled that the earlier offer of a 'swap' deal suggested by Zhou Enlai in his meetings with Nehru in April 1960 had fetched no response from India.

The visit of the Indian prime minister, Rajiv Gandhi, to China in 1988, a prime-ministerial visit after a gap of thirty-four years, was path-breaking. Even though the visit did not bring about any settlement of the border dispute, it created the right environment for the two countries to carry forward the dialogue process, which seemed to have reached a dead end after eight rounds of the official-level talks that had started in December 1981, after the India visit of the Chinese foreign minister. For the first time, India did not insist on resolution of the boundary issue as a condition for any other matters to be taken up. Both sides agreed to 'seek fair, reasonable and mutually acceptable solution to the boundary question, and agreed to expand and develop bilateral relations in all fields'.[14] The talks laid the foundation for a more vibrant, multidimensional relationship between

Asia's largest nations. A joint working group (JWG) was created at a senior level aided by an expert group at the working level for negotiations on the boundary issue and realization of a road map for reducing tensions along the frontier. A joint economic group was created too, to enhance trade and commerce between the two countries.

The next landmark visit to China was that of Prime Minister P.V. Narasimha Rao in 1993, during which it was agreed that the de facto border being manned or actively patrolled by either side would be termed as the Line of Actual Control (LAC), without prejudice to the respective positions on the boundary of either country. The signing of the Agreement on Maintaining Peace and Tranquility along the LAC was a very significant step taken during this visit. This agreement stipulated that the boundary issue would be solved through 'peaceful and friendly consultations'. Both sides agreed to respect the LAC and that 'neither side shall use or threaten to use force against the other by any means'. Besides this, it was agreed that the JWGs of both sides would evolve confidence-building measures relating to military activities, including those of the air force of both countries, so as to reduce tension along the LAC and maintain peace (Appendix 5). During the process of clarification of the LAC in the eighth meeting of the JWG in 1995, the 'two sides had identified eight pockets of dispute'[15] where they perceived the alignment of the boundary differently. Further negotiations would focus on these disputed areas—and also other areas where such differences had cropped up later (there are about fifteen of them as of 2018)—and resolve them peacefully.

These events were followed by the signing of the Agreement on Confidence-Building Measures (CBMs) along the LAC between the militaries of both sides during the India visit of President Jiang Zemin in 1996 (Appendix 6). A number of high-profile visits by national leaders to each other's countries followed. The two sides re-emphasized that any border settlement must be fair and equitable. The challenge that both sides are now confronted with is how to reconcile the known differences within a reasonable time frame. Whereas India's international boundary has been clearly and unambiguously shown on maps since 1954, the Chinese have been loathe to share large-scale maps of all sectors showing their claim line, except in the middle sector, which was done in March 2000. Further, as far as the western sector is concerned, both sides exchanged their maps very briefly during the meeting on 17 June 2002, and returned them after a cursory look. There appeared no meeting point or even a scope for discussion as both countries had shown 'maximalistic positions'.[16] There was no exchange of such maps relating to the eastern sector at any stage. As brought out earlier, it was only during the official level talks in 1960 that the Chinese gave a signed small-scale map showing their perception of the Sino-Indian boundary. This issue has not progressed till date and needs to be revived as the first step of the LAC clarification leading to the resolution of the boundary problem. This is unlikely to happen in a hurry as China is capable of waiting indefinitely until it acquires a dominant negotiating position.

During another path-breaking visit by Prime Minister A.B. Vajpayee to China in 2003, both countries forged a commitment at the highest political level to move ahead purposefully and to resolve the boundary question peacefully. The two sides agreed to raise the level of discussions and appoint 'special representatives' at the apex level, handpicked by their respective premiers, to 'explore from the political perspective of the overall bilateral relationship the framework of a boundary settlement'. This step was necessitated as the deliberations of the JWG and the Experts Group had not yielded worthwhile results, despite a decade and a half of negotiations. It was realized by both sides that without a political stimulus, resolution of the boundary problem would be impossible.

Taking note of the growing entente in Indo-US relations as the twenty-first century got under way, the Chinese were compelled to try a different tack in their strategy and begin to mend fences with India. In a very significant visit to India during April 2005 by the Chinese premier, Wen Jiabao, both sides in an accord underscored that Sino-Indian ties 'have now acquired a global and strategic character'. The two countries agreed to establish a Strategic and Cooperative Partnership for Peace and Prosperity.[17]

Along with this, a historic, and in my view one of the most important, agreement between India and China, titled Political Parameters and Guiding Principles for the Settlement of the Boundary Question, was concluded by the two sides on 11 April 2005 (Appendix 7). In this agreement, the emphasis was on finding a 'political' resolution of the boundary problem keeping in mind the countries' 'long-term interests and overall bilateral relationship'.[18] India reiterated its one-China policy and re-emphasized that Tibet was an autonomous region of China (Appendix 7). In a conciliatory and belated reciprocal gesture, the Chinese, for the first time, acknowledged that Sikkim was a state of India. Trade between Sikkim and Chumbi Valley in Tibet Autonomous Region (TAR) commenced via the historic Nathu La (as agreed in 2003). Significantly, China admitted India was an important developing country and had an increasingly important influence in the international arena. It said it understood and supported India's aspirations to play an active role in the UN and in international affairs.

Articles III, V and VII of the agreement (Appendix 7) are of great significance, as they can greatly assist in defining the framework of the proposed solution to the boundary problem in the future. Article III talks of 'mutually acceptable adjustments to their (the two countries') respective positions on the boundary question so as to arrive at a package settlement'; Article V has spelt out factors for consideration—such as 'historical evidence', 'national sentiments' and 'sensitivities' of both sides; and Article VII has underscored that 'both sides shall safeguard due interests of their settled populations'.

This agreement might pave the way forward, as considerable pragmatism and flexibility have been introduced to help achieve a breakthrough. Any mutually acceptable solution will eventually have to be an exercise carried out objectively and pragmatically, based on this agreement. Importantly, the two countries have decided to put in place a 'strategic cooperative partnership for peace and prosperity', thereby raising the level of ties between them. After arduous efforts of almost a decade, a framework for this agreement is being evolved as a 'strategic objective' by the special representatives of the prime ministers of the two nations as part of their negotiations to arrive at an 'early solution' to this thorny issue. Another agreement signed during the Wen Jiabao's visit related to the protocol governing the modalities for implementation of the CBMs along the LAC.[19]

During the China visit of India's defence minister, Pranab Mukherjee, in 2006, the first Memorandum of Understanding on Defence Cooperation was signed, ushering in an era of enhanced defence exchanges involving 'annual defence dialogue, joint military exercises and cooperation in "search and rescue", counter-terrorism and anti-piracy operations'. Building on this, in May 2007, as chairman of the Chiefs of Staff Committee, I led a tri-service delegation to China. We were very warmly welcomed and accorded high protocol. We called on Vice President Zeng Quinghong and Foreign Minister Yang Jiechie. While shaking hands with the vice-president, I summoned the courage to say, 'Excellency, when our two nations shake hands, the world sits up to watch.' He acknowledged that with a smile. Having met the Chinese military hierarchy and visited their army, naval and air force bases, we worked out the details of the first defence dialogue and the joint training exercises to be held in 2007–08 and beyond. These events have taken place regularly thereafter, barring one or two years in between. President Hu Jintao paid a four-day visit to India in November 2006, during which a 'ten-pronged strategy' was drawn up in a joint declaration intended to take the India–China relationship to a 'qualitatively new level'. Besides a number of initiatives launched under this agreement to reinforce the Strategic and Cooperative Partnership, it was agreed to establish new consulates general in Guangzhou and Kolkata.

This relationship was further extended by the articulation and signing of a protocol titled 'A Shared Vision for the 21st Century' by Prime Ministers Manmohan Singh and Wen Jiabao at Beijing on 14 January 2008, in which the two leaders resolved to 'promote the building of a harmonious world of durable peace and common prosperity'.[20] This document also underlined the countries' common positions on a number of international and regional matters, and some bilateral ones. It concluded by emphasizing that 'the two sides recognise the responsibilities and obligations of the two countries to the international community. The two sides are determined to enhance mutual understanding and friendship between the people of China and India, for the betterment of both countries and to bring about a brighter future for humanity.'[21] (See Appendix 8.)

China regards its ties with India as one of its most important bilateral relationships, said President Xi Jinping, during his meeting with Prime Minister Manmohan Singh in March 2013. He said he saw the current period as one of strategic opportunities, and said both countries had 'a similar mission to boost their social and economic development'. On the boundary issue, he said both countries should make good use of the mechanism of special representatives and 'strive for a fair and rational solution framework as soon as possible'.[22] With a new regime led by President Xi Jinping having taken charge in China from March 2013 and with the new BJP government led by Prime Minister Narendra Modi assuming power in India in 2014 with a massive mandate, the expectations of the people have risen as far as a solution to our boundary problem and other issues are concerned. The two powerful leaders represent one-third of the world's population, and are expected to mould relations between India and China to create a stable and peaceful environment in the region.

We have witnessed two important reciprocal visits by these two leaders, the first by President Xi Jinping in September 2014 and the second by Prime Minister Narendra Modi in May 2015. These visits have further consolidated our strategic partnership and strengthened the foundation of a mutually respectful relationship, with a large number of multidimensional agreements and MoUs being signed. On the complex boundary issue, Modi highlighted the importance of 'resuming the process of clarification of the LAC as a first step'. As conveyed by Prime Minister Zhou Enlai to his counterpart Nehru, on 4 November 1962, 'in the east it [the LAC] coincides with the McMahon Line and in the west and in the middle sector it coincides with the traditional boundary as put forth by the Chinese'; therefore taking the matter forward and demarcating the LAC on the ground should be feasible with some accommodation by both sides.

The Chinese could have been more forthcoming and positive on India's permanent membership of the reformed UN Security Council and for India's membership of export control regimes like Nuclear Suppliers Group,[23] thus forging closer cooperation with India in international affairs. As explained earlier, it is an acknowledged fact that the Chinese are very sensitive to the growing strategic partnership between the US and India since the beginning of this century. The four-day visit by President Bill Clinton to India in May 2000, with a five-hour halt in Pakistan en route, was a clear indicator of the direction in which relations between the US and India were headed. This wide-ranging and meaningful relationship has continued to 'blossom' during the terms of US presidents George W. Bush, Barack Obama and now Donald Trump. Accordingly, China has displayed a large measure of warmth and a positive approach to evolving a strategic and cooperative partnership for peace and prosperity with India—particularly starting with the visit of Wen Jiabao to India— hoping to lure India away from the US, or at least prevent our bonds with that country from becoming stronger. There is undoubtably an all-encompassing relationship that is emerging between India and China which, besides the security dimension, also spans the political, economic and cultural aspects, and people-to-people ties. Besides these bilateral deliberations, the aspect of cooperation on many multilateral issues relating to the war against terror, climate control and World Trade Organization (WTO) has enhanced the scope of our engagement with China. Based on policy decisions taken during the high-level meetings described above, mechanisms have been put in place to evolve answers to various complex issues we are faced with, beginning with the boundary problem.

At the highest political level are the special representatives appointed by the two governments. Based on the 'political parameters and broad framework' enunciated by this apex body, which was created in 2003 during Prime Minister Vajpayee's visit, the officials who form part of the JWG undertake follow-up actions. They are assisted by the officials of the multidisciplinary Expert Groups who work at the functional level. These bodies had been meeting regularly, and although progress appeared to be slow, it was in the right direction. However, in due course of time these groups were to be replaced by a group referred to as Working Mechanism for Consultation and Coordination on India– China Border Affairs, created in 2012 by an agreement between the two countries. The aim of this mechanism, comprising joint secretary–level officials of the MEA and MoD, including the army form the Indian side, and their counterparts from China, is to handle important border matters.

Specifically, they have been tasked with ensuring peace and tranquility and to enhance CBMs along the border, in keeping with the agreements of 1993, 1996, and 2005. They have been designated to act as mediators in case the mechanism of Border Personnel Meetings (BPMs) fails to resolve problems on the ground, and to 'study ways and means to conduct and strengthen exchanges and cooperation between military personnel and establishments of the two sides in the border areas'.

This mechanism has been seriously tested on a few occasions—when there were tense face-offs at Depsang Valley in the Daulat Beg Oldi (DBO) sector (2013), at Chumar in Demchok area (2014), both in Ladakh, and at Doklam (2017)—and has acquitted itself with credit by preventing the situations from escalating out of control.

The special representatives adopted a 'three-stage process' for their assignment. The first step was accomplished when both sides came to a landmark comprehensive agreement on the 'guiding principles and political parameters' in 2005. Now they are focusing on evolving a 'framework' for the settlement of the LAC as their second step. The third and last step will entail delineation of the boundary based on the agreed framework. They have had nineteen rounds of talks so far, during which there has been little tangible progress. It appears that the process has again been stalemated while evolving the framework for resolution of the boundary dispute. As a matter of fact, since the boundary problem is very complex, the scope of this high political-level dialogue between the special representatives has been enlarged to include macro-level bilateral and multilateral issues covering subjects such as security and counter-terrorism, sharing of river waters, trade and commerce, WTO, Shanghai Cooperation Organization (SCO), nuclear energy and the enhancing of mutual trust and cooperation. These are issues also discussed during the 'strategic dialogues' at the foreign secretary level. It is apparent that there are various layers of mechanisms ascending from the ground level to the national leadership to ensure peace on the India–China border.

That this approach has worked is borne out by the fact that there has been no armed skirmish or encounter along the long frontier of over 4,000 kilometres for the past half-century. Regular visits on a reciprocal basis have been taking place by the defence ministers and the chiefs of the three forces of the two countries, and military-to-military ties have shown a remarkable rise. Regular meetings between field commanders take place at selected places on the border to resolve local issues as part of the various CBMs in force and to create goodwill by celebrating each other's national days and holding sports competitions.

There are incursions across the LAC by both sides on account of their varying perceptions as to where the border lies in certain areas, but there has never been an armed clash since the 1967 flare-up at Nathu La in Sikkim and the tense and conflict-prone situations at a few places: the Sumdurong Chu incident in Arunachal Pradesh during 1986–87 and the Doklam crisis of 2017 being two examples. A number of CBMs are now in place in the military field along the LAC which have helped to reduce tensions at the border considerably. A hotline between the HQs of both militaries is under consideration, and the details are being worked out. These negotiations are expected to throw up solutions that would be mutually acceptable, fair and reasonable.

While this process is on, top priority must be given to determination and demarcation of the Line of Actual Control, albeit without prejudice to the position of both sides as far as the boundary is concerned. To resolve a complex problem like this it has to be understood that no straightforward or universally applicable principle can be rigidly applied. Geography does not follow cardinal directions or make available an unbroken chain of mountains to facilitate the creation of an undisputable boundary, so there are going to be problems. But mutual adjustments have to be made by both countries so that the impasse is broken. Leaving aside the populated areas, small adjustments of the boundary in the uninhabited high-altitude Himalayan wilderness would be in the interest of both countries. This would be an eminently commendable and viable step to take at this historical juncture, when both nations are moving to centre stage in world affairs. Although finding a solution to a complex problem such as the boundary dispute between China and India is not going to be easy, our understanding of present-day China must factor in the Chinese psyche and their civilizational traits, as I have explained earlier, to arrive at a resolution. Ultimately, if we take pains to study and analyse the Chinese, they would not appear 8 feet tall!

22

The Way Forward

'To follow a path of peaceful development and development through cooperation not only meets the common interests of China and India, the two largest developing countries in the world, but also does a great service to Asia and the world at large.'

—Xi Jinping (Xinhua PLA Daily)

Going by history, custom and tradition, Asian countries had frontiers that were not barriers to people-to-people contact and trade. With the advent of the colonial era, the concept of 'nation states' and colonies with defined boundaries and 'spheres of influence' was introduced in South Asia. Can South Asia become like Europe, where people live peacefully and where seamless movement from one nation to the other is possible, with only the language on the signboards indicating change of country? What we need in the twenty-first century is a peaceful environment in the region, free movement of people and ease of trade. We could begin this within some of the SAARC or BIMSTEC countries as a first step. That this has commenced to some extent is true in the case of India with respect to Nepal, Bhutan and Myanmar. Perhaps the same is achievable in the foreseeable future with Sri Lanka, Bangladesh and the Maldives too. This would definitely engender a ripple effect in other countries of South-East Asia and ASEAN too. Next we should pursue with vigour and perseverance the resolution of the boundary and other problems with China and Pakistan. This will augur well for a stable, peaceful and prosperous Asia.

Relations between the two Asian giants, barring the border war of 1962, have been friendly for centuries together. During the first decade and a half of our Independence, we were dealing with the new communist People's Republic of China, with its hard-core communist leadership and war-hardened People's Liberation Army bloodied in the Korean War. This army was led by generals who had survived the Long March and the civil war and had fought in Korea too. Chairman Mao Zedong had a demi-god kind of persona and enjoyed unquestioned political and military power. Zhou Enlai was a pragmatic and mature veteran of the civil war, endowed with a sharp mind. He had a phenomenal memory, and quickly acquired enviable diplomatic finesse. He appeared to have mastered the art of changing goalposts when required, and of adroitly fielding embarrassing questions with vague replies such as 'the time is not ripe' or referring to vexing matters as 'issues left over by history' and so on. However, this genre of leadership and their mandarins did not hesitate to employ chicanery, deceit and force to achieve their aims.

On the Indian side, there were few leaders besides Jawaharlal Nehru and Vallabhbhai Patel with any world vision. Unfortunately, Patel passed away prematurely and Nehru, though a visionary, was found wanting as far as understanding of matters military was concerned. What is of great significance is that he was held in such awe that no one questioned his policy decisions, especially on foreign affairs. At the professional and functional level, most of the leadership in the bureaucracy, foreign service, military and intelligence had been catapulted into the higher ranks at the time of Independence even when they did not possess the desired level of experience and maturity. This led to a general lack of coordination and teamwork, and to incorrect assessments and decision making. It was this flawed understanding on both sides that led to the Sino-Indian border war in 1962.

So far as China's consolidation of its hold over Tibet goes, it needs to recall the acts and gestures of goodwill and friendship by India in recent history, both during its rule by the British and post-Independence. British India had never coveted Tibet as a possession or even as a protectorate.

Having brought Tibet to its knees, Younghusband's expeditionary force was directed to fall back to India within a fortnight of the signing of their agreement with the Tibetans in 1904. Moreover, the terms of reparation by the Tibetans in the treaty were diluted by the British government. The seventy-five-year occupation of Chumbi Valley was reduced to three years and the amount of reparation brought down too. Of greater significance is that the prestige and position of the Chinese as the suzerain power over Tibet was lifted from the abyss it had dropped into. This was when the British Empire was at its zenith and the Ch'ing dynasty was tottering! Further, the Indian government allowed passage of Chinese officials, shipments of supplies (even for the military) and post and telegraph facilities through India via Calcutta, Siliguri and Kalimpong to Chumbi Valley and beyond to Lhasa as there were no roads in Tibet and movement along the tracks was unsafe, arduous and extremely time-consuming. This continued till the mid-1950s, when some of the roads from China to Tibet were constructed.

To a large extent, British India and independent India helped China to re-establish and consolidate its hold on Tibet, particularly in view of Tibet having enjoyed de facto independent status from 1913 to 1951. It must not be forgotten that India facilitated the Tibetan delegation to proceed through India to Peking to formally accept to be an autonomous part of China, even though the seventeen-point agreement signed in May 1951 has remained controversial, as something done under duress.

India's large-heartedness and its endeavours to befriend China did not end there. As a gesture of goodwill, the Panchsheel agreement of 1954 was a classic example of India's one-sided generosity and diplomatic naivety, one that resulted in its giving away all rights and privileges and, significantly, in ending India's presence in Tibet without the country gaining anything as a quid pro quo. These aspects have been elaborated on here to highlight the efforts made by India for decades to build a friendly and constructive relationship with China. We can derive some satisfaction from the fact that during the past half-century or more, after the flare-up at Nathu La during 1967, we have seen peace along the disputed frontier. Although at times there has been friction on the border issue, the maturity and statesmanship of the leaders of both nations have ensured that these problems were resolved in a peaceful manner through dialogue and diplomatic exchange, as has been demonstrated during the recent stand-off at Doklam. The landmark agreements of 1993, 1996, 2003 and the signing of the Strategic and Cooperative Partnership for Peace and Prosperity during the visit of Chinese premier Wen Jiabao in April 2005, in the course of which we also signed the 'Agreement on Political Parameters and Guiding Principles' for resolving the boundary dispute, were aimed at maintaining tranquility on the borders while addressing the border question, and at enhancing mutual trust and understanding. The same objectives were emphasized in January 2008 during Prime Minister Dr Manmohan Singh's visit to China. These agreements have far-reaching implications for our relations as they are not just confined to bilateral security issues, but also to many regional and global issues of concern to us.

The leaders of our two nations have also articulated a 'Shared Vision for the 21st Century' (Appendix 8). We have a 'historic opportunity', as stated by President Xi Jinping, to settle our boundary problem and move ahead. We must also capitalize on the tremendous scope for enhancing bilateral relations by reaching a consensus on other vital global issues like maritime security, climate control, WTO, UN reforms and sustainable development. The military-to-military cooperation between the two countries could form the pivot in our relations with China to enable creation of a secure and stable environment in the region. Analysts of India–China relations see three dimensions to this relationship: adversarial or conflict-prone, competitive and cooperative. Also to be considered are the mindsets of the leadership and of the strategic elite, the media and the people at large, and to remove from their minds misconceptions and prejudices, bringing in mutual trust between the Chinese and the Indians as well as engendering national pride in them, as has been emphasized by Prime Minister Narendra Modi.

India and China inherited an undemarcated and partly delineated boundary of approximately 4,057 kilometres along the Karakoram, Kunlun and Himalayan chain of mountains. By ancient custom and tradition, as also on account of trade, the limits and boundaries of the states were known to the local inhabitants. However, there arose complexities and differences in perception pertaining to the uninhabited and high-altitude zones and areas where the rivers cut across the mountain ranges, and some spillover of populations and areas of influence occurred over the years. Also, where boundaries had been drawn on maps using antiquated survey methods and instruments or incomplete surveys a century or more ago, there is a need to rectify the errors using more scientific satellite-based systems.

Even at the time of signing of the Simla Convention, McMahon had said that minor adjustments to the boundary would be looked at as and when additional inputs on the frontier were received. For example, leeway was provided for realignment of the border to ensure that the sacred places of the Tibetans, like Tso Karpo ('White Lake') and Tsari Sarpa ('New Tsari') were included in Tibet, even when their precise locations were not known even to the Tibetan delegation at that juncture. Southern Tibet actually relates to the areas south of Lhasa, such as Kongbo, Takpo and Pomed, which lie along the Tsangpo Valley going downstream to the famous bend of the river. The Lhasa Tibetans refer to the people of these areas as Pobas, or southerners, whose territorial limits did not extend south of the Himalayan crest. 'South Tibet' as a term for present-day Arunachal Pradesh was never part of the Chinese lexicon of boundary negotiations till the 1980s, and is a later invention.

The Chinese, given their propensity to change the goalposts, have come out with a few names of their own (like 'South Tibet') for places in Arunachal Pradesh. The Chinese claim to this 'South Tibet', which comprises a large part of the southern slopes of the eastern Himalayas, is not only preposterous but also without any historical basis. There has never been Chinese presence, let alone administration, in the tribal territories south of the Himalayas. The awareness levels of the elite, the political leadership—the Opposition leaders in particular—the media and the lay people of both countries have to be raised so that they understand the ground realities of the boundary problem. They are then likely to become facilitators rather than obstacles to solutions to the problem.

As a matter of fact, today there is a Line of Actual Control which both sides have agreed to define and respect. More importantly, we have decided to maintain peace on the border. A complex dispute like this of many dimensions—historical background, nationalistic sentiments, ethnicity, settled populations and geographical principles—cannot be resolved merely at the level of officials. A mutually beneficial solution requires visionary and bold political leadership and an exceptional level of political will. A certain amount of accommodation will have to be made by both sides if we have to move forward. A bold and mutually beneficial solution can only come about in the form of a 'high-level political coup'—a tête-à-tête executed by the apex leadership of India and China, not retarded by the cautiousness likely to be injected by officials.

China's vulnerable back door is exposed by an unstable Tibet. Some Chinese leaders and scholars have expressed their concern about China's inability to fully assimilate and consolidate their hold on the Tibet region. An autonomous Tibet, which has had close and enduring historical ties with India, is seen as much of a 'stumbling block' in the way of improving relations between the two countries as the boundary dispute. According to recently declassified Chinese documents, the Chinese have a belief that India has always had an influence on Tibet down the ages; and after the Younghusband expedition, they imagined a 'long-term design' too[1] on our part. A latent potential for unrest in Tibet, which surfaces from time to time, coupled with the fact that the Chinese efforts of the past six decades have not entirely succeeded in Sinification of Tibet, is seen as a serious security challenge by China.

The Chinese see India as a facilitator of the Tibetan 'government in exile' in Dharamsala, blessed by the Dalai Lama, which is a causative factor for friction in their relationship. The Dalai Lama's activities, though purely ecclesiastical in nature, and his religious visits to many places in India—to Arunachal Pradesh in particular—are considered by the Chinese as provocative and unfriendly acts by India. Another dimension of conflict that is talked about relates to the new reincarnation of the Dalai Lama on the eventual 'passing on to the heavenly field' of the current one. The Chinese government has already announced that the next Dalai Lama would be chosen by a draw at the Jokhang monastery in the heart of Lhasa and can assume his role only after their approval. This announcement has been rejected by the Dalai Lama, who has categorically stated that any candidate chosen on political grounds by the PRC shall not be recognized or accepted. The Grand Lama has clearly announced that if the institution of the Dalai Lama should continue—itself a decision to be made after consultations with the 'high lamas' and other stakeholders— the responsibility for discovering the reincarnation in accordance with tradition shall rest with the officials of Dalai Lama's Phodrang Trust.[2]

Even to this day the Chinese exhibit a lurking fear of India's ability to play the Tibet or Dalai Lama card if required. Tawang did not figure at all in the Sino-Indian boundary talks initially. In fact, in the unofficial 'east-west swap deal' proposed by Zhou Enlai in 1960, he 'offered to recognize India's position in the eastern sector if India accepted China's sovereignty over Aksai Chin area in the west'. This offer was repeated later by Deng Xiaoping in 1980, and the McMahon Line was to be accepted as the boundary in the east. These offers of a package deal were not accepted by the Indian side, which wanted to follow a 'sector-by-sector approach'.[3]

By 1985, the Chinese had changed the goalposts again and were now proposing a revised swap deal with a caveat that Tawang should be handed over to them. The inhabitants of the Tawang area are non-Tibetan Monpas who are adherents of Tibetan Buddhism. The Urgelling monastery, located a few miles from the seventeenth-century Tawang monastery, was the birthplace of the sixth Dalai Lama. Even though ecclesiastical dues and donations were collected by the Tibetan Dzongpens of Tsona Dzong from the Monpas of Tawang area, that did not give them temporal power over them. Let alone China, which never had any presence whatsoever in Tawang, even Tibet did not have any administrative infrastructure here. During the Simla Conference in 1914, when the Tibetan plenipotentiary raised claims for inclusion in Tibet of Batang, Litang and other Tibetan-inhabited towns and villages in the eastern frontier zone, the Chinese raised a hue and cry. Addressing the Tibetan delegation at Simla on 7 March 1914, Ivan Chen, the Chinese plenipotentiary, emphasized that ecclesiastical power does not confer territorial rights, arguing that contributions made to the monasteries cannot be construed as tax. On 13 June 1914, Sun Pao-chi, the Chinese minister for foreign affairs, unambiguously conveyed to the British minister in Peking that 'the Tibetans affected to think that they had rights over all places inhabited by Lamaists, but this was not so. The Lamas might have ecclesiastical authority but this did not necessarily mean that these places belonged to Tibet.'[4] Therefore, by the same yardstick, there is no substance in the present Chinese claim for possession of Tawang.

The Chinese are making a desperate bid for Tawang not only for the geostrategic advantages that would accrue from its possession but also because of their apprehension that reincarnation of a future Dalai Lama could take place in the Monpa area again. It is difficult to imagine the effect such an event will have on Tibet and on Tibetans the world over. Tawang is one of the most highly populated towns in Arunachal Pradesh and the nerve centre of the Monpa area. Article VII of the 'Agreement on Political Parameters and Guiding Principles' signed on 11 April 2005 during the visit of Premier Wen Jiabao clearly says: 'In reaching a boundary settlement, the two sides shall safeguard due interests of their settled populations in the border areas.' (See Appendix 7.) Therefore the question of ceding Tawang area, which has a population of over 50,000, (besides other cogent reasons and logic articulated earlier in this account) to China does not arise.

The reported possibility of Chinese diversion of waters of rivers emanating from Tibet and construction of dams on them, particularly on the Tsangpo (Brahmaputra), has led to a large degree of disquiet in India, Bangladesh and other riparian states of South-East Asia. This anxiety and alarm raised in the media is misplaced, and is based on exaggerated or incorrect reports. As has been explained earlier, there are no viable or concrete plans to divert the waters of the Tsangpo or to dam the river (only run-of-the-river power generation projects are being constructed). However, as a component of their strategy, the Chinese offer only vague or muted clarifications to these rumours, or resort to disinformation. They seem to relish indulging in mind play on their adversaries, competitors or even smaller neighbours as a tactic to exert their influence on them. The lower riparian states feel it is incumbent on a responsible China to allay their fears on the issue of river waters and to offer to share hydrological data with them.

The political and economic imperatives of the two rising powers of Asia may lead to rivalry or competition for influence, resources and markets in the region. So it is that the maritime dimension and the security of sea corridors in the Indian and Pacific Oceans have assumed vital importance. There is a perception among some researchers from China's strategic community that there exists a US–India–Japan–Australia strategy to contain China. Similarly, some strategic experts from India and the West have advanced and elaborated on the 'string of pearls' strategy of the Chinese in India's neighbourhood. The significance and impact of the 'Asia Pivot' theory of the US on the security situation in the Asia-Pacific region would have to be factored in during future security calculations. There has been a considerable increase in the presence of the Chinese navy in the Indian Ocean region in recent years, and India too has been making efforts to augment its naval capabilities. These are pointers that underscore the importance of the security of sea lanes of communication (SLOCs) passing through the Indian Ocean and the need for India to have a dominant presence there.

In order to offset the effect of the Malacca Straits as a choke point in its mercantile trade and SLOCs, China has already put into place a meticulous and well-thought-out strategy. This is to construct land routes at a cost of trillions of dollars, consisting of road, railway and oil pipeline corridors connecting China, Central Asia and the whole of Europe right through to Spain. There are initiatives such as the One Belt One Road (OBOR), and the China Pakistan Economic Corridor (CPEC) connecting the port of Gwadar (Pakistan) and passing through Pakistan Occupied Kashmir to Sinkiang (China), and the road and oil pipeline connecting the port of Sittwe (Myanmar) with Kunming (China). These routes would provide China with secure alternatives to the Malacca Straits route. Recently, a freight train brought in for the first time container loads from the UK to China, from London to Yiwu. Presently, trains are being run from China to many European destinations.

As far as India is concerned we have not agreed to be part of either the CPEC or OBOR projects, seemingly in reciprocity to China's stand on Arunachal Pradesh and our sovereignty issue over Jammu and Kashmir. India's strategic thinking has rightly held the belief that the special relationship between China and Pakistan has been born out of their intrinsic antagonism towards India. Accordingly, China's strategic interests would be best served by a friendly and, to some extent, a dependent Pakistan that would not only keep India engaged in a low-intensity conflict in Kashmir by sending in terrorists and providing support to terrorist organizations, but by also remaining a staunch ally to the Chinese in international matters. Obviously, this strategy has profound security connotations for India. However, to be fair to the Chinese, barring some symbolic gestures along the LAC, they have never overtly sided with Pakistan during the Indo-Pak wars of 1965, 1971 or during the conflict in Kargil. Notwithstanding the above argument, the Indian armed forces should be prepared to face a two-front war as a worst-case scenario. Consequently, India's military needs to acquire the desired offensive, defensive and deterrence capabilities and the required political and diplomatic 'savoir-faire' to handle such a challenge.

Going beyond the challenges discussed above, one can also see a number of positive factors that are likely to usher in a convergence of interests and cooperation between India and China. India has always striven to be a good neighbour, desirous of living in peace with its border states, and has no extraterritorial ambition or wish to promote its ideology and democratic path elsewhere. We were the first non-communist country after Burma to establish diplomatic relations with China on 1 April 1950. Following the five principles of peaceful coexistence or Panchsheel, India was unprepared for the rude shock and the humiliation caused by the Chinese attack in 1962. It was a reverse suffered by the nation politically, diplomatically as well as militarily. Although six decades have gone by since, the scars remain. In an attempt to heal these scars, Deng Xiaoping, in his discussions with Rajiv Gandhi during the Indian PM's visit to China in 1988, said he had come to the conclusion that 'Panch Sheel—the Five Principles of Peaceful Coexistence approved by Zhou En-lai and Nehru—could be the basis for taking forward the international dialogue'. Deng added, 'Since both sides did not live up to these principles, Sino-Indian relations suffered a setback.'[5] Perhaps the Chinese were suffering the pangs of a guilty conscience after the stab in the back inflicted by them on a trusting though complacent India. At the same time they had also unfairly accused India of interfering in their internal affairs in Tibet, and berated us for welcoming the Dalai Lama and sheltering thousands of Tibetan refugees. This further reinforces the premise that Tibet is the core problem between the two nations.

There are, of course, our different political systems and inherent ideological contradictions too. One hopes that with a new generation of policymakers in place in both countries, and with their enhanced defence capabilities, including nuclear weapons, the likelihood of an armed conflict is quite remote. Today, India and China have increasingly become aware of their linked destinies as neighbours and are expected to contribute to the establishment of an atmosphere of mutual understanding, trust and cooperation in Asia and the world. Peace and stability are imperative if the countries are to raise the socio-economic conditions of millions of their people. Within the ambit of the Strategic and Cooperative Partnership Agreement of 2005, greater importance is being given to relations with India by the new Chinese leadership. Chinese premier Wen Jiabao's famous comment that there has been a 'friendly relationship between our two nations for 99.9% of the period of over two millennia' does convey a message.

Indeed, there has been rapid growth of bilateral trade and commerce, which has touched $84 billion in 2017, a phenomenal increase from $0.35 billion in 1992. The complementarities in trade and commerce between the two countries, as analysed by Binod Singh in his book *India–China Relations: Future Perspectives* are interesting. He writes, 'China is perceived to be strong in manufacturing and infrastructure while India is perceived to be strong in services and information technology … The relative strengths and weaknesses of the two countries indicate a significant degree of convergence in their economies in the coming decades.'[6] However, it is crucial that the imbalance in our trade with China is addressed to make it a win-win situation for both nations. In this regard, a strategic economic dialogue has commenced between the two countries. In the wake of being recognized as emerging powers, a greater sense of responsibility devolves on India and China to contribute to peace and stability in the region and in the world. Both nations must understand that there is 'enough space for growth', as emphasized by the prime ministers of both countries. The military capabilities of both countries have been enhanced manifold, although the Chinese have a definite edge over India at present. Besides, there is the intrinsic deterrence value of nuclear weapons and missiles, which have a longer reach and are suitably vectored. There is in consequence an equilibrium and strategic balance of sorts between India and China.

This scenario is far removed from the situation obtaining in the 1950s and '60s. Looking at the possibility of an armed conflict in the Indo-Tibetan frontier zone, the challenge posed by the altitude and terrain obtaining in the region would inhibit deployment of their full might by either side. The difficulty of providing logistical support would also act as a restraining factor. History is witness to many monumental blunders committed by warring nations who forgot to factor in geography. Therefore, my reckoning is that war can no longer be a preferred option for either side. China is faced with the spectre of terrorism in the restive Uighur region of Xinjiang. Tackling the extreme radical Islamists with a heavy hand has not helped. A report by Simon Denyer in the *Washington Post* (September 2014) said: 'China's clumsy attempts to "liberate" Uighurs from the oppression of conservative Islam are only driving more people into the hands of the fundamentalists.' And in recent times these extremists have begun to target civilians—Han Chinese in particular.

Radical Islam has spawned terror that has unified the world in its efforts to eradicate this scourge from the earth. This is another field in which China and India are working together; countering terror is one of the important themes in joint military training, and there is so much that one can learn from the other's experiences. Among Indians, their perception of the Chinese oscillates between the aggressive and expansionist neighbour and the historically friendly one. It also depends on which segment of Indian society one belongs to. A young Indian professional, businessman or commoner carries little if any baggage of the past and would prefer to engage freely with our large neighbour, but on an equal footing and on a level playing field. Some strategic thinkers and individuals, particularly from the generation that experienced the war of 1962, still have a 'stabbed-in-the-back' feeling against China.

The various accords between the two nations cannot be taken lightly, of course, yet it does not mean that we can afford to lower our guard. There is still the need to continuously modernize and enhance the capabilities of our armed forces and intelligence agencies and build our infrastructure along the frontiers. Cyber and space are new dimensions that need to be addressed seriously, and the desired level of both offensive and defensive capabilities created. In fact, with our intrinsic IT acumen, India should be the leading country in the cyber domain, but we seem to be lagging behind. We need to take urgent action on this front.

Although India and China have differences in their systems of governance and their approach to regional and international issues, the predominant view of most Sinologists in India calls for 'constructive engagement' with China. As articulated by S. Bhattacharya, 'Current Chinese perceptions of India are also dominated by an appreciation of the changes that have taken place in recent times and the desire to engage in closer contacts, especially in the economic field.'[7] Bhattacharya says, 'There is a growing realization in China that the sustained growth of India is indeed a reality that cannot be ignored. To some extent, the increasing geopolitical importance of India and the improvement in bilateral relations have spurred the need to have a new look on how they perceive India.'[8]

It is now being acknowledged that India's GDP growth rate has overtaken China's during 2016–17 and that India is one of the fastest-growing economies of the world today. India's place among the leading nations of the world and in the Asian power structure is well merited. India's strong stand against Chinese interference in Arunachal Pradesh and Chinese objection to the Dalai Lama's visit to the state, and India's non-participation in the inaugural ceremony of China's OBOR initiative on the grounds of our sovereignty and territorial integrity, are telling statements. India has thereby conveyed to China that its dichotomous approach with regard to Jammu and Kashmir and Arunachal Pradesh is not appreciated, particularly when India has consistently endorsed China's sovereignty over Tibet Autonomous Region and its one-China policy.

There is no hesitation in saying that when India and China shake hands, the impact is felt by the rest of the world. The major powers already have comprehensive engagement and ties with us, and those are being further enhanced. In addition, our relations with Africa and Latin America, besides within Asia of course, are being strengthened too. India and China should make our smaller neighbours believe that the two present an opportunity and not a threat to each other's stability and growth, and that the same logic would equally apply to them. Wen Jiabao's concluding remarks at the National Peoples Conference, published in *Xinhua* in March 2005, carried a quotation, the immortal Shanti mantra from the Upanishads: 'May he protect us both together. May he nourish us both together. May we conjointly work with great energy. May our study be vigorous and effective. May we not hate anyone. Let there be peace, let there be peace, let there be peace.'[9] He expressed similar sentiments during his visit to India in May 2005, to which he accorded the highest importance. In the words of our former national security adviser Shivshankar Menon, 'Today India has few relationships which can match with China for its range, significance and the variety of emotions that it evokes in both countries.' Though already articulated by me, I wish to reinforce my viewpoint with a quotation from the noted political scientist John Garver:

> India also seems to be handicapped by a dearth of strategic thinking and real China experts. China, by contrast, has a tradition of strategic thought that is second to none in the world. It is arguably the major power best able to think strategically for long periods of time and mobilise the national resources and will needed to attain its postulated strategic objectives.[10]

Many Indian strategists have been predicting a war between China and India. First it was supposed to have happened after the Beijing Olympics, then it was forecast to take place in 2012, and a few speak of 2020 now. Some of these analysts haven't been to the high Himalayan regions on either side of the frontier zone or have merely undertaken whistle-stop tours in fair weather! To comprehend the true dimensions of fighting a war in this region, one has to see the conditions in these parts during the freezing winters when the snow, the blizzards, the high attitudes and permafrost conditions make life impossible; or during the monsoons when it rains for days on end and even small streams become raging torrents, washing away bridges and entire sections of roads. The challenge of geography in such areas can be devastating. Glibly talking of the two countries going to war is irresponsible and baseless, unless there is concrete evidence of a military build-up and concentration of forces.

India is the only country in the developing world with the potential to match China's growth and capabilities. The India–China relationship can be extrapolated from the scenario of a fight between two tigers over territory. In such a fight both end up severely mauled and bloodied, as happened in the ruinous wars bettween Athens and Sparta that went on for decades before ending in 5 BC. No one is the winner, and both adversaries are likely to suffer the pain of their wounds for years, resulting in a zero-sum game. The emergence of two potential global players from Asia would definitely tilt the balance of power in favour of Asia; therefore there is the belief in some quarters that other world powers might be content to see China engaged in a race for dominance with another rising Asian state such as India, as it would help to maintain the balance of power internationally.

However, the greatest challenge for both India and China in the forseeable future is to raise the socio-economic condition of millions of their underprivileged citizens and to improve basic infrastructure in their remote interior areas. Therefore, a conflict between the two nations would not be in the national interests of either. Although the Great Himalayas are a formidable barrier, going in an arc from the north-west of India to its north-east, at some places there aren't easily identifiable watersheds or the continuity of the mountain chain is broken, resulting in differences in perception as to where the border lies. This is particularly so where there are tri-junctions of the boundaries or major rivers cutting across from Tibet to the Indian plains and entering river basins; these are the precise areas that make boundary definition such a problem.

Hence, many of the disputed pockets are located where the McMahon Line crosses river valleys such as Namka Chu, Sumdorong Chu, Longju or Dichu (Walong sector). The most recent flare-up of 2017 was in the Doklam area, which is in the vicinity of the India–China–Bhutan trijunction. These differences need to be resolved peacefully by dialogue, until which time both countries must ensure that the status quo is maintained. Therefore, early resolution of the boundary dispute should be accorded the highest priority, without in any way impacting the other multidimensional engagements taking place between India and China. A solution to the boundary issue will have to be found not by experts or geographers but at the national political level. Before taking any decision regarding mutual adjustment and accommodation, the people of both countries need to be sensitized about the matter and be made aware of the reality on the ground.

The Chinese have, over the years, been changing the goalposts as far as their boundary claims are concerned. In 2011, Wen Jiabao was reported to have remarked that 'it may not be possible to ever fully solve the boundary question'.[11] Pending finalization of the boundary, the existing LAC could be termed as the working boundary and maintenance of peace along the border ensured. The clarification and subsequent demarcation of the LAC based on the actual situation on the ground must be accorded the highest priority in the interests of both countries. The current global security and economic situation demands that India and China consult and show greater inclination to work together and manage the differences that exist rather than adopt an antagonistic approach. Despite the major upheavals in international power equations since the end of the cold war, 'Beijing has stuck to the belief that there are more opportunities than challenges for China in today's international environment.'[12] That is India's position too. During the past three decades in particular, we have shown our ability to deal with difficult and seemingly intractable issues in a mature and pragmatic manner. Even the boundary and water issues are being handled with political sagacity and diplomatic finesse, though it would be unrealistic to expect quick results. Recently, India and China agreed to hold a bilateral dialogue on maritime issues. One must realize the impact of people-to-people contacts, which are rapidly increasing as a result of enhanced trade and tourism. For example, there are over 18,000 Indian students in China today, which is more than those studying in the UK and is unprecedented although not large enough. Of late many students are opting to learn Mandarin or other Chinese languages in universities and even schools. This congruence will grow in the years to come. It would be reasonable to assume that a similar situation exists in China, although there are fewer Chinese students in Indian universities than Indians in Chinese schools. Besides that there are 25,000 IT professionals presently working with Chinese companies in China.

Importantly, the underlying 'trust deficit' between the two countries needs to be addressed and the strategic cooperative partnership strengthened. China is very sensitive to the presence and activities of the Dalai Lama and his government-in-exile in India. Although India has made it clear that the Dalai Lama will not be allowed to carry out any political activity from Indian soil, the Chinese suspect an Indian hand whenever there are disturbances in Tibet, as was the case in 2008–09.

During the visit of the Dalai Lama to Tawang in April 2017, the Chinese raised a massive hue and cry. It was purely a monastic visit, yet China warned India of consequences. The Chinese reaction was to invent and announce Chinese names for a few places in Arunachal Pradesh in an attempt to reinforce their claim to a large part of the state. India has learnt to stand firm in such matters. At a conference during March 2018 at Dharamsala, the Dalai Lama stated: 'We Tibetans, for example, are not seeking independence' and would like to have a 'connection with China' and 'live with respect'. One hopes that such a statement would help to allay the apprehensions of the Chinese and mend the fence with them. In the near and mid-term future, I believe the way forward for both China and India is positive and constructive engagement in bilateral and multilateral issues, setting aside the boundary issue. As responsible emerging powers, both nations must endeavour to find common ground and play their role in the shaping of a new world order at forums such as the UN, G20, BRICS, SCO, ASEAN, BCIM and international financial organizations.

Till we acquire the financial and military muscle to be able to stand our ground, we should follow the Chinese example of a 'peaceful rise' to power instead of being unduly moralistic or getting bogged down by political one-upmanship. National interest must come first. Negotiations to find a mutually acceptable resolution to the boundary dispute must continue. At the same time the relationship between India and China, two great nations of Asia and proud inheritors of ancient civilizations, should not be held hostage to the outcome of the boundary negotiations. For such a relationship to be realized it is imperative that India enhances its comprehensive national power and reduces the present asymmetry between the two nations. Military strength gives us the ability to deter aggression and safeguard our core values as a nation. It is indispensable if we wish to be an economic giant and helps us to make diplomacy more effective.

In an emerging multipolar configuration, India, while ensuring its strategic autonomy, must engage with other major powers and play a meaningful role in the maintenance of an equilibrium and balance of power in the world. India with its resources, rising economic and military power and potential is being looked upon as a 'swing' nation that can contribute to the stability of a complex world. We must exploit this opportunity and enhance our stature and sphere of influence. India has engaged in strategic and mutually beneficial relationships with the US, Russia, China, Japan, UK, France, and other European nations. Going beyond the basic non-aligned structure of its foreign policy, India is displaying an increasingly mature and pragmatic approach while creating bonds with other important players on the world stage. It is part of many multilateral groupings such as BRICS, SCO, ASEAN, G20 and BIMSTEC. The 'Quad' of US, Japan, Australia and India has been revived and a meeting was held at the working level during the ASEAN meeting in 2017. This gives India enhanced leverage while dealing with China.

India is now in a happy situation and being courted by the P5 (five permanent members of the UNSC) and other nations. US president Barack Obama had remarked in 2010, 'India is not a rising power, it is a world power.' Current US president Donald Trump has put Pakistan in its place and made no bones about Pakistan having deceived, lied and conducted itself in a duplicitous manner with regard to promoting and aiding terror outfits. On the other hand, he has repeatedly stressed the importance of the growing strategic partnership with India, particularly in the domain of cooperation in defence matters, and the role this relationship will play in enabling strategic balance, stability and peace in South Asia.

Even though India–Russia relations are not at the same level as they were with the Soviet Union in the 1960s and '70s, and Russia and China are growing closer, Russia is not likely 'to take sides' as far as India and China are concerned. This was emphasized by Sergei Karaganov, economic and foreign policy adviser to Russian president Vladimir Putin, who went on to articulate that Sino-Indian hostility was 'an aberration' and 'thirty-forty years ago there was a deep distrust between Russia and China, including a territorial dispute. Now because of the wisdom of our peoples, the Russia–China border is peaceful.'[13] Both India and China ought to take a cue from this example. Today, India is deservingly poised to achieve permanent membership of the UN Security Council and has overwhelming international support to sit at the high table.[14]

China is one of our most important neighbours and the largest one. Our relations with China therefore assume the greatest significance for stability, peace and prosperity of the region. We are two emerging powers, seeking our rightful place on the world stage. It bears reiteration that together we make up a third of mankind. In the same breath, the security and prosperity of both India and China would be best served if all our neighbours evolve as viable states with stable regimes and robust economies. The leadership of both nations, despite hawks on both sides of the Himalayas, realize the significance of peace in the region so that the aspirations of the people may be met. We have a 'strategic and cooperative' partnership and a shared vision for the twenty-first century. There is enough space for sustained economic growth, social development and trade for both of us and the paths we have chosen may be different, but our goal is common—the well-being and prosperity of our people and peaceful growth.

I believe therefore that we may be competitors but not rivals. It is important that we keep in mind the lessons of the past, yet we must not allow the acrimonious decades of the 1950s and 1960s to cloud our judgement and hold hostage a promising future and prosperity for our people. India should engage China with self-confidence and on an equal footing. While it is a fact that China has progressed enormously, it merits recognition that India too is no longer the India of 1962.

India's defence strategy vis-à-vis China must aim at achieving a more robust deterrence capability, thereby taking the cost of an armed conflict to a prohibitive level so far as the political, economic, diplomatic and military dimensions are concerned. As a matter of fact, the approach taken by both countries to enhance military-to-military cooperation and mutual trust while strengthening CBMs along the LAC is pragmatic and militarily sound. This in my opinion is beyond doubt the most beneficial option for both nations.

India's bumbling, elephantine and almost chaotic democracy will keep moving forward, albeit fitfully, and the people are looking forward with mixed feelings to the national elections of 2019. On the other hand, Xi Jinping's totalitarian 'New China' is, as brilliantly argued by Francois Godement of the European Council on Foreign Relations, akin to Mao's model, 'but with the benefit of technological tools that Mao could only dream of'. Yet interestingly, many international experts on China like David Shambaugh and Gordon Chang have predicted the end of the 'regime due to economic vulnerabilities and social tensions', 'political repression', 'corruption' and so on.[15]

Further in his narrative, Francois Bougon has concluded that if 'he [Xi] succeeds, China may well become the perfect twenty-first-century dictatorship'.[16] However, sceptics doubt whether the Middle Kingdom would be transformed into a 'great modern socialist country' and a 'global leader' by 2049, as envisioned by Xi, or is it only a chimera? At this juncture it is not easy to predict and time alone will tell.

Finally, we should not assume that our place at the high table of the world is assured; we have to get our act together and work hard to realize our dream. We need to remember the axiom 'strength begets respect', and also the words of Thucydides in *Median Dialogue*: 'Right, as the world goes, is only in question between equals in power, while the strong do what they can and the weak suffer what they must.' These words hold good to this day. We have to become strong militarily while we forge ahead in other fields.

With the strong leadership that we see at the helm of affairs in both countries, it is hoped that their statesman-like, pragmatic and visionary approach will resolve the boundary and other issues as expeditiously as possible. When this happens in a fair, mutually acceptable and beneficial manner, the two rising nations can move forward and ensure that we and our future generations see a conflict-free, stable and prosperous world. A constructive relationship between India and China can redefine the contours of the twenty-first century, and the leadership that can make it happen will be remembered by history.

Notes

1. Roof of the World: Geography of Tibet

1. Mike Searle, *Colliding Continents*, Oxford: Oxford University Press, 2013, p. 331.
2. Name given by Eduard Suess, an eminent Austrian geographer and scientist.
3. While in the army, we often came across such fossils while patrolling along the Indo-Tibetan border in the Joshimath sector in the 1970s.
4. Mike Searle, *Colliding Continents*, p. 3.
5. Ibid., p. 367.
6. Sir Charles Bell, *Portrait of the Dalai Lama*, London: Collins, 1946, p. 19.
7. John W. Garver, *Protracted Contest: Sino-Indian Rivalry in the Twentieth Century*, Seattle and London: University of Washington Press, 2001, p. 37.
8. Ibid., p. 37.
9. Sir Charles Bell, *Portrait of the Dalai Lama*, London: Collins, 1946, p. 21.
10. Ibid., p. 17.
11. British Library and Archives, *Military Report on Tibet, 1910/12*, p. 10 (IOR L/MIL/17/14/92). Hereafter this will be referred to as BLA, *Military Report on Tibet*, 1910/12.
12. Mike Searle, *Colliding Continents*, p. 299.

13. Gondker Narayana Rao, *The India-China Border – A Reappraisal*, Delhi: Motilal Banarsidass Publishers Pvt. Ltd, 1968, p. 7.

14. BLA, *Military Report on Tibet*, 1910/12, p. 1.

15. Ibid., pp. 8–13.

16. R.D. Pradhan, *India China Gridlock Over Arunachal*, Pune: Chinar Publishers, 2013, p. 143.

17. BLA, *Military Report on Tibet*, 1910/12, p. 68.

2. History and Geopolitics

1. Claude Arpi, *Tibet: The Lost Frontier*, New Delhi: Lancer Publishers, 2008, Back Cover.

2. Sir Charles Bell, *Tibet: Past and Present*, Delhi: Low Price Publications, 1924, pp. 23–31; BLA, *Military Report on Tibet*, 1910/12, p. 94.

3. Claude Arpi, *Tibet: The Lost Frontier*, New Delhi: Lancer Publishers, 2008, pp. 34–35.

4. L. Austine Waddell, *Lhasa and its Mysteries*, Delhi: Sanskaran Prakashak, 1905/1975, p. 24.

5. Ibid.

6. Timotheus A. Bodt, *The New Lamp Clarifying the History, Peoples, Languages and Traditions of Eastern Bhutan and Eastern Mon*, Wageningen, the Netherlands: Monpasang Publications, 2012, p. 4.

7. Claude Arpi, *Tibet: The Lost Frontier*, New Delhi: Lancer Publishers, 2008, pp. 24–25.

8. Ibid., p.25.

9. H.E. Richardson, *Short History of Tibet*, New York: E.P. Dutton & Co. Inc., 1962, p. 30.

10. L. Austine Waddell, *Lhasa and Its Mysteries*, pp. 30–31; Claude Arpi, *Tibet: The Lost Frontier*, pp. 38–39.

11. Timotheus A. Bodt, *The New Lamp Clarifying the History, Peoples, Languages and Traditions of Eastern Bhutan and Eastern Mon*, Wageningen, the Netherlands: Monpasang Publications, 2012, p. 113.

12. Claude Arpi, *Tibet: The Lost Frontier*, New Delhi: Lancer Publishers, 2008, p. 41.

13. Eric Teichmann, *Travels of a Consular Officer in Eastern Tibet*, Cambridge: Cambridge University Press, 1922, p. 2.

14. Alastair Lamb, *The McMahon Line, Vol. I,* London: Routledge & Kegan Paul Ltd, 1966, *Vol. I,* p. 184.

15. L. Austine Waddell, *Lhasa and Its Mysteries,* pp. 34–35.

16. Eric Teichmann, *Travels of a Consular Officer in Eastern Tibet,* p. 4.

17. BLA, *Military Report on Tibet,* 1910/12, p. 99.

18. L. Austine Waddell, *Lhasa and Its Mysteries,* pp. 46–50; BLA, *Military Report on Tibet,* 1910/12, p. 102.

19. Alastair Lamb, *The McMahon Line, Vol. I,* p. 110 (Morley to Minto, 6 July 1906).

20. BLA, *Military Report on Tibet,* 1910/12, p. 103; Warren W. Smith Jr, *A History of Tibetan Nationalism and Sino-Tibetan Relations,* New Delhi: HarperCollins Publishers, 1996, p. 156.

3. Clouds over Lhasa

1. Sir Charles Bell, *Portrait of the Dalai Lama,* London: Collins, 1946, p. 22.

2. Tsepon W.D. Shakabpa, *Tibet: A Political History,* New York: Potala Publications, 1984, p. 219.

3. Warren W. Smith Jr, *Tibetan Nation: A History of Tibetan Nationalism and Sino-Tibetan Relations,* New Delhi: HarperCollins Publishers, 1996, p. 155.

4. L. Austine Waddell, *Lhasa and Its Mysteries,* Delhi: Sanskaran Prakashak, 1905/1975, pp. 56–57.

5. Amar Kaur Jasbir Singh, *Himalayan Triangle,* London: The British Library, 1988, pp. 8–9, n. 127.

6. Maj. Gen. Shubhi Sood, *Younghusband: The Troubled Campaign,* New Delhi: India Research Press, 2005, p. 51.

7. L. Austine Waddell, *Lhasa and Its Mysteries,* 1905/1975, p. 80.

8. Ibid.

9. Maj. Gen. Shubhi Sood, *Younghusband: The Troubled Campaign,* p. 56.

10. https://en.wikipedia.org/wiki/British_expedition_to_Tibet#cite_note-VirtualTibet-17

11. L. Austine Waddell, *Lhasa and Its Mysteries,* p. 198.

12. Ibid., p. 245.

13. Ibid., p. 269.

4. Tibet on Its Knees

1. L. Austine Waddell, *Lhasa and Its Mysteries*, Delhi: Sanskaran Prakashak 1905/1975, p. 22. This mantra of six symbols is chanted repetitiously by adherents of Buddhism and painted on rocks everywhere in Tibet. Each of these symbols has a profound meaning. It is singing 'praises to the jewel in the lotus' and has many other interesting interpretations, such as 'Hail! The Jewel [Grand Lama] in the Lotus flower!'

2. Ibid., p. 279.

3. Ibid., p. 278.

4. Parshotam Mehra, *The McMahon Line and After*, Delhi: The Macmillan Company of India Ltd., 1975, p. 26.

5. L. Austine Waddell, *Lhasa and Its Mysteries*, p. 332.

6. Ibid., p. 400.

7. H.E. Richardson, *Short History of Tibet*, New York: E.P. Dutton & Co. Inc., 1962, p. 254.

8. Ibid., pp. 254–55.

9. L. Austine Waddell, *Lhasa and Its Mysteries*, p. 418.

10. Ibid., p. 418–9.

11. S. S. Khera, *India's Defence Problem*, New Delhi: Orient Longman Ltd, 1968, p. 150.

12. Parshotam Mehra, *The McMahon Line and After*, p. 67.

13. Warren W. Smith Jr, *Tibetan Nation: A History of Tibetan Nationalism and Sino-Tibetan Relations*, Delhi: HarperCollins Publishers India, 1996, p. 159.

14. Sir Charles Bell, *Portrait of the Dalai Lama*, London: Collins, 1946, p. 135.

15. Warren W. Smith Jr, *Tibetan Nation: A History of Tibetan Nationalism and Sino-Tibetan Relations*, p. 159

16. Hull, A.M.A., *Colonel Younghusband's Mission to Lhasa, 1904*, Durham, UK.: Durham theses, Durham University, 1989, p. 43.

17. Ibid., p. 42.

18. Hull, A.M.A., *Colonel Younghusband's Mission to Lhasa, 1904*, p. 43.

19. Ibid., and Francis Younghusband, *India and Tibet*, Hong Kong: Oxford University Press, 1985, p. 133.

5. First Exile of the Dalai Lama (1904–1909)

1. Parshotam Mehra, *The McMahon Line and After*, Delhi: The Macmillan Company of India Ltd., 1975, pp. 26–27.
2. Sir Charles Bell, *Portrait of the Dalai Lama*, London: Collins, 1946, p. 65.
3. Ibid., p.66.
4. Parshotam Mehra, *The McMahon Line and After*, p. 27.
5. Warren W. Smith, *Tibetan Nation: A History of Tibetan Nationalism and Sino-Tibetan Relations*, p.164.
6. Sir Charles Bell, *Portrait of the Dalai Lama*, p. 69.
7. Ibid., p. 66.
8. Parshotam Mehra, *The McMahon Line and After*, p. 49.
9. C.G.E. Mannerheim, *Across Asia From West to East* 1906–08, Oosterhout N.B. Netherlands: Anthropological Publications, 1969, pp. 693–694.
10. Elliott Sperling, *JIATS,* No. 6, 2011, THL#5720, pp. 389–410.
11. Ibid. Vicomte Henri d'ollone, *In Forbidden China*, Boston: Maynard and Company Publishers, 1906–09, pp. 306–7.
12. Alastair Lamb, *The McMahon Line, Vol. I,* London: Routledge & Kegan Paul Ltd., 1966, p. 174.
13. Warren W. Smith Jr, *Tibetan Nation*, p.112.
14. Amar Kaur Jasbir Singh, *Himalayan Triangle*, London: The British Library, 1988, p. 20, note 348.
15. Warren W. Smith Jr, *Tibetan Nation: A History of Tibetan Nationalism and Sino-Tibetan Relations*, p. 168.
16. Parshotam Mehra, *The McMahon Line and After,* p. 29.
17. Warren W. Smith Jr, *Tibetan Nation: A History of Tibetan Nationalism and Sino-Tibetan Relations*, p. 174.

6. Chinese Subjugation of Tibet (1905–1911)

1. Alastair Lamb, *The McMahon Line, Vol. I,* London: Routledge & Kegan Paul Ltd, 1966, p. 35.
2. Parshotam Mehra, *The McMahon Line and After*, Delhi: The Macmillan Company of India Ltd, 1975, p. 18.

3. Alastair Lamb, *Britain and Chinese Central Asia: The Road to Lhasa, 1767 to 1905*, London: Routledge and Kegan Paul, 1960, p. 260.
4. Firuz Kazemzadeh, *Russia and Britain in Russia: Imperial Ambition in Qajar Iran*, London: I.B. Tauris, 2013.
5. Warren W. Smith Jr, *Tibetan Nation: A History of Tibetan Nationalism and Sino-Tibetan Relations*, p.88.
6. Alastair Lamb, *The McMahon Line, Vol. I*, pp. 186–189.
7. Ibid., p. 188.
8. Ibid., pp. 187–8
9. Warren W. Smith Jr, *Tibetan Nation*, p. 170.
10. Alastair Lamb, *The McMahon, Line* Vol. I, p. 188.
11. BLA, IOR L/P&S/10/343, p. 123.
12. Parshotam Mehra, *The McMahon Line and After*, p.77.
13. Alastair Lamb, *The McMahon Line, Vol. I*, p. 132.
14. H.E. Richardson, *A Short History of Tibet*, New York: E.P Dutton & Co Inc., 1962, p. 96.
15. Alastair Lamb, *The McMahon Line, Vol. I*, p. 193.
16. H.E. Richardson, *A Short History of Tibet*, New York: E.P Dutton & Co. Inc., p. 99.
17. Parshotam Mehra, *The North-Eastern Frontier, Vol. I, 1906-14*, New Delhi: Oxford University Press, 1979, p.188.
18. Warren W. Smith Jr, 1996, p. 180.
19. Ibid.
20. BLA, *Military Report on Tibet*, 1910/12, pp. 2–4.
21. BLA, Mr Alston's Memorandum on Tibet, January 1–30 August 1913, No. 352 of September 8, 1913–5062.

7. Southern Frontiers of Tibet

1. Dorothy Woodman, *Himalayan Frontiers*, London: Barrie & Rockliff, The Cresset Press, 1969, pp. 130–31.
2. Alastair Lamb, *The McMahon Line, Vol. II*, London: Routledge & Kegan Paul Ltd, 1966, p. 291.
3. Captain F.M. Bailey, '*Report on an Exploration of the North East Frontier 1913*', Simla: Government of India, 1914, p. 22.

4. Ibid., p. 23.

5. Parshotam Mehra, *The North-Eastern Frontier Vol. I, 1906-14*, New Delhi: Oxford University Press, 1979, p. 35.

6. Alastair Lamb, *The McMahon Line, Vol. II*, p.333.

7. Dorothy Woodman, *Himalayan Frontier*, p. 128.

8. Parshotam Mehra, *The North-Eastern Frontier, Vol. I, 1906-14*, p.37.

9. Ibid., pp. 37–39. According to information gained by Captain Hardcastle of the Mishmi Mission 1911–12, this Chinaman's name was Chang or Chiang and his title was Ta Lao-yeh. He was 'evidently a military officer'. Further, he was described 'as wearing a black uniform with a belt' and had reportedly served with the garrison in Chikung for a year.

10. Dorothy Woodman, *Himalayan Frontiers*, pp. 129–30.

11. Ibid., p. 130.

12. Alastair Lamb, *The McMahon Line, Vol. II*, pp. 287–89, 357–58.

13. *McMahon's Final Memorandum*, 1914, BLA, IOR L/P&S/18/B206, p. 2. (Hereafter will be referred to as *Final Memorandum of McMahon*, 1914).

8. The Dalai Lama Flees to India

1. Sir Charles Bell, *Portrait of the Dalai Lama*, London: Collins, 1946, p. 86.

2. Ibid.

3. Ibid., p. 92.

4. Warren W. Smith, *Tibetan Nation: A History of Tibetan Nationalism and Sino-Tibetan Relations*, New Delhi: HarperCollins Publishers, 1996, p. 177–79, and letter of the 13th Dalai Lama to Lo T'i-t'ai, Notes 98–99.

5. Tsepon W.D. Shakabpa, *Tibet: A Political History*, New York: Potala Publications, 1984, p. 245.

6. Ibid., pp. 246–49.

7. Sir Charles Bell, *Portrait of the Dalai Lama*, p. 129.

8. Warren W. Smith, *Tibetan Nation*, p. 181

9. H.E. Richardson, *A Short History of Tibet*, New York: E.P. Dutton & Co. Inc., 1962, p. 105.

10. Parshotam Mehra, *The McMahon Line and After*, Delhi: The Macmillan Company of India Ltd, 1975, p. 128.
11. Sir Charles Bell, *Portrait of the Dalai Lama*, p.135.
12. Parshotam Mehra, *The McMahon Line and After*, p. 126.
13. Tsepon W.D. Shakabpa, *Tibet: A Political History*, pp. 246–47.
14. Ibid., pp. 248–49.

9. Tibet Policy of the British

1. Dorothy Woodman, *Himalayan Frontiers*, London: Barrie & Rockliff, The Cresset Press, 1969, p.149.
2. BLA, IOR L/P&S/10/432 dated 21 February 1914. Note from H. Porter, consul general, Chengtu, on 21 February 1914, to J. Jordan, minister in British Legation in Peking.
3. BLA, *Military Report on Tibet*, 1910/12, pp. 9–10.
4. Heather Spence, *British Policy and the 'Development' of Tibet 1912-1933*, Sydney: University of Wollongong, 1993, p. 41.
5. Ibid., p. vii.
6. Ibid., pp. vii–viii.
7. Ibid.
8. Ibid., p. 43
9. Ibid., pp. 45–46.
10. BLA, *Military Report on Tibet*, 1910/12, p. 9.
11. Eric Teichmann, *Travels of a Consular Officer in Eastern Tibet*, Cambridge: Cambridge University Press, 1922, p. 16; Warren W. Smith Jr, *A History of Tibetan Nationalism and Sino-Tibetan Relations*, HarperCollins Publishers, 1996, p.175.
12. Eric Teichmann, *Travels of a Consular Officer in Eastern Tibet*, p. 16.
13. Alastair Lamb, *The McMahon Line, Vol. I*, London: Routledge & Kegan Paul Ltd, 1966, pp. 199–200.
14. Tsepon W.D. Shakabpa, *Tibet: A Political History*, New York: Potala Publications, 1984, p. 230.

10. Eastern Himalayan Frontier

1. Zorawar Daulet Singh, *The Himalayan Stalemate*, New Delhi: KW Publishers Pvt. Ltd, 2011, p. 1.
2. Timotheus A. Bodt, *The New Lamp Clarifying the History, Peoples, Languages and Traditions of Eastern Bhutan and Eastern Mon*, Wageningen, the Netherlands: Monpasang Publications, 2012, p. 4.
3. Gondker Narayana Rao, *The India-China Border*, Delhi: Motilal Banarsidass Publishers Pvt. Ltd, 1968, pp. 62–63.
4. Captain F.M. Bailey, *Report on an Exploration of the North East Frontier 1913*, Simla: Government of India, 1914, p. 14.
5. Ibid., p. 79.
6. Ibid., pp. 10–11.
7. Ibid., p. 2.
8. Ibid., pp. 2–3.
9. Alastair Lamb, *The McMahon Line, Vol. II*, London: Routledge & Kegan Paul Ltd, 1966, p. 277.
10. Captain F.M. Bailey, *Report on an Exploration of the North East Frontier 1913*, pp. 10–11.

11. British Administration of Eastern Himalayan Region

1. Manilal Bose, *Historical and Constitutional Documents of North Eastern India*, (1824–1973), Delhi: Concept Publishing Company, 1979, p. 21.
2. Dorothy Woodman, *Himalayan Frontiers*, London: Barrie and Rockliff, The Cresset Press, 1969, p. 112.
3. Verrier Elwin, *A Philosophy for NEFA*, Itanagar: Government of Arunachal Pradesh, 2006, p. 2.
4. Gondker Narayana Rao, *The India-China Border: A Reappraisal*, Delhi: Motilal Banarasidass Publishers Private Limited, 1968, p. 71.
5. Report of the Officials of the Governments of India and the Peoples Republic of China on the Boundary Question, Part II, p. 102. Hereafter will be referred to as Officials' Report.

6. Ibid.

7. Ibid.

8. Alastair Lamb, *The McMahon Line, Vol. II*, London: Routledge & Kegan Paul Ltd, 1966, p. 313.

9. Dorothy Woodman, *Himalayan Frontiers*, p. 109.

10. Parshotam Mehra, *The McMahon Line and After*, Delhi: The Macmillan Company of India Ltd, 1975, p. 90.

11. Sadiya was completely destroyed by the severe earthquake of 1950 and the Brahmaputra and its tributaries changed their course at many places resulting in the loss of many lives and property.

12. Manilal Bose, *Historical and Constitutional Documents of North-Eastern India (1824-1973)*, p. 157.

13. Dorothy Woodman, *Himalayan Frontiers*, p. 135.

14. Captain F. M. Bailey, *Report on an Exploration of the North-East Frontier 1913*, Simla: Government of India, 1914, p. 25.

15. Alastair Lamb, *The McMahon Line, Vol. II*, p. 346.

16. Ibid., p. 335.

17. Parshotam Mehra, *The McMahon Line and After*, p.96.

18. Ibid., p. 97.

19. Alastair Lamb, *The McMahon Line, Vol. II*, p. 345, n. 33.

20. Parshotam Mehra, *The North-Eastern Frontier, Vol. I, 1906-14*, Delhi: Oxford University Press, 1979, p. 41.

21. Captain H. T. Morshead, *Report on an Exploration on the North East Frontier 1913*, Dehradun: Government of India, 1914, p. 4.

22. Sir Robert Reid, *History of the Frontier Areas Bordering on Assam from 1883–1941*, Guwahati: Spectrum Publications, 1942, p. 181.

23. Ibid.

24. Ibid.

25. Dorothy Woodman, *Himalayan Frontiers*, p. 369.

26. Ibid., p. 135.

27. Ibid., p. 369.

28. Sir Robert Reid, *History of the Frontier Areas Bordering on Assam from 1883–1941*, p. 283.

29. Alastair Lamb, *The McMahon Line, Vol. II*, p. 361.

30. Ibid., p. 406.

31. Ibid., pp. 361–62.
32. Dorothy Woodman, *Himalayan Frontiers*, p. 132.
33. Alastair Lamb, *The McMahon Line, Vol. II*, p. 356.
34. Ibid., p. 543. See also O'Callaghan's Tour Diary, 7 March 1914.
35. Ibid., p. 357.
36. H.E. Richardson, *A Short History of Tibet*, New York: E.P Dutton & Co. Inc., 1962, p. 73.
37. Ibid., pp. 73–74.
38. Parshotam Mehra, *The McMahon Line and After*, p. 34.
39. Sir Charles Bell, *Portrait of the Dalai Lama*, London: Collins, 1946, p. 42.
40. Ibid., pp. 61–62.
41. Alastair Lamb, *The McMahon Line, Vol. I*, p. 44.
42. L. Austine Waddell, *Lhasa and Its Mysteries*, Delhi: Sanskaran Prakashak, 1905, p. 416.
43. Alastair Lamb, *The McMahon Line, Vol. I*, pp. 149–51.
44. Heather Spence, *British Policy and the 'Development' of Tibet 1912–1933*, Sydney: University of Wollongong, 1993, p. 7.
45. Sir Charles Bell, *Portrait of the Dalai Lama*, p. 76.
46. Alastair Lamb, *The McMahon Line, Vol. I*, p. 54.

12. The Prelude

1. Viceroy to Foreign Office, 15 June 1913, BLA, IOR L/P&S/18/B 201, p. 2376, hereafter referred to as BLA.
2. Mr Alston's No. 352 of 8 September 1913, to Viceroy, Tibet: Memorandum from Jan 1 to Aug 30, 1913, BLA, IOR, L/P&S/18/B201, p. 5062.
3. Mr Alston's No. 266 of 30 June 1913, BLA, IOR L/P&S/18/B 201.
4. Alston's Tibet: Memorandum from Jan 1 to Aug 30, 1913, BLA, IOR L/P&S/18/B202, p. 17.
5. Ibid., p. 18.
6. W. Langley, Foreign Office to Under Secy of State, India Office, dated 13 Aug 1913, BLA, IOR L/P&S/18/B 201, p. 299.

7. Colonel A.H. McMahon, in his address 'International Boundaries', published in *Journal of the Royal Society of Arts*, London, 15 November, 1935, p. 2.

8. Parshotam Mehra, *The McMahon Line and After*, Delhi: The Macmillan Company of India Ltd, 1975, p. 173, n. 10.

9. BLA, IOR L/P&S/18/B 201, p. 2564.

10. Ibid., p. 2279, Sir J. Jordan to Sir Edward Gray, 5 June 1913.

11. Mr Alston's No. 352 of 8 September 1913, Tibet: Memorandum from Jan 1 to Aug 30, 1913, BLA, IOR L/P&S/18/B 202.

12. Dorothy Woodman, *Himalayan Frontiers*, London: Barrie & Rockliff, The Cresset Press, 1969, p. 155.

13. Alastair Lamb, *The McMahon Line, Vol-II*, London: Routledge & Kegan Paul Ltd, 1966, p. 474.

14. Mr Alston's No. 352, 8 September 1913, Tibet: Memorandum from Jan 1 to Aug 30, 1913, p. 13, BLA, IOR L/P&S/18/B 202.

15. Dorothy Woodman, *Himalayan Frontiers*, p. 155.

16. Sir Charles Bell, *Tibet Past and Present*, Delhi: Low Price Publications, 1924, p. 158.

17. Ibid., pp. 157–58.

18. Claude Arpi, 'The Border is Fixed: The Simla Conference', *Indian Defence Review*, 17 Aug 2015.

19. Sir Charles Bell, *Tibet Past and Present*, pp. 157–58; *Final Memorandum of McMahon*, 1914, p. 13, BLA, IOR L/P&S/B 206.

13. The Conference Proceedings

1. Parshotam Mehra, *The North-Eastern Frontier, Vol. I, 1906-14*, New Delhi: Oxford University Press, 1979, p. 209.

2. Alston's Memorandum from Jan 1 to Aug 30, 1913, British Legation, Peking, p. 18, BLA, IOR L/P&S/18/B 202.

3. BLA, IOR L/P&S/10/432 dated 20 Apr 1914, p. 1751.

4. Neville Maxwell, *India's China War*, New Delhi: Natraj Publishers, 1970, p. 37.

5. Dorothy Woodman, *Himalayan Frontiers*, London: Barrie & Rockliff, The Cresset Press, 1969, p. 157.

6. Alastair Lamb, *The McMahon Line, Vol. II*, London: Routledge & Kegan Paul Ltd, 1966, p. 477.

7. BLA, IOR L/P&S/18/B 201, p. 4229.

8. Ibid., p. 4215.

9. Ibid.

10. McMahon's Memorandum of Progress of Negotiations from 06 October 1913–20 March 1914, p. 5014, BLA, IOR L/P&S/18/B 206.

11. BLA, IOR L/P&S/18/B 201, p. 4215.

12. Ibid.

13. Ibid.

14. Ibid.

15. Sir Charles Bell, *Tibet Past and Present*, Delhi: Low Price Publications, 1924, p. 152.

16. Ivan Chen to McMahon, 30 October 1913, p. 1, BLA, IOR L/P&S/18/B 206.

17. Ibid.

18. Ibid.

19. Ibid.

20. Ibid.

21. Ibid.

22. Ibid., p. 4473. Viceroy to Secy of State London, 30 October 1913.

23. Alastair Lamb, *The McMahon Line, Vol. II*, p. 480.

24. Proceeding of the 2nd Meeting of the Tibet Conference (18 November 1913), BLA, IOR L/P&S/18/B 206.

25. Ibid., p. 480.

26. BLA, IOR L/P&S/18/B 206, p. 4798.

27. Parshotam Mehra, *The McMahon Line and After*, Delhi: The Macmillan Company of India Ltd, 1975, p. 187.

28. Simla Conference, Proceeding of Informal Meetings, Dec 1913, BLA, IOR/P&S/10/343, p. 194.

29. Ibid., p. 195.

30. Ibid.

31. Ibid.

32. Ibid.

33. Ibid., p.196.

34. Ibid.

35. Ibid.

36. Ibid., p. 197.

37. Ibid., p. 196.

38. Ibid., p. 197.

39. Parshotam Mehra, *The McMahon Line and After*, p. 197.

40. Progress of Simla Convention Viceroy State Dept 18 Dec 1913, BLA, IOR L/P&S 18/ B 201, p. 5092.

41. Proceedings of the 3rd Meeting, BLA, IOR L/P&S/10/343, p. 481.

42. Ibid.

43. Ibid.

44. Ibid.

45. Ibid.

46. Ibid.

47. Parshotam Mehra, *The North-Eastern Frontier, Vol. I, 1906-14*, pp. 159–60.

48. Ibid.

49. Ibid., and Progress of Simla Convention, Viceroy to State Department, 18 December 1913, BLA, IOR L/P&S 18/ B 201.

50. BLA IOR LP&S/10/343, p. 14.

51. Parshotam Mehra, *The McMahon Line and After*, p. 195.

52. Foreign Office to India Office, London, BLA, IOR L/P&S/10/432.

53. Secretary of State to Viceroy, 6 January 1914, BLA, IOR L/P&S/10/343, p. 201.

54. Viceroy to Secretary of State, 17 February 1914, BLA, IOR LP&S/10/343, p. 621.

55. John Rowland, *A History of Sino- Indian Relations*, Dvan Nostrand Company Inc., 1967, p. 49.

56. Final Memorandum of McMahon, 1914, Enclosure 3, p. 9, BLA IOR L/P&S/18/B 202.

57. Ibid.

58. BLA, IOR L/P&S/18/B 202.

59. Alston's Memorandum, from Jan 1 to Aug 30, 1913, British Legation, Peking, 30 August 1913, BLA, IOR/L/P&S/18/B 202.

60. Parshotam Mehra, *The North-Eastern Frontier Vol. I, 1906-14*, p. 211.

61. Parshotam Mehra, *The McMahon Line and After*, p. 210.
62. Parshotam Mehra, *Essays in Frontier History*, New Delhi: Oxford University Press, 2007, p. 67.
63. Parshotam Mehra, *The North-Eastern Frontier Vol. I, 1906-14*, p. 171.
64. Final Memorandum of McMahon, 1914, p. 10.
65. Parshotam Mehra, *The McMahon Line and After*, p. 216.
66. Final Memorandum of McMahon, 1914, p. 10.
67. Parshotam Mehra, *The McMahon Line and After*, p. 216; BLA, IOR L/P&S/10/432-11584 of 16 March 1914.
68. Final Memorandum of McMahon, 1914, p. 10.
69. Ibid., p. 11.
70. Ibid.
71. Ibid.
72. Ibid., p. 12.
73. Ibid.
74. Dorothy Woodman, *Himalayan Frontiers*, p. 172.
75. Parshotam Mehra, *The North-Eastern Frontier Vol. I, 1906-14*, p. 159.
76. Ibid.
77. BLA, IOR L/P&S/10/343, p. 1021.
78. Alastair Lamb, *The McMahon Line*, Vol. II, p. 505.
79. Ibid., p. 509.
80. Ibid., p. 507.
81. Ibid., p. 509.
82. Parshotam Mehra, *The McMahon Line and After*, pp. 255–256.
83. Ibid., pp. 256–60.
84. Final Memorandum of McMahon, 1914, p. 10. Encl 4, p. 2.
85. Ibid.
86. Ibid., p. 3.
87. Proceedings of the 8th Meeting at Simla, 3 July 1914, p. 2, sourced from Peking 1940, 'The Boundary Question Between China and Tibet: A Valuable Record of the Tripartite Conference between China, Britain and Tibet held in India, 1913–14, pp. 145–50. Hereafter will be referred to as Procs of the 8th Meeting, 1914.
88. Ibid., p. 2.
89. Ibid., p. 3.

90. H.E. Richardson, *A Short History of Tibet*, p. 114.
91. Procs of the 8th Meeting, 1914, p. 3.
92. Ibid., p. 4.
93. BLA, IOR L/P&S/18/B 206, No. 90 of 1914.

14. Defining and Delineating the McMahon Line

1. T.H. Holditch, *Political Frontiers and Boundary Making*, London: Macmillan and Co. Ltd 1916, p. 174. An eminent geographer and authority on Frontier Surveys of the Indian subcontinent, he was the president of the Royal Geographic Society.
2. Parshotam Mehra, *The McMahon Line and After*, Delhi: The Macmillan Company of India Ltd., 1975, pp. 96–97; also Hardinge to Crewe, 21 September 1911, BLA, IOR, P&EF 1910/13.
3. Final Memorandum of McMahon, 1914, Enclosure 5, p. 6, BLA, IOR L/P&S/18/B 202.
4. Alston's Memorandum of 30 August 1913, BLA, IOR L/P&S/18/B 202.
5. Dorothy Woodman, *Himalayan Frontiers*, London: Barrie & Rockliff, The Cresset Press, 1969, p. 370.
6. Ibid., p. 376.
7. Ibid., p. 377.
8. Captain F.M. Bailey, *Report on an Exploration of the North East Frontier 1913*, Simla: Government of India, 1914, pp. 13, 14, 34.
9. McMahon Memorandum of 28 March 1914, BLA, IOR L/P&S/10/343, p. 1517.
10. Officials Report 1960, Part 2, p. 103; also Gondker Narayana Rao, *The India-China Border A Reappraisal*, Delhi: Motilal Banarsidass Publishers Pvt. Ltd, 1968, p. 62.
11. W. H. Wilkinson, British Consul General, Chengtu, 22 April 1912 to Lord Hardinge, 114.
12. Ibid.
13. BLA, IOR L/P&S/10/343, p. 6, and Final Memorandum of McMahon, 1914.

14. McMahon's Memorandum of 28 March 1914, BLA, IOR L/P&S/10/343, p.1517.

15. Dalai Lama's Temporal, Spiritual Rule Reinstated

1. Heather Spence, *British Policy and the 'Development' of Tibet 1912-1933*, Sydney: University of Wollongong, 1993, p. 234.
2. H.E. Richardson, *A Short History of Tibet*, New York: E.P. Dutton & Co. Inc., 1962, p. 117.
3. Ibid., p. 116.
4. Dorothy Woodman, *Himalayan Frontiers*, London: Barrie & Rockliff, The Cresset Press, 1969, pp. 185–87.
5. Ibid., p. 187.
6. Tsepon W.D. Shakabpa, *Tibet: A Political History*, New York: Potala Publications, 1984, p. 262.
7. Ibid.
8. Amar Kaur Jasbir Singh, *Himalayan Triangle*, London: The British Library, 1988, p. 28.
9. Parshotam Mehra, *The McMahon Line and After*, Delhi: The Macmillan Company of India Ltd, 1975, p. 331.

16. Tibet: A Political Chessboard; Panchen Lama; Death of Dalai Lama

1. Dorothy Woodman, *Himalayan Frontiers*, London: Barrie & Rockliff, The Cresset Press, 1969, p. 188.
2. Amar Kaur Jasbir Singh, *Himalayan Triangle*, London: The British Library, 1988, p. 28; also, Viceroy to Secretary of State, 29 August 1919, BLA, IOR L/P&S/10/715, p. 4657.
3. Dorothy Woodman, *Himalayan Frontiers*, p. 190.
4. Parshotam Mehra, *The McMahon Line and After*, Delhi: The Macmillan Company of India Ltd, 1975, p. 350.
5. Ibid., p. 348.
6. Dorothy Woodman, *Himalayan Frontiers*, p. 191.

7. Amar Kaur Jasbir Singh, *Himalayan Triangle*, p. 28.

8. Warren W. Smith Jr, *Tibetan Nation: A History of Tibetan Nationalism and Sino-Tibetan Relations*, Delhi: HarperCollins Publishers, 1996, p. 211.

9. Parshotam Mehra, *The McMahon Line and After*, p. 367.

10. H.E. Richardson, *A Short History of Tibet*, New York: E.P. Dutton & Co., 1962, p. 124.

11. Amar Kaur Jasbir Singh, *Himalayan Triangle*, p. 30.

12. Parshotam Mehra, *The McMahon Line and After*, p. 375.

13. Bell to Government of India, 19 January 1921, BLA, IOR L/P&S/10/971; also Heather Spence, *British Policy and The 'Development' of Tibet 1912-1933*, Sydney: University of Wollongong, 1993, p. 217.

14. Ibid., p. 221.

15. Tsepon W.D. Shakabpa, *Tibet: A Political History*, New York: Potala Publications, 1984, p. 249.

16. W.W. Rockhill, *The Dalai Lamas of Lhasa and their Relations with the Manchu Emperor of China, 1644–1908*, Leyden: Oriental Printing Office, 1910.

17. Warren W. Smith Jr, *Tibetan Nation: A History of Tibetan Nationalism and Sino-Tibetan Relations*, pp. 216–17.

18. Sir Charles Bell, *Portrait of the Dalai Lama*, London: Collins, 1946, p. 363.

19. Warren W. Smith Jr, *Tibetan Nation: A History of Tibetan Nationalism and Sino-Tibetan Relations*, pp. 216–17.

20. Melvyn C. Goldstein, *A History of Modern Tibet, 1913-1951*, Oakland: University of California Press, 1989, p. 63.

21. Warren W. Smith Jr, *Tibetan Nation: A History of Tibetan Nationalism and Sino-Tibetan Relations*, pp. 216–17.

22. Ludlow Diaries, entry on 28 October 1926, BLA, IOR: MSS D 979, also, Heather Spence, *British Policy and The 'Development' of Tibet 1912-1933*, p. 269.

23. Amar Kaur Jasbir Singh, *Himalayan Triangle*, p. 30.

24. Alexander Berzin, April 2003, http://studybuddhism.com/en/advanced studies/history-culture/shambhala/use-of-shambhala-in-russian-japanese-schemes-in-tibet, accessed on 12 August 2018.

25. Parshotam Mehra, *The McMahon Line and After*, p. 366.

26. Tsepon W.D. Shakabpa, *Tibet: A Political History*, p. 280.

27. Warren W. Smith Jr, *Tibetan Nation: A History of Tibetan Nationalism and Sino-Tibetan Relations*, 1996, p. 240.

28. Ibid., p.219.

29. Tsepon W.D. Shakabpa, *Tibet: A Political History*, p. 271.

30. Ibid.

31. Ibid., p. 274.

32. Sir Charles Bell, *Tibet: Past and Present*, Delhi: Low Price Publications, 1924, p. 270.

33. Tsepon W.D. Shakabpa, *Tibet: A Political History*, p. 270.

34. H.E. Richardson, *A Short History of Tibet*, p.132.

35. Sir Charles Bell, *Portrait of the Dalai Lama*, p. 380.

36. Ibid.

37. H.E. Richardson, *Short History of Tibet*, p. 139.

38. Tsepon W.D. Shakabpa, *Tibet: A Political History*, p. 275.

39. H.E. Richardson, *Short History of Tibet*, p. 140.

40. Sir Charles Bell, *Portrait of the Dalai Lama*, p. 380.

41. H.E. Richardson, *A Short History of Tibet*, p.142.

42. Ibid., p. 143.

43. Ibid., p. 145.

44. Dorothy Woodman, *Himalayan Frontiers*, p. 204.

45. Heather Spence, *British Policy and the 'Development' of Tibet 1912-1933*, p. iv.

46. Parshotam Mehra, *The McMahon Line and After*, p. 460.

17. Bonhomie, Appeasement, Imprudence, Deception

1. S. S. Khera, *India's Defence Problem*, New Delhi: Orient Longman Ltd, 1968, p. 152.

2. John W. Garver, *Protracted Contest: Sino-Indian Rivalry in the Twentieth Century*, Seattle and London: University of Washington Press, 2001, p. 14.

3. Amar Kaur Jasbir Singh, *Himalayan Triangle*, London: The British Library, 1988, p. 42.

4. Home Minister Vallabhbhai Patel's note to Prime Minister, New Delhi, 7 November 1950.

5. Ranjit Singh Kalha, *India-China Boundary Issues*, New Delhi: Pentagon Press, 2014, p. 48

6. P. B. Sinha and A.A. Athale, *History of The Conflict with China, 1962*, New Delhi: History Division Ministry of Defence, 1992, p. 48.

7. A. G. Noorani, *India-China Boundary Issues Problem 1846-1947*, New Delhi: Oxford University Press, 2011, p. 221.

8. Martin Jacques, *When China Rules the World*, Delhi: Penguin Group, 2009, p. 298.

9. Ibid., p. 299.

10. Nancy Jetly, *India-China Relations 1947-1977*, New Delhi: Radiant Publishers, 1979, p. 251.

11. Wing Commander (Retd) R. V. Parasnis, *Remembering a War, The 1962 India-China Conflict*, Bharat Rakshak, A Consortium of Indian Defence websites, 5 December 2002, p. 3.

12. Ibid.

13. Jagat S. Mehta, *The Tryst Betrayed*, New Delhi: Penguin Group, 2010, p. 308.

14. Lt Gen. B.M. Kaul, *Untold Story*, New Delhi: Allied Publishers, 1967, p. 280.

15. M.L. Sali, *India-China Border Dispute*, New Delhi: A.P.H. Publishing Corporation, 1998, p. 74.

16. John W. Garver, *Protracted Contest*, p. 50.

17. Amar Kaur Jasbir Singh, *Himalayan Triangle*, p. 41.

18. Dorothy Woodman, *Himalayan Frontiers*, London: Barrie & Rockliff, The Cresset Press, 1969, pp. 226–27.

19. D. R. Mankekar, *The Guilty Men of 1962*, Bombay: The Tulsi Shah Enterprises, 1968, p. 112.

20. Jagat S. Mehta, *The Tryst Betrayed*, p. 107.

21. Ranjit Singh Kalha, *India-China Boundary Issues*, p. 72.

22. D. R. Mankekar, *The Guilty Men of 1962*, p. 27.

23. B. N. Mullik, *The Chinese Betrayal*, New Delhi: Allied Publishers, 1971, pp. 196–99.

24. Ibid., p.206.

25. Ranjit Singh Kalha, *India-China Boundary Issues*, p. 167.

26. D. R. Mankekar, *The Guilty Men of 1962*, p. 138.

27. Ibid.

28. Ashok Karnik, 'Intelligence An Insider's View', http://freedomfirst. in/issue/articles.aspx?id=8453, p. 3.

29. Verrier Elwin, *A Philosophy for NEFA*, Itanagar: Government of Arunachal Pradesh, 2006, p. 3.

30. Jagat S. Mehta, *The Tryst Betrayed*, p. 292.

18. Disputed Areas in the Ladakh and Central Sectors

1. A.G. Noorani, *India-China Boundary Problem 1846-1947*, New Delhi: Oxford University Press, 2011, pp. 113–16.

2. Xuecheng Liu, 'The Sino Indian Border Dispute and Sino-Indian Relations', Lanham, Maryland: University Press of America, 1994, p. 70, The author has stated that in 1938 British and Chinese representatives discussed the border question and it was brought out by the Chinese representative General Jiang that 'the Chinese did not agree to negotiate the 1899 border proposal, mainly because they did not want to accept the British annexation of Hunza, not because they disagreed with the proposed boundary alignment.' The fact however remains that the Chinese did not accept the 1899 boundary proposal and the offer was not on the table thereafter.

3. Ibid.

4. H. N. Kaul, *India-China Boundary in Kashmir*, New Delhi: Gyan Publishing House, 2003, pp. 17–19.

5. Peace Treaty between the Ruler of Jammu, The Emperor of China and the Lama Guru of Lhasa, 1842. (Appendix 1)

6. A.G. Noorani, *India-China Boundary Problem 1846-1947*, p. 23.

7. Ibid., p. 24.

8. Xuecheng Liu, *The Sino-Indian Border Dispute and Sino-Indian Relations*, p. 67.

9. P.C. Chakravarti, *The Evolution of India's Northern Borders*, Bombay: Asia Publishing House, 1969, p. 151.

10. Xuecheng Liu, *The Sino-Indian Border Dispute and Sino-Indian Relations*, pp. 6–7.
11. Gondker Narayan Rao, *The Indo-China Border: A Reappraisal*, Delhi: Motilal Banarsidass Publishers Pvt. Ltd, 1968, pp. 14–32.
12. Prime Minister Jawaharlal Nehru addressing Parliament on 12 September 1959.
13. P.C. Chakravarti, *The Evolution of India's Northern Borders*, p. 94.
14. Ibid., p.96.
15. Ibid.

19. Hurtling Towards the Border War

1. George Ginsburg and Michiel Mathos, *Communist China and Tibet: The First Dozen Years*, Leiden: Martinus Nijhoff, 1964, p. 210.
2. Henry Kissinger, *On China*, Delhi: Penguin Books, 2011, p. 25.
3. B. N. Mullik, *The Chinese Betrayal*, New Delhi: Allied Publishers, 1971, p. 148.
4. D. R. Mankekar, *The Guilty Men of 1962*, Bombay: The Tulsi Shah Enterprises, 1968, p. 138.
5. Jagat S. Mehta, *The Tryst Betrayed*, New Delhi: The Penguin Group, 2010, p. 115.
6. D. R. Mankekar, *The Guilty Men of 1962*, pp. 17–18.
7. Government of India, White Paper I (1954-1959), p. 77.
8. Ibid., p. 77–8.
9. Ranjit Singh Kalha, *India-China Boundary Issues*, New Delhi: Pentagon Press, 2014, p. 129.
10. Lorenz Luthi, *Sino-Soviet Split*, Princeton, New Jersey: Princeton University Press, 2008, pp. 158–60.
11. Henry Kissinger, *On China*, p. 181.
12. Neville Maxwell, *India's China War*, New Delhi: Natraj Publishers, 1970, p. 164; John W. Garver, *Protracted Contest: Sino-Indian Rivalry in the Twentieth Century*, Seattle and London: University of Washington Press, 2001, p. 102.

13. Dorothy Woodman, *Himalayan Frontiers*, London: Barrie & Rockliff, The Cresset Press, 1969, p. 305; see also *People's Daily*, Peking, 1 February, 1960.

14. Jagat S. Mehta, *Negotiating for India*, New Delhi: Manohar Publishers & Distributors, 2006, p.78.

15. Nevill Maxwell, *India's China War*, p. 164; and *The Hindu*, 26 April 1960.

16. John W. Garver, *Protracted Contest Sino-Indian Rivalry in the Twentieth Century*, p. 100.

17. Ranjit Singh Kalha, *India-China Boundary Issues*, pp. 132–3.

18. Henry Kissinger, *On China*, p. 187.

19. Natwar Singh, *Daily Mail*, London, 19 March 2014.

20. Jagat S. Mehta, *Negotiating for India*, New Delhi: Manohar Publishers & Distributors, 2006, p. 83.

21. Ibid., p. 84.

22. Ibid., p. 25.

23. Ranjit Singh Kalha, *India-China Boundary Issues*, pp. 134–35.

24. D. R. Mankekar, *The Guilty Men of 1962*, p. 32.

25. Ranjit Singh Kalha, *India-China Boundary Issues*, p. 114.

26. Jagat S. Mehta, *The Tryst Betrayed*, p. 117.

27. Ranjit Singh Kalha, *India-China Boundary Issues*, p.121.

28. Jagat S. Mehta, *The Tryst Betrayed*, p. 138.

29. Maj. Gen. D. K. Palit, VrC, *War in High Himalaya*, London: Lancer International C. Hurst & Co Publishers Ltd, 1991, p. 103.

30. Ibid., p. 104.

31. Ibid., p. 103.

32. Neville Maxwell, *India's China War*, p. 255.

33. Maj. Gen. D. K. Palit, VrC, *War in High Himalaya*, p. 104.

34. The Times, London, 23 September 1962; and later confirmed to the press by Prime Minister Jawaharlal Nehru before leaving for Colombo on 13 October 1962; see also D. R. Mankekar, *The Guilty Men of 1962*, p. 50.

35. Lt Gen. B.M. Kaul, *Untold Story*, New Delhi: Allied Publishers, 1967, p. 365.

36. Brig. J. P. Dalvi, *Himalayan Blunder*, Dehra Dun: Nataraj Publishers, 1969, pp. 292–93.

37. Ranjit Singh Kalha, *India-China Boundary Issues*, p. 162.

38. Jagat S. Mehta, *The Tryst Betrayed*, p.119.

39. Jagat S. Mehta, *Negotiating for India*, p.79.

40. *The Asian Age*, 20 October 2012.

41. Henry Kissinger, *On China*, Delhi: Penguin Books, 2011, pp. 189.

42. Sun Xiao and Chen Zhibin, *The Snows of the Himalayas: The True History of the China–India War, April 1991*, p. 9. (This is a Chinese account of the 1962 war.)

43. Brig. J. P. Dalvi, *Himalayan Blunder*, p. 356.

44. Jagat S. Mehta, *The Tryst Betrayed*, p. 262.

20. Understanding the Middle Kingdom and the Dragon

1. Henry Kissinger, *On China*, Delhi: Penguin Books, 2011, p. 188.

2. Cooperation without trust: India-China relations today by Abhilash Roy Nalpathamkalam, http://in.boell.org/sites/default/files/downloads/India-China_Relations_-_Abhilash_10.10.pdf.

3. Jagat S. Mehta, *Negotiating for India*, New Delhi: Manohar Publishers & Distributors, 2006, p. 117.

4. Ibid., p. 118.

5. John W. Garver, *Protracted Contest: Sino-Indian Rivalry in the Twentieth Century*, Seattle and London: University of Washington Press, 2001, p. 37.

6. Rebecca Cairns, 'Agrarian Reform', *Alpha History*, available at 18 July 2015, at: http://alphahistory.com/chineserevolution/agrarian-reform/#sthash.zNlEswxG. dpuf (accessed on 18 July 2015).

7. K. Natwar Singh, *My China Diary*, New Delhi: Rupa and Co., 2009, pp. 98–9.

8. D. R. Mankekar, *The Guilty Men of 1962*, Bombay: The Tulsi Shah Enterprises, 1968, p. 16.

9. Neville Maxwell, *India's China War*, New Delhi: Natraj Publishers, 1970, p. 93.

10. Sir Charles Bell, *Portrait of The Dalai Lama*, London: Collins, 1946, p. 99.

11. Jagat S. Mehta, *Negotiating for India*, p. 55.

12. K. Subrahmanyam, 'Strategy and Mind Games', in *India China Neighbours Strangers*, New Delhi: India International Centre Quarterly, Vol. 36, No 3/4, pp. 104–15.

13. John W. Garver, *Protracted Contest Sino-Indian Rivalry in the Twentieth Century*, p. 118.

14. Ibid., p. 119.

15. Ibid.

16. Jagat S. Mehta, *Negotiating for India*, p. 79.

17. John W. Garver, *Protracted Contest: Sino-Indian Rivalry in the Twentieth Century*, p. 121.

18. Amar Kaur Jasbir Singh, *Himalayan Triangle*, London: The British Library, 1988, p. 41.

19. D. R. Mankekar, *The Guilty Men of 1962*, p. 27.

20. Bertil Lintner, 'Not a Border DISPUTE', *India Today*, 22 January 2018.

21. Henry Kissinger, *On China*, p. 170.

22. Claude Arpi, 'China Becomes Red', Part 2, http://www.friendsoftibet. org/ articles/ claude2.html (accessed on 26 Jun 2015).

23. Ibid.

24. Henry Kissinger, *On China*, Penguin Books, Delhi, 2011, p. 191.

25. Teresita C. Shaffer and Howard B. Schaffer, New Delhi: *India at the Global High Table*, HarperCollins Publishers, 2016, p. 267.

26. Henry Kissinger, *On China*, p. 26.

27. Zheng Bijian, 'China's Peaceful Rise to Great-Power Status', *Foreign Affairs*, 84, 2005, p. 18.

28. Quoted portions have been extracted from the full text of Xi Jinping's speech contained in chinadaily.com.en. See also Ananth Krishnan's articles in *India Today* of 23 October and 6 November 2017 titled 'The Xi Supremacy' and 'One Man's Army'.

29. Francois Bougon, *Inside the Mind of Xi Jinping*, Chennai: Context, Westland Publications Private Limited, 2018, p. 4.

30. Luo Zhaohui, 'A Chinese View of the New Global Order', *The Tribune*, 16 Nov 2017.

21. India–China Boundary Negotiations

1. Excerpts from statements of Prime Minister Narendra Modi and President Xi Jinping during the Wuhan Summit in April 2018.
2. L. Oppenheim, *International Law: A Treatise, Vol. I - Peace,* London: Longmans, Green and Co., 1905, p. 534.
3. Memorandum signed by A.H. McMahon on 28 March 1914 that accompanied the notes exchanged between the British and Tibetan plenipotentiaries dated 24 and 25 March 1914 respectively.
4. The Eastern Sentinel, Guwahati, 21 October 2012.
5. Lord Curzon, *Frontiers, The Romanes Lecture 1907*, Oxford: Clarendon Press, 1907, p. 49.
6. Simla Conference, Proceedings of the Third Meeting in Delhi on 12 January 1914, BLA, IOR L/P&S/10/343, Enclosure 2, p. 123.
7. Ibid.
8. Ibid., p. 197.
9. P.B. Sinha and A.A. Athale, *History of The Conflict with China, 1962,* New Delhi: History Division, Government of India, Ministry of Defence, 1992, p. 29.
10. Ranjit Singh Kalha, *India-China Boundary Issues*, New Delhi: Pentagon Press, 2014, p. 107.
11. Eric Hayer, *The Pragmatic Dragon: China's Grand Strategy and Boundary Settlements*, Vancouver: UBC Press, 2015, p. 32.
12. Henry Kissinger, *On China*, Delhi: Penguin Books, pp. 217–20.
13. Ibid.
14. Wenwen Shen, 'China and its Neighbours: Troubled Relations', http://www.eu.asiacentre.eu/pub_details.php?pub_id=46(accessed on 01 March 2012).
15. MEA, GOI, Prime Minister's visit to China, http://www.chinadaily.com.cn /china/2015modivisitchina/2015-05/15/content_20729162.Htm (accessed on 30 Jan 2016).
16. Pravin Sawhney and Ghazala Wahab, 'When Narasimha Rao Visited China', *The Pioneer*, 12 February 2017.
17. Ranjit Singh Kalha, *India-China Boundary Issues*, p. 215.

18. Zhang Yan, *India-China Relations: Future Perspectives*, New Delhi: Vij Books India Pvt Ltd, 2012, p. 8.

19. Vidya Nadkarni, *Strategic Partnerships in Asia*, London and New York: Routledge Taylor & Francis Group, 2010, p. 119.

20. Xinhua News Agency, Beijing, 12 April 2005.

21. D.P. Tripathi and B.R. Deepak, *India-China Relations: Future Perspectives*, New Delhi: Vij Books India Pvt. Ltd, 2012, p. 244.

22. Ibid., p. 249.

23. Xinhua News Agency, 27 March 2013.

24. Ranjit Singh Kalha, *PM Modi's Visit to China: The Myths and Realities*, Institute of Defence Studies and Analyses (IDSA), New Delhi, 25 May 2015.

22. The Way Forward

1. Ananth Krishnan, 'Behind the War, a Genesis in Tibet', *The Hindu*, 20 October 2012.

2. Ranjit Singh Kalha, 'The Politics of Reincarnation', https://thewire.in/124075/dalai-lama-china-india-tibet/ (accessed on 14 April 2017).

3. Jeff M. Smith, *Cold Peace: China-India Rivalry in the Twenty-First Century*, New York: Lexington Books, 2013, pp. 61–62.

4. Officials Report on the Boundary Question, Part 2, p. 131 (Comments on the Eastern Sector under Item 2)

5. K. Natwar Singh, *My China Diary*, New Delhi: Rupa Publications, 2009, p. 130.

6. Binod Singh, *India China Relations: Future Perspectives,* New Delhi: Vij Books India Pvt. Ltd, 2012, pp. 197–202.

7. Sanjay Bhattacharya, *Indian Foreign Policy: Challenges and Opportunities*, New Delhi: Academic Foundation, 2007, p. 697.

8. Ibid., pp. 699–700.

9. S. Kulkarni, *India China Relations: Future Perspectives*, New Delhi: Vij Books India Pvt. Ltd, 2012, p. 40.

10. John W. Garver, *Protracted Contest: Sino-Indian Rivalry in the Twentieth Century*, Seattle and London: University of Washington Press, 2001, p. 377.

11. Ranjit Singh Kalha, *India-China Boundary Issues*, New Delhi: Pentagon Press, 2014, p. 228.

12. Zheng Bijian, 'China's Peaceful Rise to Great-Power Status', *Foreign Affairs*, Vol. 18, 2005, p. 84.

13. Interaction between Indrani Bagchi and Sergei Karaganov, *The Times of India*, 28 February 2018.

14. General J.J. Singh, *A Soldier's General*, New Delhi: HarperCollins Publishers, 2012 p. 250. The author led a tri-service delegation to China as the Chairman of the Chiefs of Staff Committee and army chief.

15. Francois Bougon, *Inside the Mind of Xi Jinping*, Chennai: Context, Westland Publications Private Limited, 2018, pp. 176-78.

16. Ibid, p.178.

Appendix 1

Excerpts of the Peace Treaty between the Ruler of Jammu, the
Emperor of China and the Lama Guru of Lhasa (1842).

As on this auspicious day, the 2nd of Assuj, Sambhat 1899 [16th
or 17th September AD 1842], we, the officers of the Lhasa
(Government), Kalon of Sokan and Bakshi Shajpuh, Commander of the
Forces, and two officers on behalf of the most resplendent Sri Khalsaji
Sahib, the asylum of the world, King Sher Singhji and Sri Maharaj Sahib
Raja-i-Rajagan Raja Sahib Bahadur Raja Gulab Singhji i.e., the Mukhtar-
ud-Daula Diwan Hari Chand and the asylum of vizirs, Vizir Ratnun,
in a meeting called together for the promotion of peace and unity, and
by profession and vows of friendship, unity and sincerity of heart and
by taking oaths like those of Kunjak Sahib, have arranged and agreed
that relations of peace, friendship and unity between Sri Khalsaji and
Sri Maharaj Sahib Bahadur Raja Gulab Singhji and the Emperor of
China and the Lama Guru of Lhasa will henceforward remain firmly
established for ever; and we declare in the presence of the Kunjak Sahib
that on no account whatsoever will there be any deviation, difference
or departure (from this agreement). We shall neither at present nor in
future have anything to do or interfere at all with the boundaries of
Ladakh and its surrounding as fixed from ancient times and will allow
the annual export of wool, shawls and tea by way of Ladakh according
to old established custom.

Should any of the opponents of Sri Khalsaji and Sri Raja Sahib Bahadur at any time enter our territories, we shall not pay any heed to his words or allow him to remain in our country.

We shall offer no hindrance to traders of Ladakh who visit our territories. We shall not, even to the extent of a hair's breadth, act in contravention of the terms that we have agreed to above regarding firm friendship, unity, the fixed boundaries of Ladakh and the keeping open of the route for wool, shawls and tea. We call Kunjak Sahib, Kairi, Lassi, Zhoh Mahan, and Khushal Choh as witnesses to this treaty.

This Treaty was signed in September, A.D. 1842. The Parties to the Treaty were on the one hand, Shri Khalsaji and Shri Maharaj Sahib Bahadur Raja Gulab Singh, and on the other hand the Emperor of China and the Lama Guru of Lhasa. By this Treaty the traditional boundary between Ladakh and Tibet was reaffirmed.

APPENDIX 2

Excerpts of the Anglo–Tibetan Treaty of 1904.
(7 September 1904)

WHEREAS doubts and difficulties have arisen as to the meaning and validity of the Anglo-Chinese Convention of 1890, and the Trade Regulations of 1893, and as to the liabilities of the Thibetan Government under these Agreements; and whereas recent occurrences have tended towards a disturbance of the relations of friendship and good understanding which have existed between the British Government and the Government of Thibet; and whereas it is desirable to restore peace and amicable relations, and to resolve and determine the doubts and difficulties as aforesaid, the said Governments have resolved to conclude a Convention with these objects, and the following Articles have been agreed upon by Colonel F.E. Younghusband, C.I.E., in virtue of full powers vested in him by his Britannic Majesty's Government, and on behalf of that said Government, and Lo-Sang Gyal-Tsen, the Ga-den Ti-Rimpoche, and the representatives of the Council, of the three monasteries Se-ra, Dre-pung, and Ga-den, and of the ecclesiastical and lay officials of the National Assembly on behalf of the Government of Thibet:-

1. The Government of Thibet engages to respect the Anglo-Chinese Convention of 1890, and to recognize the frontier between Sikkim

and Thibet, as defined in Article I of the said Convention, and to erect boundary pillars accordingly.

2. The Thibetan Government undertakes to open forthwith trade marts to which all British and Thibetan subjects shall have free right of access at Gyangtse and Gartok, as well as at Yatung.

The Regulations applicable to the trade mart at Yatung, under the Anglo-Chinese agreement of 1893, shall subject to such amendments as may hereafter be agreed upon ....

In addition to establishing trade marts at the places mentioned, the Thibetan Government undertakes to place no restrictions on the trade by existing routes, and to consider the question of establishing fresh trade marts under similar conditions if development of trade requires it.

3. The question of the amendment of the regulations of 1893 is reserved for separate consideration, ...

4. The Thibetan Government undertakes to levy no dues of any kind other than those provided for in the tariff to be mutually agreed upon.

5. The Thibetan Government undertakes to keep the roads to Gyangtse and Gartok from the frontier clear of all obstruction and in a state of repair suited to the needs of the trade marts that may hereafter be established, a Thibetan Agent who shall receive from the British Agent appointed to watch over British trade at the marts in question any letter which the latter may desire to send to the Thibetan or to the Chinese authorities. The Thibetan Agent shall also be responsible for the due delivery of such communications and for the transmission of replies.

6. As an indemnity to the British Government for the expense incurred in the dispatch of armed troops to Lhasa, to exact reparation for breaches of Treaty obligations, and for the insults offered to and attacks upon the British Commissioners and his following and escort, the Thibetan Government engages to pay a sum of £ 500,000/- equivalent to 75 lakhs of rupees - to the British Government.

The indemnity shall be payable at such place as the British Government may from time to time, after due notice, indicate, whether in Thibet or in the British districts of Darjeeling or Jalpaiguri, in seventy-five annual installments of one lakh of rupees each on the 1st January in each year, beginning fron the 1st January, 1906.

7. As security for the payment of the above mentioned indemnity, and for the fulfillment of the provision relative to trade marts specified in Articles II, III, IV and V, the British Government shall continue to occupy the Chumbi Valley until the indemnity has been paid, and until the trade marts have been effectively opened for three years, whichever date may be the later.

8. ....

9. The Government of Thibet engages that, without the previous consent of the British Government –

(a) No portion of Thibetan territory shall be ceded, sold, leased, mortgaged or otherwise given for occupation, to any Foreign Power;

(b) No such Power shall be permitted to intervene in Thibetan affairs;

(c) No Representatives or Agents of any Foreign Power shall be admitted to Thibet;

(d) No concessions for railways, roads, telegraphs, mining or other rights, shall be granted to any foreign power, or the subject of any foreign power. In the event of consent to such concessions being granted, similar or equivalent concessions shall be granted to the British Government;

(e) No Thibetan revenues, whether in kind or in cash, shall be pledged or assigned to any foreign power, or to the subject of any foreign power.

10. In witness whereof the negotiators have signed the Thibetan date, the 27th of the seventh month of the Wood Dragon year.

(Thibet Frontier Commission)	F.E. Younghusband, Colonel,	(Seal of the Dalai Lama affixed by
(Seal of British Commissioner)	British Commissioner.	the Ga-den Ti-Rimpoche.)
(Seal of Council.)	(Seal of Dre-pung Monastery.)	(Seal of Sera Monastery.) (Seal of National Assembly).
(Seal of Gaden Monastery)		

The Viceroy and Governor - General of India ratified the Convention on 11 November 1904, subject to reduction of indemnity to Rs 25,00,000 and a declaration that British occupation of the Chumbi valley would cease after payment of three annual installments, provided that the Tibetans Comply with the other terms of the Convention.

Appendix 3

Excerpts of the Convention between Great Britain and Russia
relating to Persia, Afghanistan and Tibet (31 August 1907).

His Majesty the King of the United Kingdom of Great Britain and
Ireland and of the British Dominious beyond the Seas, Emperor
of India, and His Majesty the Emperor of All the Russias, animated
by the sincere desire to settle by mutual agreement different questions
concerning the interests of their states on the Continent of Asia, have
determined to conclude Agreements destined to prevent all cause of
misunderstanding between Great Britain and Russia in regard to the
questions referred to, and have nominated for this purpose their respective
Plenipotentiaries to wit:

His Majesty the King of the United Kingdom of Great Britain and
Ireland and of the British Dominions beyond the Seas, Emperor of India,
the Right Honourable Sir Arthur Nicolson, His Majesty's Ambassador
Extraordinary and plenipotentiary to His Majesty the Emperor of all the
Russias;

His Majesty the Emperor of all the Russias, the Master of his Court
Alexander Isworsky, Minister for Foreign Affairs;

Who, having communicated to each other their full powers, found in
good and due form, have agreed on the following :-

405

Arrangement concerning Thibet

The Governments of Great Britain and Russia recognizing the suzerain rights of China in Thibet, and considering the fact Great Britain, by reason of her geographical position, has a special interest in the maintenance of the status quo in the external relations of Thibet, have made the following arrangement :-

ARTICLE I

The two High Contacting Parties engage to respect the territorial integrity of Thibet and to abstain from all interference in the internal administration.

ARTICLE II

In conformity with the admitted principle of the suzerainty of China over Thibet, Great Britain and Russia engage not to enter into negotiations with Thibet except through the intermediary of the Chinese Government............

It is dearly understood that Buddhists, subjects of Great Britain or of Russia, may enter into direct relations on strictly religious matters with the Dalai Lama and the other representatives of Buddhism in Thibet;...........

ARTICLE III

The British and Russian Governments respectively engage not to send Representatives to Lhassa.

ARTICLE IV

The two High Contracting Parties engage neither to seek nor to obtain, whether for themselves or their subjects, any Concessions for railways, roads, telegraphs, and mines, or other rights in Thibet.

ARTICLE V

The two Governments agree that no part of the revenues of Thibet, whether in kind or in cash, shall be pledged or assigned to Great Britain or Russia or to any of their subjects.

Annex to the Arrangement Between Great Britain and Russia Concerning Thibet...........

The present Convention shall be ratified, and the ratifications exchanged at St. Petersburgh as soon as possible.

In witness whereof the respective Plenipotentiaries have signed the present Convention and affixed thereto their seals.

Done in duplicate at St. Petersburgh, the 18th (31st) of August, 1907.

APPENDIX 4

Excerpts of the Convention Between Great Britain,
China and Tibet, Simla (1913-14).

His Majesty the King of the United Kingdom of Great Britain and Ireland and of the British Dominions beyond the Seas, Emperor of India, His Excellency the President of the Republic of China, and His Holiness the Dalai Lama of Tibet, being sincerely desirous to settle by mutual agreement various questions concerning the interests of their several States on the Continent of Asia, and further to regulate the relations of their several Governments, have resolved to conclude a Convention on this subject and have nominated for this purpose their respective Plenipotentiaries, that is to say:

His Majesty the King of the United Kingdom of Great Britain and Ireland and of the British Dominions beyond the Seas, Emperor of India, Sir Arthur Henry McMahon, Knight Grand Cross of the Royal Victorian Order, Knight Commander of the Most Eminent Order of the Indian Empire, Companion of the Most Exalted Order of the Star of India, Secretary to the Government of India, Foreign and Political Department;

His Excellency the President of the Republic of China, Monsieur Ivan Chen, Officer of the Order of the Chia Ho;

His Holiness the Dalai Lama of Tibet, Lonchen Ga-den Shatra Paljor Dorje; who having communicated to each other their respective full powers and finding them to be in good and due form have agreed upon and concluded the following Convention in eleven Articles :-

ARTICLE 1

The Conventions specified in the Schedule to the present Convention shall, except in so far as they may have been modified by, or may be inconsistent with or repugnant to, any of the provisions of the present Convention, continue to be binding upon the High Contracting Parties.

ARTICLE 2

The Governments of Great Britain and China recognizing that Tibet is under the suzerainty of China, and recognizing also the autonomy of Outer Tibet, engage to respect the territorial integrity of the country, and to abstain from interference in the administration of Outer Tibet (including the selection and installation of the Dalai Lama), which shall remain in the hands of the Tibetan Government at Lhasa.

The Government of China engages not to convert Tibet into a Chinese province. The Government of Great Britain engages not to annex Tibet or any portion of it.

ARTICLE 3

Recognizing the special interest of Great Britain, in virtue of the geographical position of Tibet, in the existence of an effective Tibetan Government, and in the maintenance of peace and order in the neighbourhood of the frontiers of India and adjoining States, the Government of China engages, except as provided in Article 4 of this Convention, not to send troops into Outer Tibet, nor to station civil or military officers, nor to establish Chinese colonies in the country. Should any such troops or officials remain in Outer Tibet at the date of the signature of this Convention, they shall be withdrawn within a period not exceeding three months.

The Government of Great Britain engages not to station military or civil officers in Tibet (except as provided in the Convention of September 7, 1904, between Great Britain and Tibet) nor troops (except the Agents' escorts), nor to establish colonies in that country.

ARTICLE 4

The foregoing Article shall not be held to preclude the continuance of the arrangement by which, in the past, a Chinese high-official with suitable escort has been maintained at Lhasa, but it is hereby provided that the said escort shall in no circumstances exceed 300 men.

ARTICLE 5

The Governments of China and Tibet engage that they will not enter into any negotiations or agreements regarding Tibet with one another, or with any other Power, excepting such negotiations and agreements between Great Britain and Tibet as are provided for by the Convention of September 7, 1904, between Great Britain and Tibet and the Convention of April 27, 1906, between Great Britain and China.

ARTICLE 6

Article III of the Convention of April 27, 1906, between Great Britain and China is hereby cancelled, and it is understood that in Article IX(d) of the Convention of September 7, 1904, between Great Britain and Tibet the term 'Foreign Power' does not include China.

Not less favourable treatment shall be accorded to British commerce than to the commerce of China or the most favoured nation.

ARTICLE 7

(a)   The Tibet Trade Regulations of 1893 and 1908 are hereby cancelled.

(b)   The Tibetan Government engages to negotiate with the British Government new Trade Regulations for Outer Tibet to give effect to Articles II, IV and V of the Convention of September 7, 1904, between Great Britain and Tibet without delay; provided always that such Regulations shall in no way modify the present Convention except with the consent of the Chinese Government.

ARTICLE 8

The British Agent who resides at Gyantse may visit Lhasa with his escort whenever it is necessary to consult with the Tibetan Government regarding matters arising out of the Convention of September 7, 1904, between Great Britain and Tibet, which it has been found impossible to settle at Gyantse by correspondence or otherwise.

ARTICLE 9

For the purpose of the present Convention the borders of Tibet, and the boundary between Outer and Inner Tibet, shall be as shown in red and blue respectively on the map attached hereto.

Nothing in the present Convention shall be held to prejudice the existing rights of the Tibetan Government in Inner Tibet, which include the power to select and appoint the high priests of monasteries and to retain full control in all matters affecting religious institutions.

ARTICLE 10

....

ARTICLE 11

The present Convention will take effect from the date of signature.

In token whereof the respective Plenipotentiaries have signed and sealed this Convention, three copies in English, three in Chinese and three in Tibetan.

Done at Simla this third day of July, A.D., one thousand nine hundred and fourteen, corresponding with the Chinese date, the third day of the seventh month of the third year of the Republic, and the Tibetan date, the tenth day of the fifth month of the Wood-Tiger year.

Initial of the Lonchen Shatra   Initial of A.H. McMahon
Seal of the Lonchen Shatra   Seal of the British Plenipotentiary

Schedule

(1) Convention between Great Britain and China relating to Sikkim and Tibet, signed at Calcutta the 17th March 1890.

(2) Convention between Great Britain and Tibet, signed at Lhasa the 7th September 1904.

(3) Convention between Great Britain and China respecting Tibet, signed at Peking the 27th April 1906.

The notes exchanged are to the following effect:

(1) It is understood by the High Contracting Parties that Tibet forms part of Chinese territory.

(2) After the selection and installation of the Dalai Lama by the Tibetan Government, the latter will notify the installation to the Chinese Government whose representative at Lhasa will then formally communicate to His Holiness the titles consistent with his dignity, which have been conferred by the Chinese Government.

(3) It is also understood that the selection and appointment of all officers in Outer Tibet will rest with the Tibetan Government.

(4) Outer Tibet shall not be represented in the Chinese Parliament or in any other similar body.

(5) It is understood that the escorts attached to the British Trade Agencies in Tibet shall not exceed seventy-five per centum of the escort of the Chinese Representative at Lhasa.

(6) The Government of China is hereby released from its engagements under Article III of the Convention of March 17, 1890, between Great Britain and China to prevent acts of aggression from the Tibetan side of the Tibet-Sikkim frontier.

(7) The Chinese high official referred to in Article 4 will be free to enter Tibet as soon as the terms of Article 3 have been fulfilled to the satisfaction of representatives of the three signatories to this Convention, who will investigate and report without delay.

Initial of the Lonchen Shatra   Initial of A.H. McMahon
Seal of the Lonchen Shatra   Seal of the British Plenipotentiary

APPENDIX 5

Agreement on the Maintenance of Peace and Tranquility along the
Line of Actual Control in the India-China Border Areas.
(7 September 1993)

The Government of the Republic of India and the Government of
the People's Republic of China (hereinafter referred to as the two
sides), have entered into the present Agreement in accordance with the
Five Principles of mutual respect for sovereignty and territorial integrity,
mutual non-aggression, non-interference in each other's internal affairs,
equality and mutual benefit and peaceful coexistence and with a view to
maintaining peace and tranquility in areas along the line of actual control
in the India-China border areas.

ARTICLE 1

The two sides are of the view that the India-China boundary question shall
be resolved through peaceful and friendly consultations. Neither side shall
use or threaten to use force against the other by any means. Pending an
ultimate solution to the boundary question between the two countries,
the two sides shall strictly respect and observe the line of actual control
between the two sides. No activities of either side shall overstep the line
of actual control. In case personnel of one side cross the line of actual
control, upon being cautioned by the other side, they shall immediately
pull back to their own side of the line of actual control. When necessary,

the two sides shall jointly check and determine the segments of the line of actual control where they have different views as to its alignment.

ARTICLE 2

Each side will keep its military forces in the areas along the line of actual control to a minimum level compatible with the friendly and good neighbourly relations between the two countries. The two sides agree to reduce their military forces along the line of actual control in conformity with the requirements of the principle of mutual and equal security to ceilings to be mutually agreed. The extent, depth, timing, and nature of reduction of military forces along the line of actual control shall be determined through mutual consultations between the two countries. The reduction of military forces shall be carried out by stages in mutually agreed geographical locations sector-wise within the areas along the line of actual control.

ARTICLE 3

Both sides shall work out through consultations effective confidence building measures in the areas along the line of actual control. Neither side will undertake specified levels of military exercises in mutually identified zones. Each side shall give the other prior notification of military exercises of specified levels near the line of actual control permitted under this Agreement.

ARTICLE 4

In case of contingencies or other problems arising in the areas along the line of actual control, the two sides shall deal with them through meetings and friendly consultations between border personnel of the two countries. The form of such meetings and channels of communications between the border personnel shall be mutually agreed upon by the two sides.

ARTICLE 5

The two sides agree to take adequate measures to ensure that air intrusions across the line of actual control do not take place and shall undertake mutual consultations should intrusions occur. Both sides shall also consult on possible restrictions on air exercises in areas to be mutually agreed near the line of actual control.

ARTICLE 6

The two sides agree that references to the line of actual control in this Agreement do not prejudice their respective positions on the boundary question.

ARTICLE 7

The two sides shall agree through consultations on the form, method, scale and content of effective verification measures and supervision required for the reduction of military forces and the maintenance of peace and tranquility in the areas along the line of actual control under this Agreement.

ARTICLE 8

Each side of the India-China Joint Working Group on the boundary question shall appoint diplomatic and military experts to formulate, through mutual consultations, implementation measures for the present Agreement. The experts shall advise the Joint Working Group on the resolution of differences between the two sides on the alignment of the line of actual control and address issues relating to redeployment with a view to reduction of military forces in the areas along the line of actual control. The experts shall also assist the Joint Working Group in supervision of the implementation of the Agreement, and settlement of differences that may arise in that process, based on the principle of good faith and mutual confidence.

ARTICLE 9

The present Agreement shall come into effect as of the date of signature and is subject to amendment and addition by agreement of the two sides.

Signed in duplicate at Beijing on the Seventh day of September 1993 in the Hindi, Chinese and English languages, all three texts having equal validity.

[Signed:]

R. L. Bhatia Minister of State for External Affairs Republic of India Tang Jiaxuan Vice-Foreign Minister People's Republic of China.

APPENDIX 6

Agreement between the Government of the Republic of India and the Government of the People's Republic of China on Confidence Building Measures in the Military Field along the Line of Actual Control in the India-China Border Areas.

The Government of the November 29, 1996 Republic of India and the Government of the People's Republic of China (hereinafter referred to as the two sides),Believing that it serves the fundamental interests of the peoples of India and China to foster a long-term good-neighbourly relationship in accordance with the five principles of mutual respect for sovereignty and territorial integrity, mutual non-aggression, non-interference in each other's internal affairs, equality and mutual benefit and peaceful coexistence, Convinced that the maintenance of peace and tranquility along the Line of Actual Control in the India-China border areas accords with the fundamental interests of the two peoples and will also contribute to the ultimate resolution of the boundary question, Reaffirming that neither side shall use or threaten to use force against the other by any means or seek unilateral military superiority, Pursuant to the Agreement between the Government of the Republic of India and Government of the People's Republic of China on the Maintenance of Peace and Tranquility Along the Line of Actual Control in the India-China Border Areas, signed on 7 September 1993, Recognizing the need for effective confidence building measures in the military field along the line of actual control in the border areas between the two sides, Noting the utility of confidence building measures already in place along the Line of Actual Control in the India-China border areas, Committed to enhancing mutual confidence and transparency in the military field, Have agreed as follows:

ARTICLE I

Neither side shall use its military capability against the other side. No armed forces deployed by either side in the border areas along the Line of Actual Control as part of their respective military strength shall be used to attack the other side, or engage in military activities that threaten the other side or undermine peace, tranquility and stability in the India-China border areas.

ARTICLE II

The two sides reiterate their determination to seek a fair, reasonable and mutually acceptable settlement of the boundary question. Pending an ultimate solution to the boundary question, the two sides reaffirm their commitment to strictly respect and observe the Line of Actual Control in the India-China border areas. No activities of either side shall overstep the Line of Actual Control.

ARTICLE III

The two sides agree to take the following measures to reduce or limit their respective military forces within mutually agreed geographical zones along the Line of Actual Control in the India-China border areas:

(1)   The two sides reaffirm that they shall reduce or limit their respective military forces within mutually agreed geographical zones along the Line of Actual Control in the India-China border areas to minimum levels compatible with friendly and good-neighbourly relations between the two countries and consistent with the principle of mutual and equal security.

(2)   The two sides shall reduce or limit the number of field army, border defence forces, paramilitary forces and any other mutually agreed category of armed force deployed in mutually agreed geographical

zones along the Line of Actual Control to ceilings to be mutually agreed upon. The major categories of armaments to be reduced or limited are as follows: combat tanks, infantry combat vehicles, guns (including howitzers) with 75 mm or bigger calibre, mortars with 120 mm or bigger calibre, surface-to-surface missiles, surface-to-air missiles and any other weapon system mutually agreed upon.

(3) The two sides shall exchange data on the military forces and armaments to be reduced or limited and decide on ceilings on military forces and armaments to be kept by each side within mutually agreed geographical zones along the Line of Actual Control in the India-China border areas. The ceilings shall be determined in conformity with the requirement of the principle of mutual and equal security, with due consideration being given to parameters such as the nature of terrain, road communication and other infrastructure and time taken to induct/de-induct troops and armaments.

ARTICLE IV

In order to maintain peace and tranquility along the Line of Actual Control in the India-China border areas and to prevent any tension in the border areas due to misreading by either side of the other side's intentions:

(1) Both sides shall avoid holding large scale military exercises involving more than one Division (approximately 15,000 troops) in close proximity of the Line of Actual Control in the India-China border areas. However, if such exercises are to be conducted, the strategic direction of the main force involved shall not be towards the other side.

(2) If either side conducts a major military exercise involving more than one Brigade Group (approximately 5,000 troops) in close proximity of the Line of Actual Control in the India-China border areas, it shall give the other side prior notification with regard to type, level, planned duration and area of exercise as well as the number and type of units or formations participating in the exercise.

(3) The date of completion of the exercise and de-induction of troops from the area of exercise shall be intimated to the other side within five days of completion or de-induction.

(4) Each side shall be entitled to obtain timely clarification from the side undertaking the exercise in respect of data specified in Pargragh 2 of the present Article.

ARTICLE V

With a view to preventing air intrusions across the Line of Actual Control in the India-China border areas and facilitating overflights and landings by military aircraft:

(1) Both sides shall take adequate measures to ensure that air intrusions across the Line of actual control do not take place. However, if an intrusion does take place, it should cease as soon as detected and the incident shall be promptly investigated by the side operating the aircraft. The results of the investigation shall be immediately communicated, through diplomatic channels or at border personnel meetings, to the other side.

(2) Subject to Paragraphs 3 and 5 of this Article, combat aircraft (to include fighter, bomber, reconnaissance, military trainer, armed helicopter and other armed aircraft) shall not fly within ten kilometres of the Line of Actual Control.

(3) If either side is required to undertake flights of combat aircraft within ten kilometres from the line of actual control, it shall give the following information in advance to the other side, through diplomatic channels:

(a) Type and number of combat aircraft;

(b) Height of the proposed flight (in meters);

(c) Proposed duration of flights (normally not to exceed ten days);

(d) Proposed timing of flights; and

(e) Area of operations, defined in latitude and longitude.

(4) Unarmed transport aircraft, survey aircraft and helicopters shall be permitted to fly up to the Line of Actual Control.

(5) No military aircraft of either side shall fly across the Line of Actual Control, except by prior permission. Military aircraft of either side may fly across the line of actual control or overfly the other side's airspace or land on the other side only after obtaining the latter's

prior permission after providing the latter with detailed information on the flight in accordance with the international practice in this regard. Notwithstanding the above stipulation, each side has the sovereign right to specify additional conditions, including at short notice, for flights or landings of military aircraft of the other side on its side of the line of actual control or through its airspace.

(6) In order to ensure flight safety in emergency situations, the authorities designated by the two sides may contact each other by the quickest means of communications available.

ARTICLE VI

With a view to preventing dangerous military activities along the Line of Actual Control in the India-China border areas, the two sides agree as follows:

(1) Neither side shall open fire, cause bio-degradation, use hazardous chemicals, conduct blast operations or hunt with guns or explosives within two kilometres from the Line of Actual Control. This prohibition shall not apply to routine firing activities in small arms firing ranges.

(2) If there is a need to conduct blast operations within two kilometres of the Line of Actual Control as part of developmental activities, the other side shall be informed through diplomatic channels or by convening a border personnel meeting, preferably five days in advance.

(3) While conducting exercises with live ammunition in areas close to the line of actual control, precaution shall be taken to ensure that a bullet or a missile does not accidentally fall on the other side across the Line of Actual Control and causes harm to the personnel or property of the other side.

(4) If the border personnel of the two sides come in a face-to-face situation due to differences on the alignment of the Line of Actual Control or any other reason, they shall exercise self-restraint and take all necessary steps to avoid an escalation of the situation. Both sides shall also enter into immediate consultations through diplomatic and/or other available channels to review the situation and prevent any escalation of tension.

ARTICLE VII

In order to strengthen exchanges and cooperation between their military personnel and establishments in the border areas along the Line of Actual Control, the two sides agree:

(1) To maintain and expand the regime of scheduled and flag meetings between their border representatives at designated places along the Line of Actual Control;

(2) To maintain and expand telecommunication links between the border meeting points at designated places along the Line of Actual Control;

(3) To establish step-by-step medium and high-level contacts between the border authorities of the two sides.

ARTICLE VIII

(1) Should the personnel of one side cross the line of actual control and enter the other side because of unavoidable circumstances like natural disasters, the other side shall extend all possible assistance to them and inform their side, as soon as possible regarding the forced or inadvertent entry across the line of actual control. The modalities of return of the concerned personnel to their own side shall be settled through mutual consultations.

(2) The two sides shall provide each other, at the earliest possible, with information pertaining to natural disasters and epidemic diseases in contiguous border areas which might affect the other side. The exchange of information shall take place either through diplomatic channels or at border personnel meetings.

ARTICLE IX

In case a doubtful situation develops in the border region, or in case one of the sides has some questions or doubts regarding the manner in which the other side is observing this Agreement, either side has the right to seek a clarification from the other side. The clarifications sought and replies to them shall be conveyed through diplomatic channels.

ARTICLE X

(1)   Recognizing that the full implementation of some of the provisions of the present Agreement will depend on the two sides arriving at a common understanding of the alignment of the line Line of Actual Control in the India-China border areas, the two sides agree to speed up the process of clarification and confirmation of the Line of Actual Control. As an initial step in this process, they are clarifying the alignment of the Line of Actual Control in those segments where they have different perceptions. They also agree to exchange maps indicating their respective perceptions of the entire alignment of the Line of Actual Control as soon as possible.

(2)   Pending the completion of the process of clarification and confirmation of the Line of Actual Control, the two sides shall work out modalities for implementing confidence building measures envisaged under this Agreement on an interim basis, without prejudice to their respective positions on the alignment of the line of actual control as well as on the boundary question,

ARTICLE XI

Detailed implementation measures required under Article I to Article X of this Agreement shall be decided through mutual consultations in the India-China Joint Working Group on the Boundary Question. The India-China Diplomatic and Military Expert Group shall assist the China India Joint Working Group.

ARTICLE XII

This Agreement is subject to ratification and shall enter into force on the date of exchange of instruments of ratification. It shall remain in effect until either side decides to terminate it after giving six months notice in writing. It shall become invalid six months after the notification.

This Agreement is subject to amendment and addition by mutual agreement in writing between the two sides.

Signed in duplicate in New Delhi on 29 November 1996 in the Hindi, Chinese and English languages, all three texts being equally authentic. In case of divergence, the English text shall prevail.

Appendix 7

Agreement between the Government of the Republic of India and the Government of the People's Republic of China on the Political Parameters and Guiding Principles for the Settlement of the India-China Boundary Question (11 April 2005).

The Government of the Republic of India and the Government of the People's Republic of China (hereinafter referred to as the two sides), Believing that it serves the fundamental interests of the peoples of India and China to foster a long-term constructive and cooperative partnership on the basis of the Five Principles of Peaceful Co-existence, mutual respect and sensitivity for each other's concerns and aspirations, and equality, Desirous of qualitatively upgrading the bilateral relationship at all levels and in all areas while addressing differences through peaceful means in a fair, reasonable and mutually acceptable manner, Reiterating their commitment to abide by and implement the Agreement on the Maintenance of Peace and Tranquility along the Line of Actual Control in the India-China Border Areas, signed on 7 September 1993, and the Agreement on Confidence Building Measures in the Military Field along the Line of Actual Control in the India-China Border Areas, signed on 29 November 1996, Reaffirming the Declaration on Principles for Relations and Comprehensive Cooperation between India and China, signed on 23 June 2003, Recalling that the two sides have appointed Special Representatives to explore the framework of settlement of the

India-China boundary question and the two Special Representatives have been engaged in consultations in a friendly, cooperative and constructive atmosphere, Noting that the two sides are seeking a political settlement of the boundary question in the context of their overall and long-term interests, Convinced that an early settlement of the boundary question will advance the basic interests of the two countries and should therefore be pursued as a strategic objective, Have agreed on the following political parameters and guiding principles for a boundary settlement:

ARTICLE I

The differences on the boundary question should not be allowed to affect the overall development of bilateral relations. The two sides will resolve the boundary question through peaceful and friendly consultations. Neither side shall use or threaten to use force against the other by any means. The final solution of the boundary question will significantly promote good neighbourly and friendly relations between India and China.

ARTICLE II

The two sides should, in accordance with the Five Principles of Peaceful Coexistence, seek a fair, reasonable and mutually acceptable solution to the boundary question through consultations on an equal footing, proceeding from the political perspective of overall bilateral relations.

ARTICLE III

Both sides should, in the spirit of mutual respect and mutual understanding, make meaningful and mutually acceptable adjustments to their respective positions on the boundary question, so as to arrive at a package settlement to the boundary question. The boundary settlement must be final, covering all sectors of the India-China boundary.

ARTICLE IV

The two sides will give due consideration to each other's strategic and reasonable interests, and the principle of mutual and equal security.

ARTICLE V

The two sides will take into account, inter alia, historical evidence, national sentiments, practical difficulties and reasonable concerns and sensitivities of both sides, and the actual state of border areas.

ARTICLE VI

The boundary should be along well-defined and easily identifiable natural geographical features to be mutually agreed upon between the two sides.

ARTICLE VII

In reaching a boundary settlement, the two sides shall safeguard due interests of their settled populations in the border areas.

ARTICLE VIII

Within the agreed framework of the final boundary settlement, the delineation of the boundary will be carried out utilising means such as modern cartographic and surveying practices and joint surveys.

ARTICLE IX

Pending an ultimate settlement of the boundary question, the two sides should strictly respect and observe the line of actual control and work together to maintain peace and tranquility in the border areas. The India-China Joint Working Group and the India-China Diplomatic and Military Expert Group shall continue their work under the Agreements of 7 September 1993 and 29 November 1996, including the clarification of the line of actual control and the implementation of confidence building measures.

ARTICLE X

The Special Representatives on the boundary question shall continue their consultations in an earnest manner with the objective of arriving at an agreed framework for a boundary settlement, which will provide the basis for the delineation and demarcation of the India-China boundary to be subsequently undertaken by civil and military officials and surveyors of the two sides.

ARTICLE XI

This Agreement shall come into force as of the date of signature and is subject to amendment and addition by mutual agreement in writing between the two sides.

Signed in duplicate in New Delhi on 11 April, 2005, in the Hindi, Chinese and English languages, all three texts being equally authentic.

In case of divergence, the English text shall prevail.

For the Government of the Republic of India.

For the Government of the People's Republic of China.

New Delhi
April 11, 2005

Appendix 8

A Shared Vision for the 21st Century of the Republic of India and the People's Republic of China.

H.E. Dr Manmohan Singh, Prime Minister of the Republic of India and H.E. Mr Wen Jiabao, Premier of the State Council of the People's Republic of China, meeting in Beijing on 14 January 2008, resolve to promote the building of a harmonious world of durable peace and common prosperity through developing the Strategic and Cooperative Partnership for Peace and Prosperity between the two countries.

India and China (hereinafter referred to as the 'two sides') are the two largest developing nations on earth representing more than one-third of humanity. The two sides recognize that both India and China bear a significant historical responsibility to ensure a comprehensive, balanced and sustainable economic and social development of the two countries and to promote peace and development in Asia and the world as a whole.

The two sides are convinced that it is time to look to the future in building a relationship of friendship and trust, based on equality, in which each is sensitive to the concerns and aspirations of the other. The two sides reiterate that India-China friendship and common development will have a positive influence on the future of the international system. India-China relations are not targeted at any country, nor will it affect their friendship with other countries.

The two sides believe that in the new century, *Panchsheel*, the Five Principles of Peaceful Co-existence, should continue to constitute the basic guiding principles for good relations between all countries and for creating the conditions for realizing peace and progress of humankind. An international system founded on these principles will be fair, rational, equal and mutually beneficial, promote durable peace and common prosperity, create equal opportunities and eliminate poverty and discrimination.

The two sides hold that the right of each country to choose its own path of social, economic and political development in which fundamental human rights and the rule of law are given their due place, should be respected. An international system founded in tolerance and respect for diversity will promote the cause of peace and reduce the use, or threat of use, of force. The two sides favour an open and inclusive international system and believe that drawing lines on the ground of ideologies and values, or on geographical criteria, is not conducive to peaceful and harmonious coexistence.

The two sides believe that the continuous democratization of international relations and multilateralism are an important objective in the new century. The central role of the United Nations in promoting international peace, security and development should be recognized and promoted. The two sides support comprehensive reform of the United Nations, including giving priority to increasing the representation of developing countries in the Security Council. The Indian side reiterates its aspirations for permanent membership of the UN Security Council. The Chinese side attaches great importance to India's position as a major developing country in international affairs. The Chinese side understands and supports India's aspirations to play a greater role in the United Nations, including in the Security Council.

The two sides support and encourage the processes of regional integration that provide mutually beneficial opportunities for growth, as an important feature of the emerging international economic system. The two sides positively view each others' participation in regional processes and agree to strengthen their coordination and consultation within regional cooperation mechanisms including the East Asia Summit, to explore together and with other countries a new architecture for closer regional cooperation in Asia, and to make joint efforts for further regional integration of Asia. The two sides will strengthen their coordination under the framework of Asia-Europe Meeting, and are committed to strengthening and deepening Asia-Europe comprehensive partnership.

The two sides take a positive view on each other's participation in sub-regional multilateral cooperation processes between like-minded countries, including South Asian Association for Regional Cooperation, Bay of Bengal Initiative for Multi-Sectoral Technical and Economic Cooperation and Shanghai Cooperation Organization. The two sides hold that this does not affect either country's existing friendly relations or cooperation with other countries.

The two sides welcome the positive facets of economic globalization, and are ready to face and meet its challenges, and will work with other countries towards balanced and mutually beneficial economic globalization. The two sides believe that the establishment of an open, fair, equitable, transparent and rule-based multilateral trading system is the common aspiration of all countries. The two sides favour the early conclusion of the Doha Development Round, placing the issues that affect the poorest of the poor at its core. The two sides are determined to strengthen their coordination with other developing countries in order to secure their shared objectives.

The two sides are convinced that it is in the common interest of the international community to establish an international energy order that is fair, equitable, secure and stable, and to the benefit of the entire international community. The two sides are committed to making joint efforts to diversify the global energy mix and enhance the share of clean and renewable energy, so as to meet the energy requirements of all countries.

The two sides welcome the opportunity for their outstanding scientists to work together in the International Thermonuclear Experimental Reactor (ITER) project, which is of great potential significance in meeting the global energy challenge in an environmentally sustainable manner. As two countries with advanced scientific capabilities, the two sides pledge to promote bilateral cooperation in civil nuclear energy, consistent with their respective international commitments, which will contribute to energy security and to dealing with risks associated with climate change.

The two sides recognize the challenge that humankind faces from climate change. The two sides take the issue of climate change seriously and reiterate their readiness to join the international community in the efforts to address climate change. The two sides also stand ready to enhance technological cooperation between the two countries. The two sides welcome the outcome of the United Nations Framework Convention on Climate Change (UNFCCC) meeting in Bali in December 2007 and agree to work closely during the negotiation process laid out in the Bali Road Map for long term cooperative action under the Convention. The two sides emphasize the importance of addressing climate change in accordance with principles and provisions of the UNFCCC and its Kyoto Protocol, in particular the principle of common but differentiated responsibilities.

The two sides appeal to the international community to move forward the processes of multilateral arms control, disarmament and non-proliferation. Outer space is the common heritage of humankind. It is the responsibility of all space-faring nations to commit to the peaceful uses of outer space. The two sides express their categorical opposition to the weaponization and arms race in outer space.

The two sides strongly condemn the scourge of terrorism in all its forms and manifestations, and in all regions of the world. The two sides pledge to work together and with the international community to strengthen the global framework against terrorism in a long-term, sustained and comprehensive manner.

The two sides believe that cultural and religious tolerance and dialogue between civilizations and peoples will contribute to overall peace and stability of our world. The two sides endorse all efforts to promote inter-civilizational and inter-faith dialogues.

The two sides believe that their bilateral relationship in this century will be of significant regional and global influence. The two sides will therefore continue to build their strategic and cooperative partnership in a positive way. As major economies in their region, the two sides believe that the strong growth in their trade and economic relations is mutually beneficial, and welcome the conclusion of a feasibility study on a Regional Trading Arrangement (RTA) between the two countries. According to the report of the Feasibility Study, an India-China RTA will be mutually advantageous. Against the backdrop of accelerating regional economic integration in Asia, the two sides agree to explore the possibility of commencing discussions on a mutually beneficial and high-quality RTA that meets the common aspirations of both countries, and will also benefit the region.

The two sides will continuously promote confidence building measures through steadily enhanced contacts in the field of defence. The two sides, therefore, welcome the commencement of the India-China Defence Dialogue and express their satisfaction at the successful conclusion of the first joint anti-terrorism training between their armed forces in December 2007. The two sides also welcome their efforts to set an example on trans-border rivers by commencing cooperation since 2002. The Indian side highly appreciates the assistance extended by China on the provision of flood season hydrological data which has assisted India in ensuring the safety and security of its population in the regions along these rivers. The two sides agree that this has contributed positively to building mutual understanding and trust.

The two sides remain firmly committed to resolving outstanding differences, including on the boundary question, through peaceful negotiations, while ensuring that such differences are not allowed to affect the positive development of bilateral relations. The two sides reiterate their determination to seek a fair, reasonable and mutually acceptable solution to the boundary question and to build a boundary of peace and friendship on the basis of the Agreement on Political Parameters and Guiding Principles for the Settlement of the India-China Boundary Question concluded in April 2005. The Special Representatives shall complete at an early date the task of arriving at an agreed framework of settlement on the basis of this Agreement.

The Indian side recalls that India was among the first countries to recognize that there is one China and that its one China policy has remained unaltered. The Indian side states that it would continue to abide by its one China policy, and oppose any activity that is against the one China principle. The Chinese side expresses its appreciation for the Indian position.

The two sides recognize the responsibilities and obligations of the two countries to the international community. The two sides are determined to enhance mutual understanding and friendship between the peoples of India and China, for the betterment of both countries and to bring about a brighter future for humanity.

(Dr Manmohan Singh)   (Wen Jiabao)
Prime Minister of the   Premier of the State Council of
Republic of India   the People's Republic of China
Beijing
14 January 2008

Index

About the Author

General J.J. Singh (retd), PVSM, AVSM, VSM, has served as the Chief of Army Staff and the Chairman of the Chiefs of Staff Committee. During his forty-seven-year stint in the army, he commanded two infantry battalions and was closely associated with the planning and execution of the Kargil War at the army headquarters. After retirement, he was appointed Governor of Arunachal Pradesh. He has also received a number of civilian honours and awards for his outstanding leadership. He was conferred with the 'Officier de l'Ordre national de la Légion d'Honneur' (Officer of the Legion of Honour), the highest civilian distinction bestowed by the Government of France, in 2015. His autobiography, *A Soldier's General*, was published in 2012.